Kitchen Princess

6

Natsumi Ando

Story by Miyuki Kobayashi

Translated by Satsuki Yamashita

Adapted by Nunzio DeFilippis and Christina Weir

Lettered by North Market Street Graphics

Ballantine Books · New York

A Del Rey Manga/Kodansha Trade Paperback Original

Kitchen Princess copyright © 2007 by Natsumi Ando and Miyuki Kobayashi
English translation copyright © 2008 by Natsumi Ando and Miyuki Kobayashi

Published in the United States by Del Rey Books, an imprint of The Random House Publishing Group, a division of Random House, Inc., New York.

DEL REY is a registered trademark and the Del Rey colophon is a trademark of Random House, Inc.

Publication rights arranged through Kodansha Ltd.

First published in Japan in 2007 by Kodansha Ltd., Tokyo

ISBN 978-0-345-50194-3

Printed in the United States of America

www.delreymanga.com

9 8 7 6 5 4 3

Translator: Satsuki Yamashita
Adaptors: Nunzio DeFilippis and Christina Weir
Lettering: North Market Street Graphics
Original cover design by Akiko Omo

Contents

The bento box in the picture above was made by
Kasumin-san, who makes wonderful lunches featuring the
faces of popular fictional characters.
This one is her "Najika bento!" It looks exactly like
Najika! I was so excited when I saw it.

—Natsumi Ando

Honorifics Explained

Throughout the Del Rey Manga books, you will find Japanese honorifics left intact in the translations. For those not familiar with how the Japanese use honorifics and, more important, how they differ from American honorifics, we present this brief overview.

Politeness has always been a critical facet of Japanese culture. Ever since the feudal era, when Japan was a highly stratified society, use of honorifics—which can be defined as polite speech that indicates relationship or status—has played an essential role in the Japanese language. When addressing someone in Japanese, an honorific usually takes the form of a suffix attached to one's name (example: "Asuna-san"), is used as a title at the end of one's name, or appears in place of the name itself (example: "Negi-sensei," or simply "Sensei!").

Honorifics can be expressions of respect or endearment. In the context of manga and anime, honorifics give insight into the nature of the relationship between characters. Many English translations leave out these important honorifics and therefore distort the feel of the original Japanese. Because Japanese honorifics contain nuances that English honorifics lack, it is our policy at Del Rey not to translate them. Here, instead, is a guide to some of the honorifics you may encounter in Del Rey Manga.

-*san:* This is the most common honorific and is equivalent to Mr., Miss, Ms., or Mrs. It is the all-purpose honorific and can be used in any situation where politeness is required.

-*sama:* This is one level higher than "-san" and is used to confer great respect.

-*dono:* This comes from the word "tono," which means "lord." It is an even higher level than "-sama" and confers utmost respect.

-*kun:* This suffix is used at the end of boys' names to express familiarity or endearment. It is also sometimes used by men among friends, or when addressing someone younger or of a lower station.

-chan: This is used to express endearment, mostly toward girls. It is also used for little boys, pets, and even among lovers. It gives a sense of childish cuteness.

Bozu: This is an informal way to refer to a boy, similar to the English terms "kid" and "squirt."

**Sempai/
Senpai:** This title suggests that the addressee is one's senior in a group or organization. It is most often used in a school setting, where underclassmen refer to their upperclassmen as "sempai." It can also be used in the workplace, such as when a newer employee addresses an employee who has seniority in the company.

Kohai: This is the opposite of "sempai" and is used toward underclassmen in school or newcomers in the workplace. It connotes that the addressee is of a lower station.

Sensei: Literally meaning "one who has come before," this title is used for teachers, doctors, or masters of any profession or art.

-[blank]: This is usually forgotten in these lists, but it is perhaps the most significant difference between Japanese and English. The lack of honorific means that the speaker has permission to address the person in a very intimate way. Usually, only family, spouses, or very close friends have this kind of permission. Known as *yobisute*, it can be gratifying when someone who has earned the intimacy starts to call one by one's name without an honorific. But when that intimacy hasn't been earned, it can be very insulting.

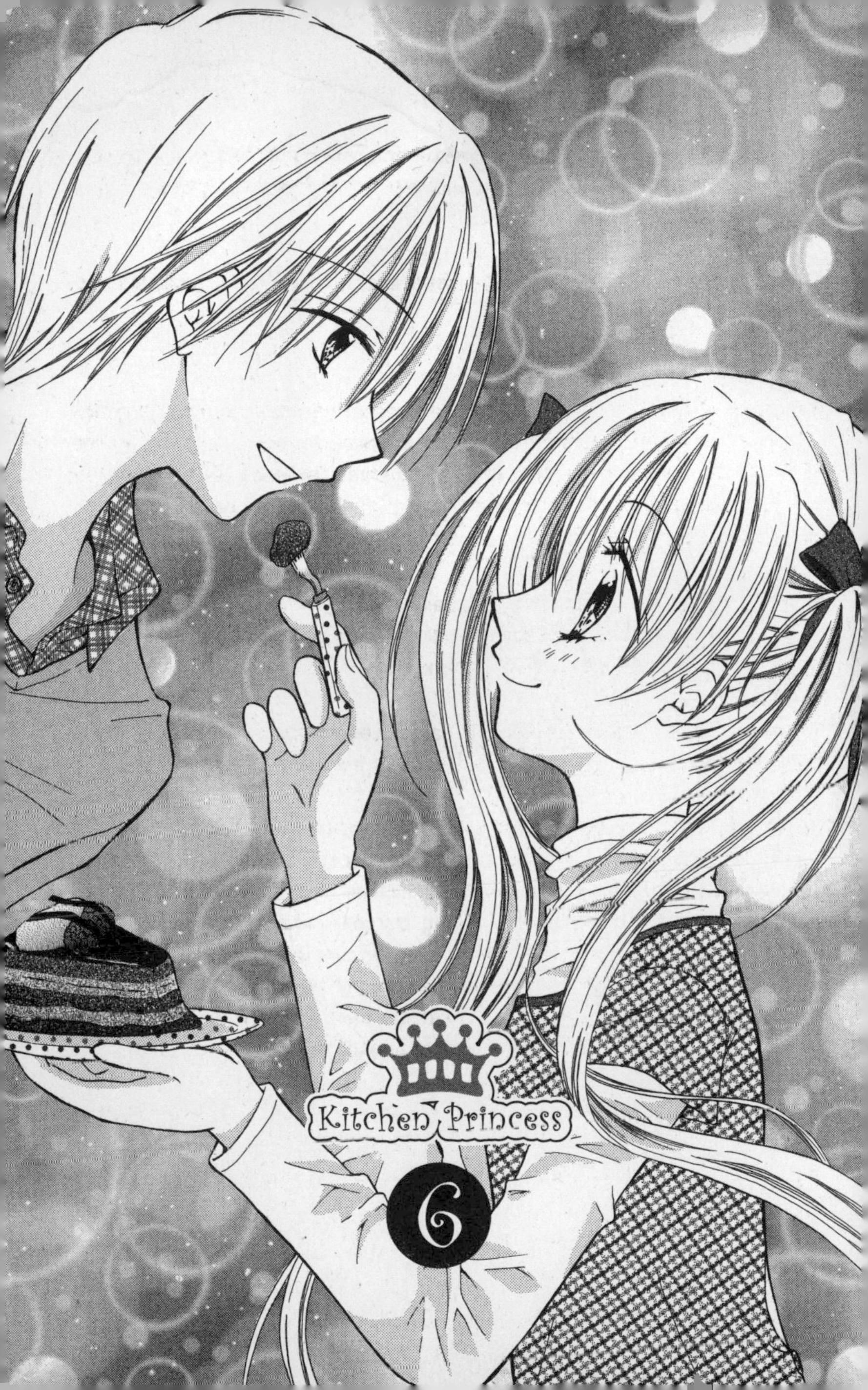
Kitchen Princess
6

Kitchen Princess

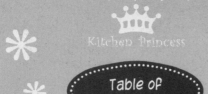

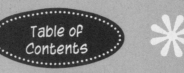

Table of Contents

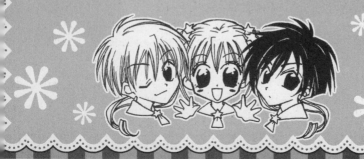

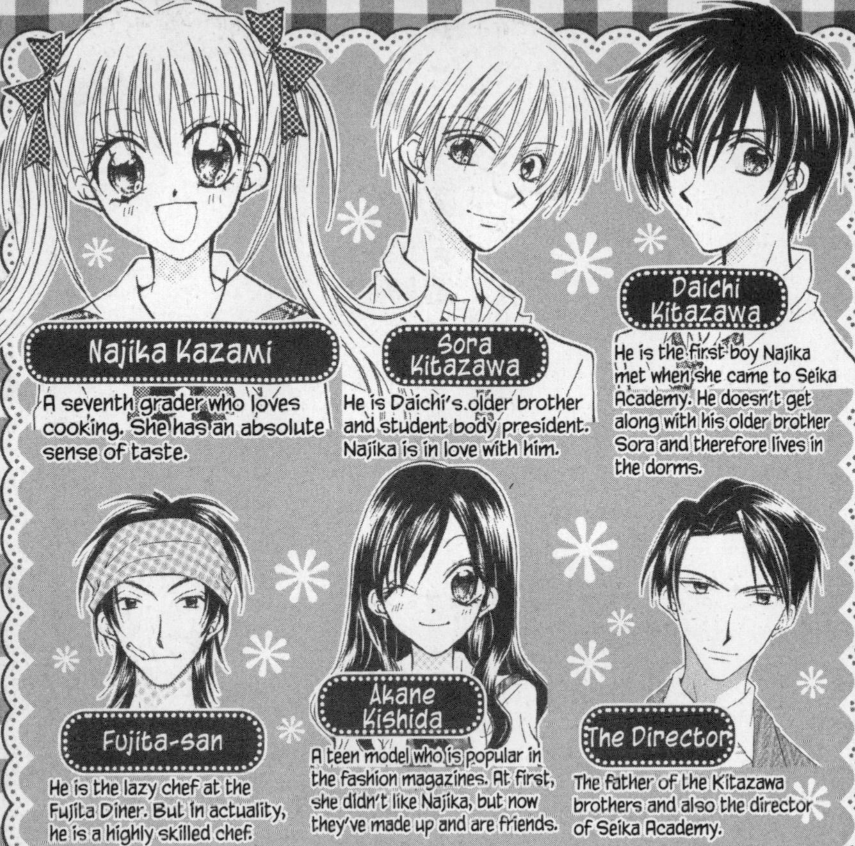

Najika Kazami
A seventh grader who loves cooking. She has an absolute sense of taste.

Sora Kitazawa
He is Daichi's older brother and student body president. Najika is in love with him.

Daichi Kitazawa
He is the first boy Najika met when she came to Seika Academy. He doesn't get along with his older brother Sora and therefore lives in the dorms.

Fujita-san
He is the lazy chef at the Fujita Diner. But in actuality, he is a highly skilled chef.

Akane Kishida
A teen model who is popular in the fashion magazines. At first, she didn't like Najika, but now they've made up and are friends.

The Director
The father of the Kitazawa brothers and also the director of Seika Academy.

The Story So Far...

Najika lost her parents when she was young and was sent to live in Lavender House, an orphanage in Hokkaido. She enrolled in Seika Academy in Tokyo to find her Flan Prince, a boy who saved her from drowning when she was young. There she met Sora, Daichi, and Akane. Najika entered the National Confectionary Competition, not knowing that Sora and the director were trying to use her to get media attention for the academy. But she believed that Sora was sincere. And because he told her that he was her "Flan Prince," Najika told Sora how she felt about him. Sora promised to tell her how he felt after the competition. But on the day of the final round, Sora was involved in an accident!!

Greetings

Hello ✿

I'm really hooked on cooking right now.

But I still don't have a stove...I can't make sweets. ¿

In this volume, I reduced the amount of extra text in the open spaces...

I didn't include any behind-the-scenes either because I figured it'd get in the way of the flow of the story.

Please enjoy.

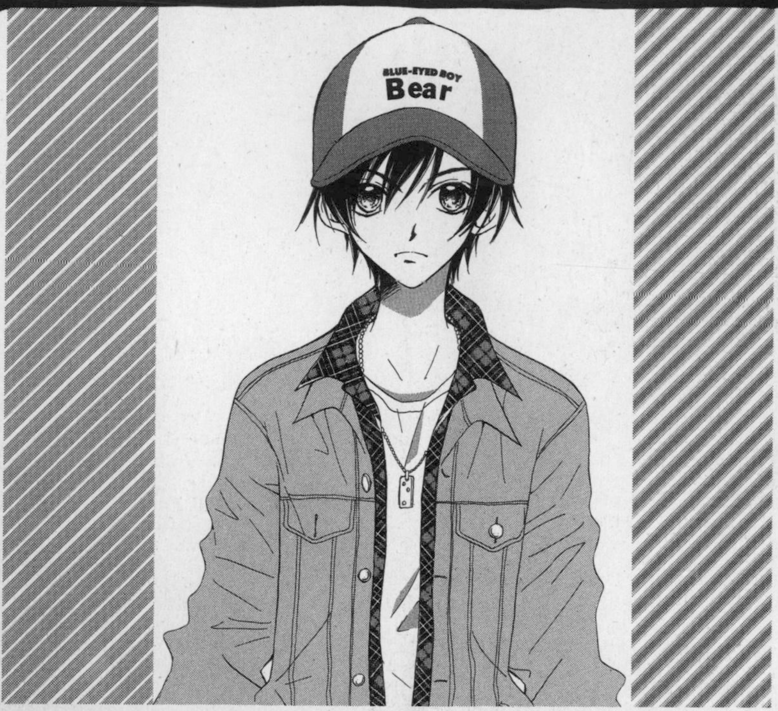
BLUE-EYED BOY
Bear

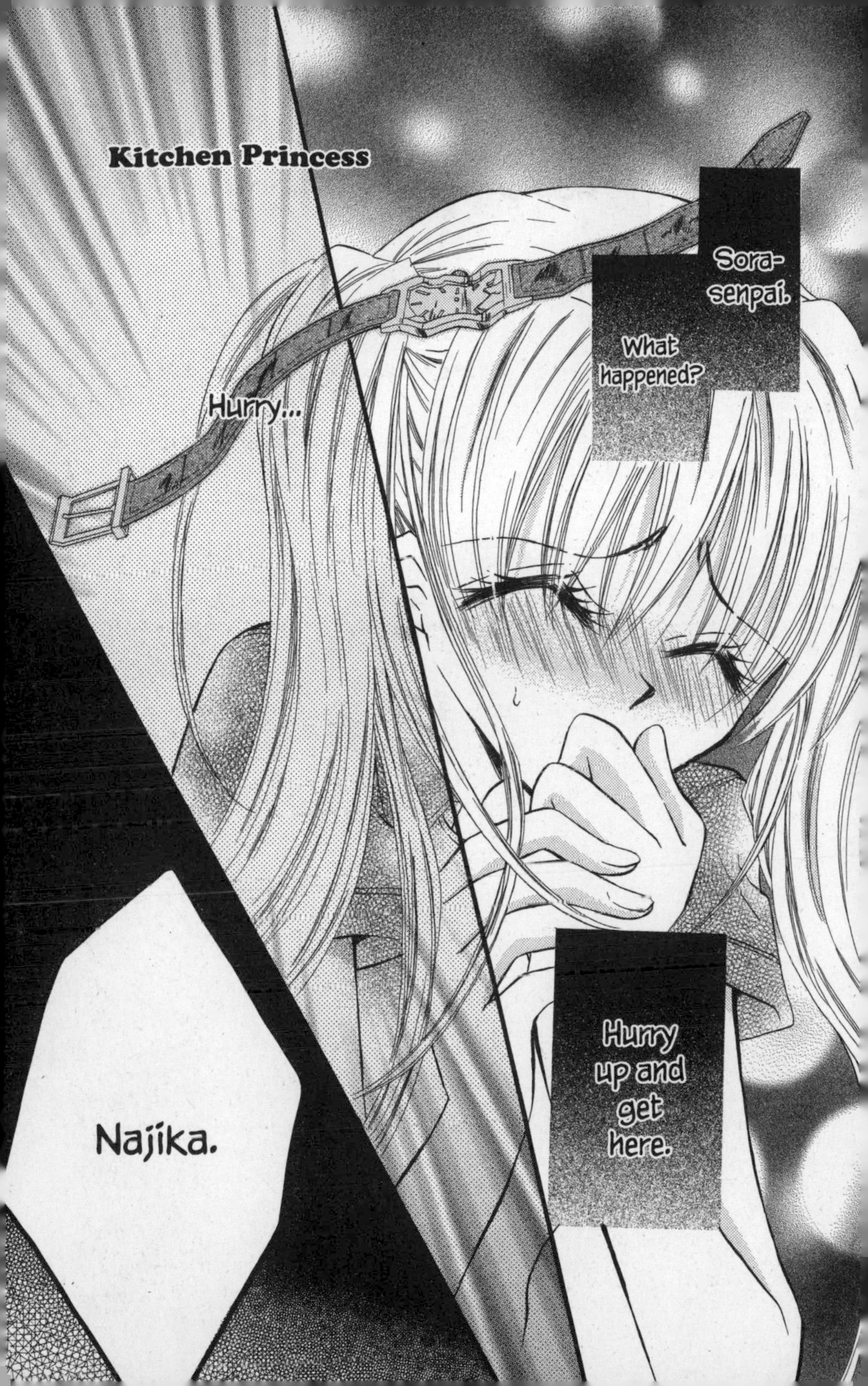
Sora-senpai.
What happened?
Hurry up and get here.
Hurry...
Najika.

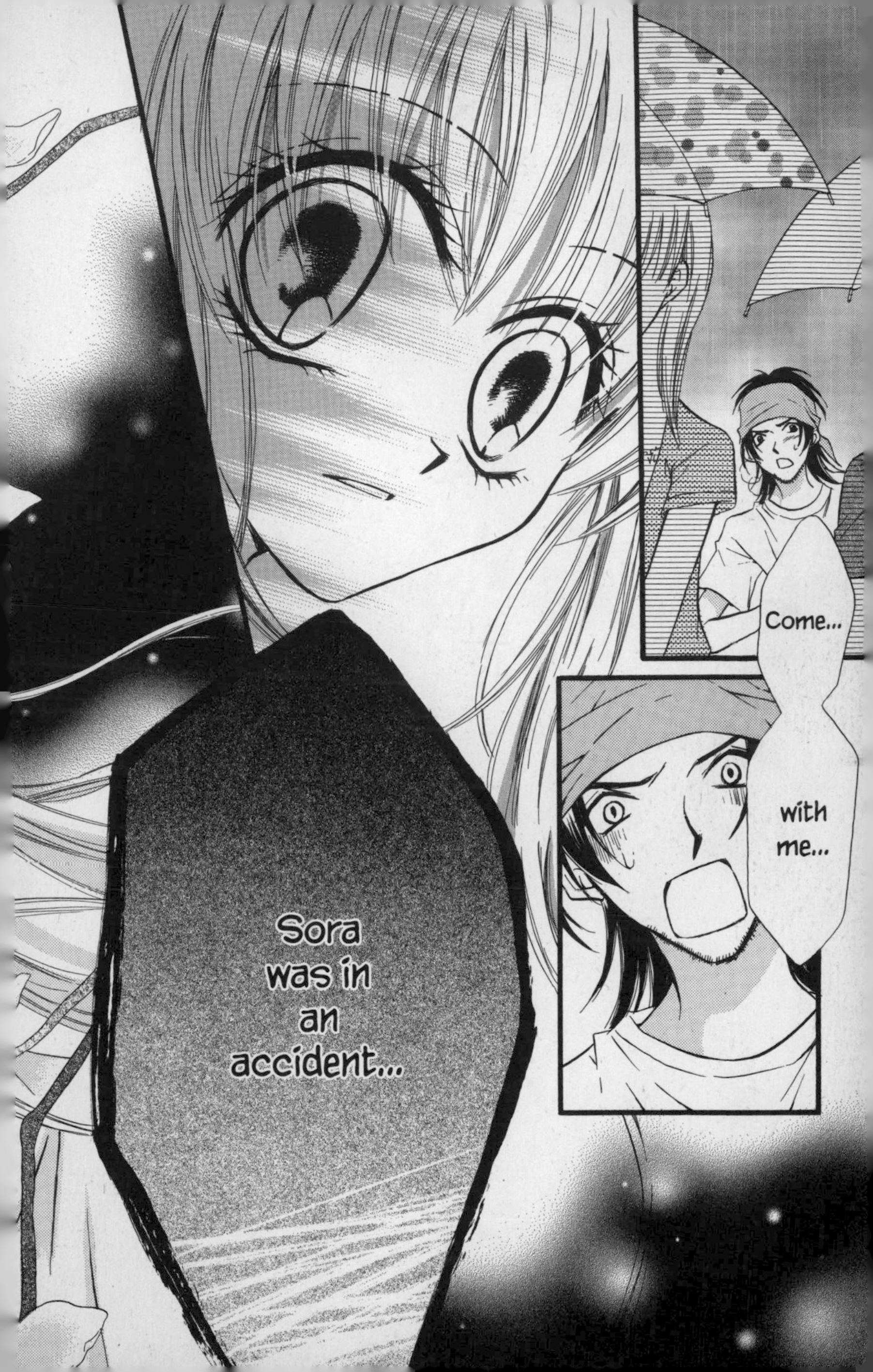
Come...
with me...
Sora was in an accident...

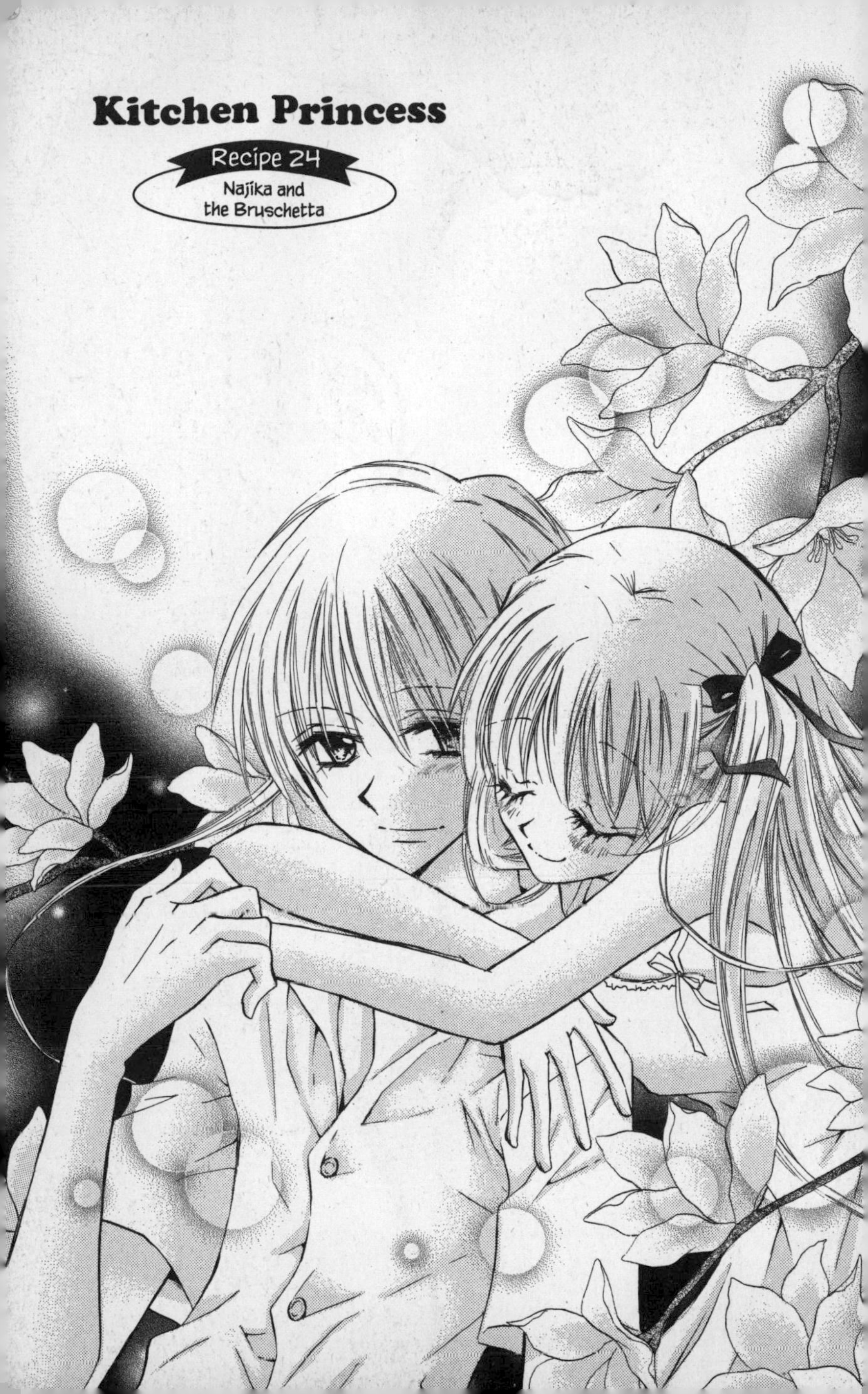
Kitchen Princess
Recipe 24
Najika and
the Bruschetta

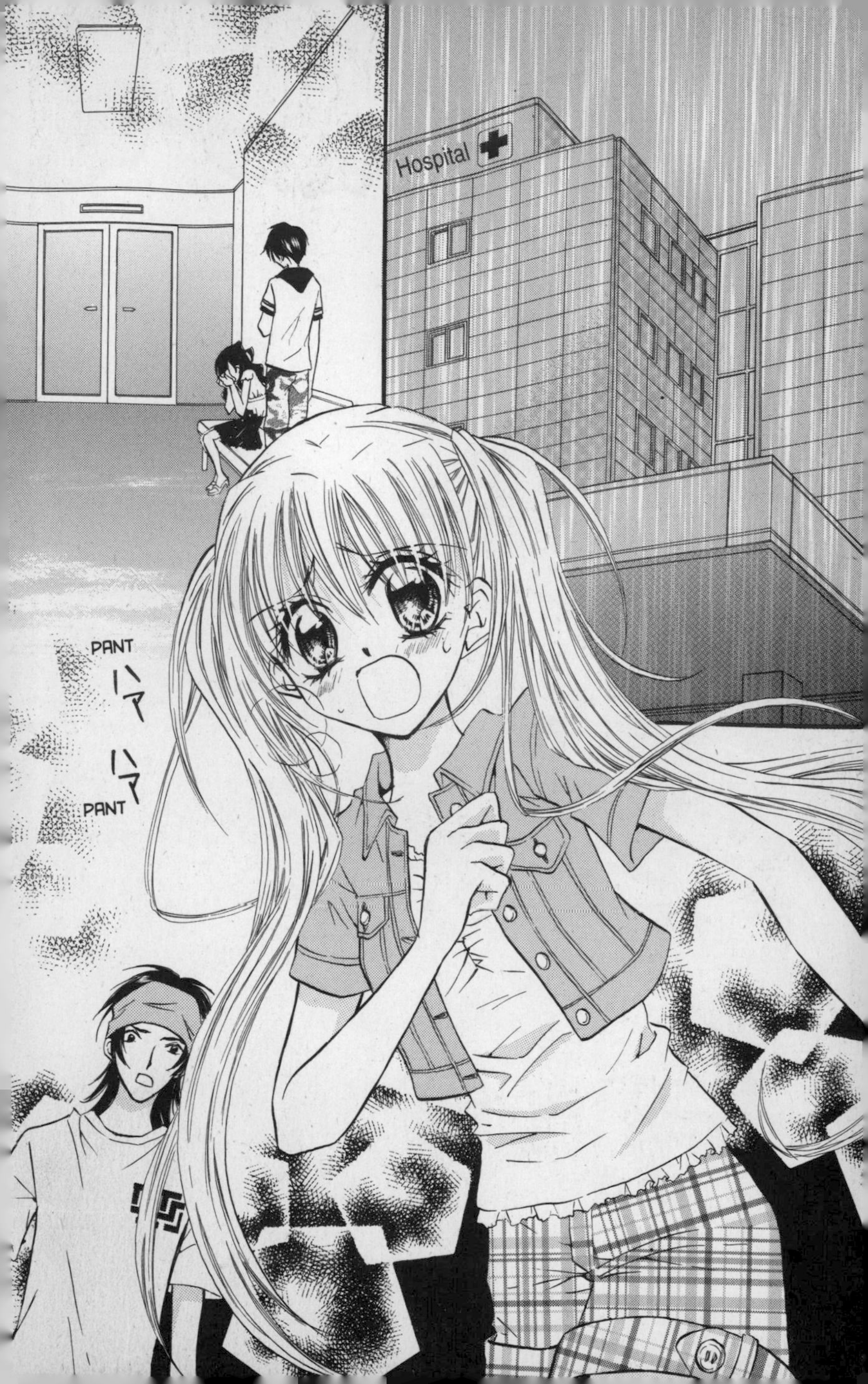
Hospital
PANT
ハア
ハア
PANT

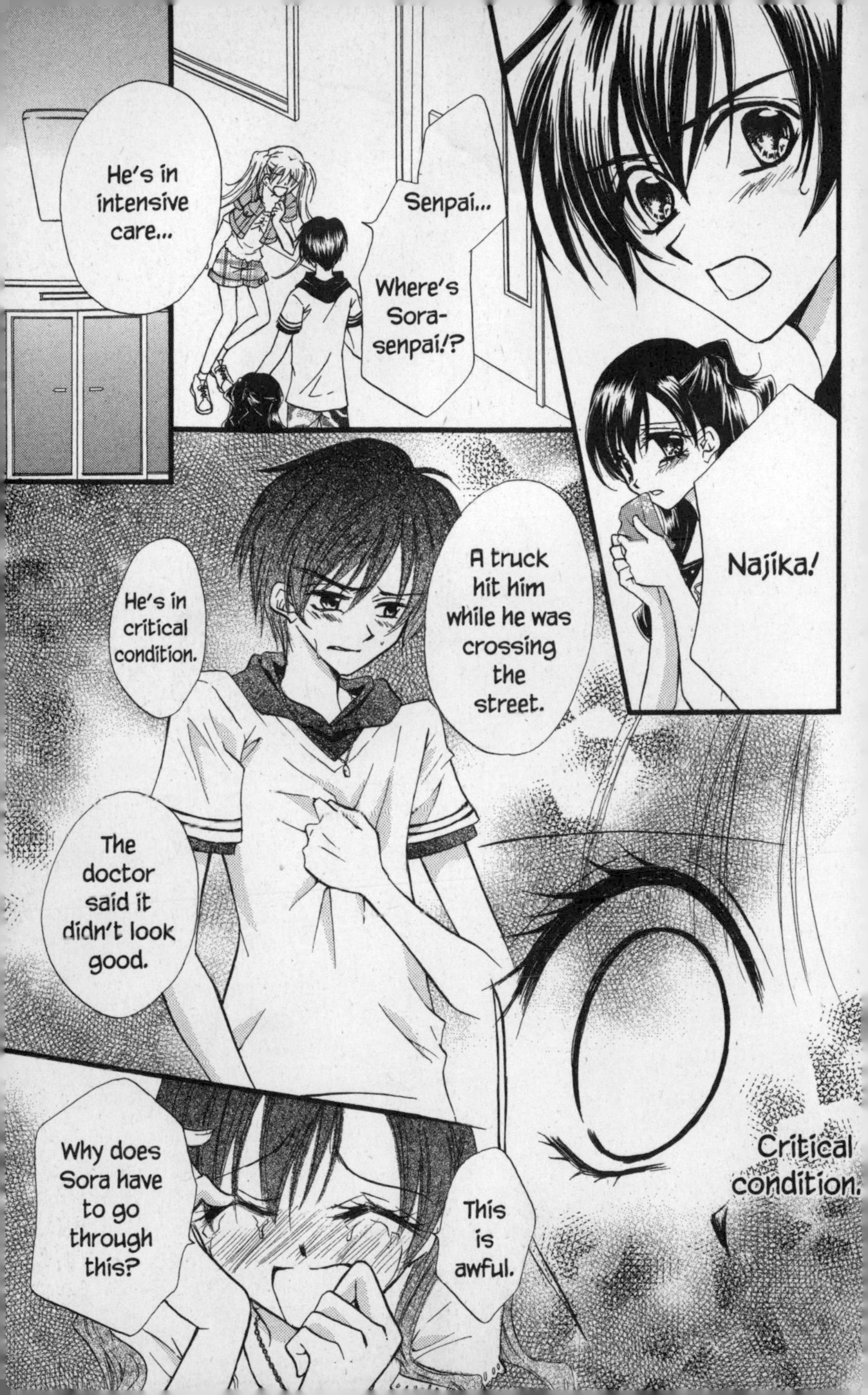
Najika!
Senpai...
Where's Sora-senpai!?
He's in intensive care...
Critical condition.
A truck hit him while he was crossing the street.
He's in critical condition.
The doctor said it didn't look good.
This is awful.
Why does Sora have to go through this?

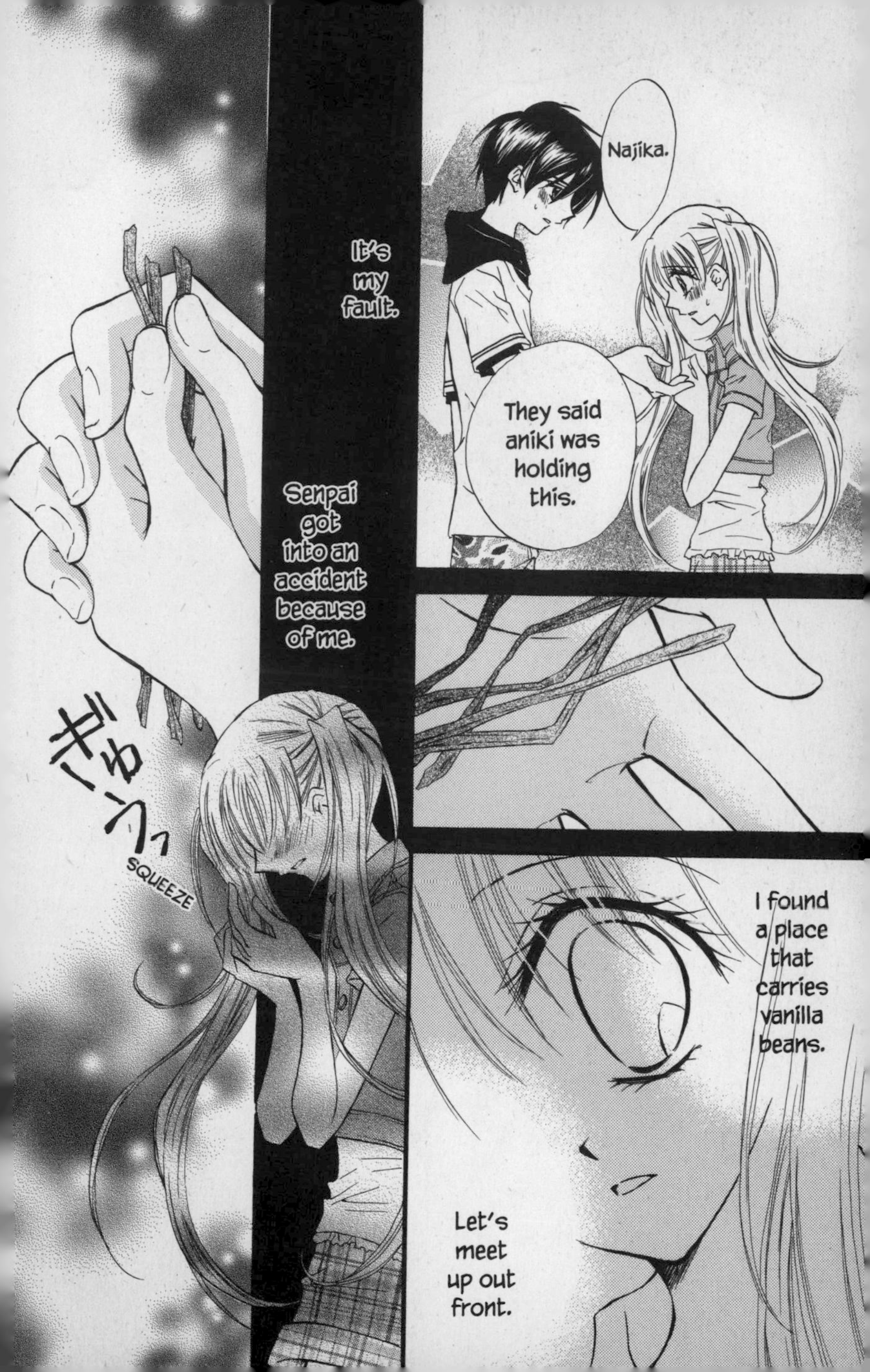
Najika.
They said aniki was holding this.
I found a place that carries vanilla beans.
Let's meet up out front.
It's my fault.
Senpai got into an accident because of me.
ぎゅうっ
SQUEEZE

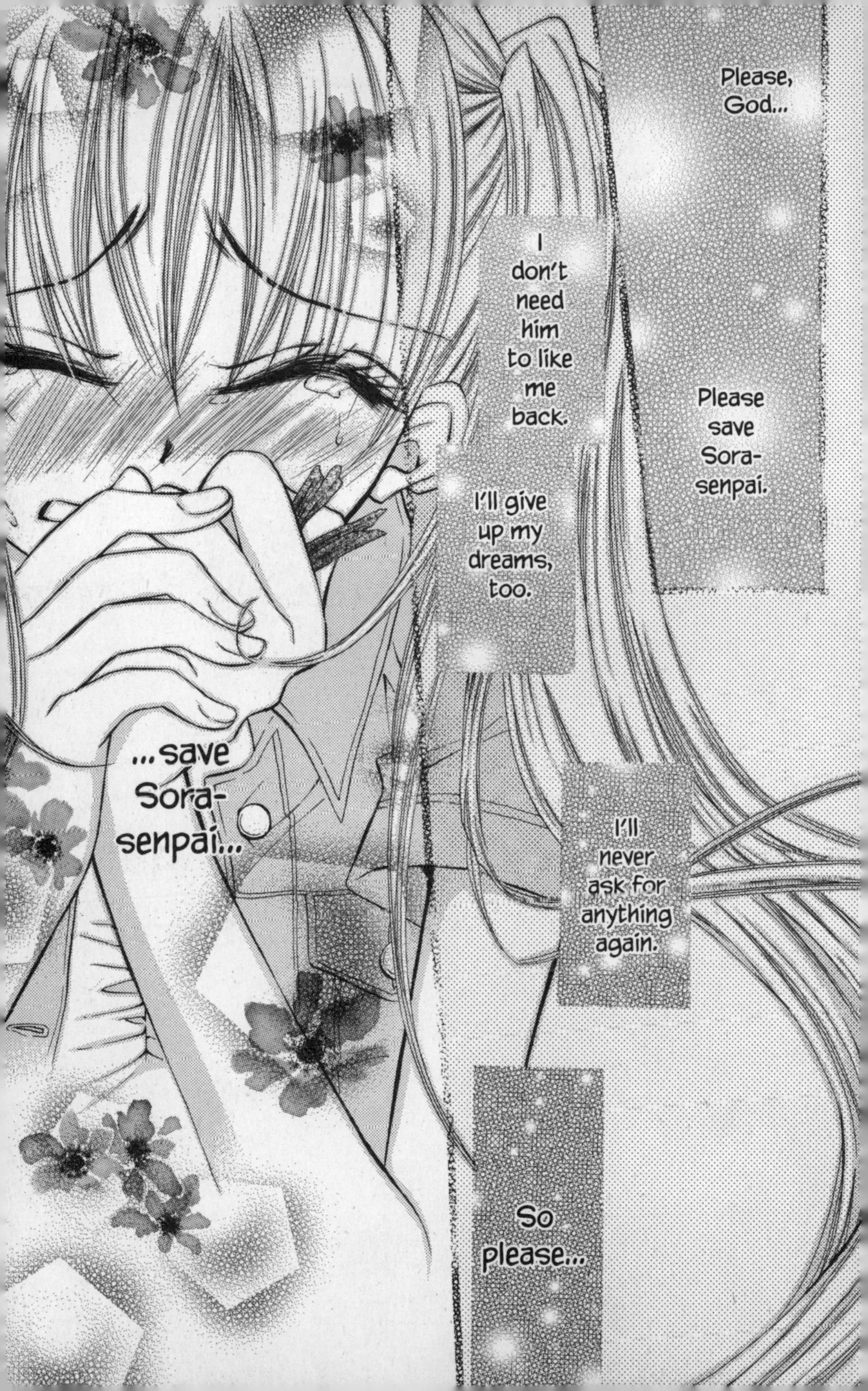
Please, God...
Please save Sora-senpai.
I don't need him to like me back.
I'll give up my dreams, too.
I'll never ask for anything again.
So please...
...save Sora-senpai...

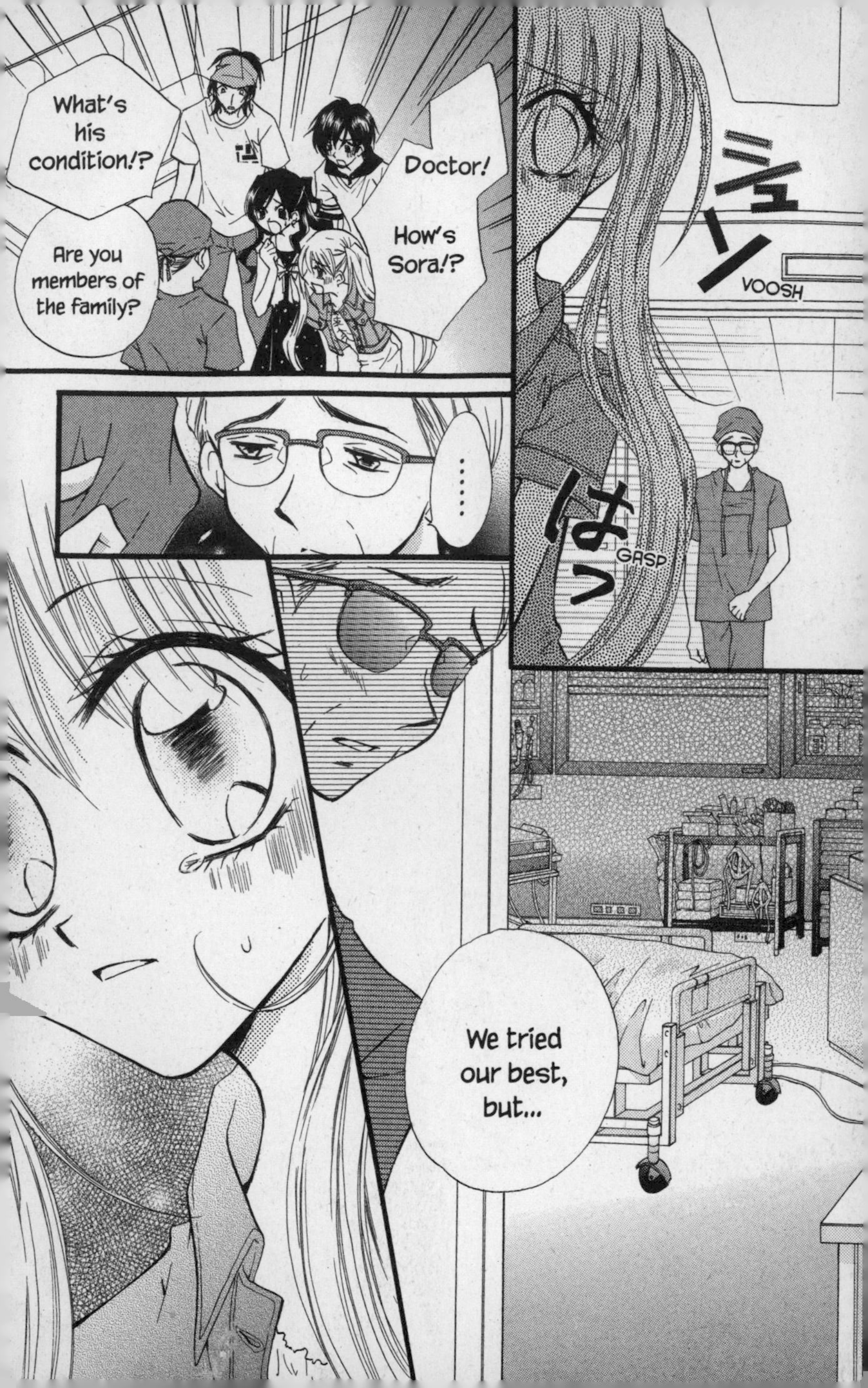
シュン
VOOSH
はっ
GASP
Doctor!
How's Sora!?
What's his condition!?
Are you members of the family?
......
We tried our best, but...

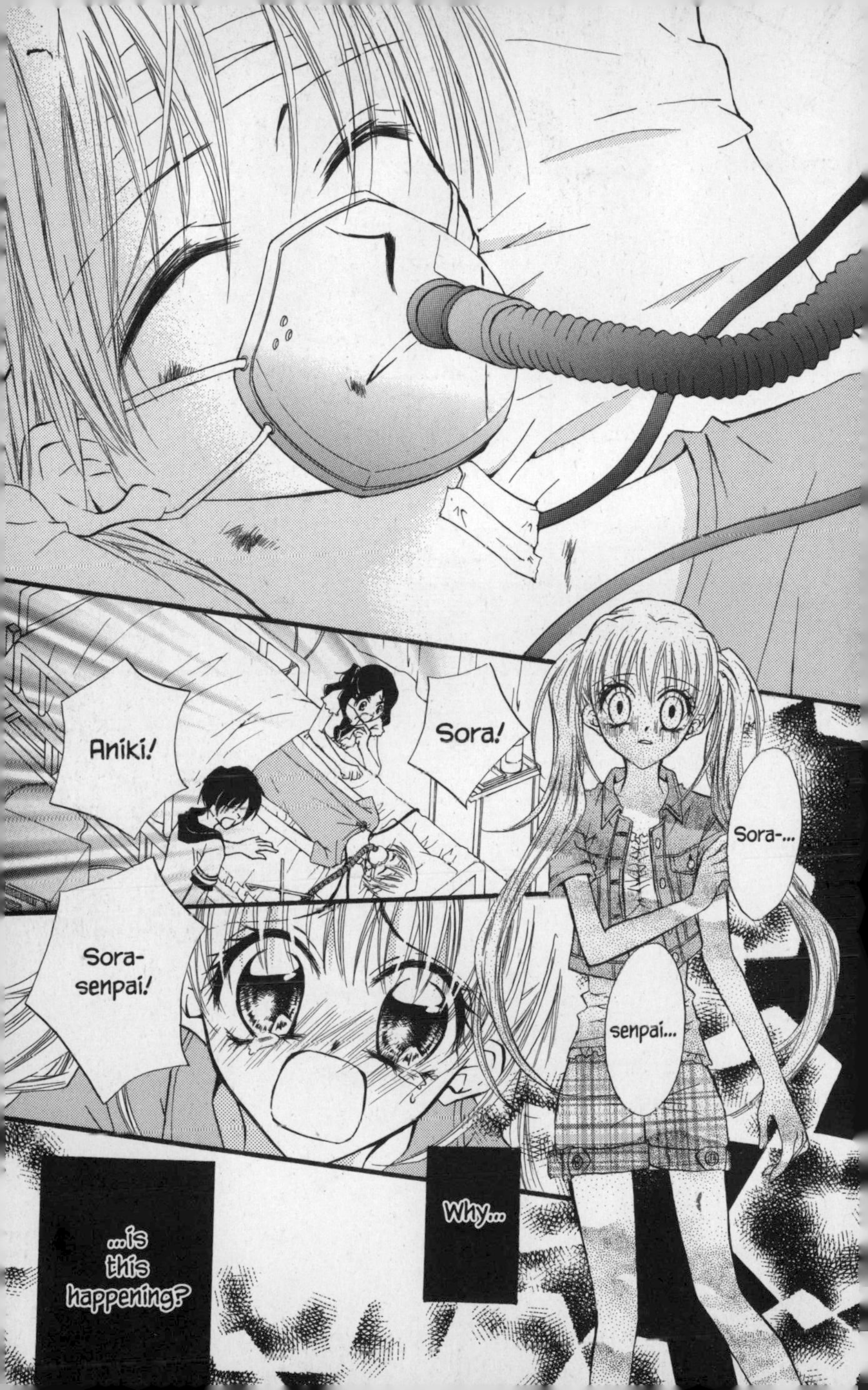
Sora-...
senpai...
Why...
Sora!
Aniki!
Sora-senpai!
...is this happening?

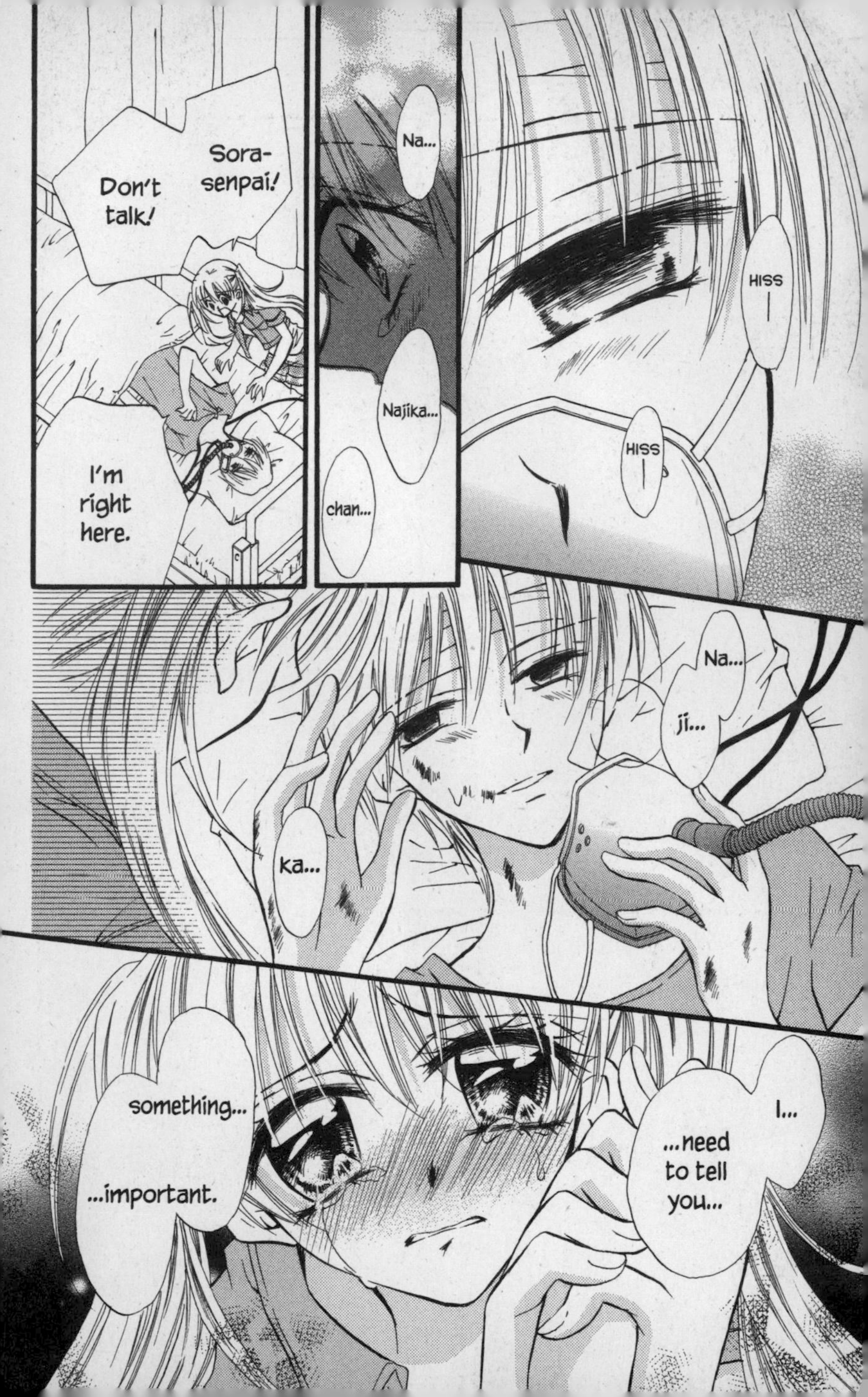
HISS
HISS
Na...
Najika...
chan...
Sora-senpai!
Don't talk!
I'm right here.
Na...
ji...
ka...
I...
...need to tell you...
something...
...important.

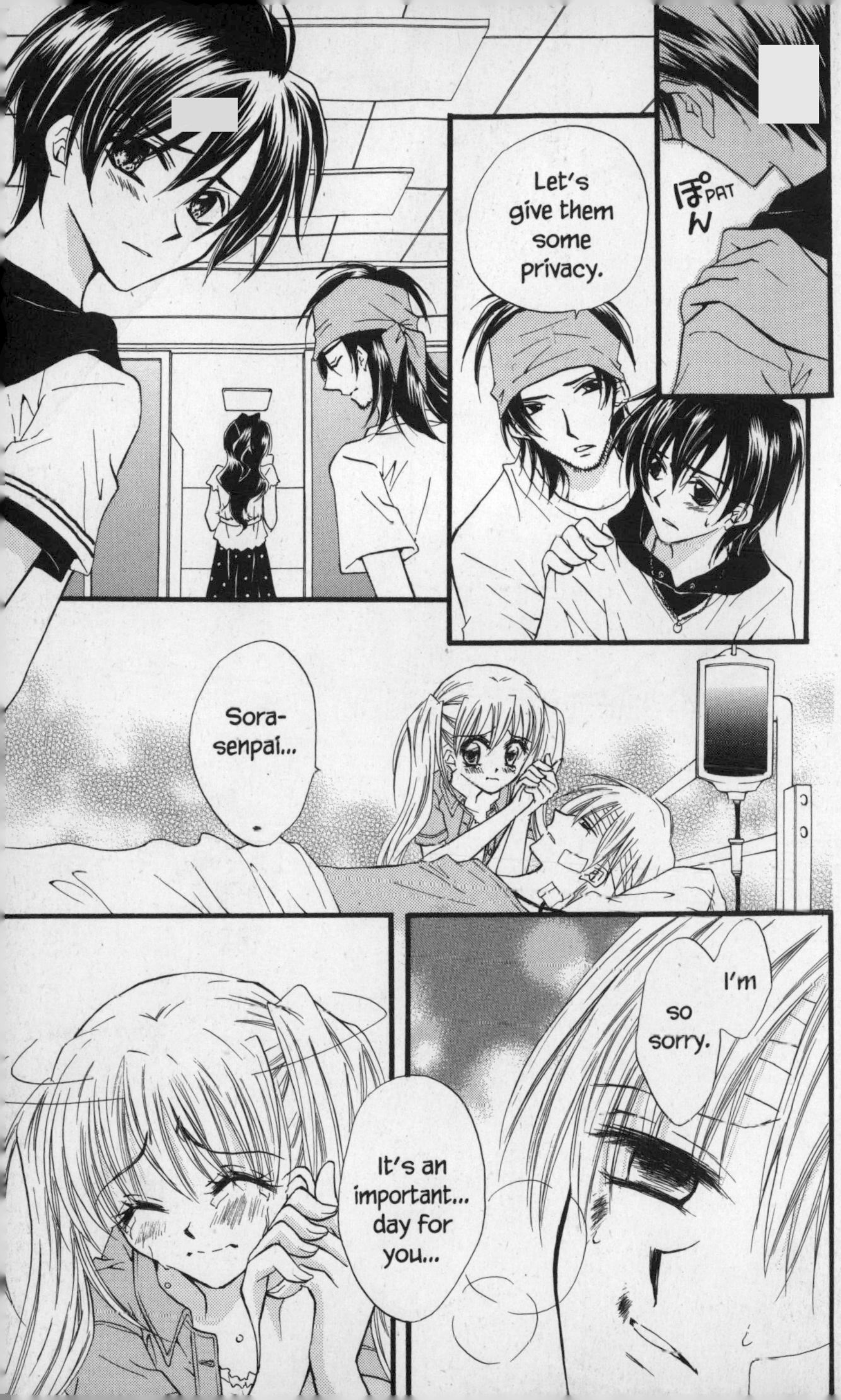
ぽん PAT
Let's give them some privacy.
Sora-senpai...
I'm so sorry.
It's an important... day for you...

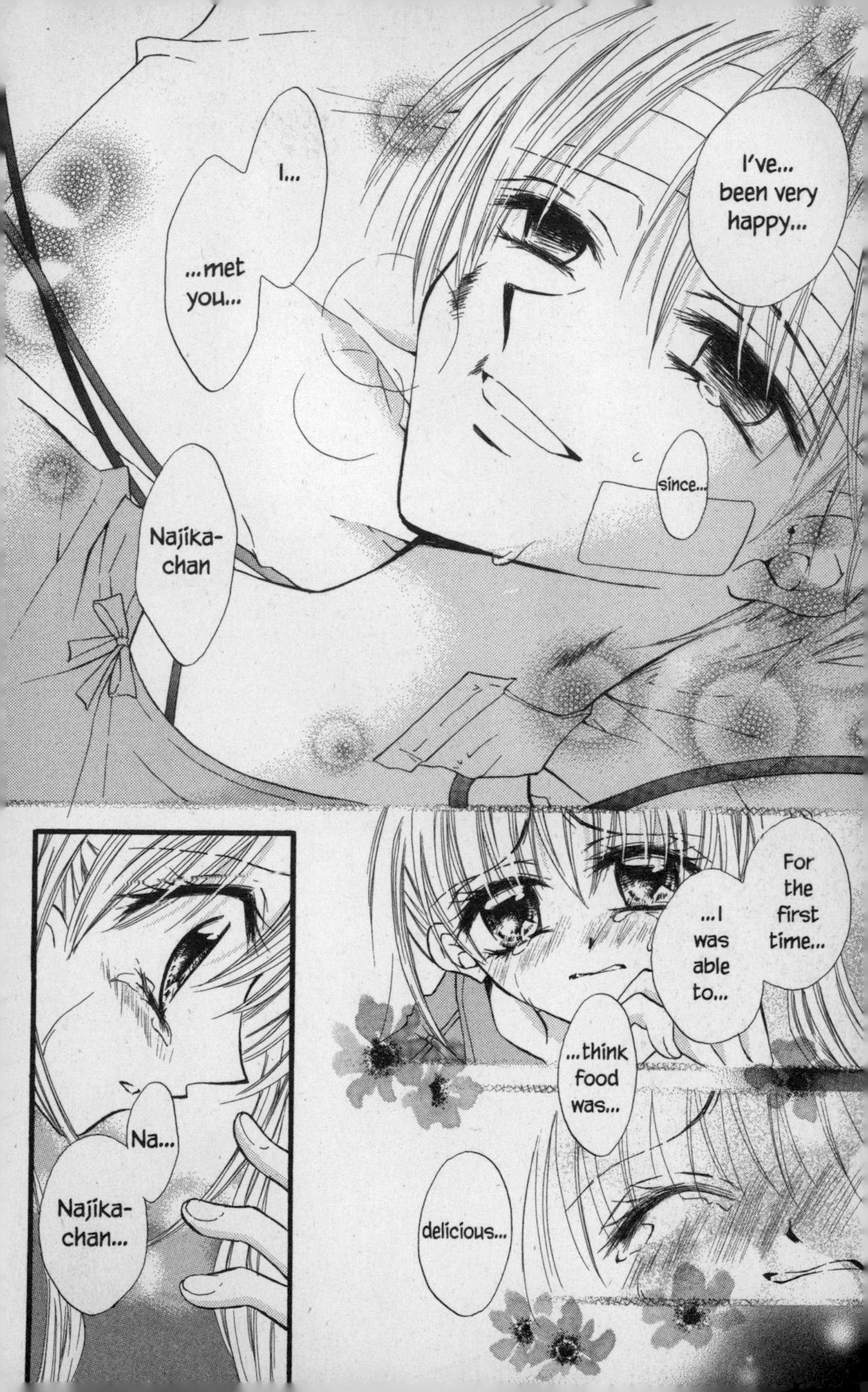
I've... been very happy...
since...
I...
...met you...
Najika-chan
For the first time...
...I was able to...
...think food was...
delicious...
Na...
Najika-chan...

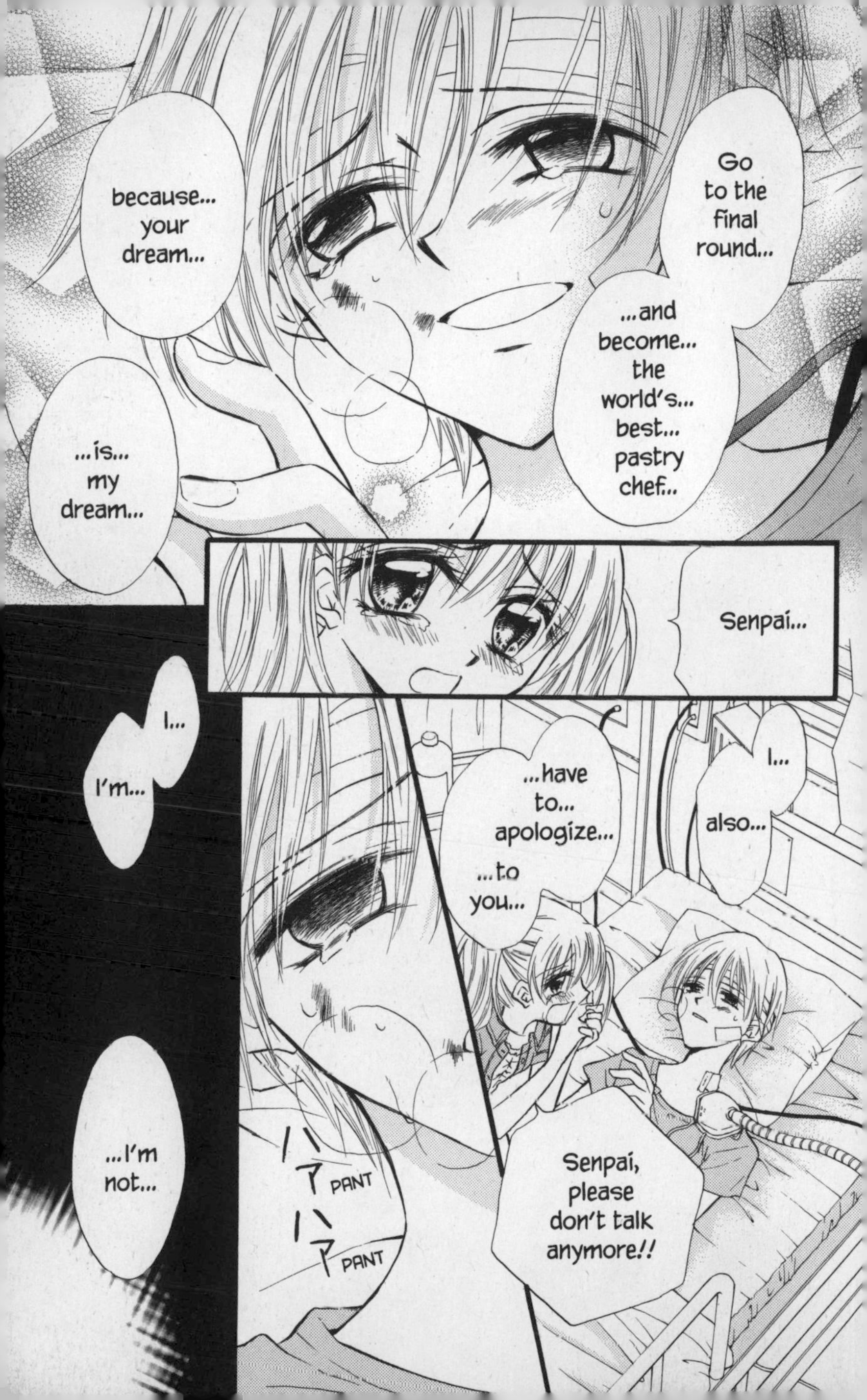

Go to the final round...
...and become... the world's... best... pastry chef...
because... your dream...
...is... my dream...
Senpai...
I... also...
...have to... apologize...
...to you...
Senpai, please don't talk anymore!!
ハア PANT
ハア PANT
I... I'm...
...I'm not...

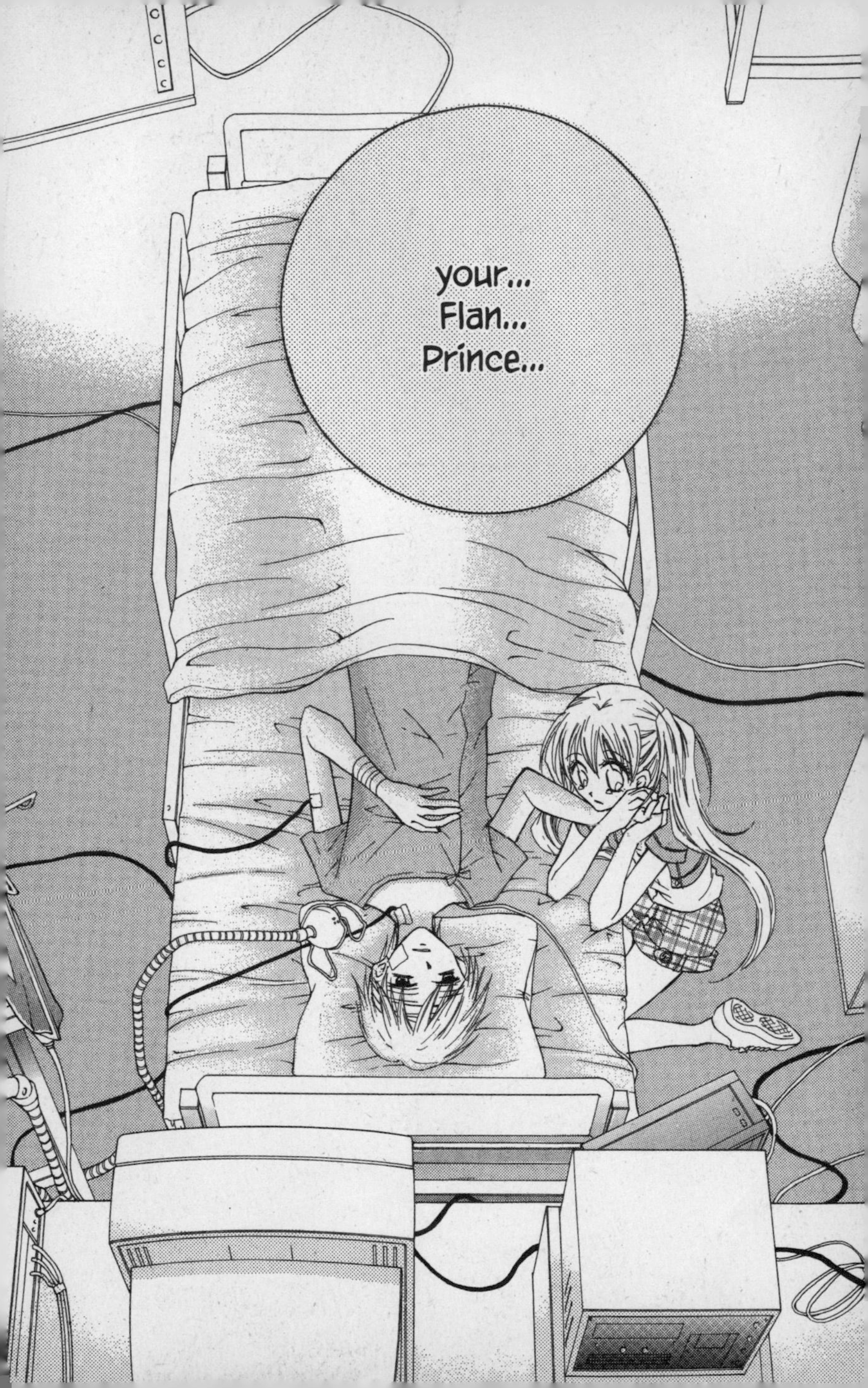
your... Flan... Prince...

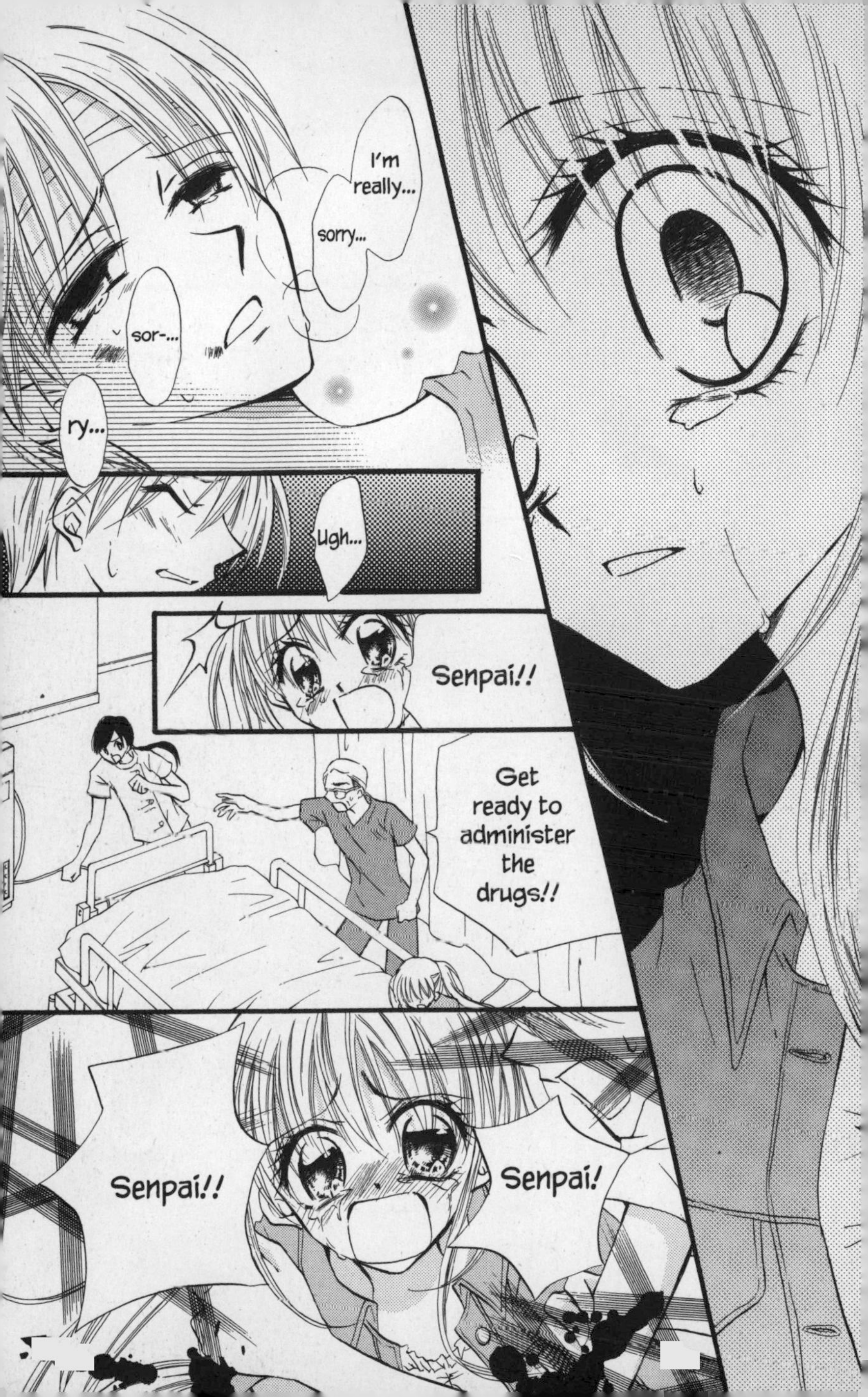
I'm really...
sorry...
sor-...
ry...
Ugh...
Senpai!!
Get ready to administer the drugs!!
Senpai!
Senpai!!

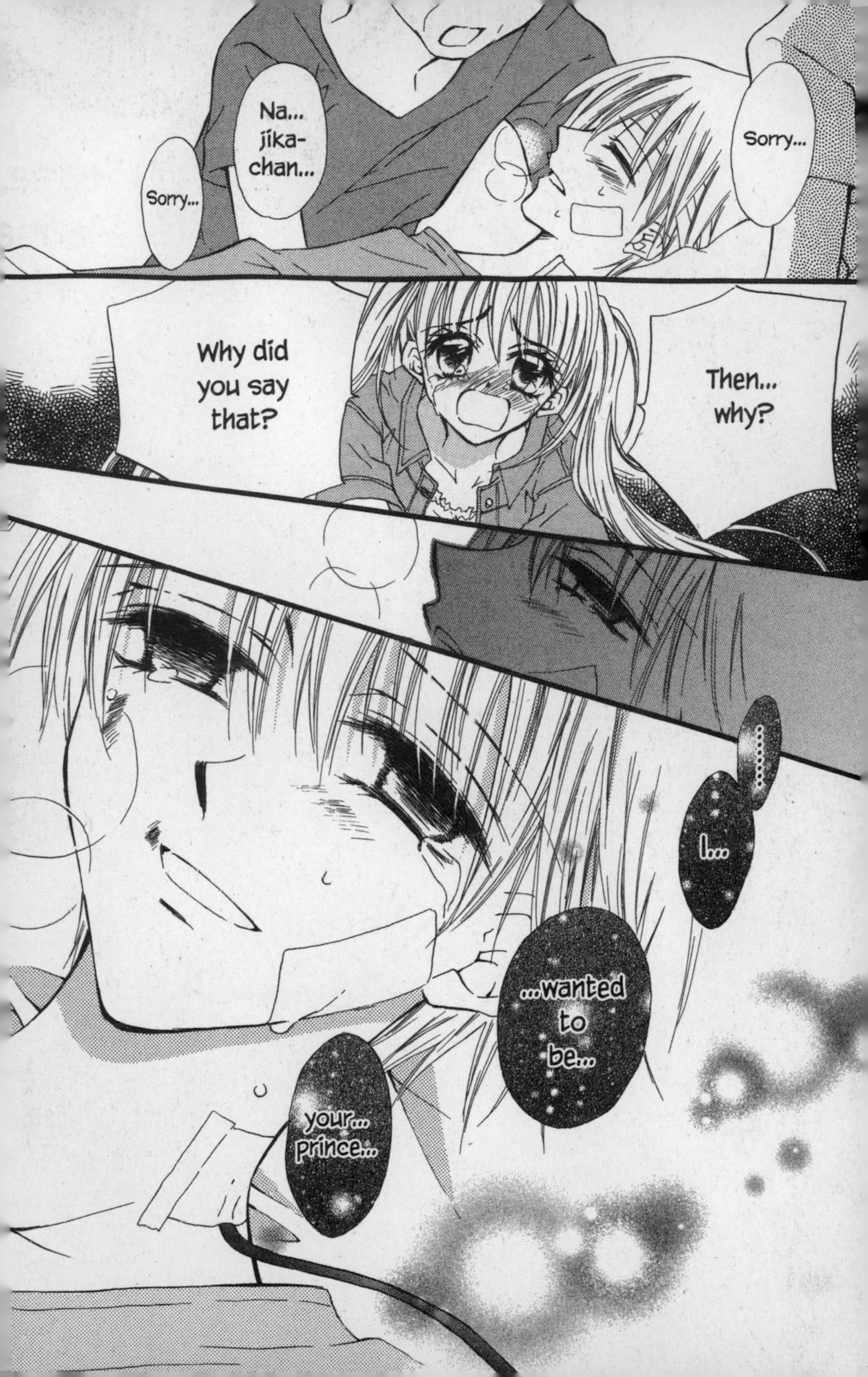
Sorry...
Na... jika-chan...
Sorry...
Then... why?
Why did you say that?
......
I...
...wanted to be...
your... prince...

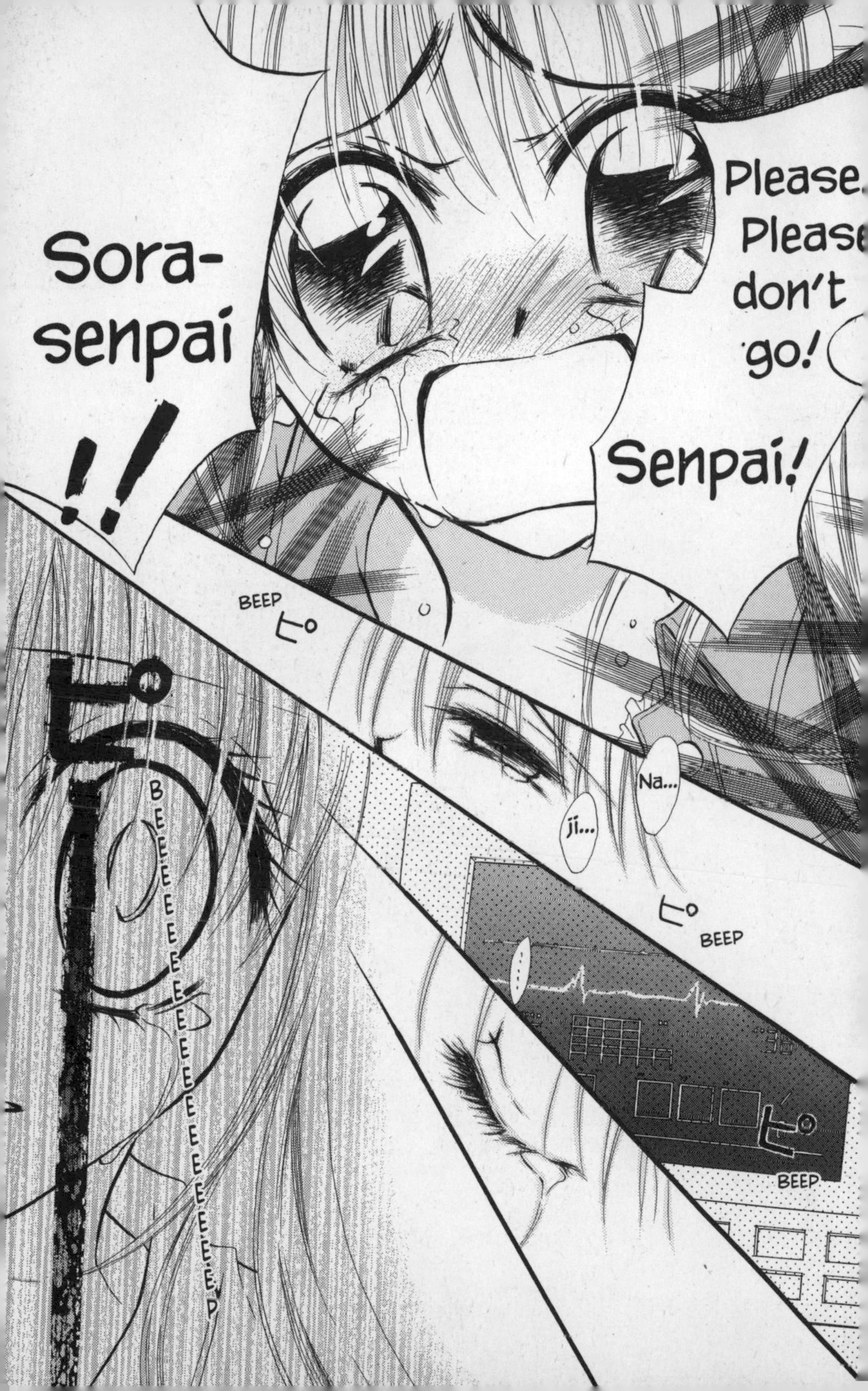

Please. Please don't go!
Senpai!
Sora-senpai
!!
BEEP
Na...
ji...
BEEP
...
BEEP
BEEEEEEEEEEEEEEEEEP

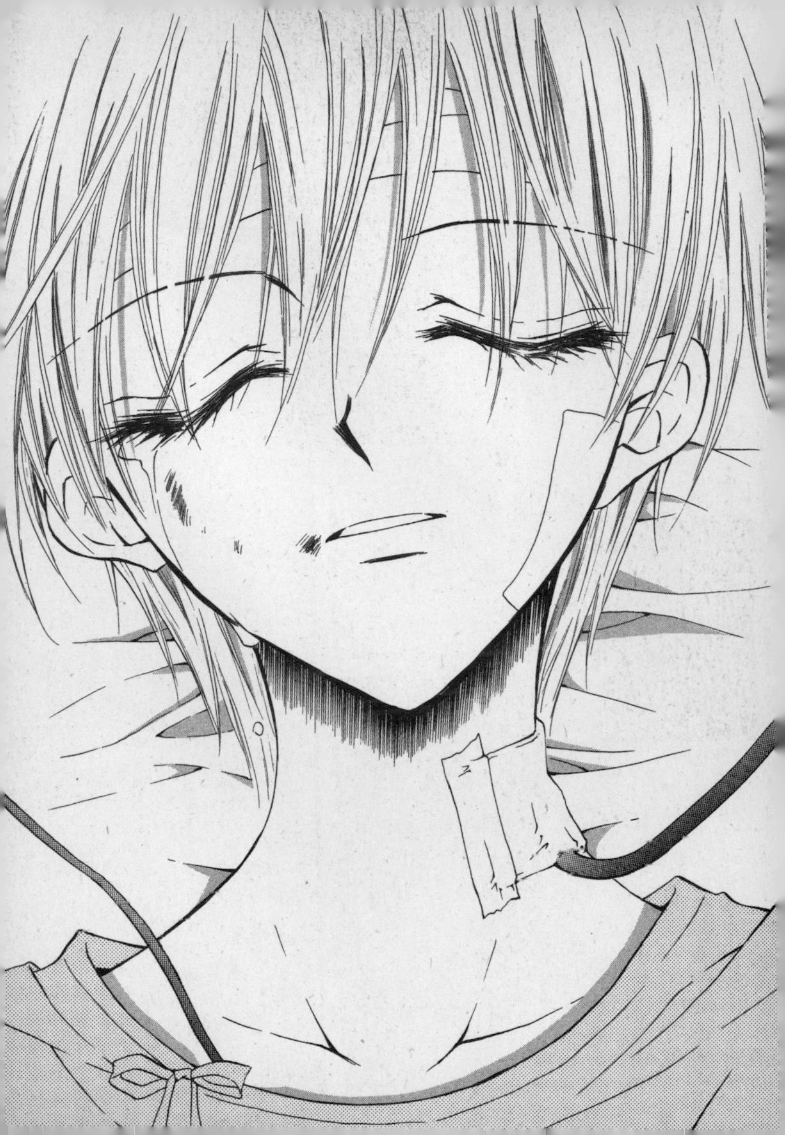

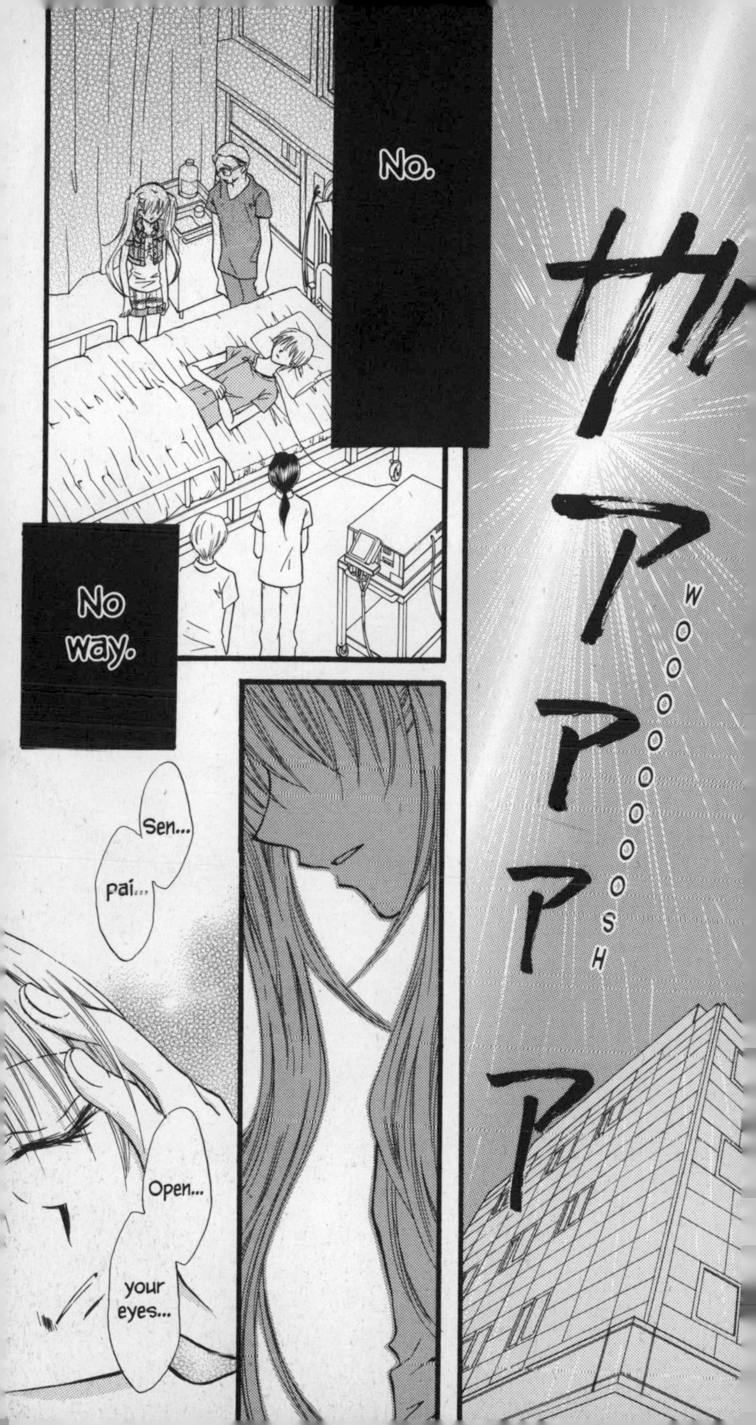

サアアアア
WOOOOOOOOOSH
No.
No way.
Sen... pai...
Open... your eyes...

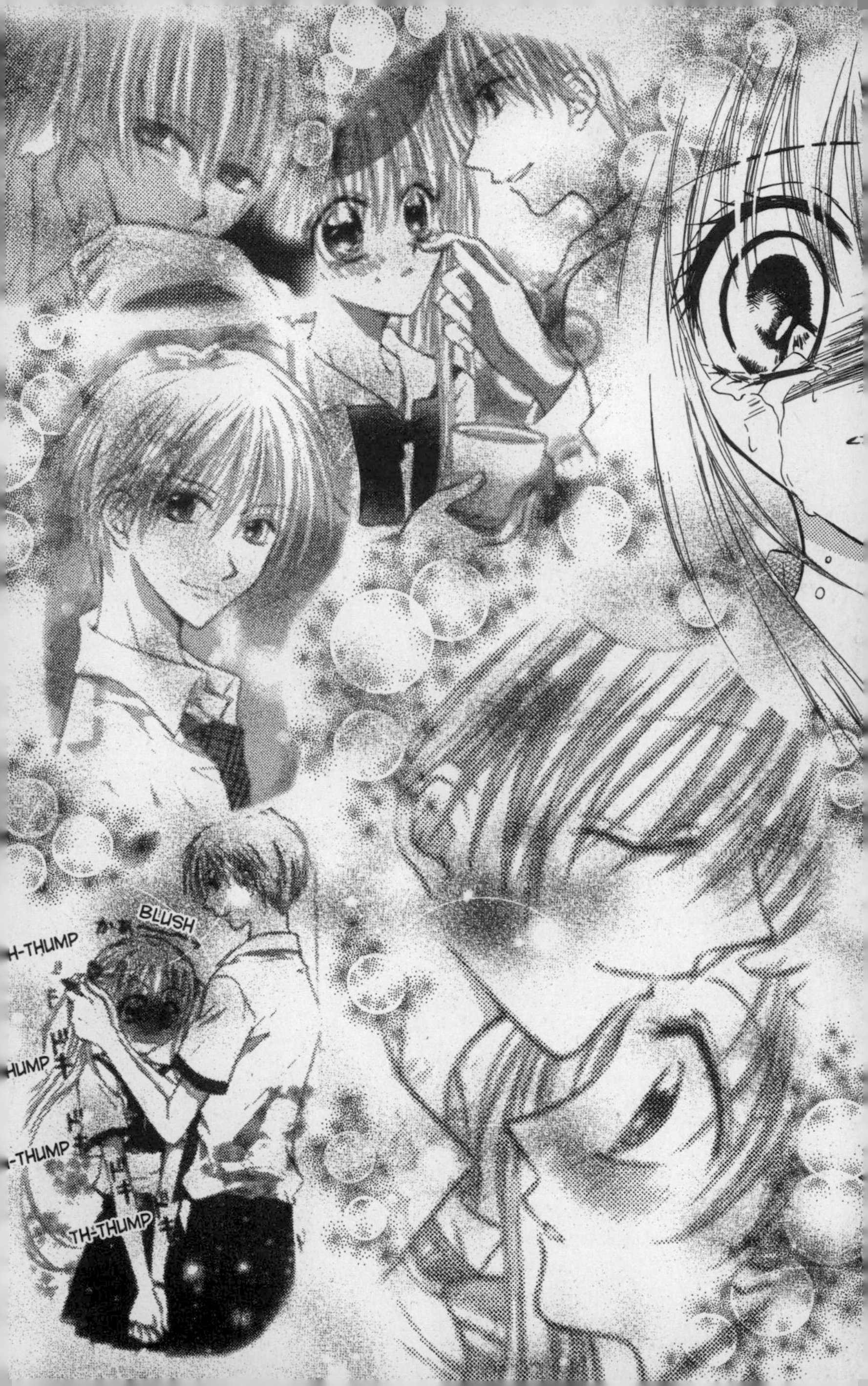
BLUSH
H-THUMP
HUMP
-THUMP
TH-THUMP

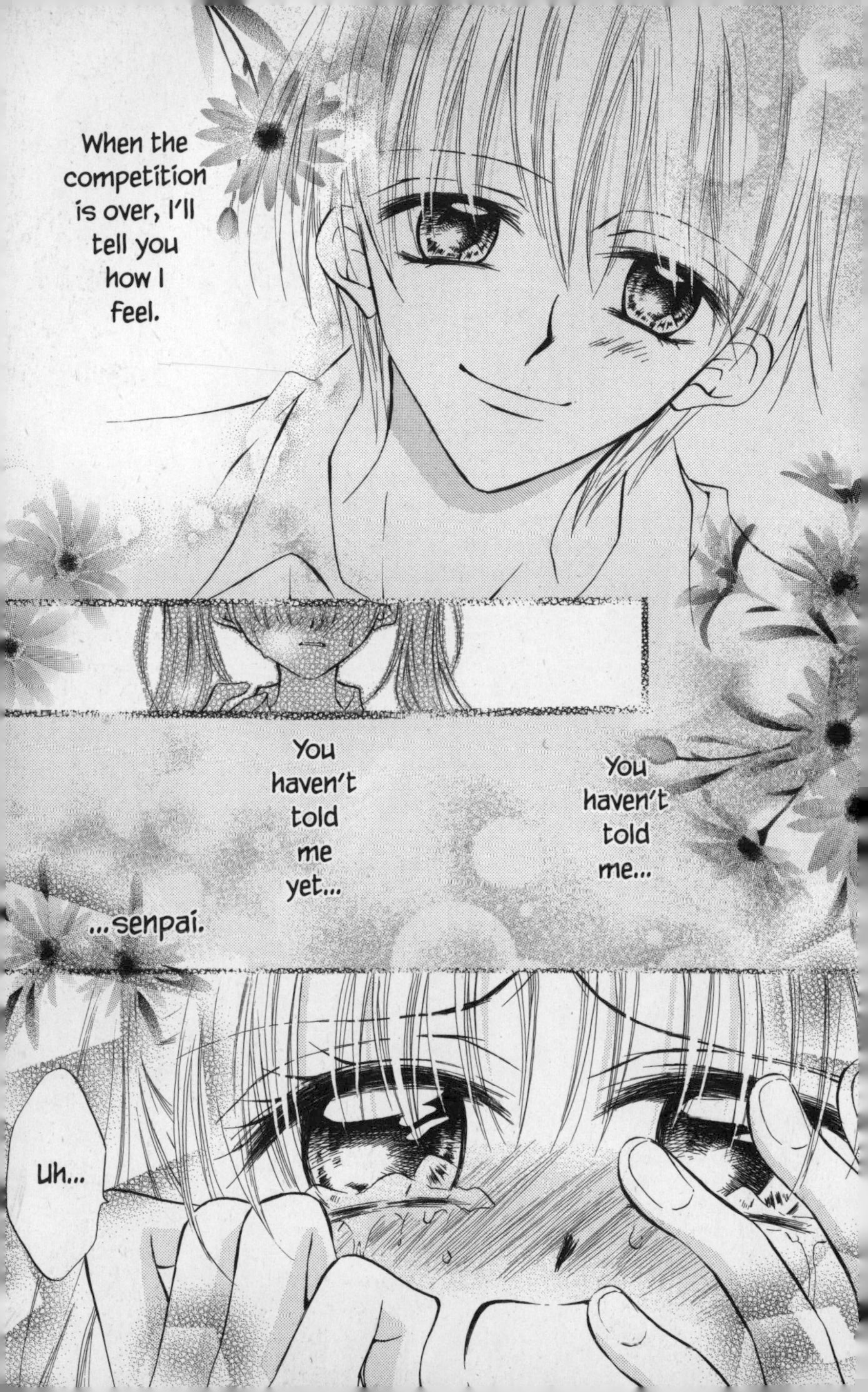
When the competition is over, I'll tell you how I feel.
You haven't told me...
You haven't told me yet...
...senpai.
Uh...

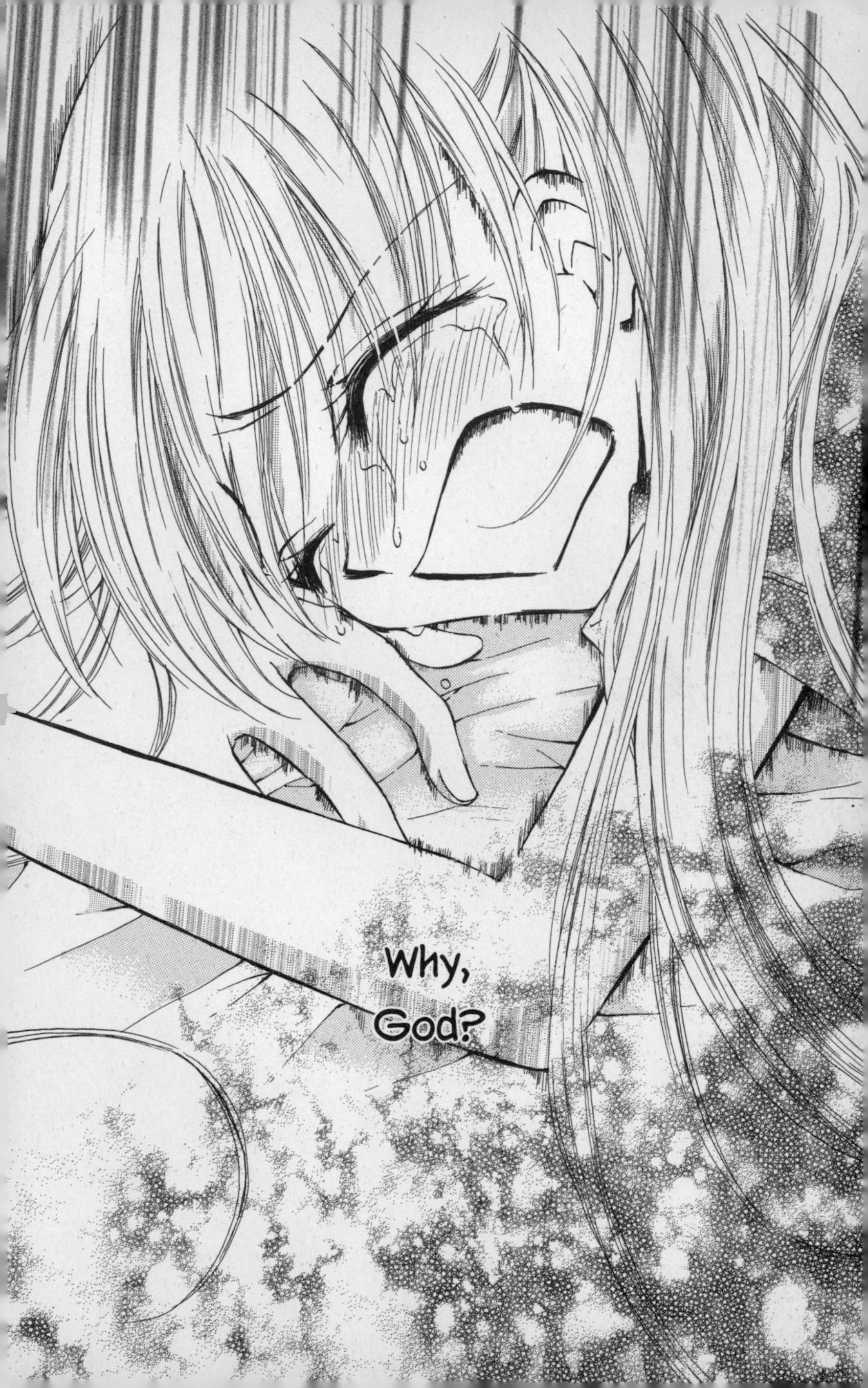
Why, God?

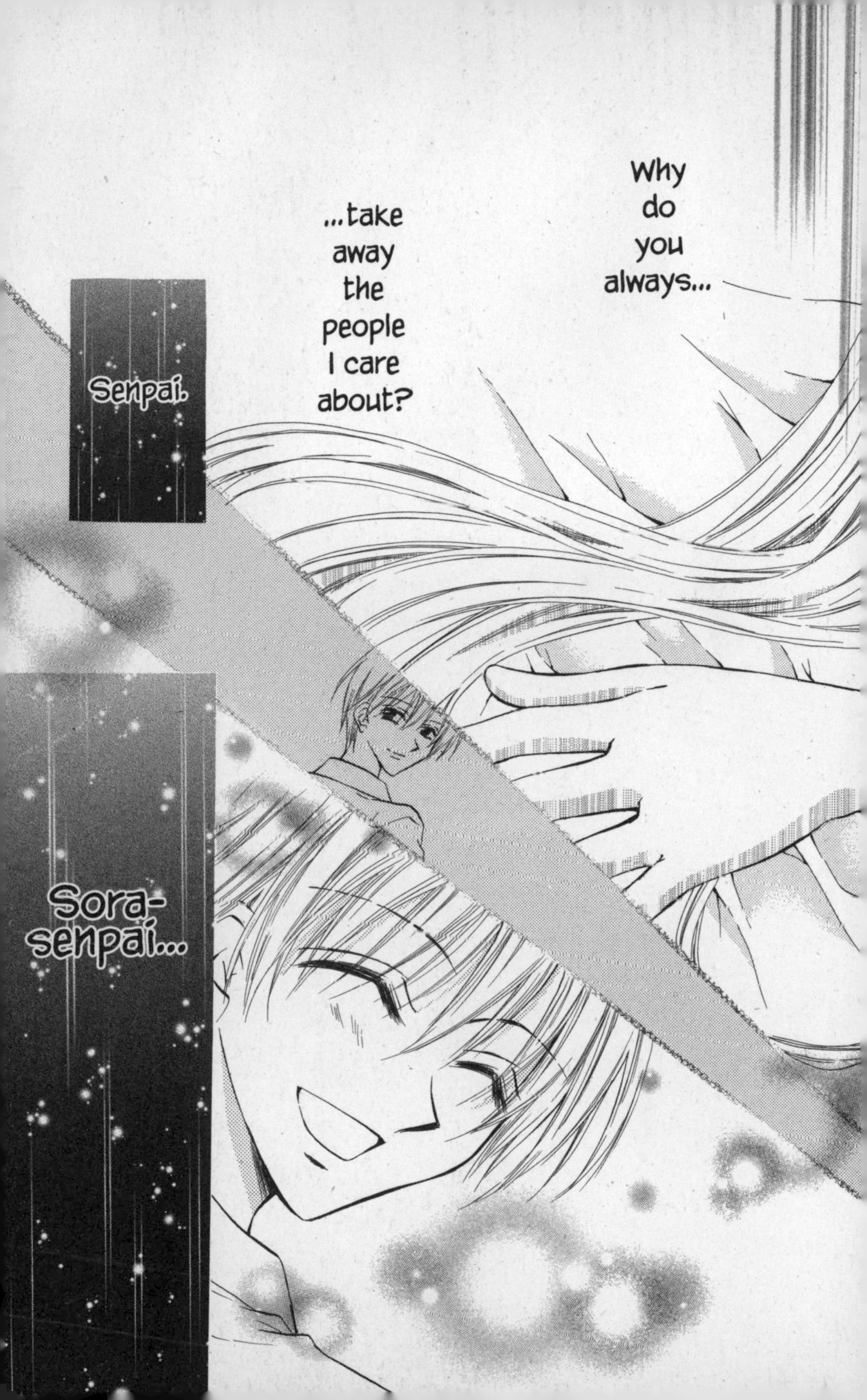
Why do you always...
...take away the people I care about?
Senpai.
Sora-senpai...

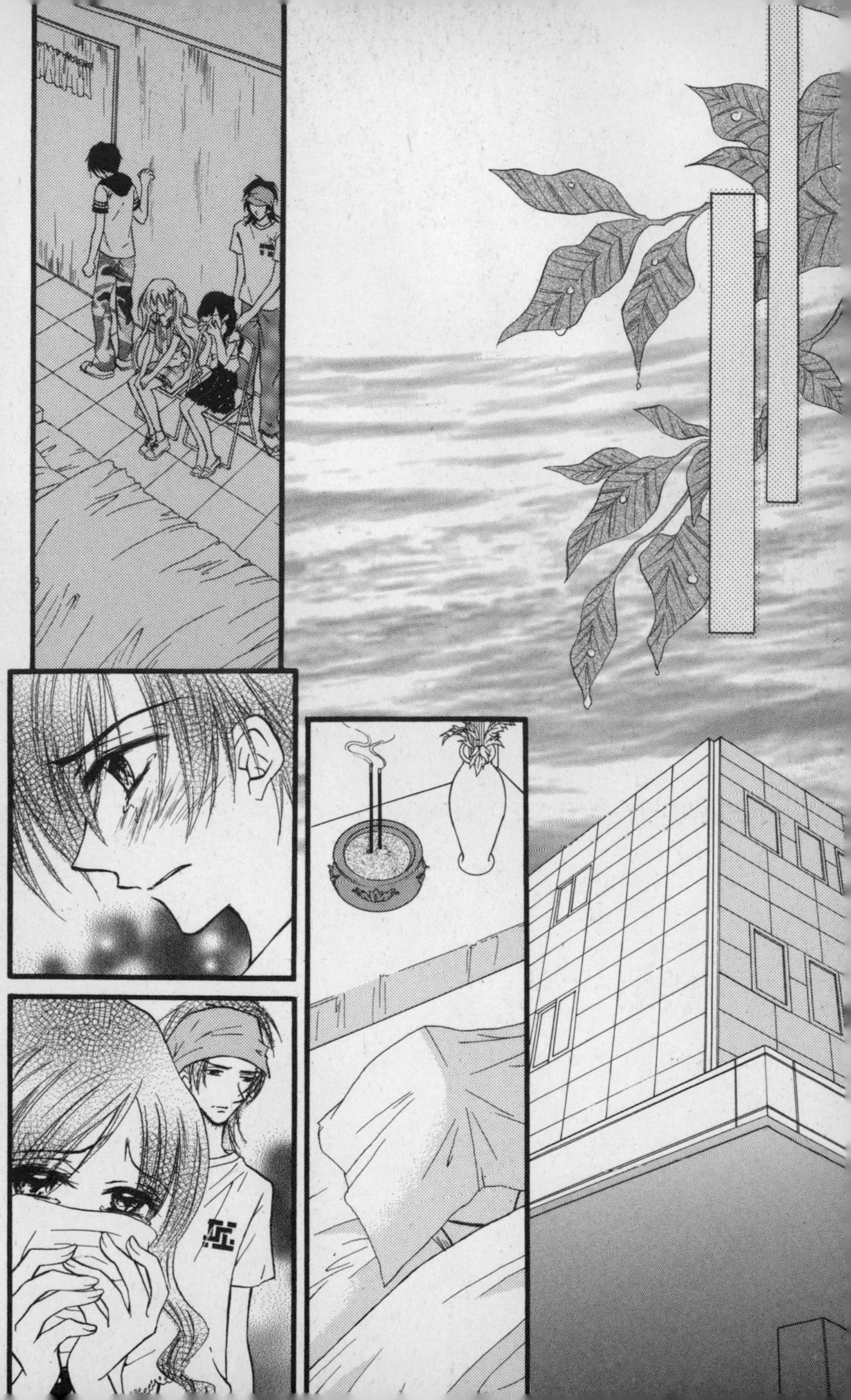

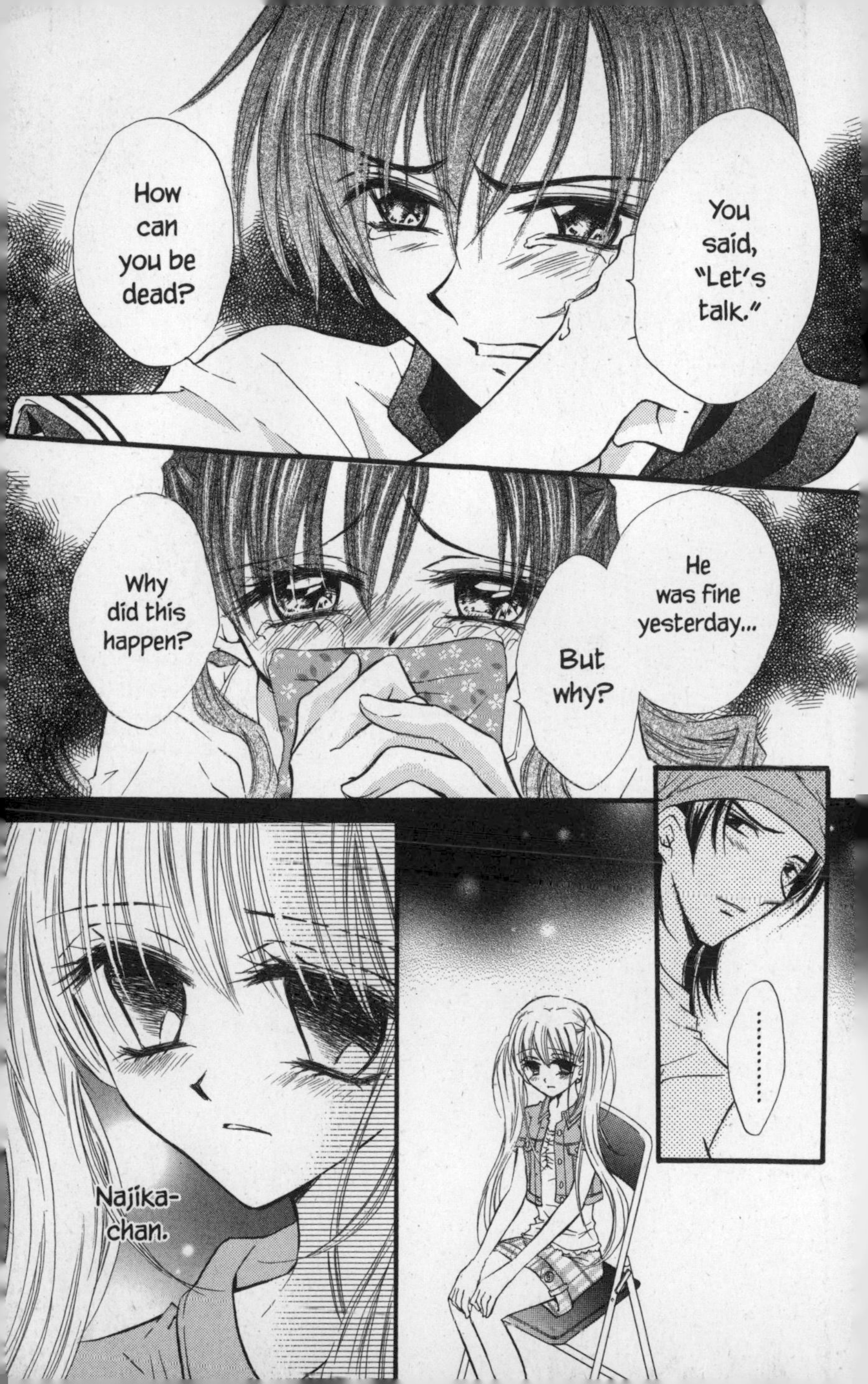
You said, "Let's talk."
How can you be dead?
He was fine yesterday...
But why?
Why did this happen?
......
Najika-chan.

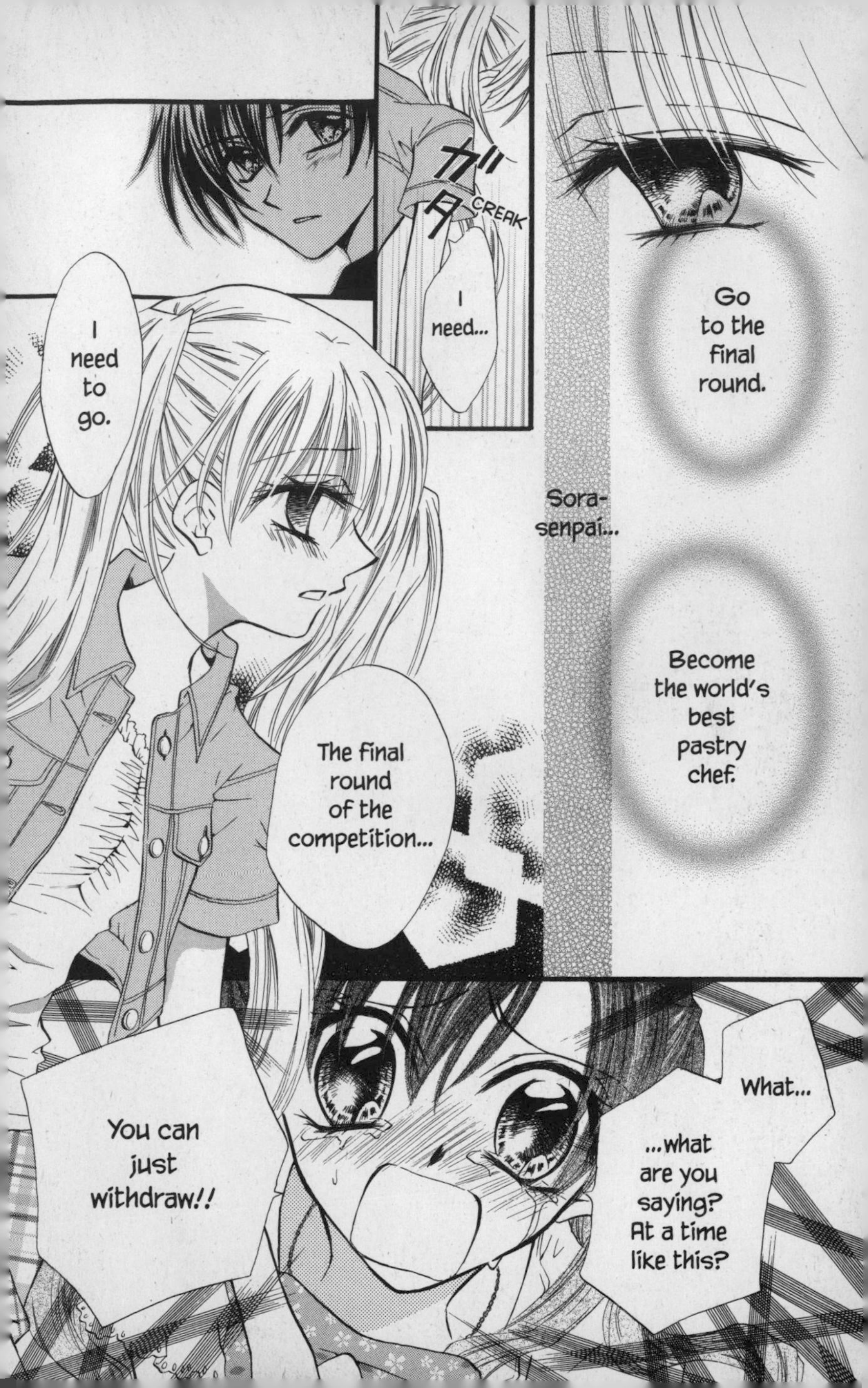

Go to the final round.
Sora-senpai...
Become the world's best pastry chef.
CREAK
I need...
I need to go.
The final round of the competition...
What...
...what are you saying? At a time like this?
You can just withdraw!!

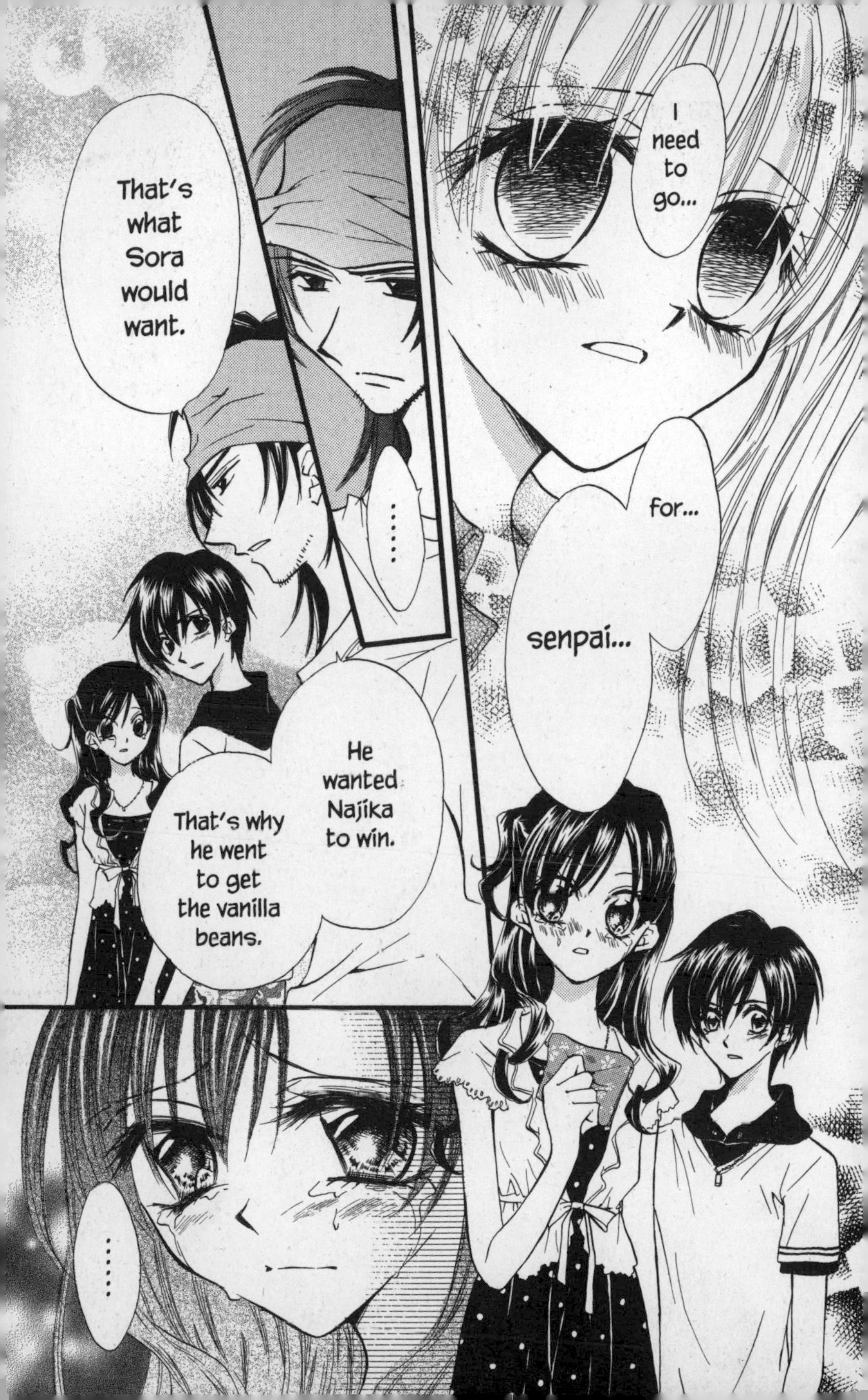
I need to go...
for...
senpai...
......
That's what Sora would want.
He wanted Najika to win.
That's why he went to get the vanilla beans.
......

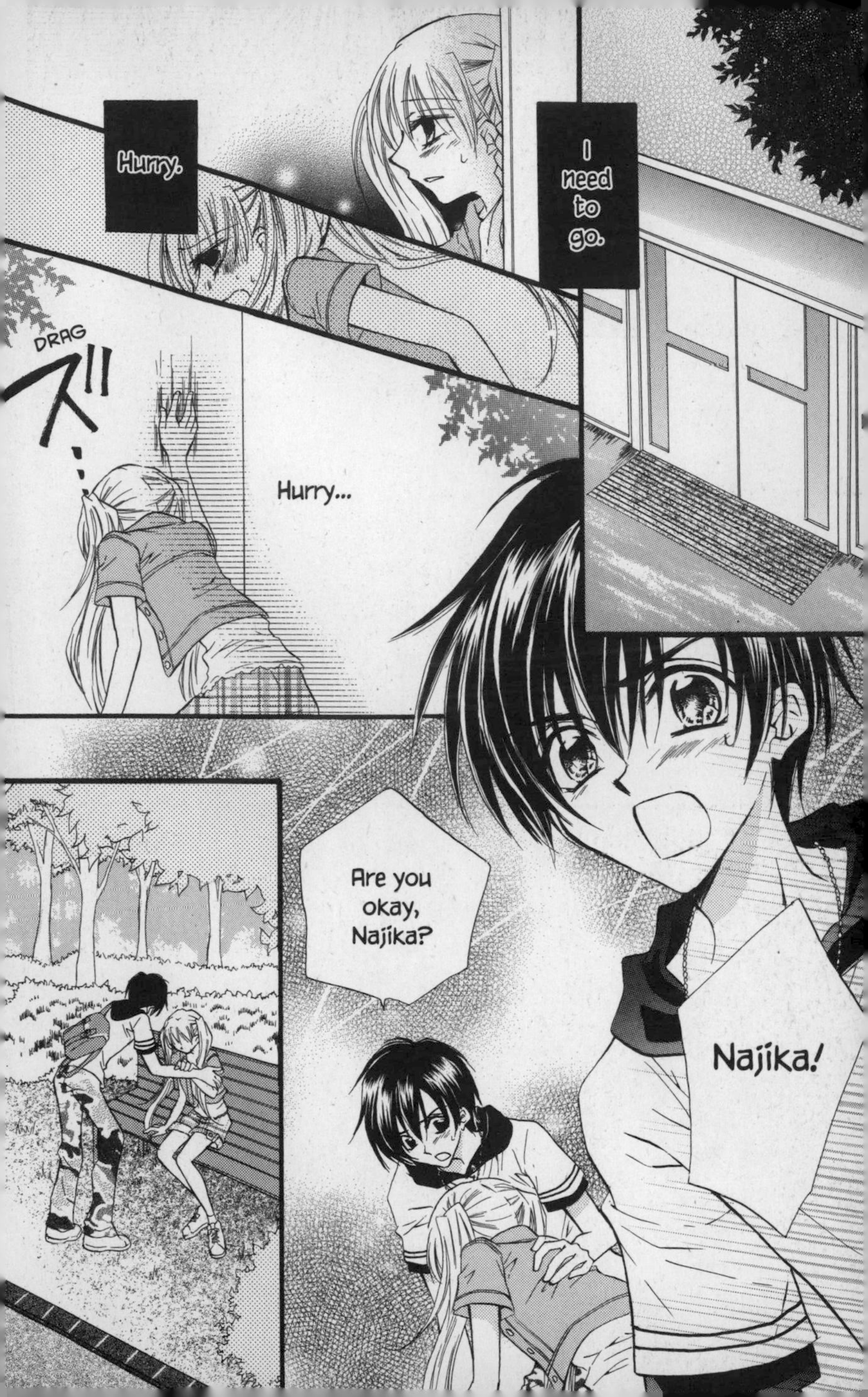
I need to go.
Hurry.
DRAG
Hurry...
Najika!
Are you okay, Najika?

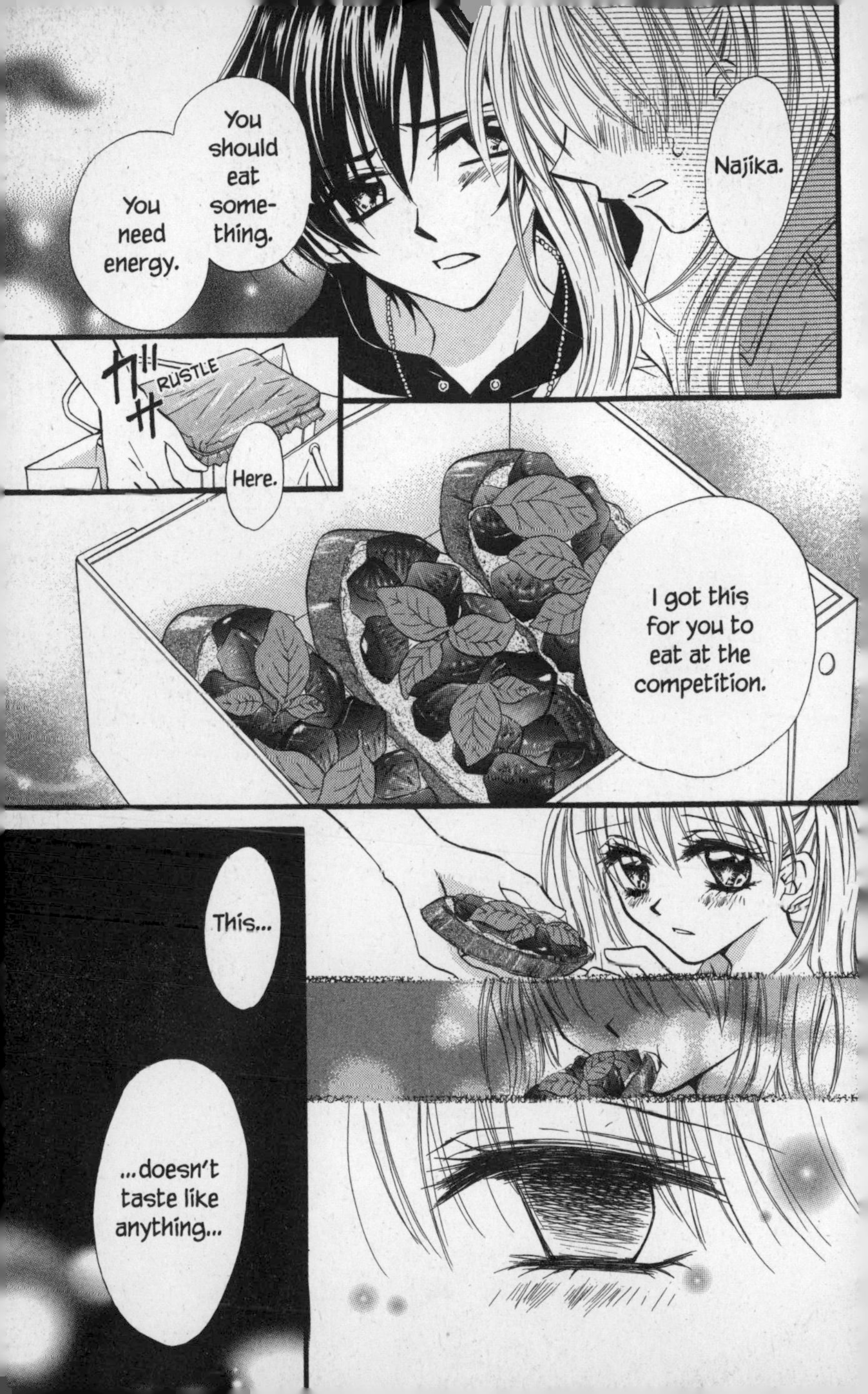
Najika.
You should eat some-thing.
You need energy.
RUSTLE
Here.
I got this for you to eat at the competition.
This...
...doesn't taste like anything...

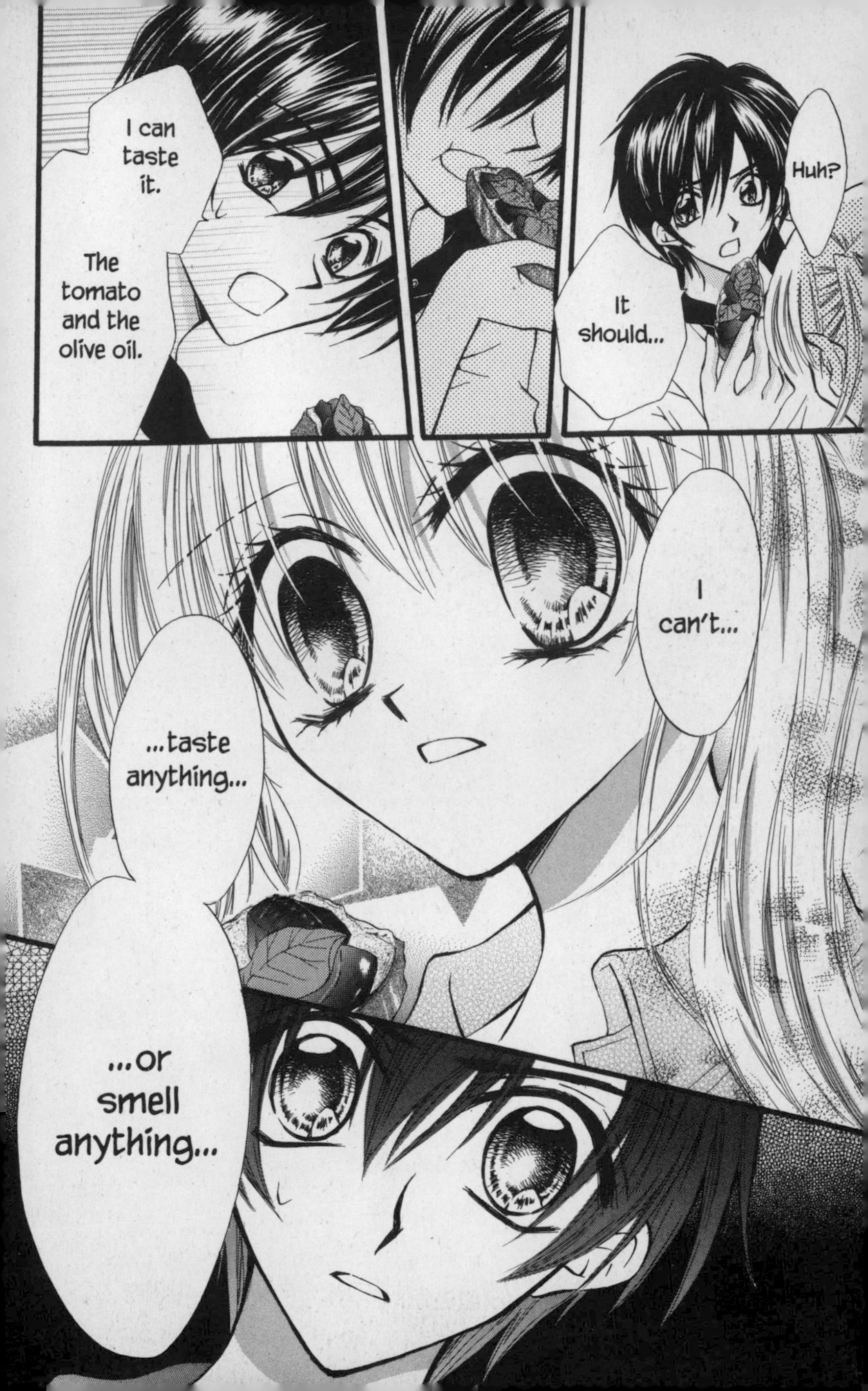
Huh?
It should...
I can taste it.
The tomato and the olive oil.
I can't...
...taste anything...
...or smell anything...

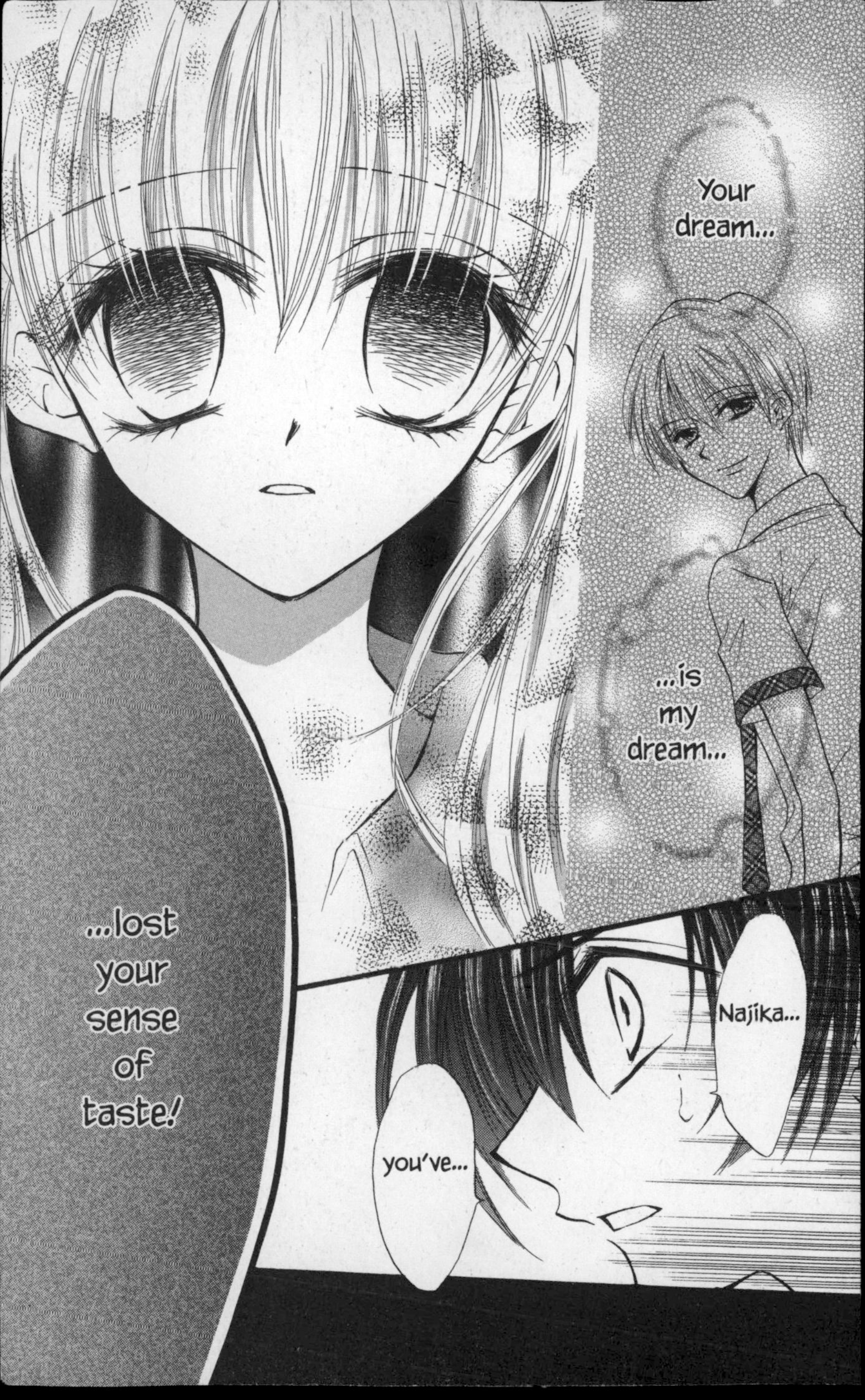
Your dream...
...is my dream...
Najika...
you've...
...lost your sense of taste!

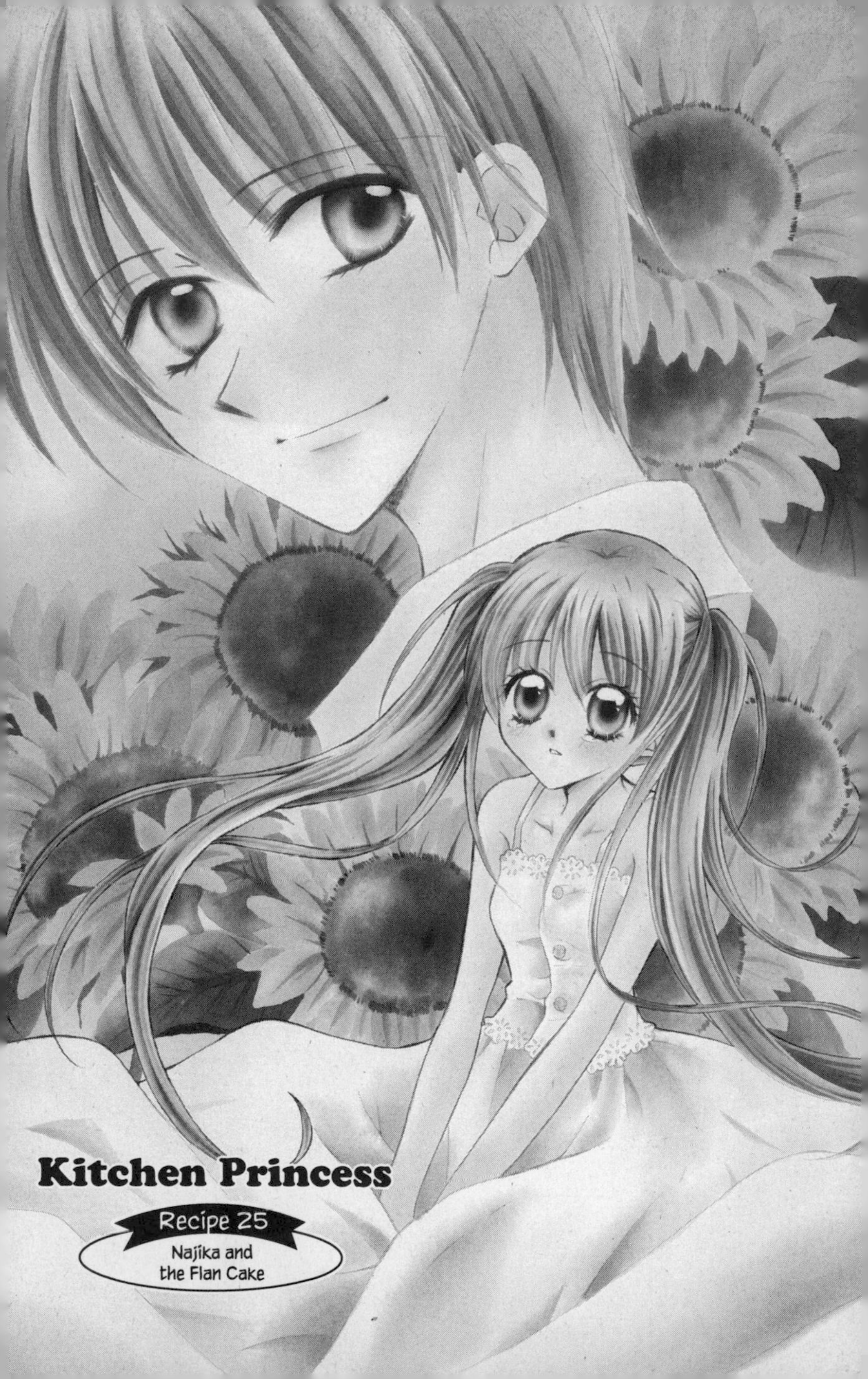
Kitchen Princess
Recipe 25
Najika and the Flan Cake

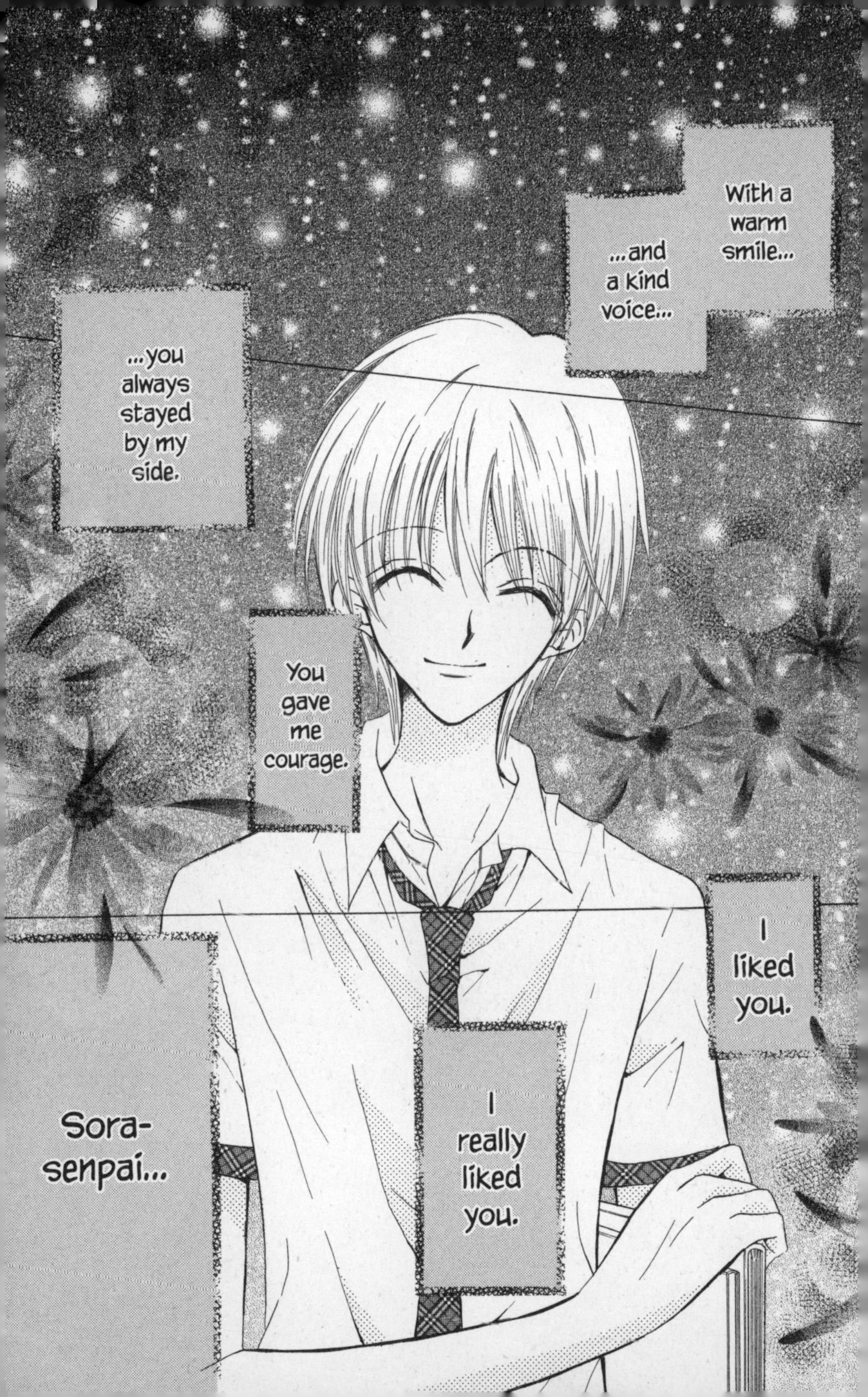

With a warm smile...
...and a kind voice...
...you always stayed by my side.
You gave me courage.
I liked you.
I really liked you.
Sora-senpai...

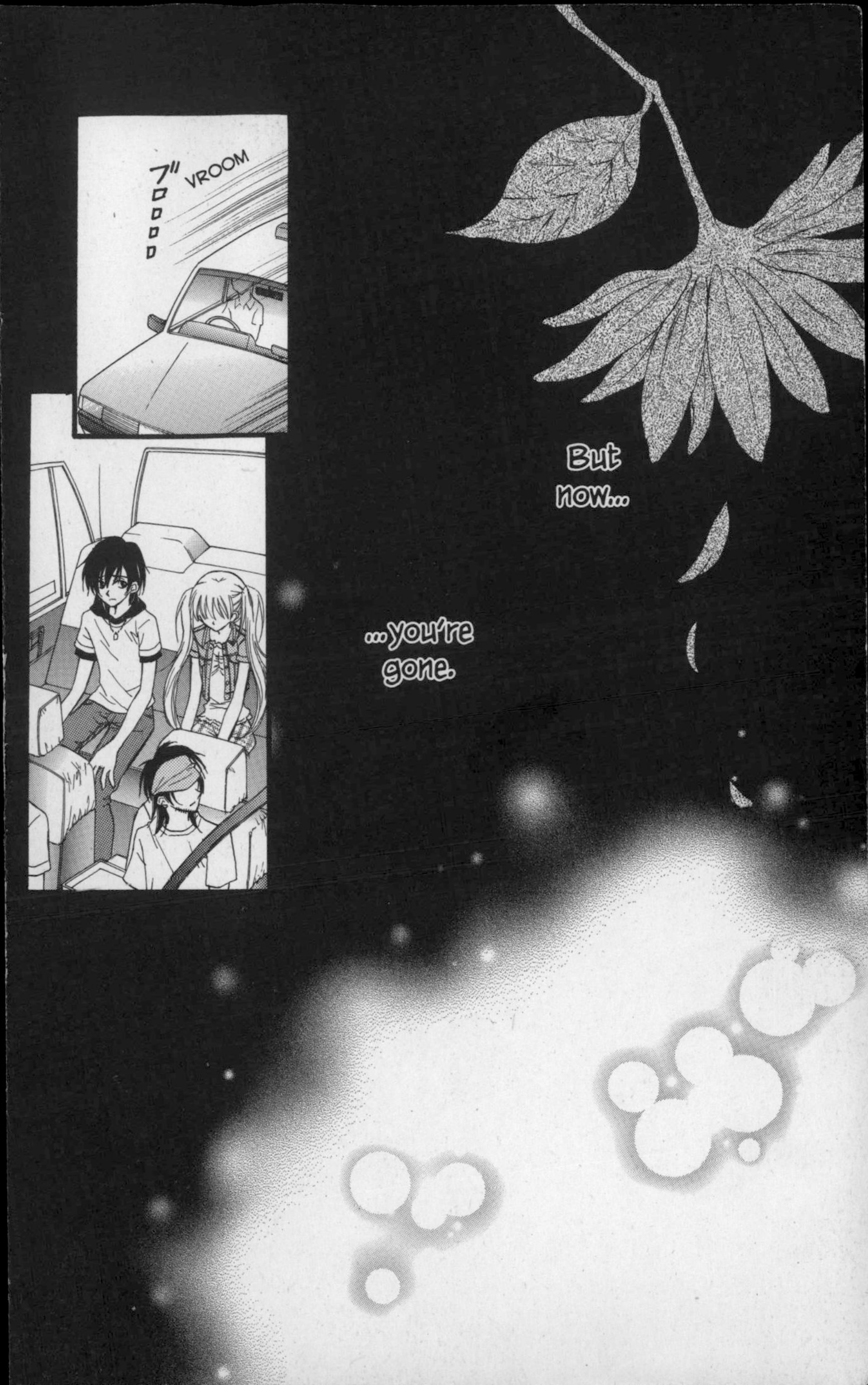
But now...
...you're gone.
ブロロロロ
VROOM

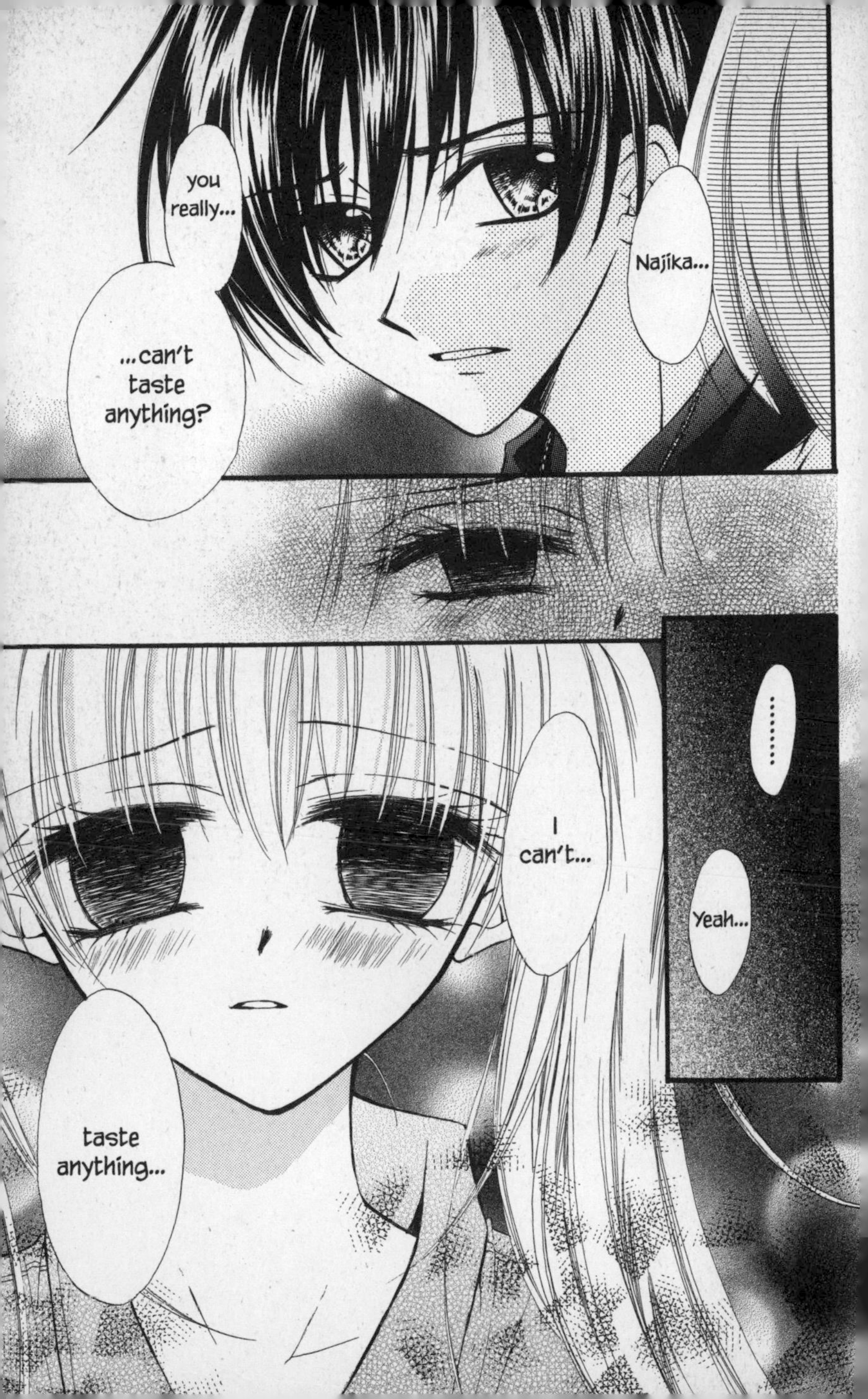
Najika...
you really...
...can't taste anything?
......
Yeah...
I can't...
taste anything...

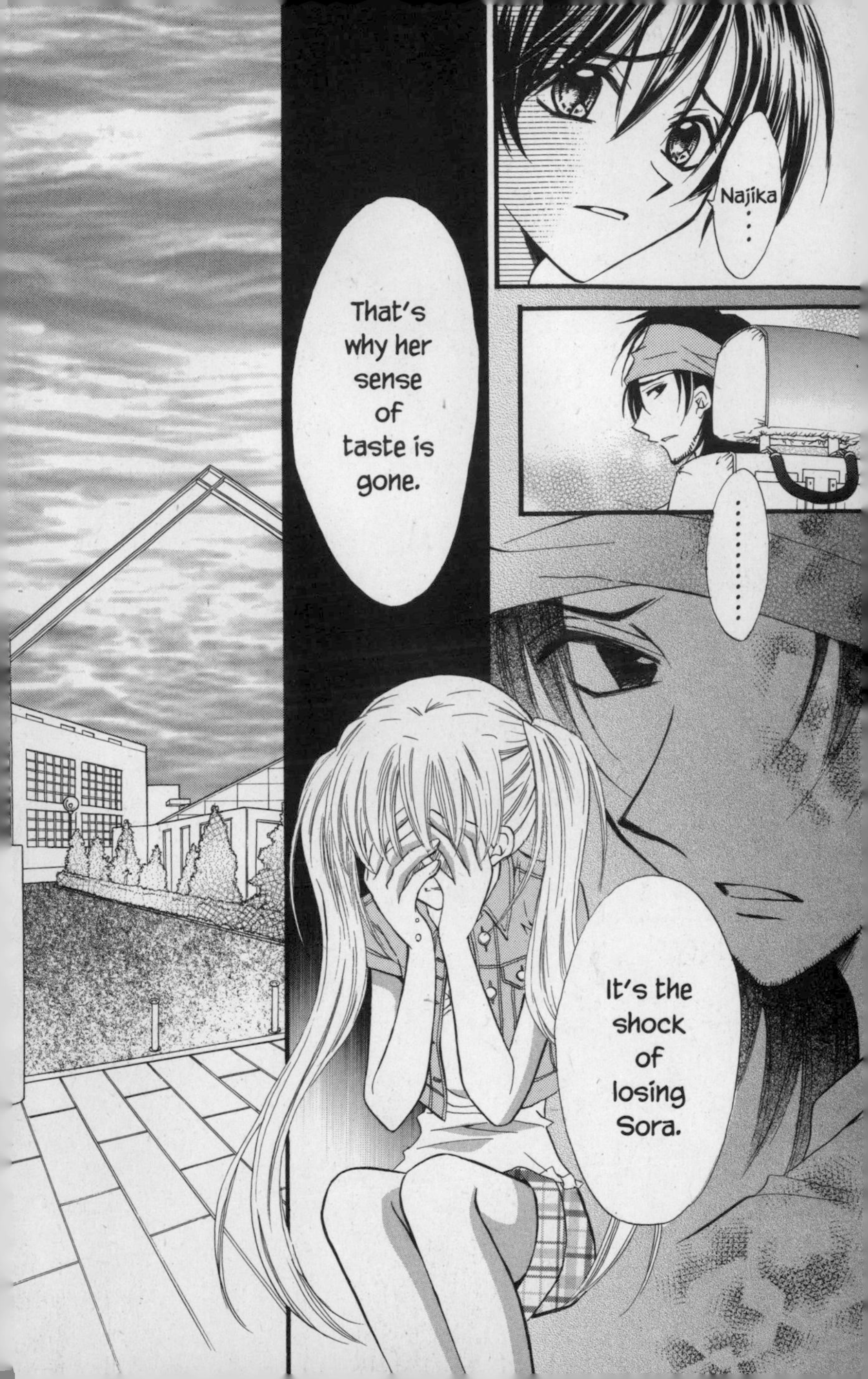
Najika
...
......
It's the shock of losing Sora.
That's why her sense of taste is gone.

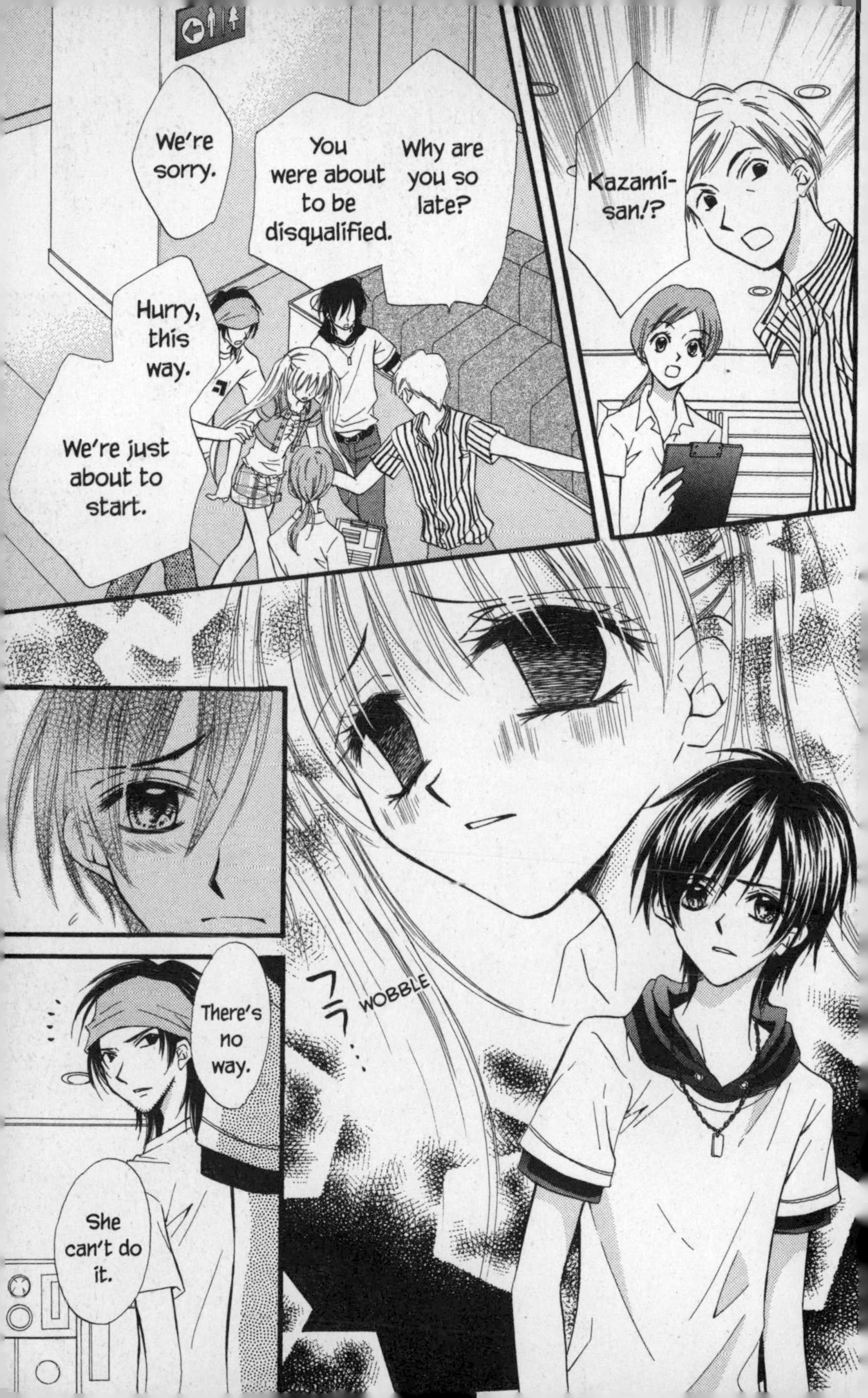
Kazami-san!?
Why are you so late?
You were about to be disqualified.
We're sorry.
Hurry, this way.
We're just about to start.
WOBBLE
There's no way.
She can't do it.

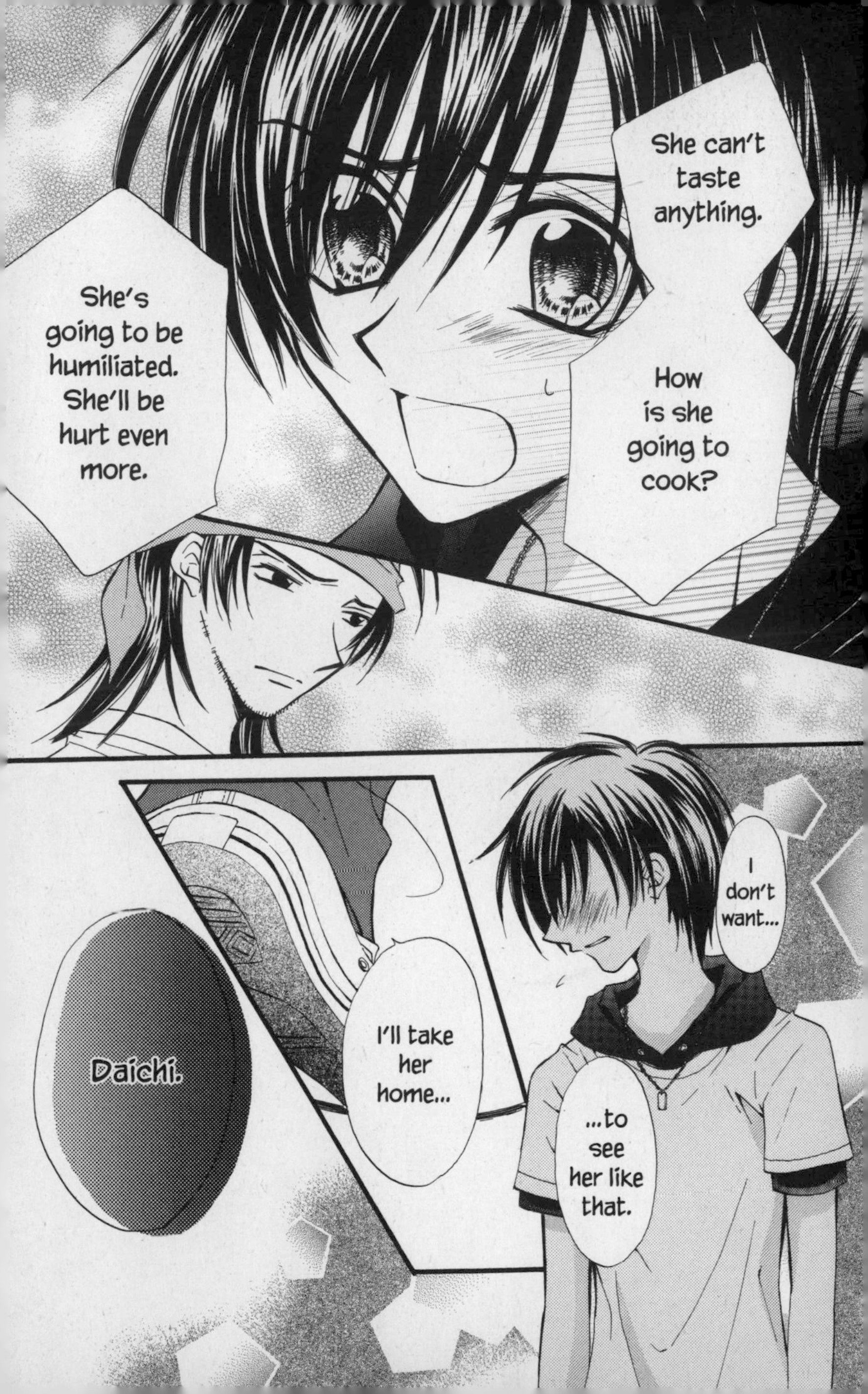
She can't taste anything.
How is she going to cook?
She's going to be humiliated. She'll be hurt even more.
I don't want...
...to see her like that.
I'll take her home...
Daichi.

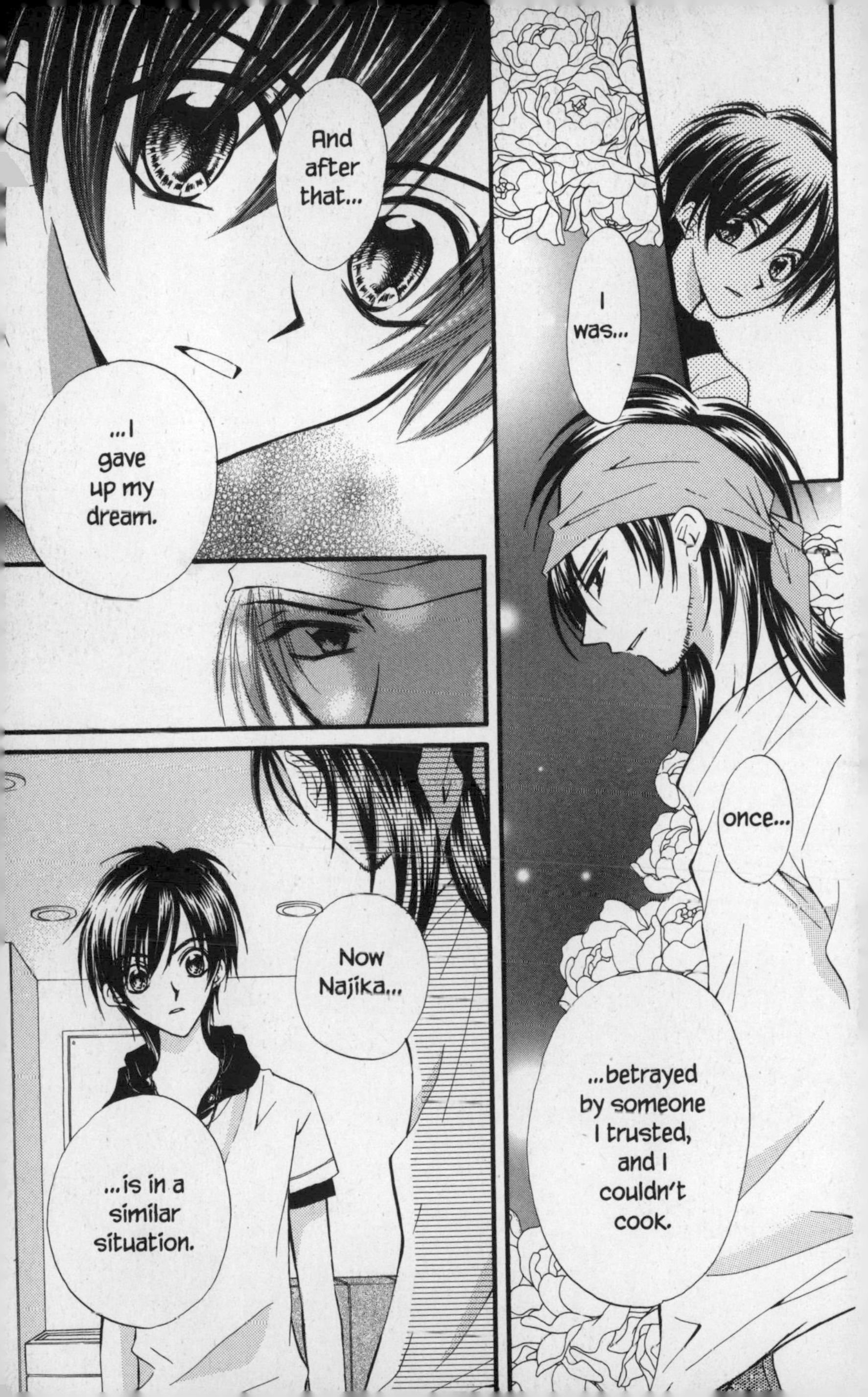
I was...
once...
...betrayed by someone I trusted, and I couldn't cook.
And after that...
...I gave up my dream.
Now Najika...
...is in a similar situation.

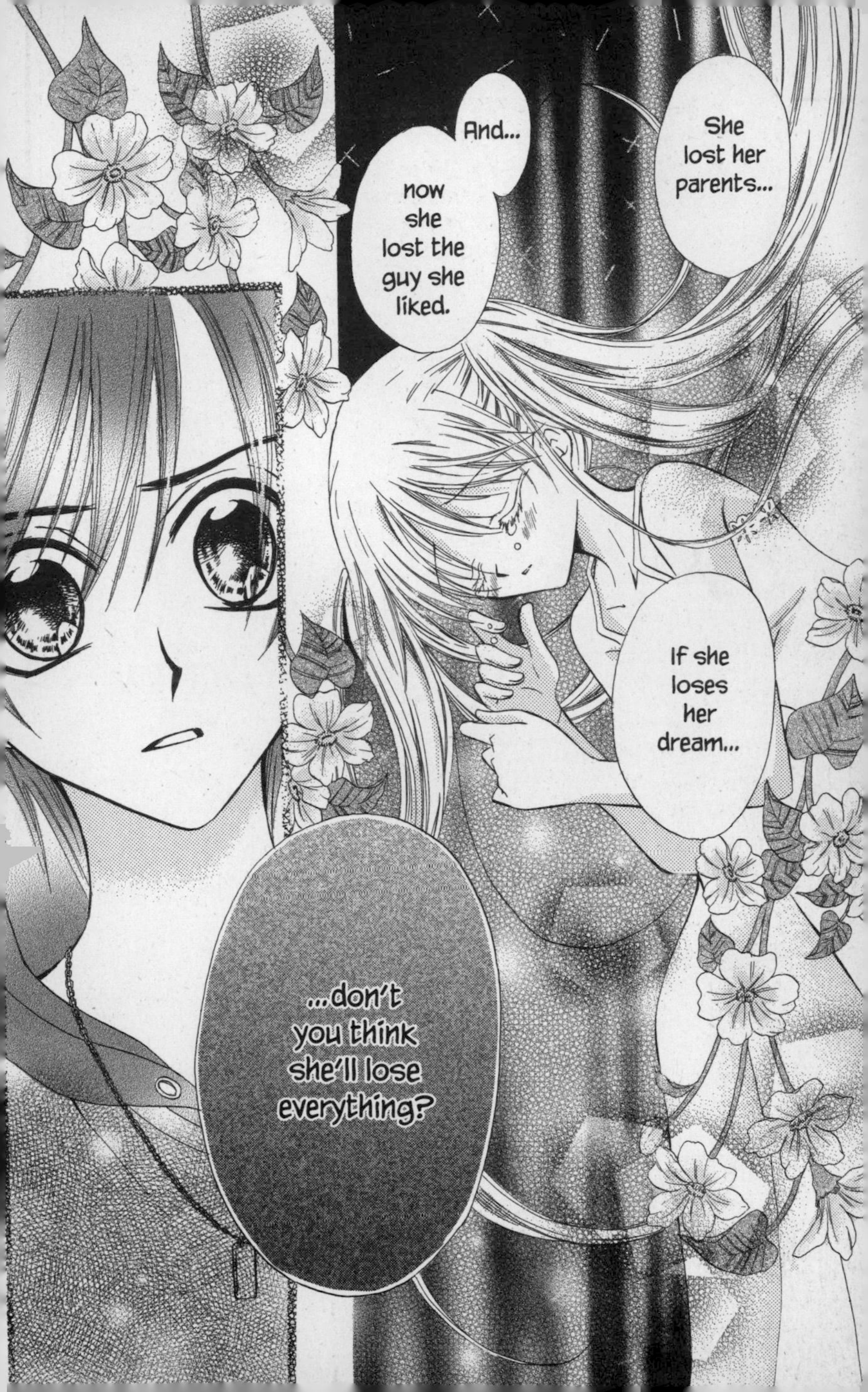
She lost her parents...
And...
now she lost the guy she liked.
If she loses her dream...
...don't you think she'll lose everything?

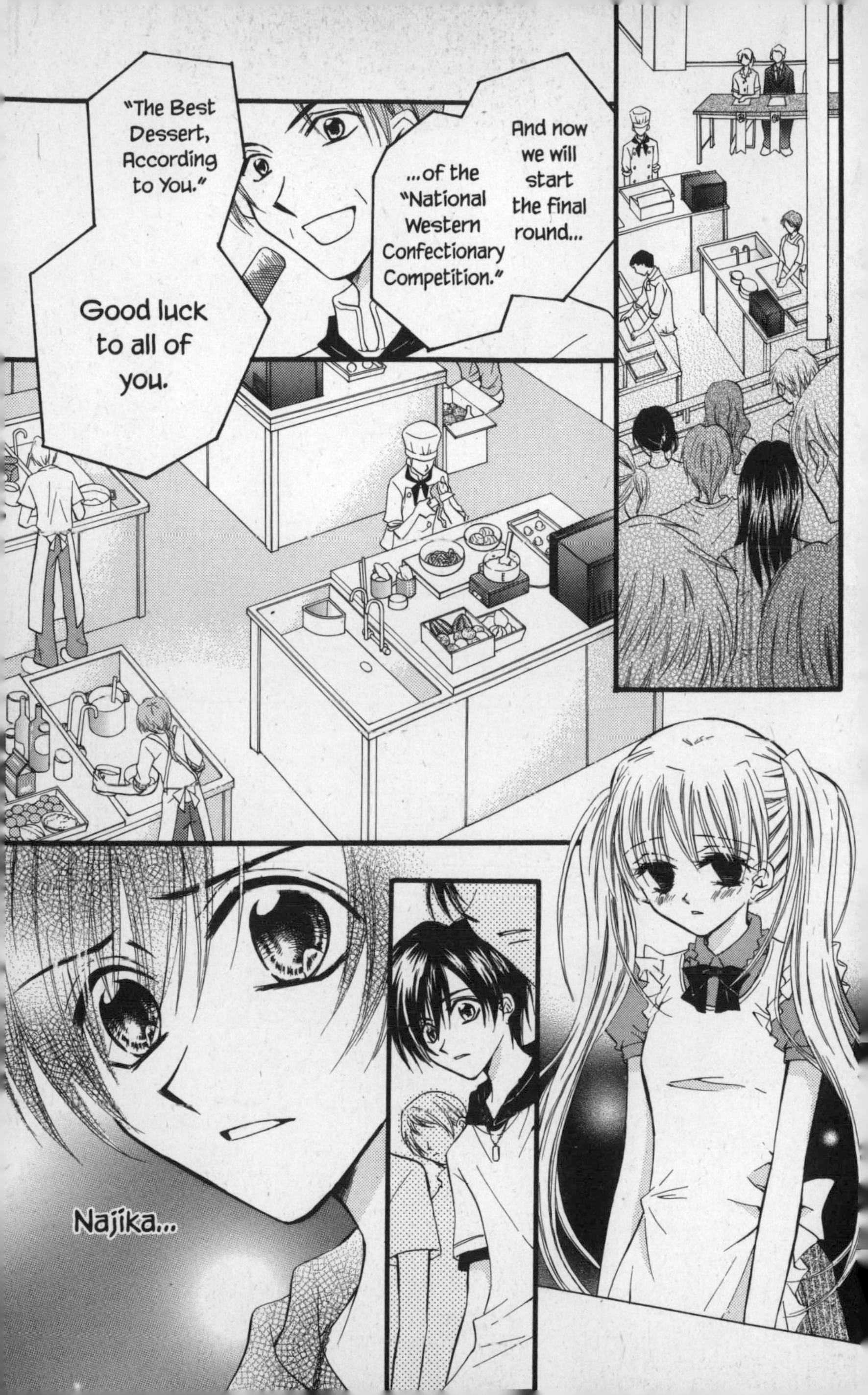
And now we will start the final round...
...of the "National Western Confectionary Competition."
"The Best Dessert, According to You."
Good luck to all of you.
Najika...

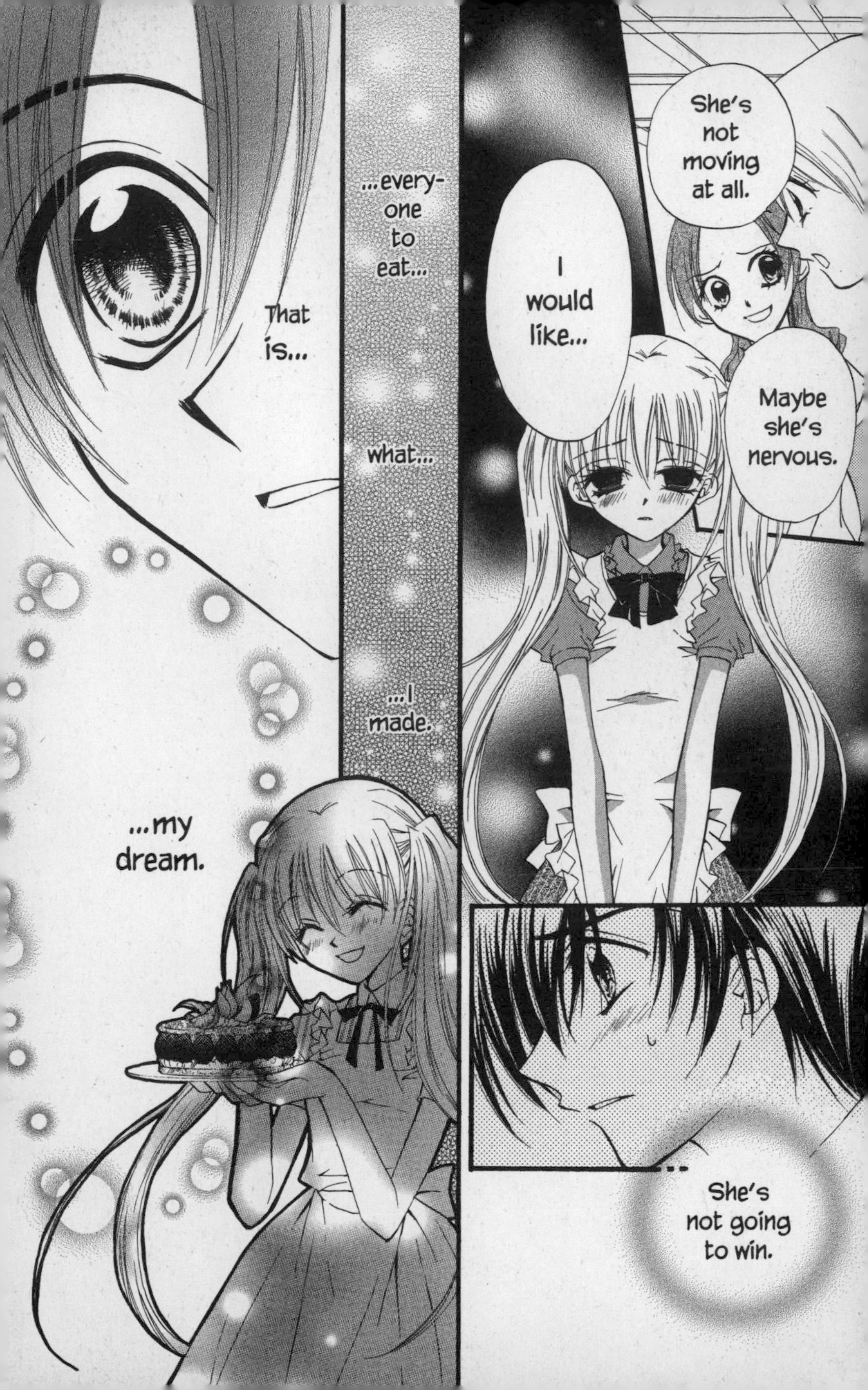
She's not moving at all.
Maybe she's nervous.
I would like...
She's not going to win.
...every-one to eat...
what...
...I made.
That is...
...my dream.

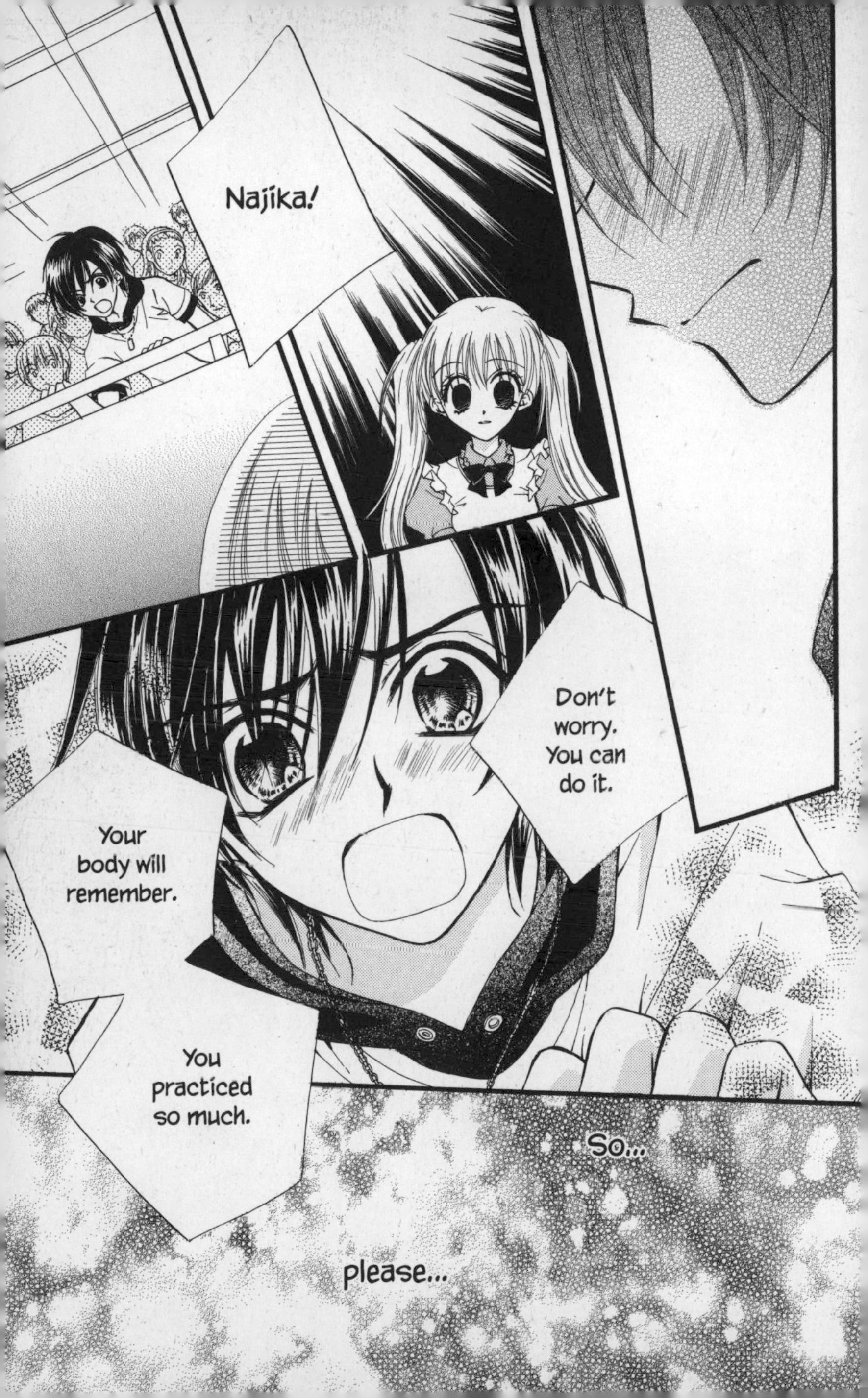
Najika!
Don't worry. You can do it.
Your body will remember.
You practiced so much.
So...
please...

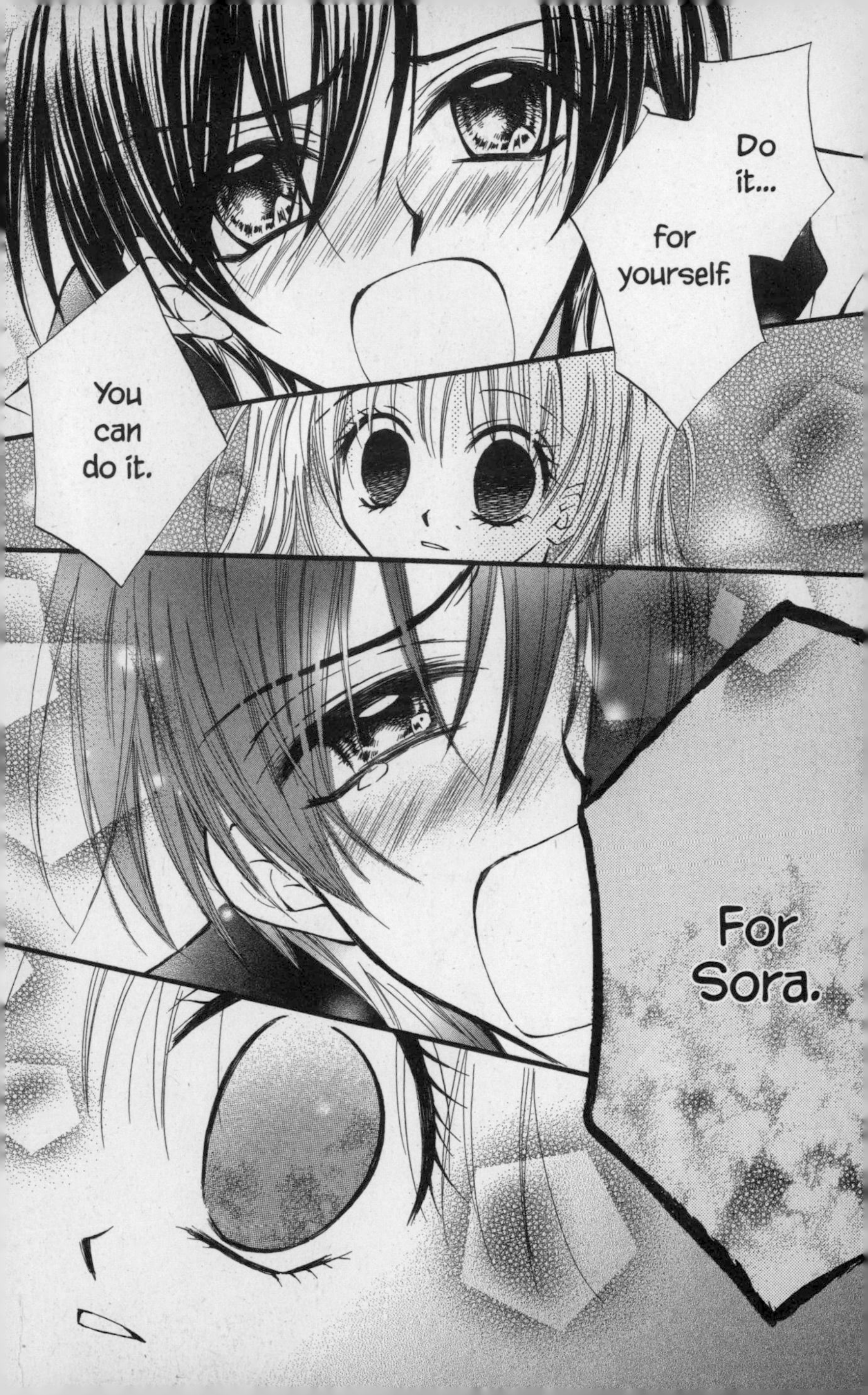
Do it...
for yourself.
You can do it.
For Sora.

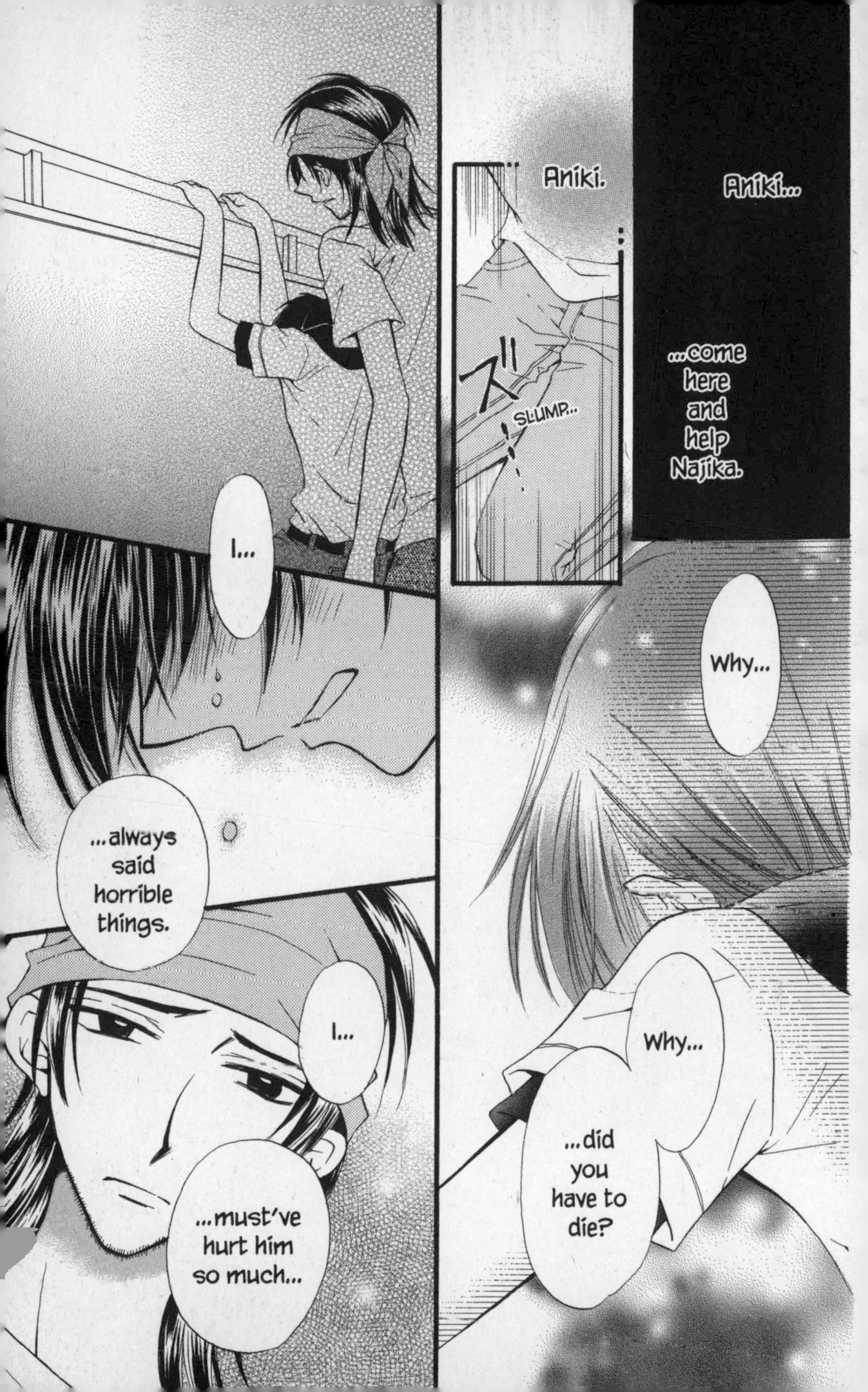
Aniki...
Aniki.
...come here and help Najika.
ズ
SLUMP...
Why...
Why...
...did you have to die?
I...
...always said horrible things.
I...
...must've hurt him so much...

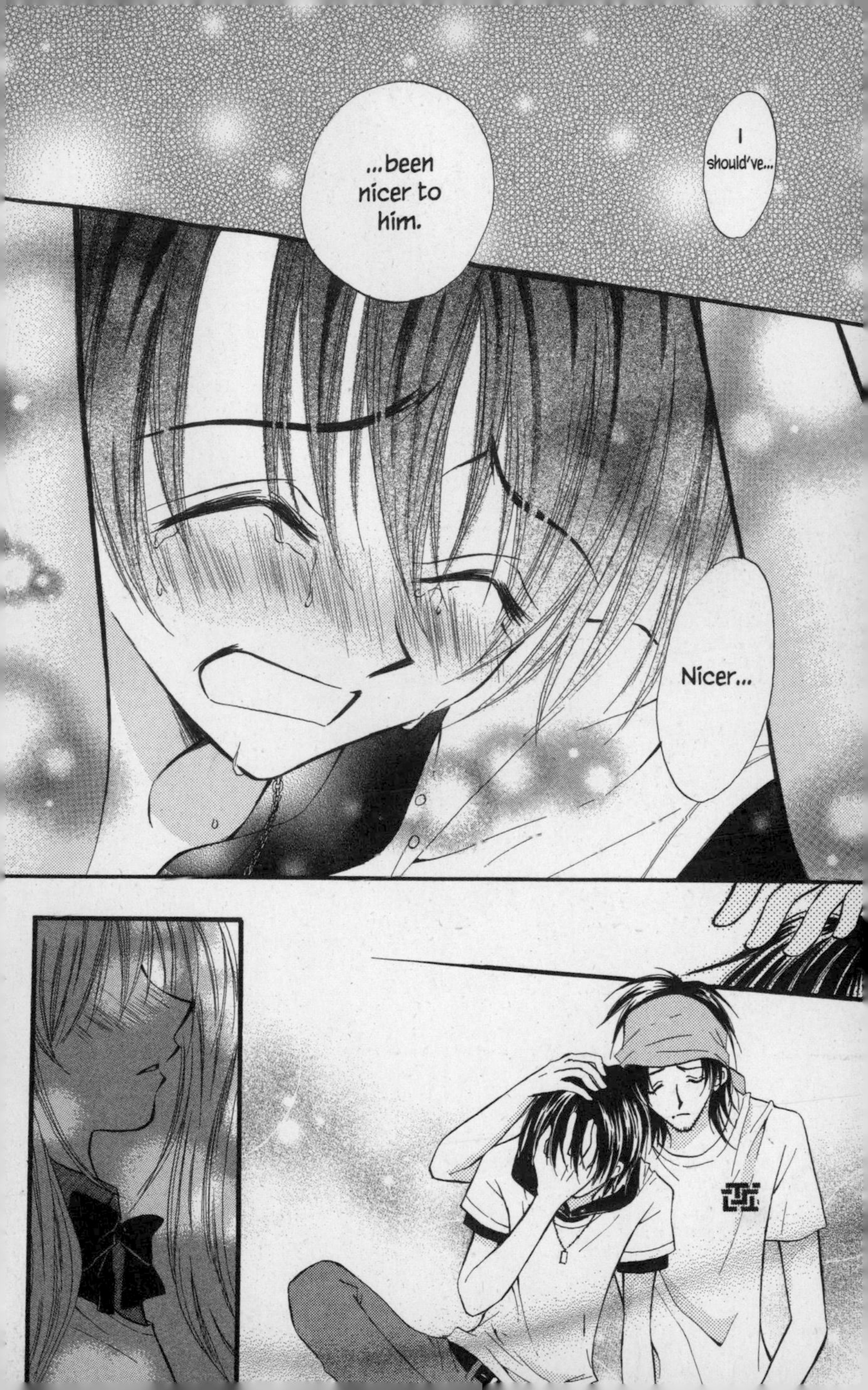
I should've...
...been nicer to him.
Nicer...

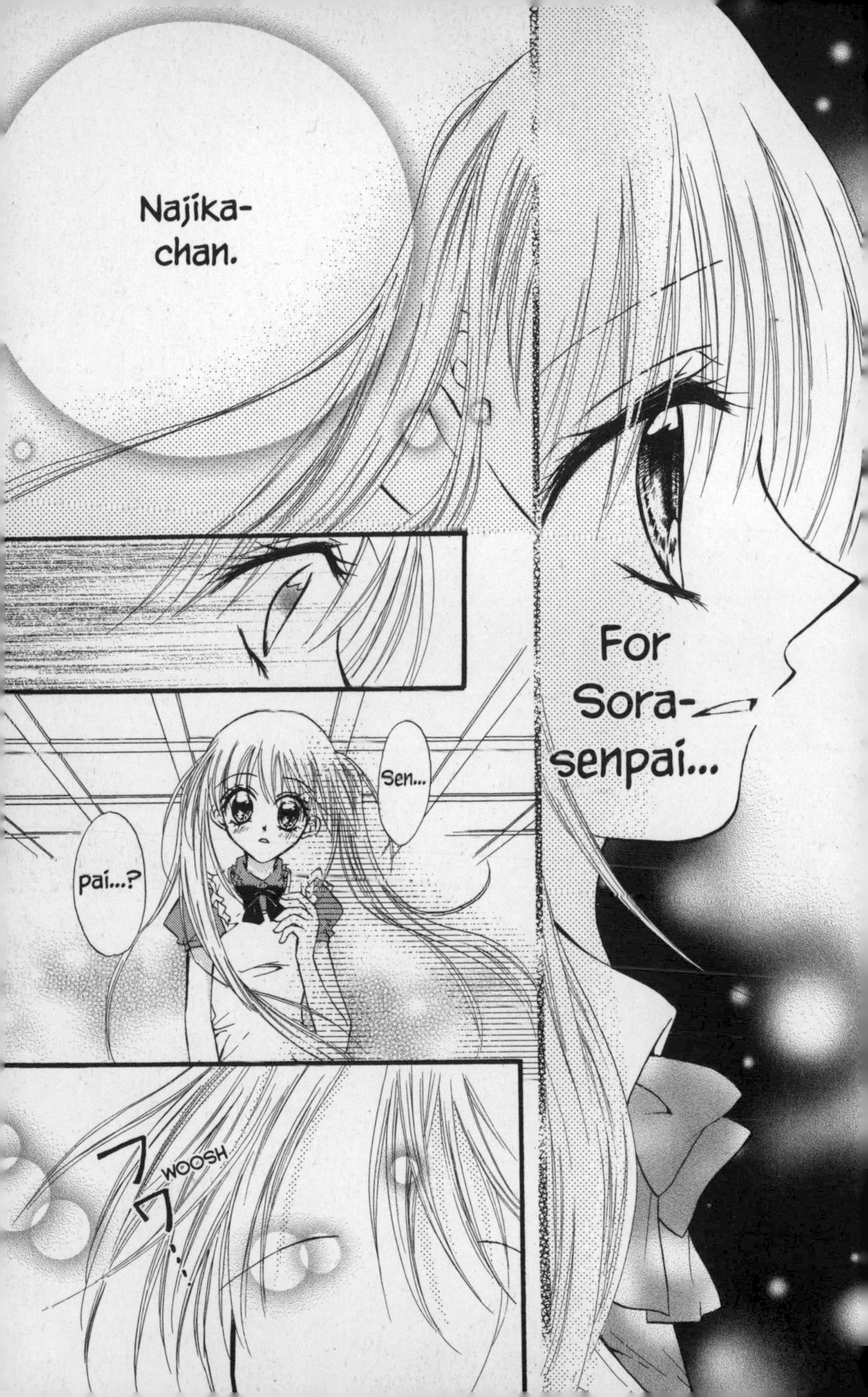
For Sora-senpai...
Najika-chan.
Sen...
pai...?
WOOSH

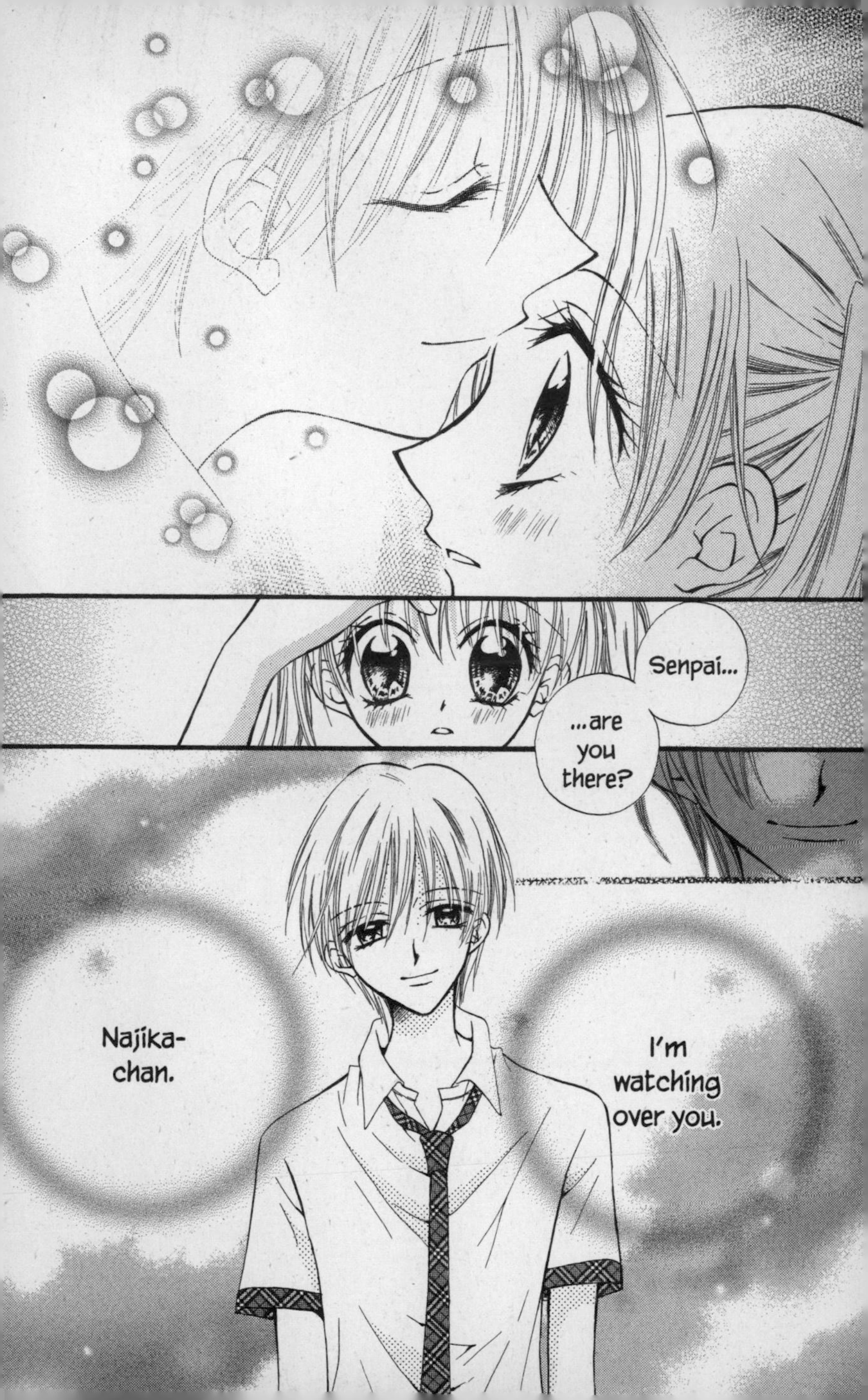
Senpai...
...are you there?
I'm watching over you.
Najika-chan.

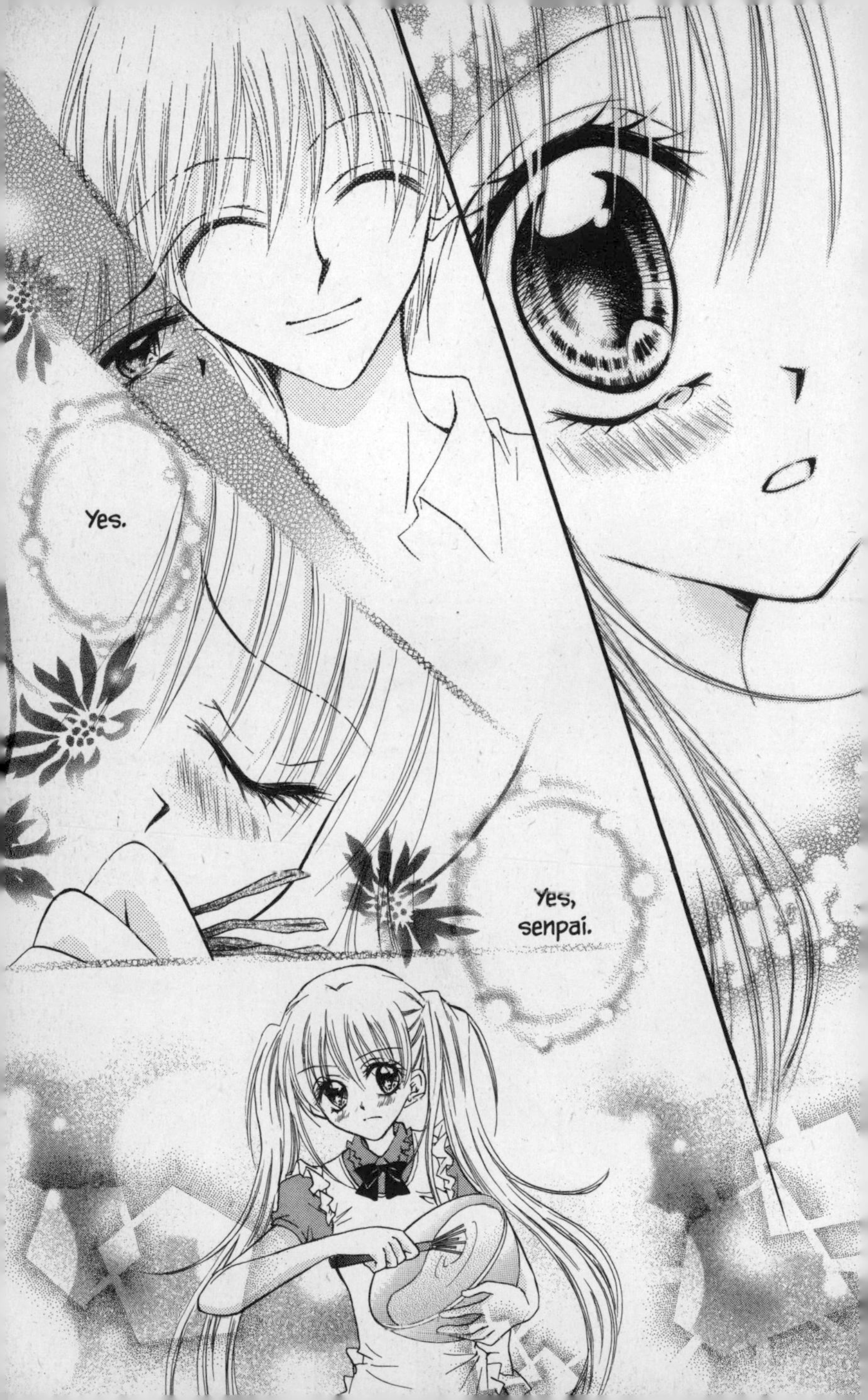
Yes.
Yes, senpai.

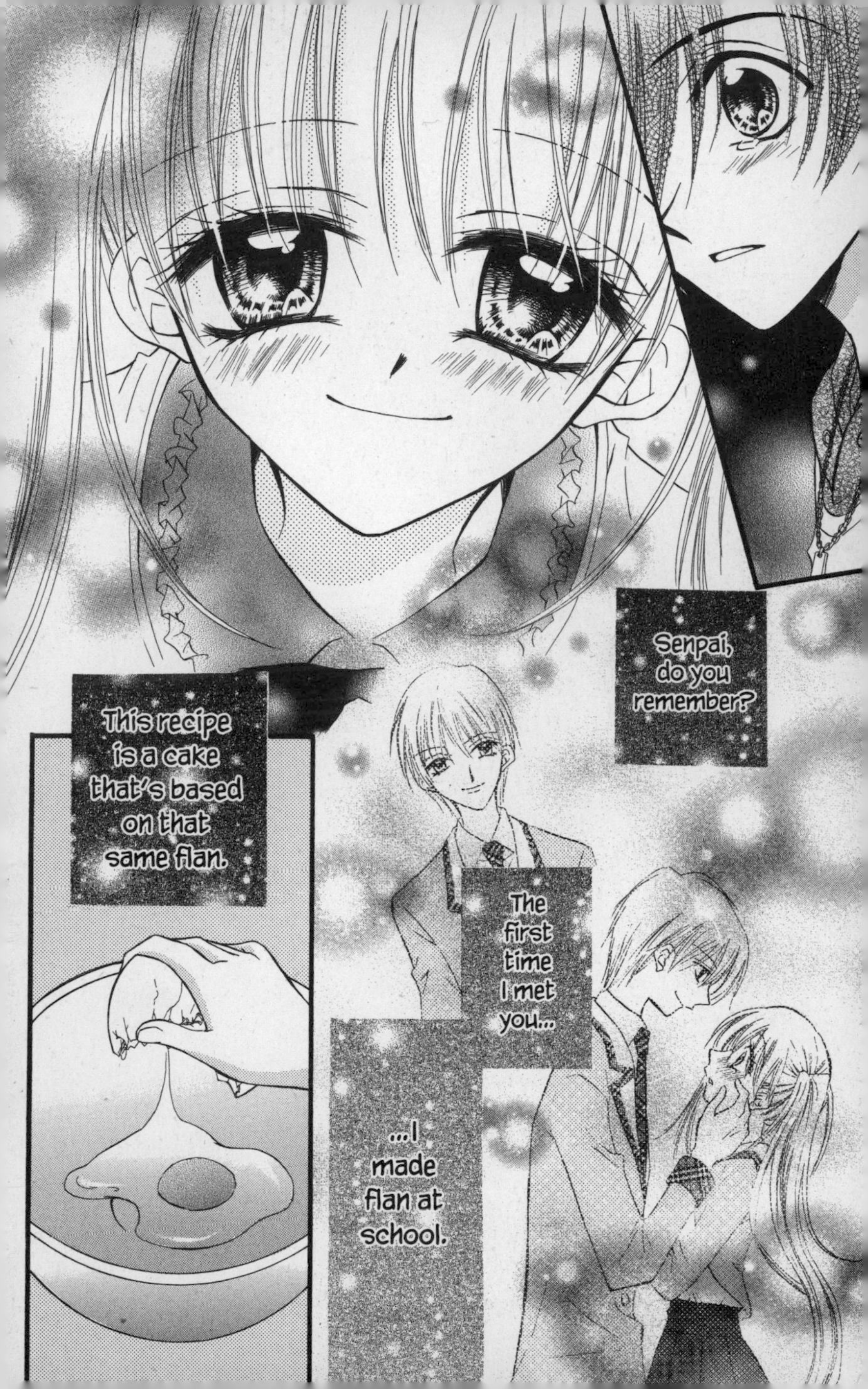
Senpai, do you remember?
This recipe is a cake that's based on that same flan.
The first time I met you...
...I made flan at school.

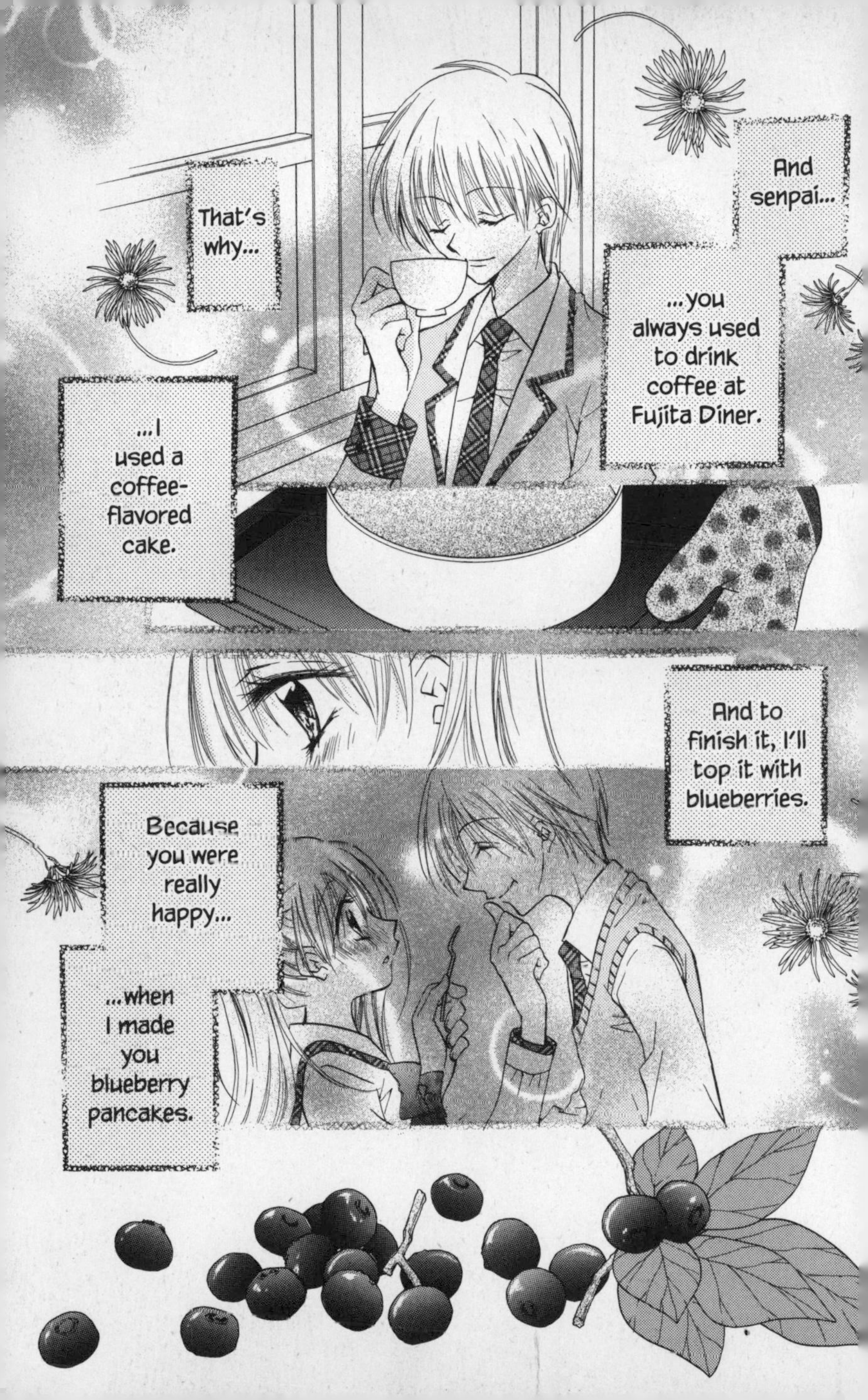

And senpai...
...you always used to drink coffee at Fujita Diner.
That's why...
...I used a coffee-flavored cake.
And to finish it, I'll top it with blueberries.
Because you were really happy...
...when I made you blueberry pancakes.

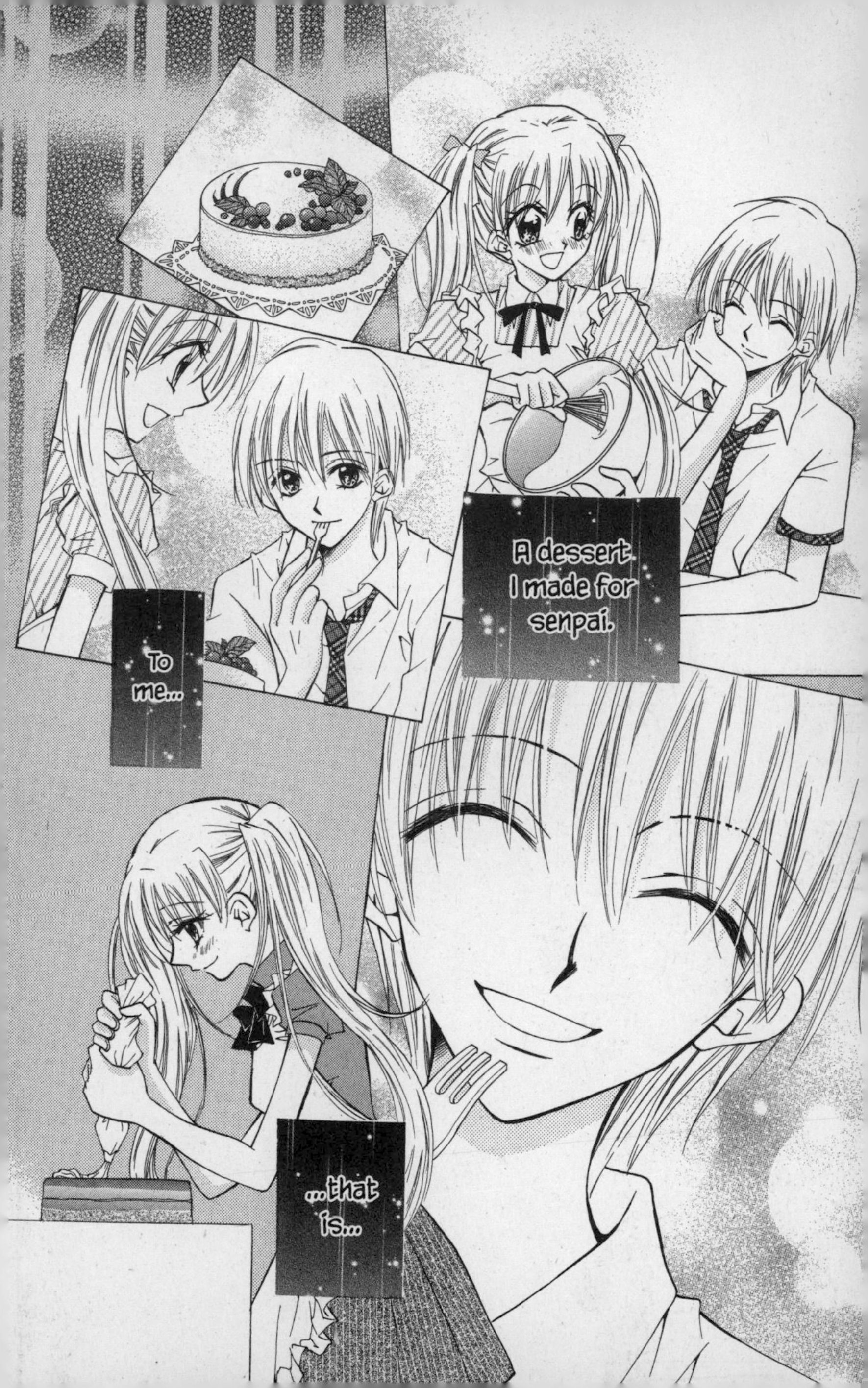
A dessert I made for senpai.
To me...
...that is...

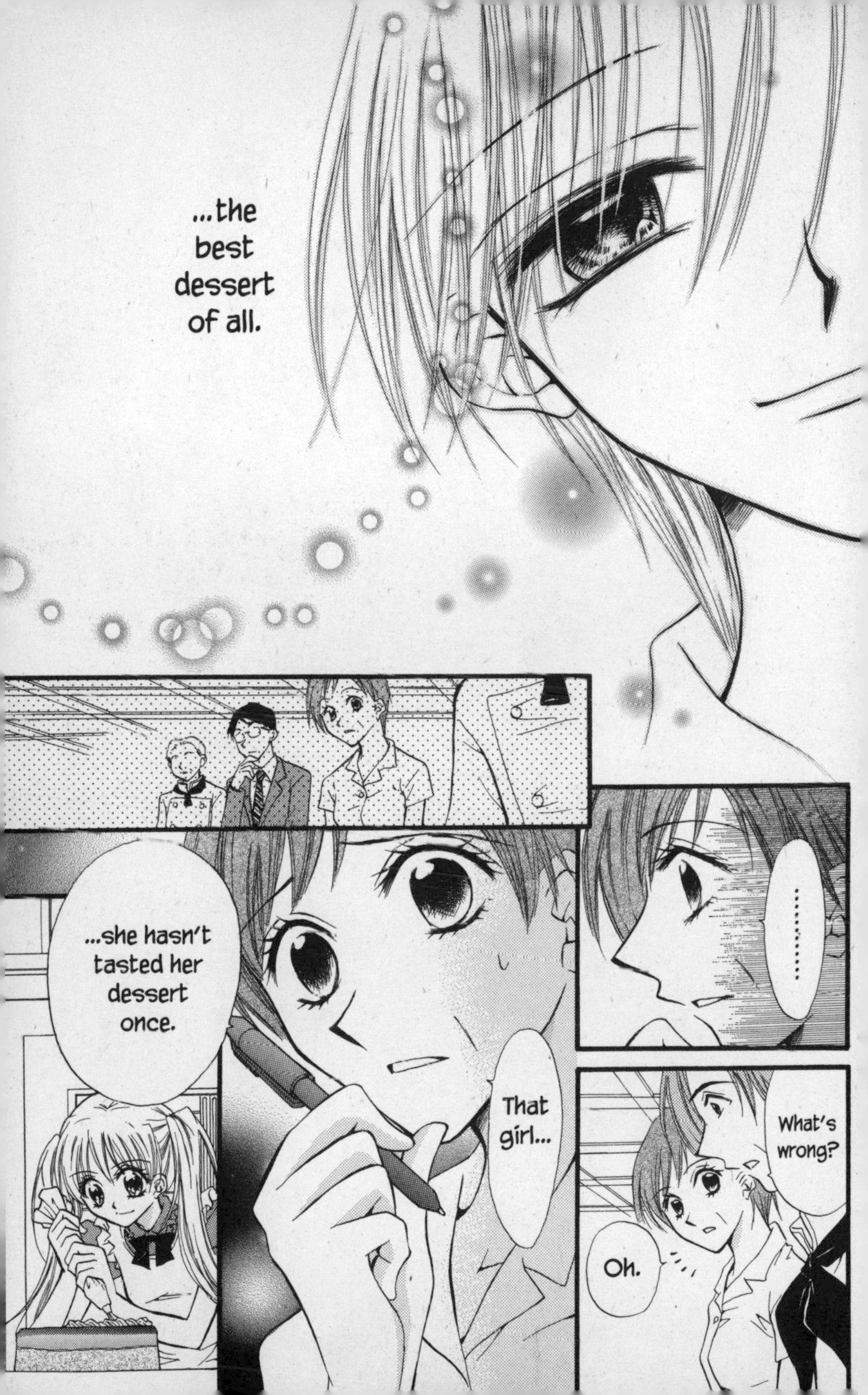
...the best dessert of all.
......
What's wrong?
Oh.
That girl...
...she hasn't tasted her dessert once.

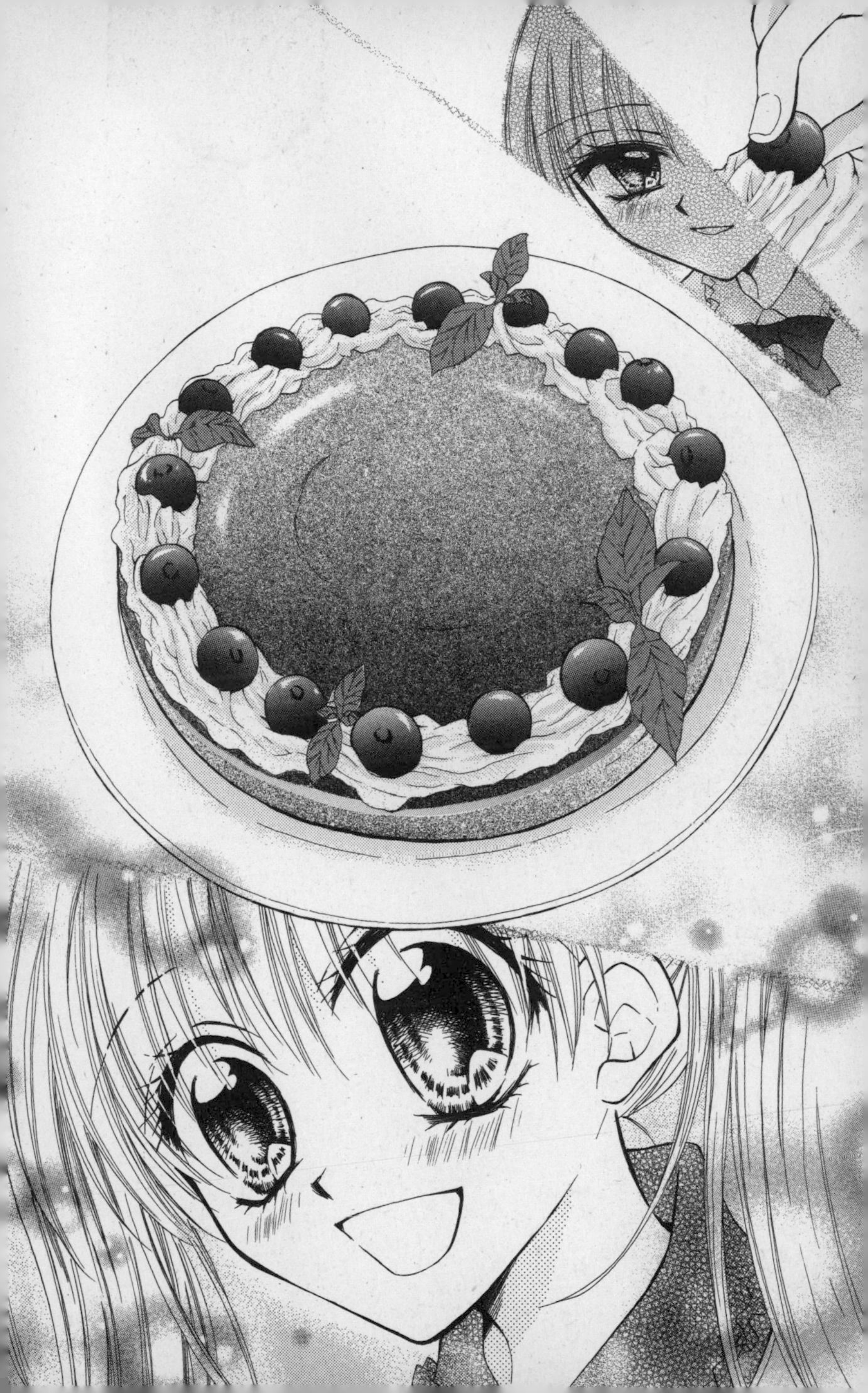

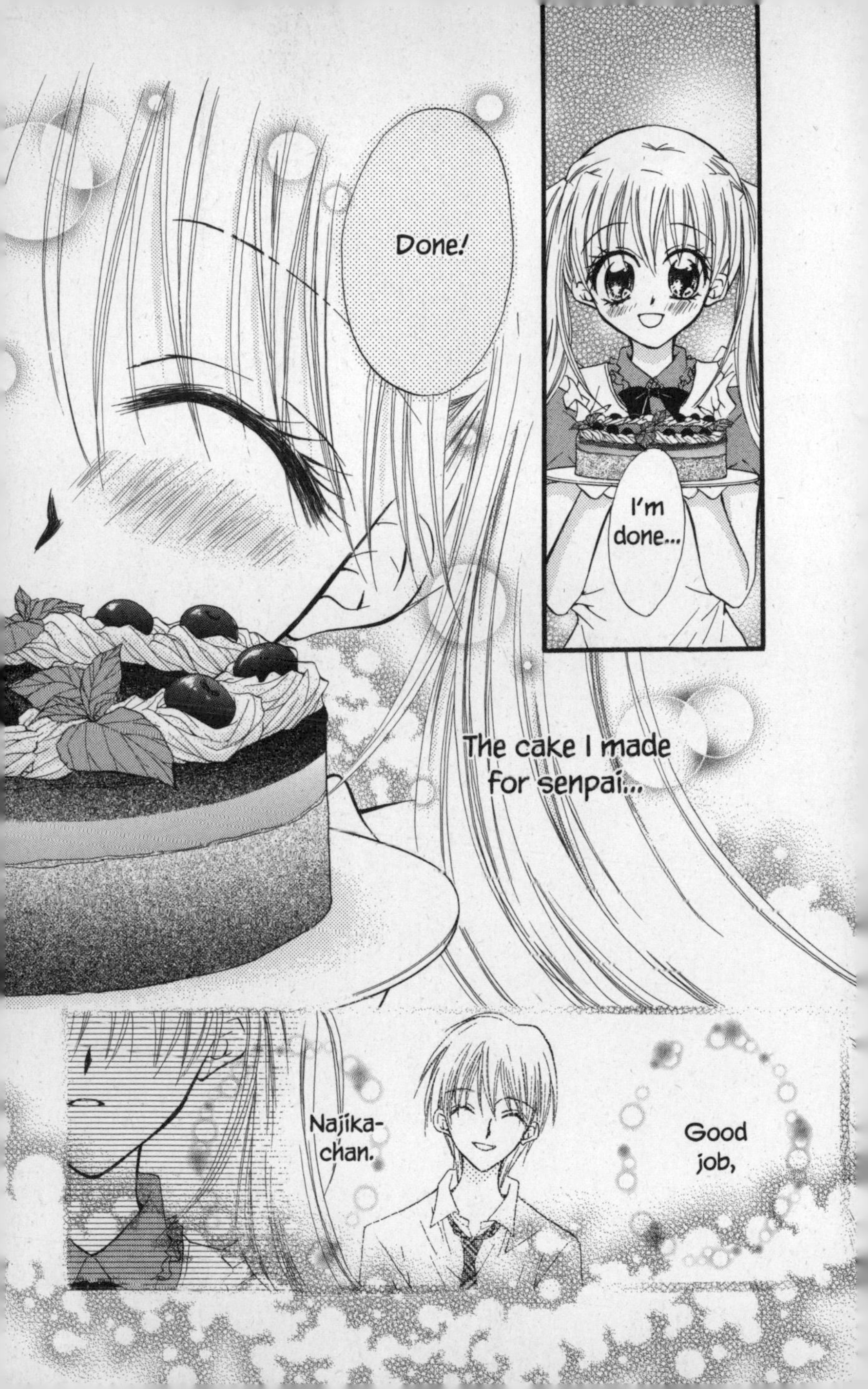
I'm done...
Done!
The cake I made for senpai...
Good job,
Najika-chan.

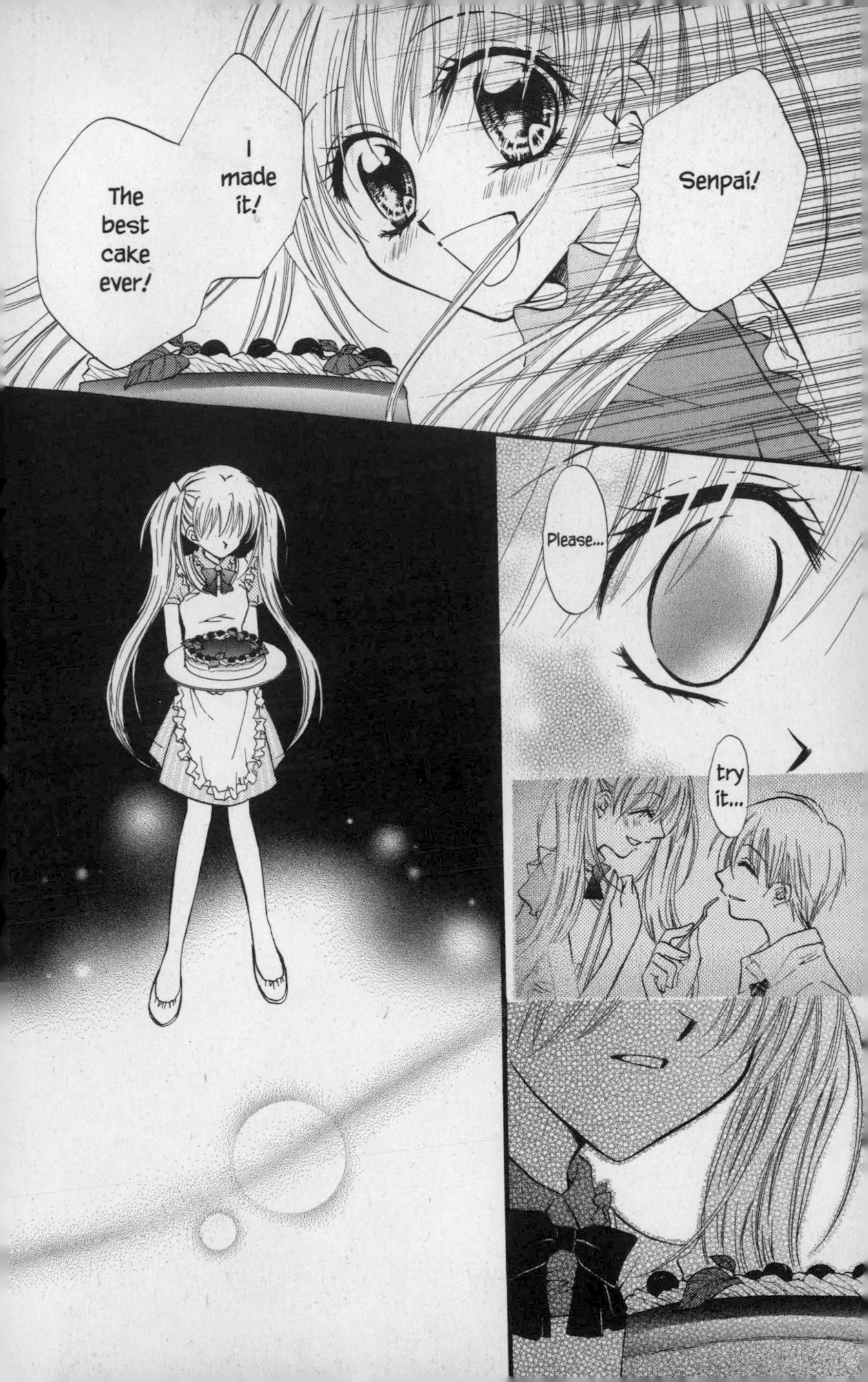
Senpai!
I made it!
The best cake ever!
Please...
try it...

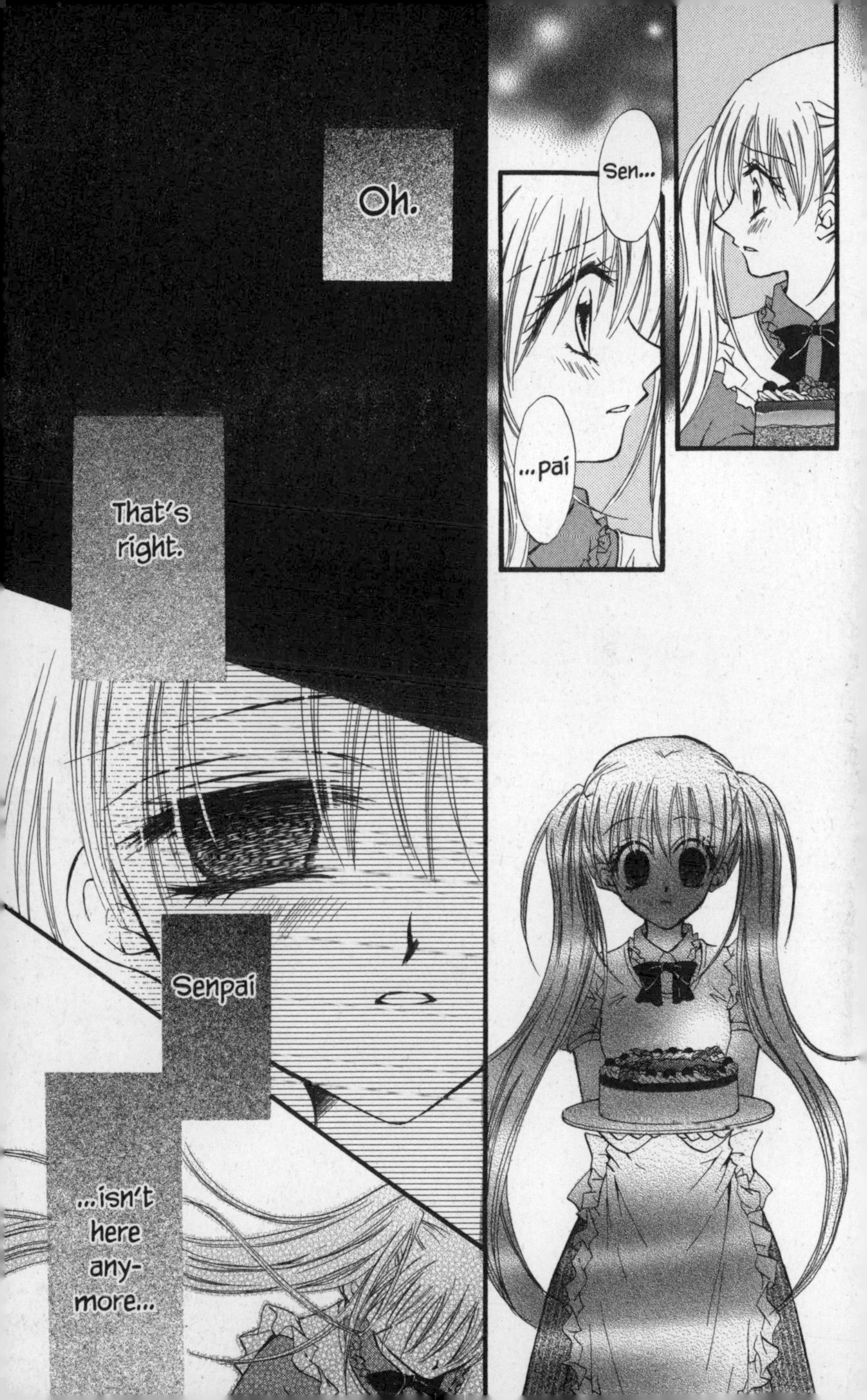
Sen...
...pai
Oh.
That's right.
Senpai
...isn't here any-more...

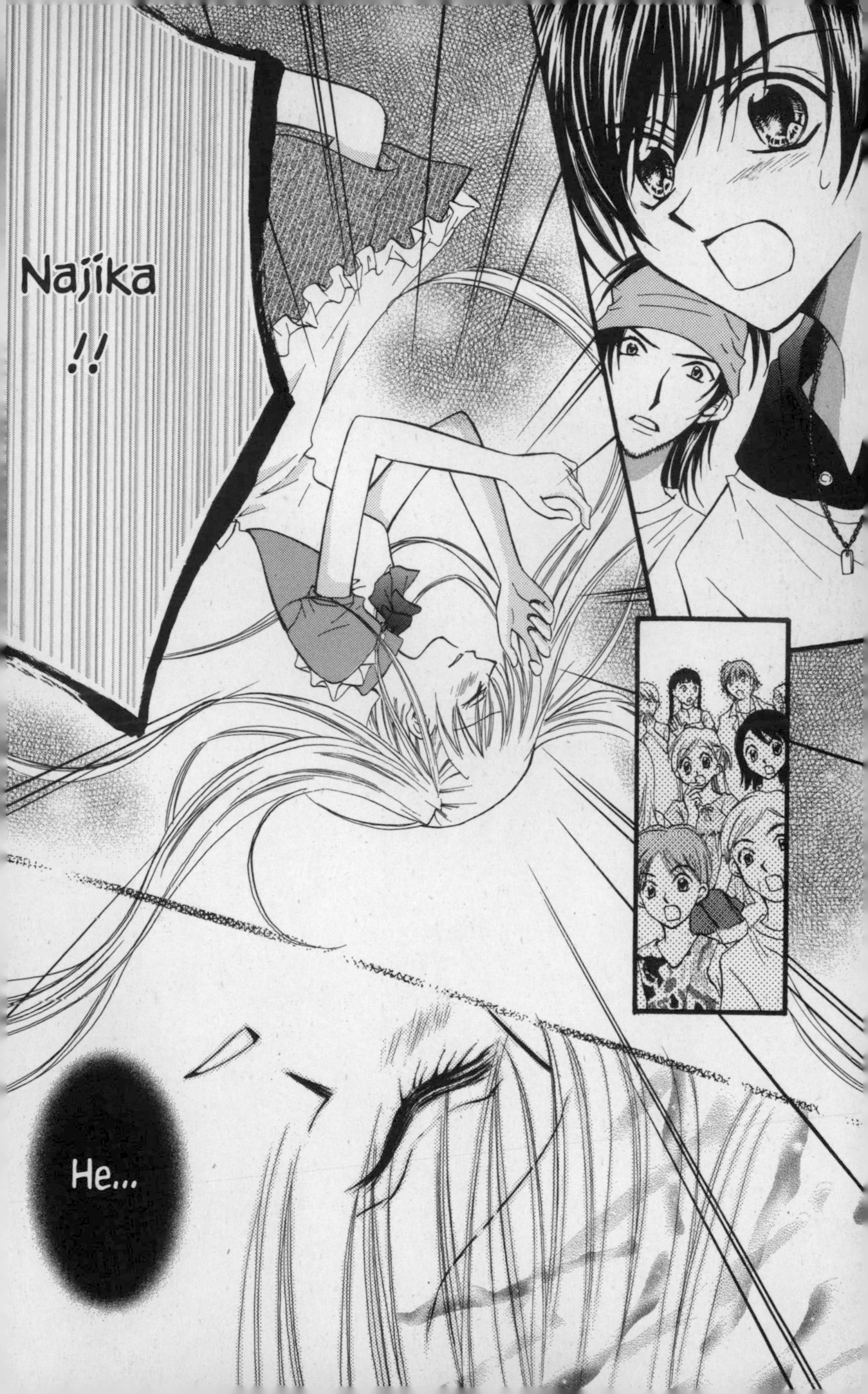
Najika !!
He...

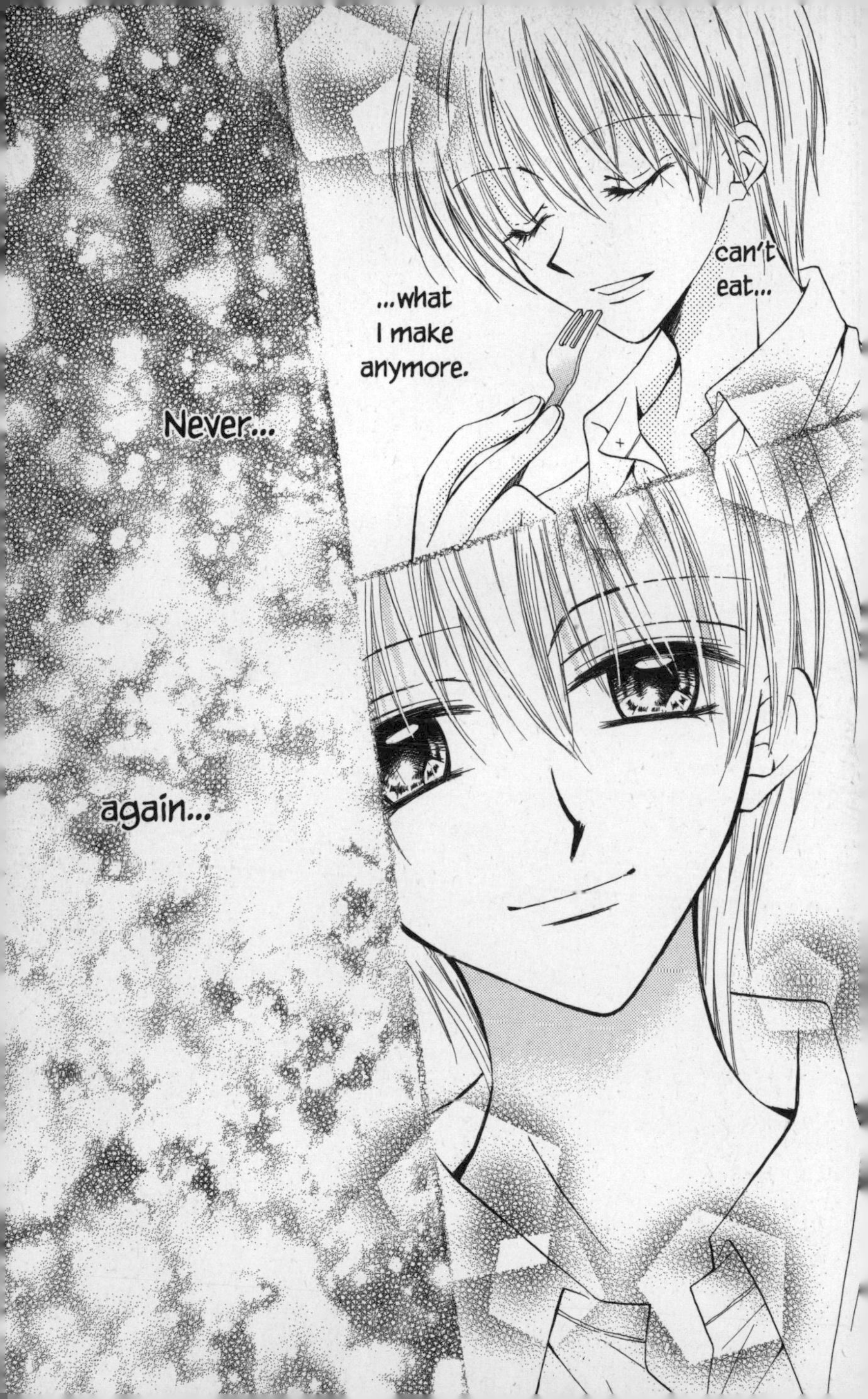
can't eat...
...what I make anymore.
Never...
again...

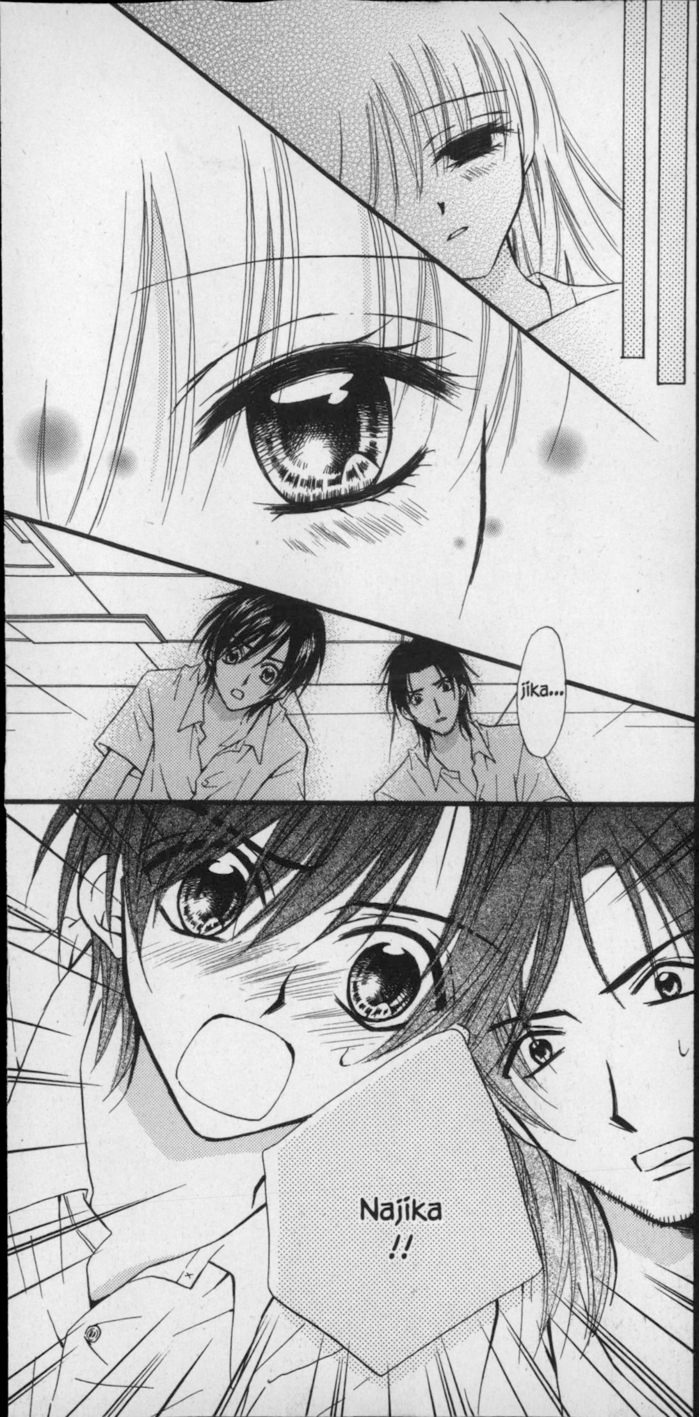
jika...
Najika !!

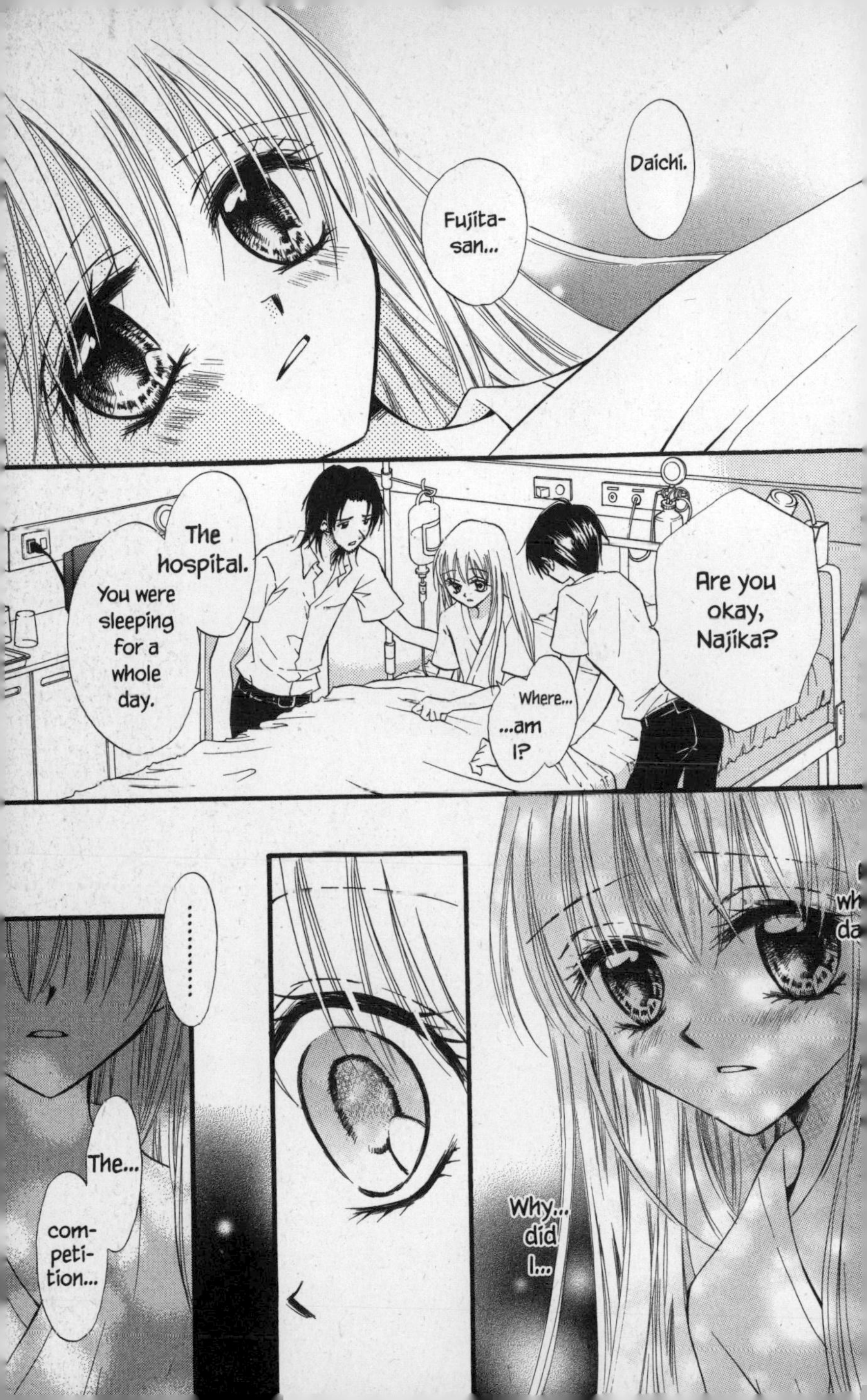
Daichi.
Fujita-san...
Are you okay, Najika?
Where... ...am I?
The hospital.
You were sleeping for a whole day.
Why... did I...
......
The...
competition...

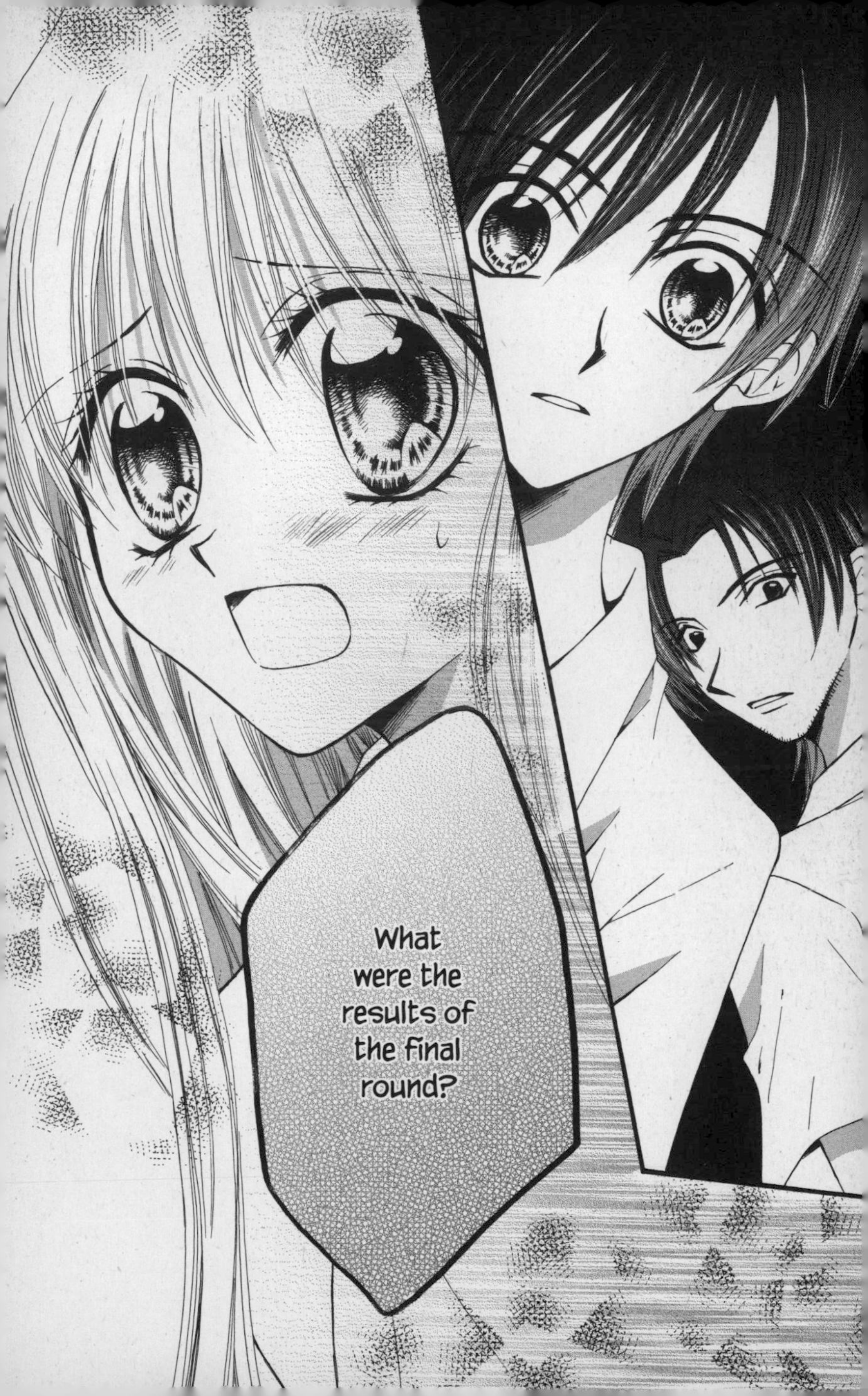
What were the results of the final round?

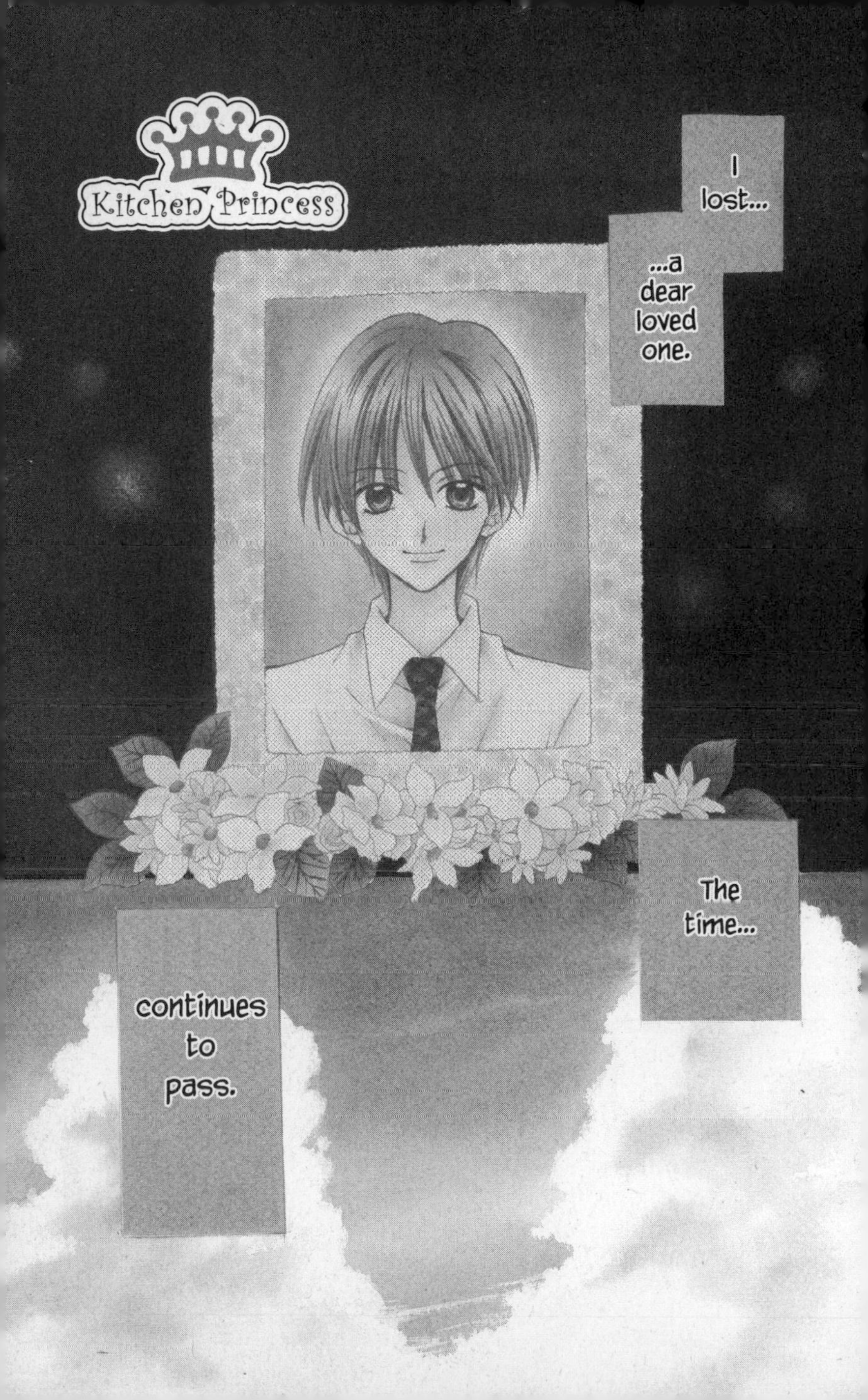
Kitchen Princess
I lost...
...a dear loved one.
The time...
continues to pass.

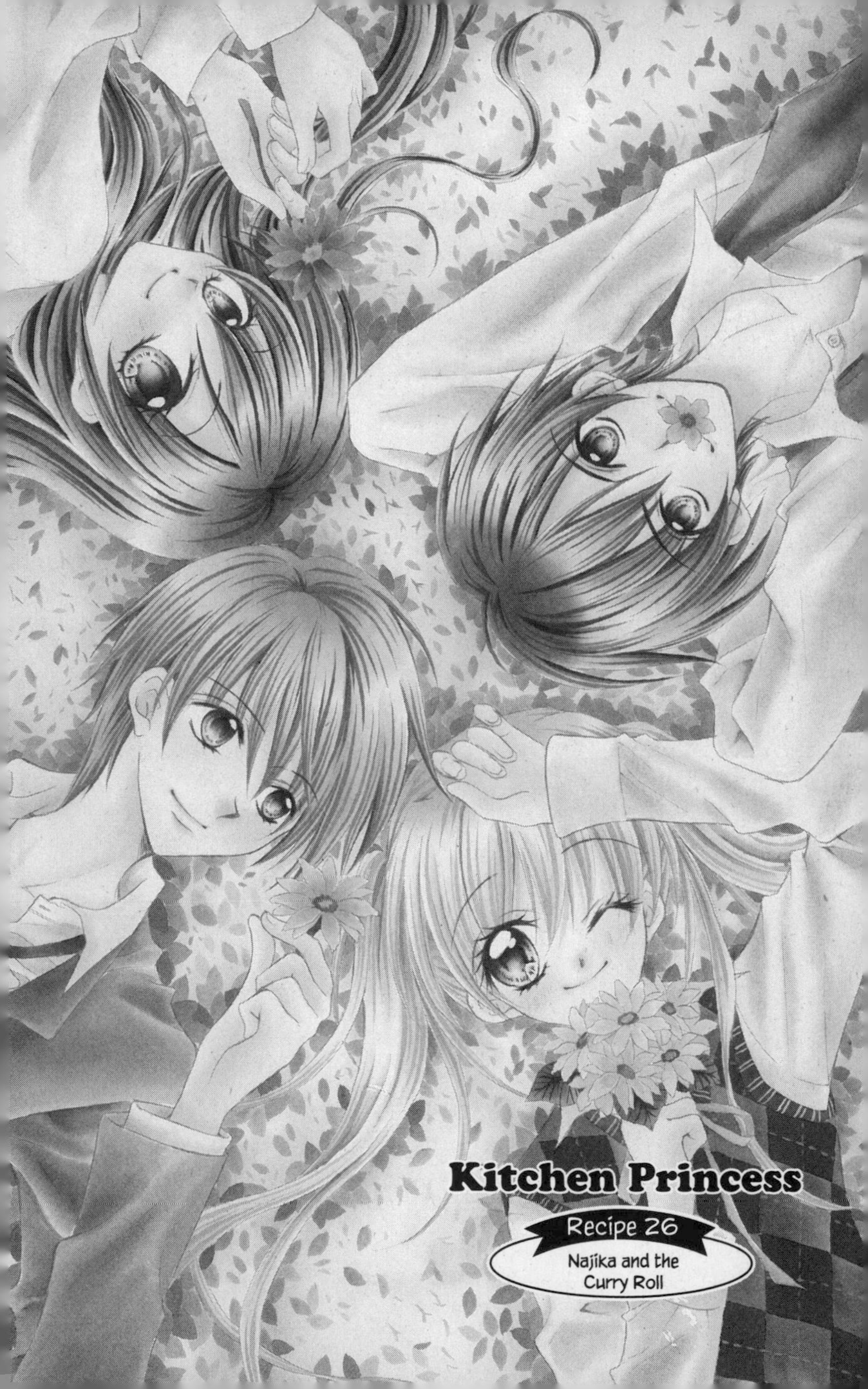
Kitchen Princess
Recipe 26
Najika and the Curry Roll

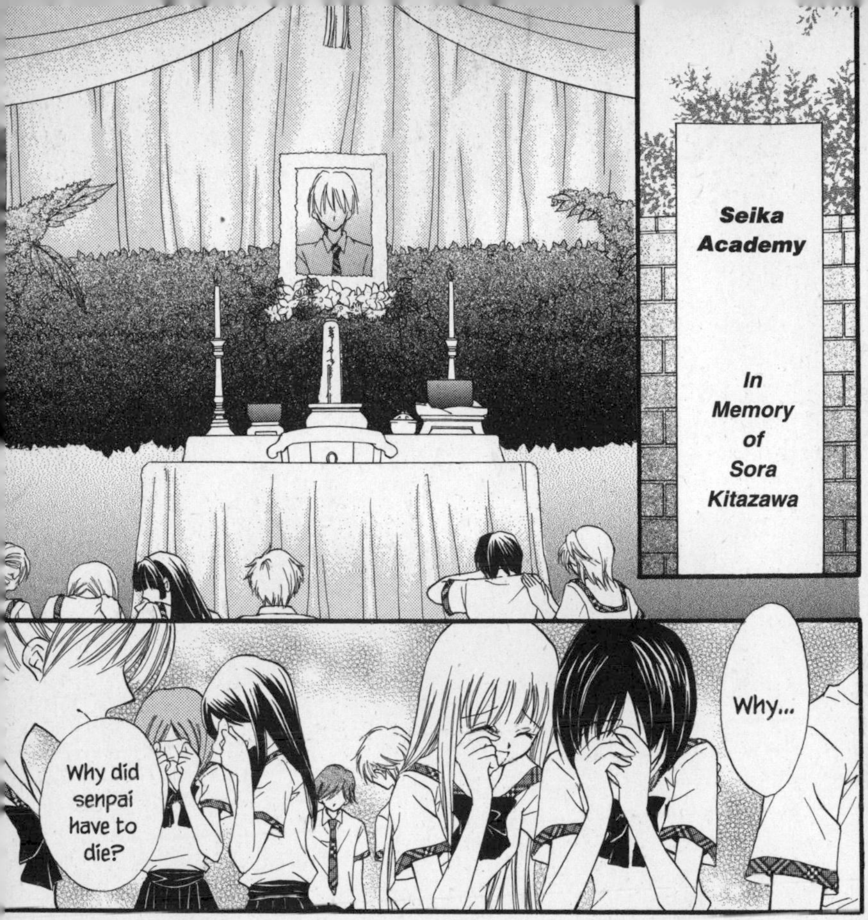
Seika Academy
In Memory of Sora Kitazawa
Why...
Why did senpai have to die?

About Recipe 25's Splash Page

The magazine was released in autumn, but the story was set during the summer, so I drew it on the theme of "A memorable and unforgettable summer." I wanted to express the transience of life, so I made the lines thin.

About Recipe 26's Splash Page

Since the last splash ignored seasons, this time I wanted to make it look like autumn and added fallen leaves. I always wanted to do a composition with all of them sleeping, but it was hard fitting all four characters in.

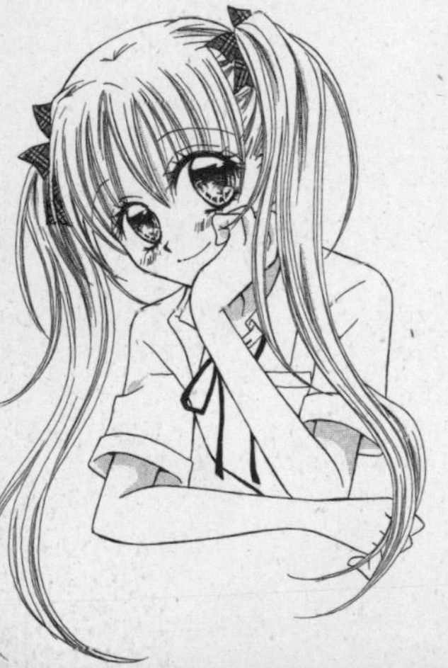

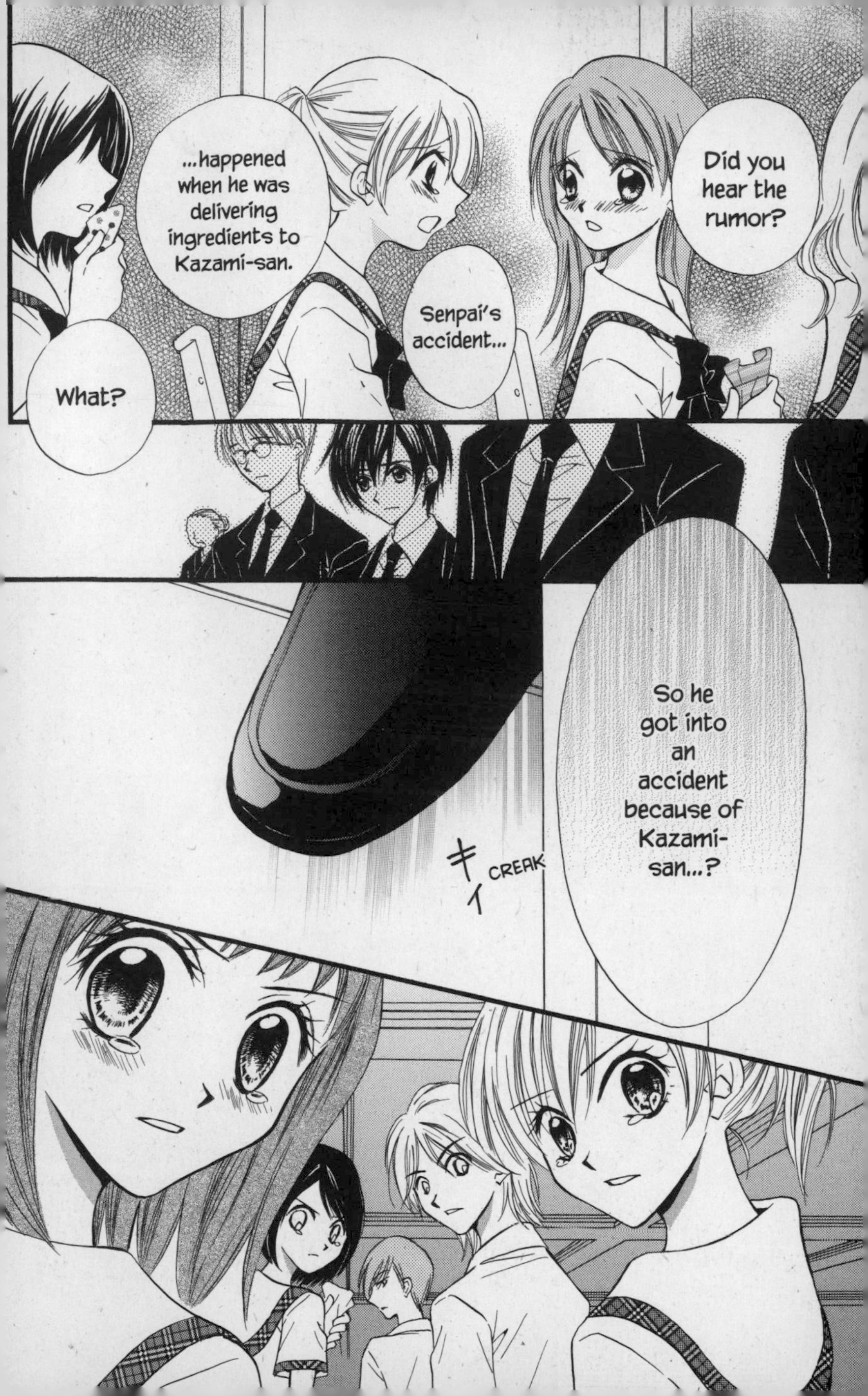
Did you hear the rumor?
Senpai's accident...
...happened when he was delivering ingredients to Kazami-san.
What?
So he got into an accident because of Kazami-san...?
キイ
CREAK

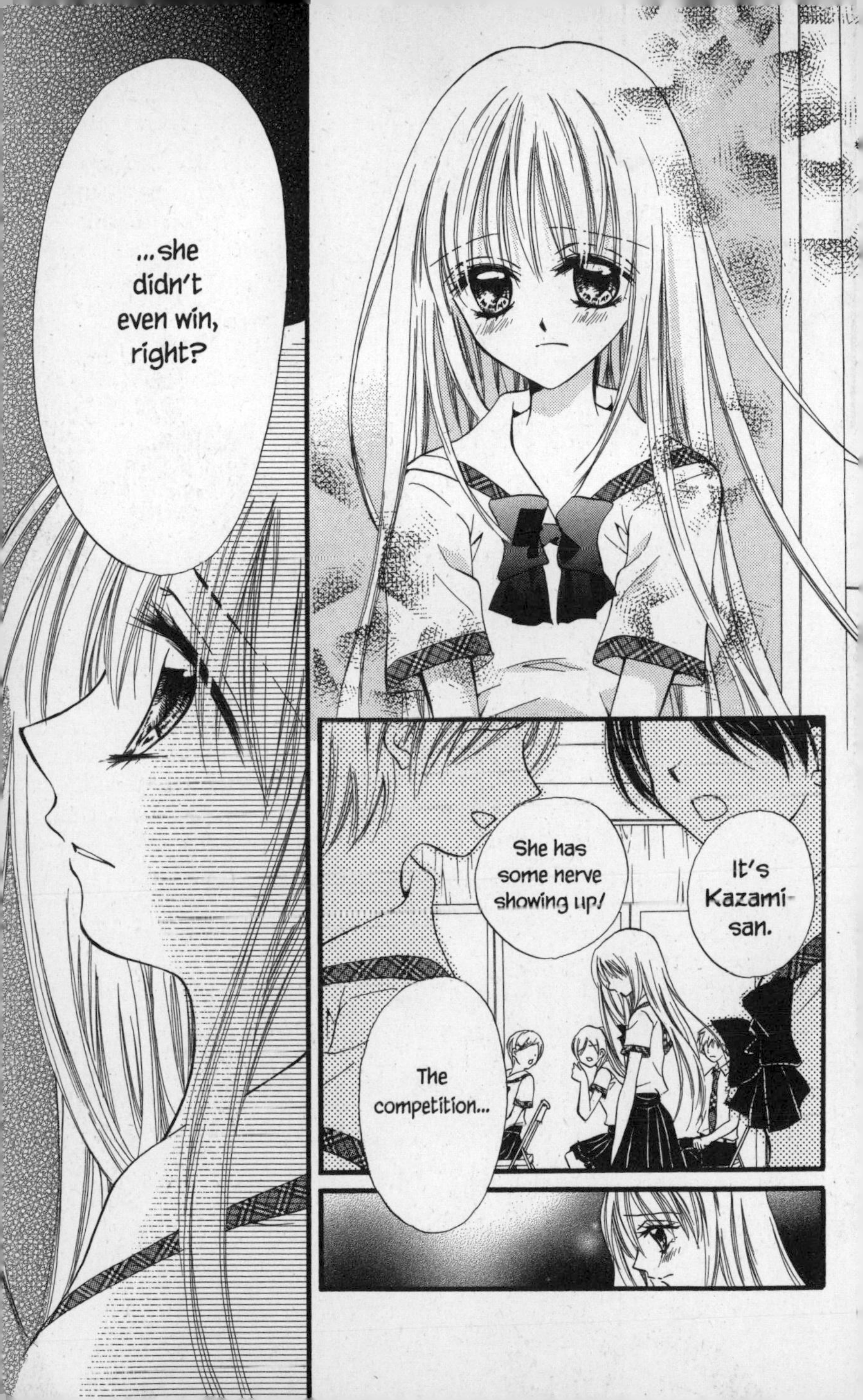
It's Kazami-san.
She has some nerve showing up!
The competition...
...she didn't even win, right?

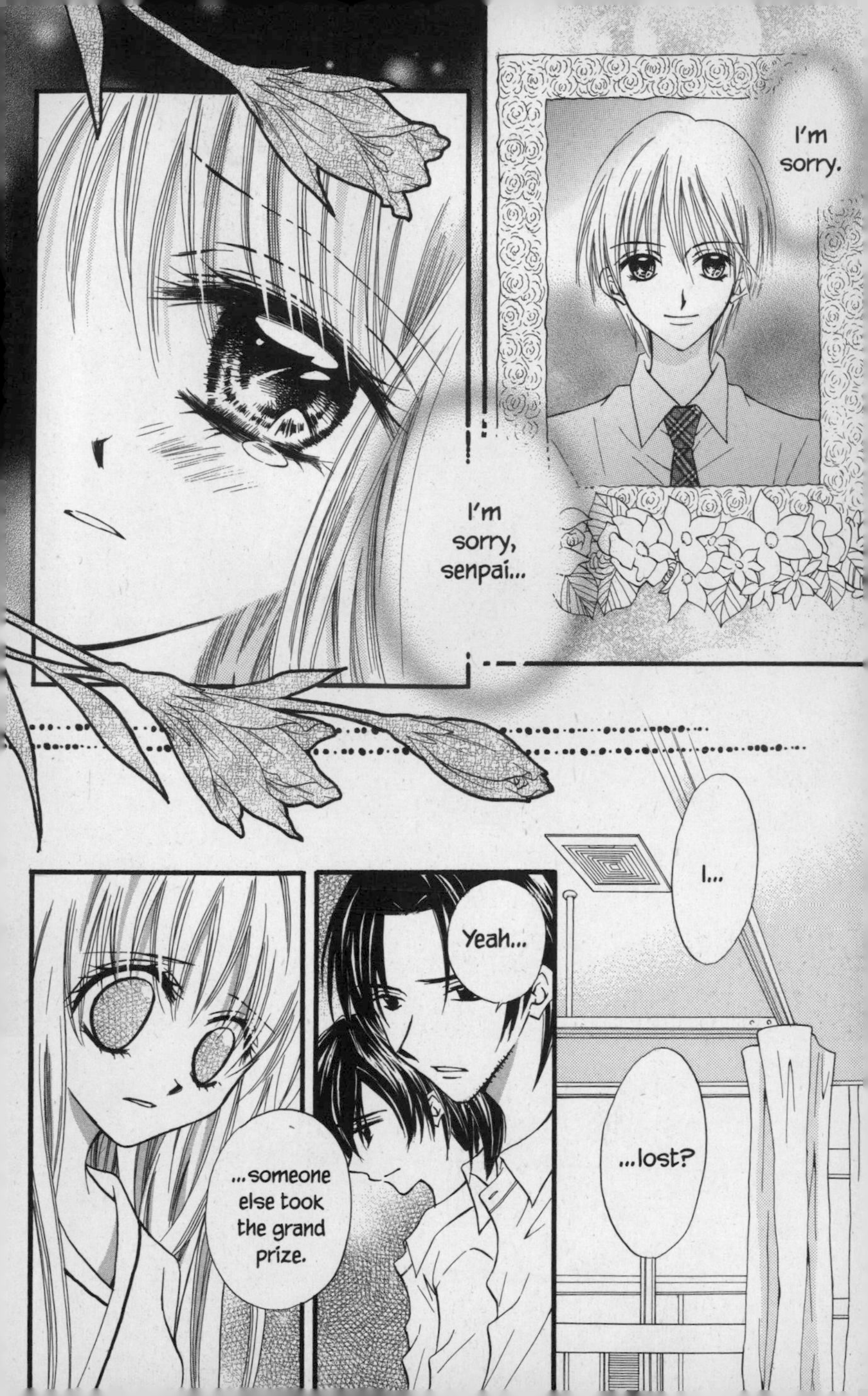
I'm sorry.
I'm sorry, senpai...
I...
...lost?
Yeah...
...someone else took the grand prize.

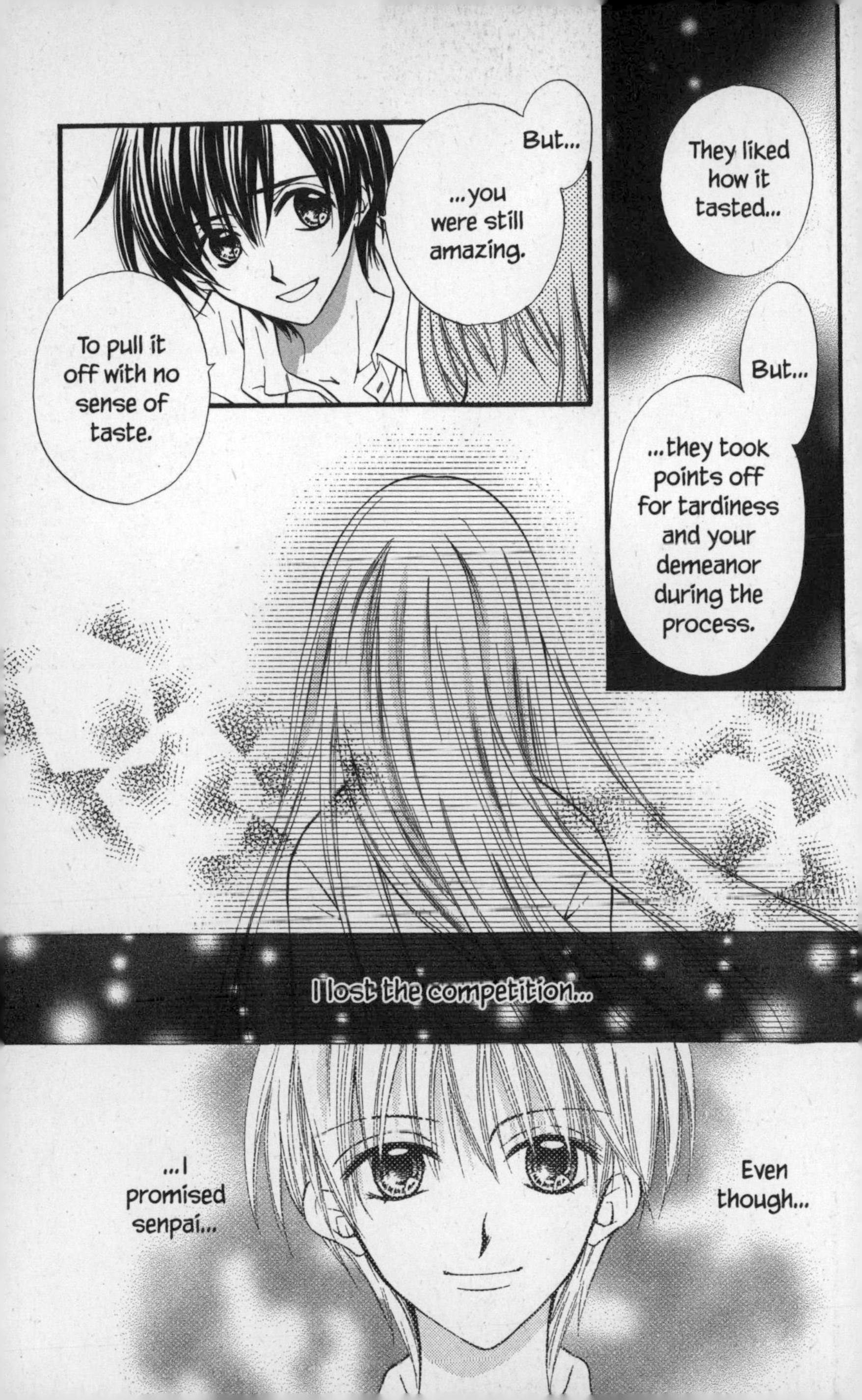
They liked how it tasted...
But...
...they took points off for tardiness and your demeanor during the process.
But...
...you were still amazing.
To pull it off with no sense of taste.
I lost the competition...
Even though...
...I promised senpai...

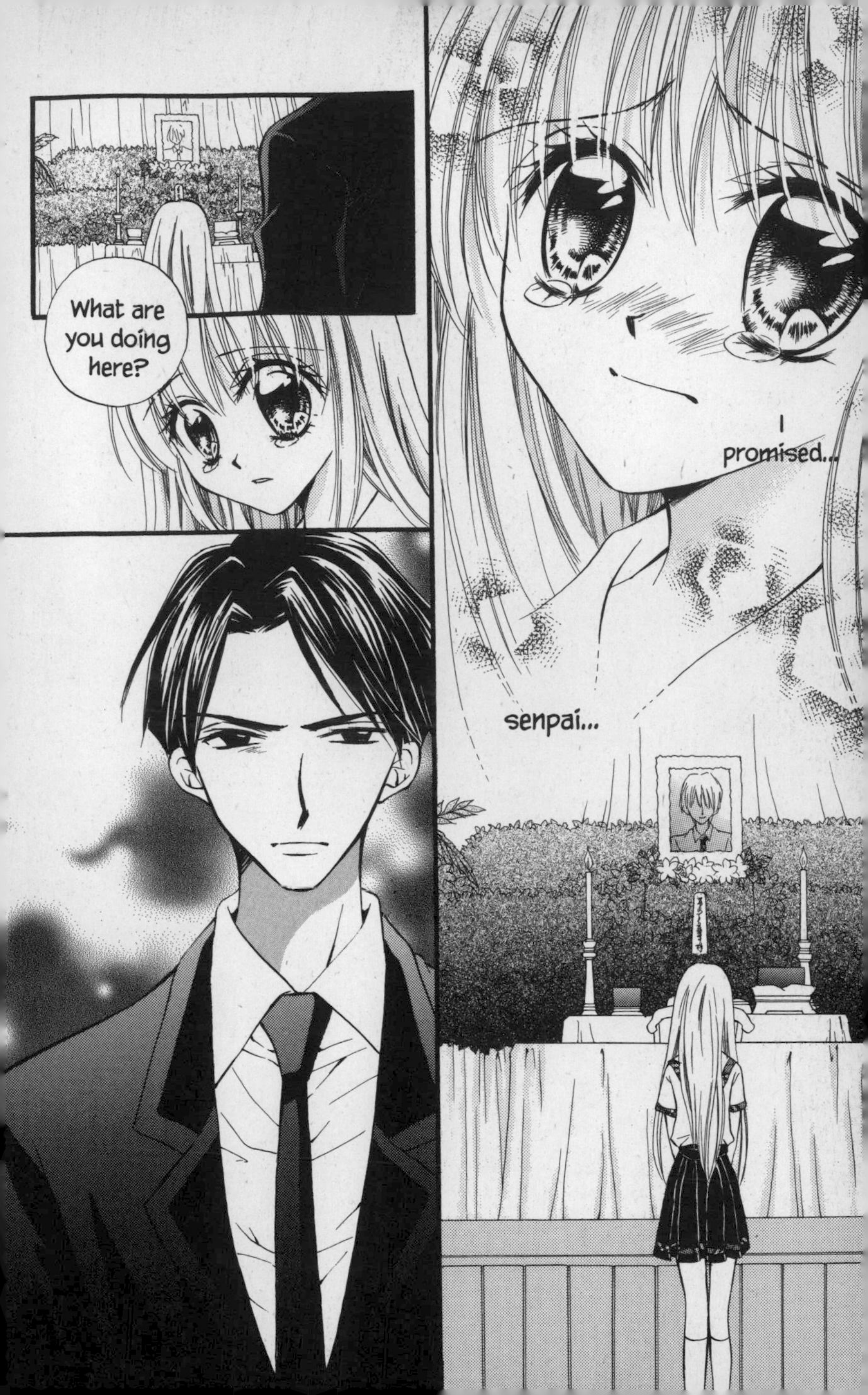
I promised...
senpai...
What are you doing here?

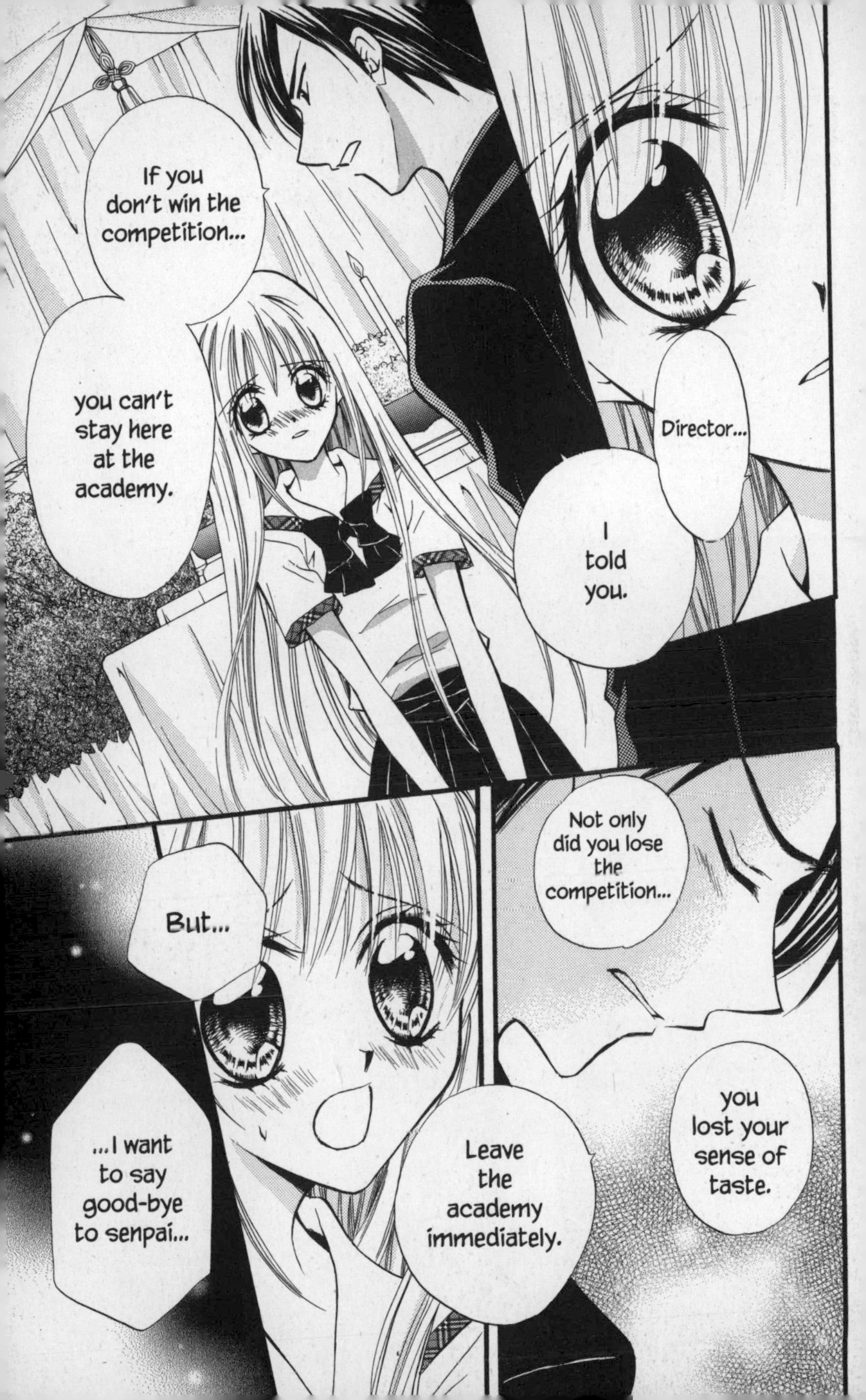
Director...
I told you.
If you don't win the competition...
you can't stay here at the academy.
Not only did you lose the competition...
you lost your sense of taste.
Leave the academy immediately.
But...
...I want to say good-bye to senpai...

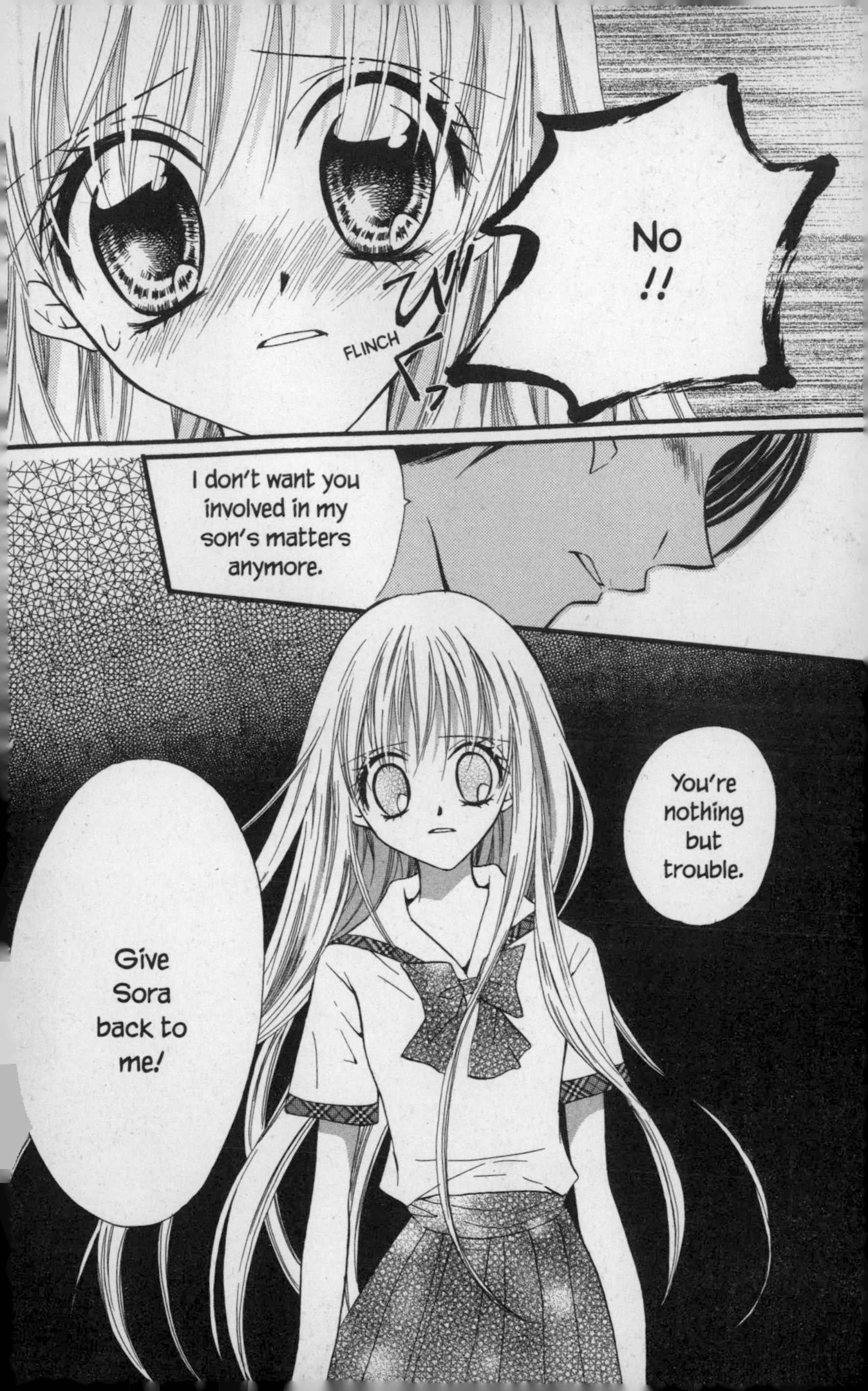
No !!
FLINCH
I don't want you involved in my son's matters anymore.
You're nothing but trouble.
Give Sora back to me!

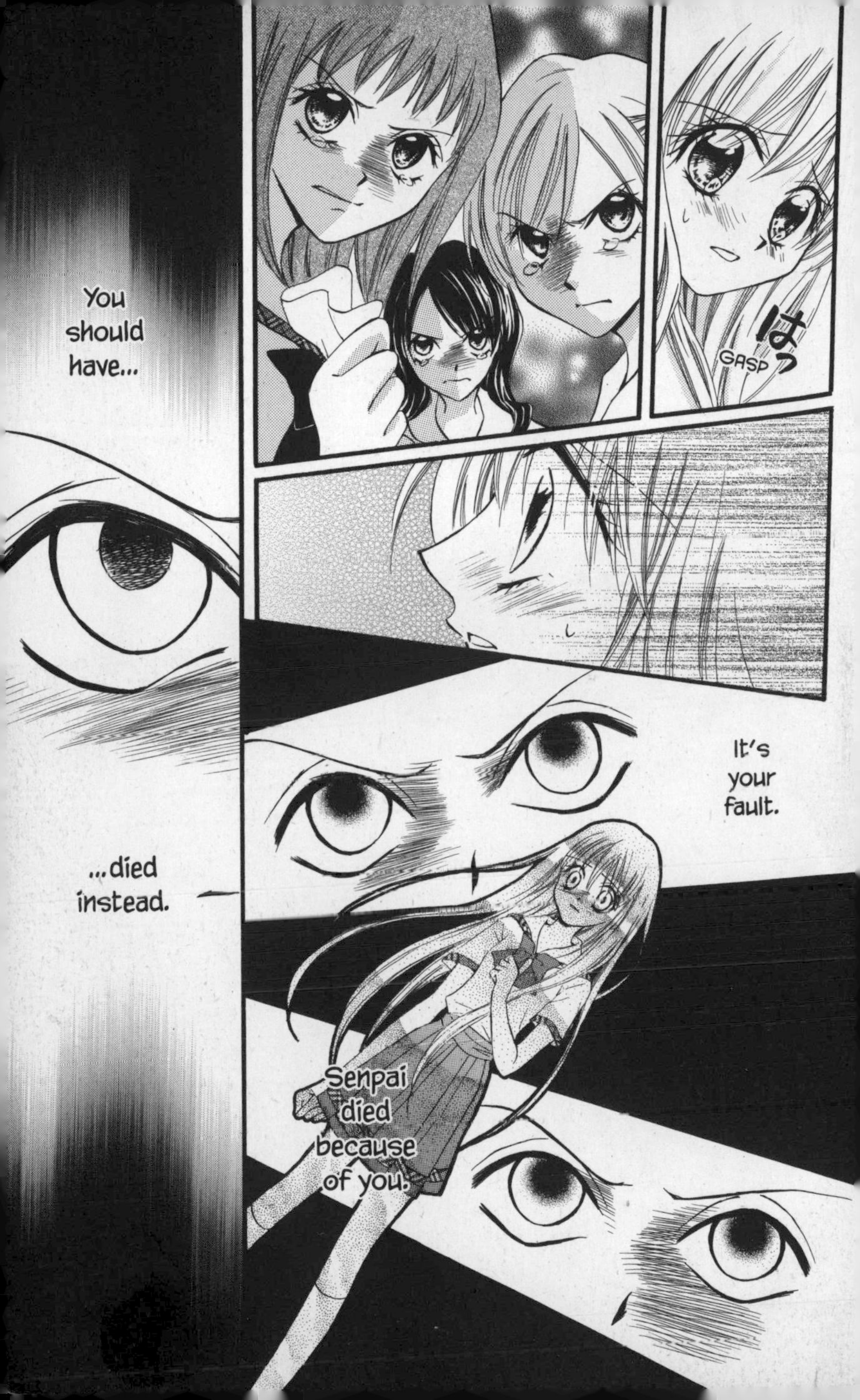
はっ
GASP
It's your fault.
Senpai died because of you.
You should have...
...died instead.

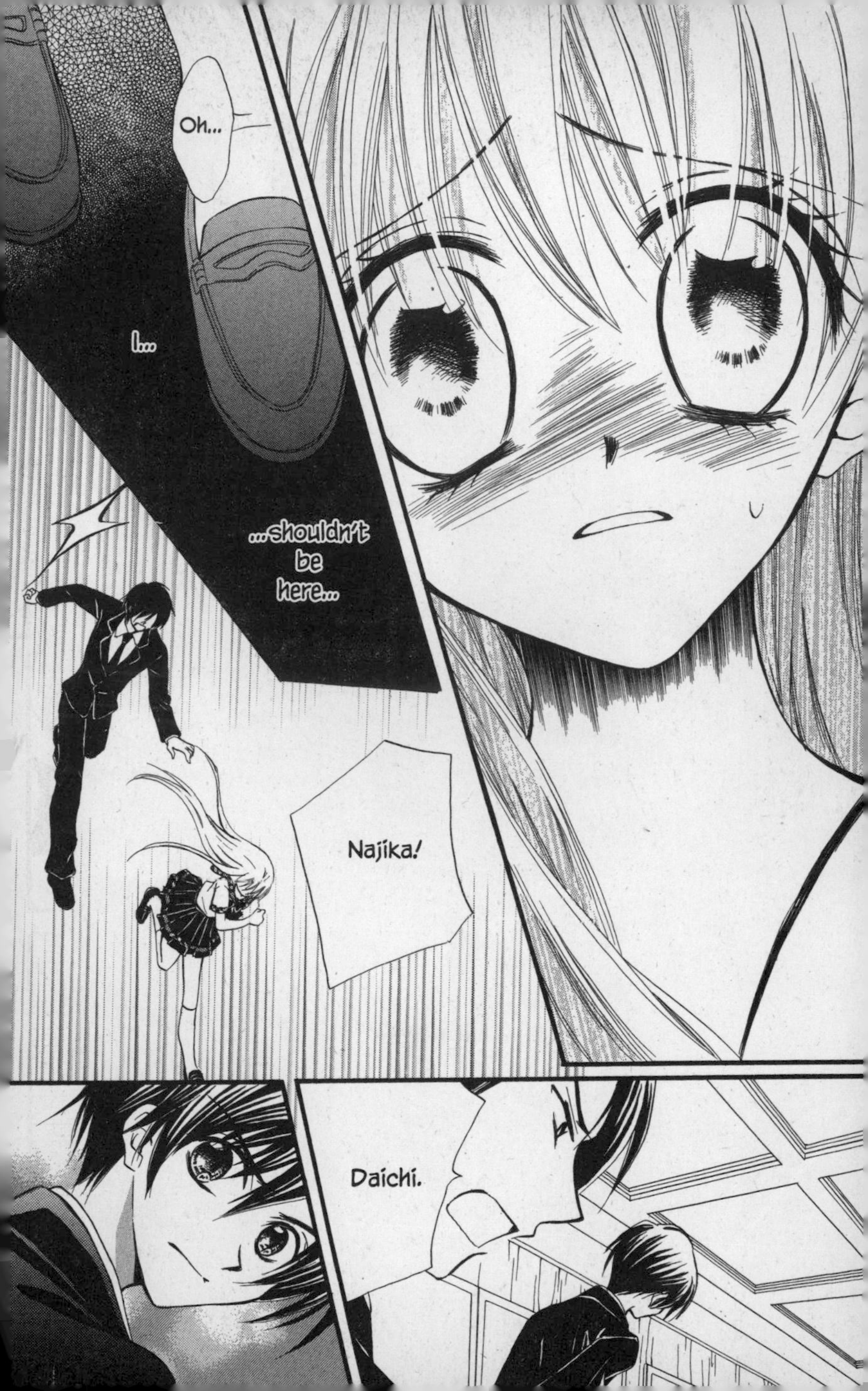
Oh...
I...
...shouldn't be here...
Najika!
Daichi.

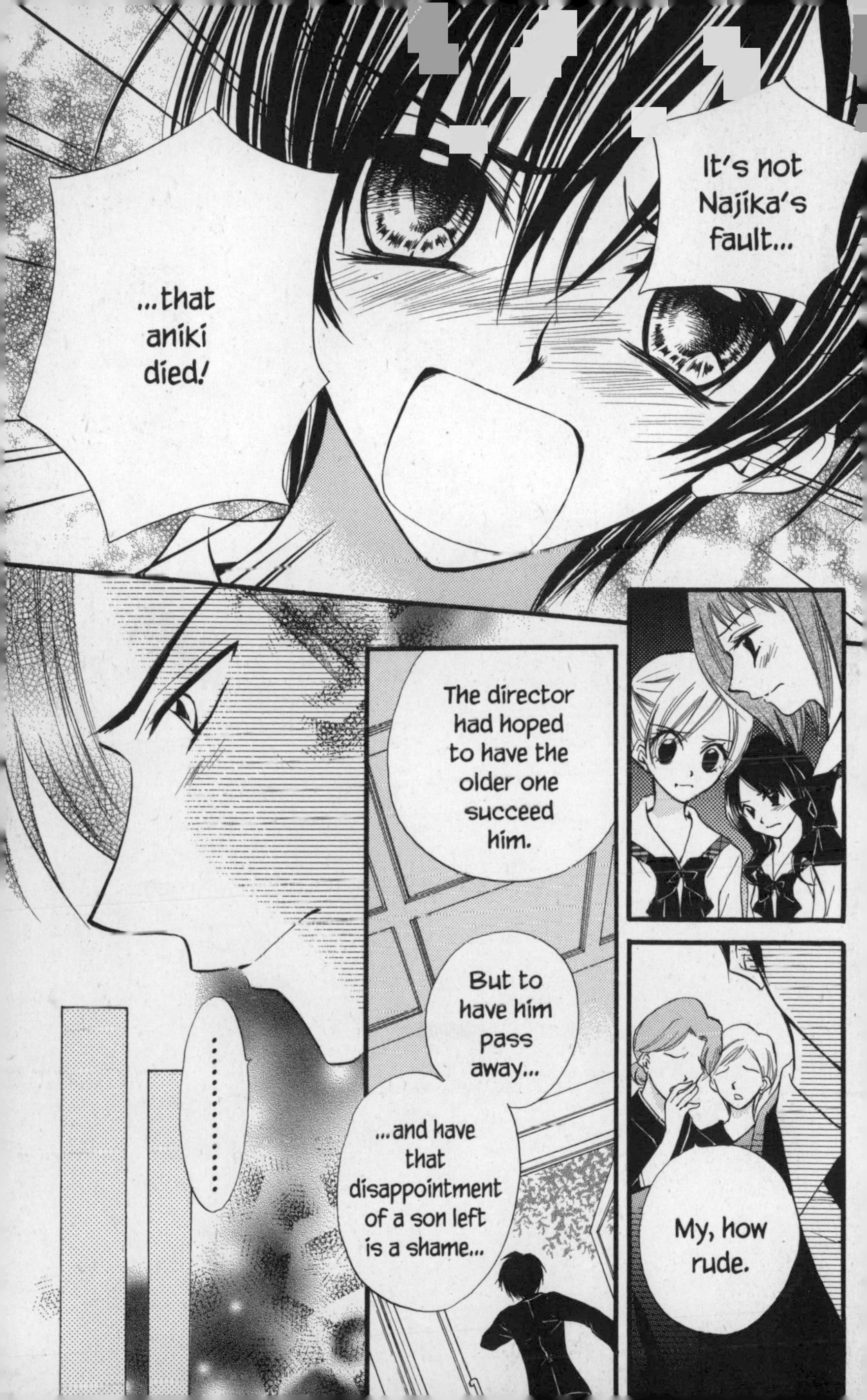
It's not Najika's fault...
...that aniki died!
My, how rude.
The director had hoped to have the older one succeed him.
But to have him pass away...
...and have that disappointment of a son left is a shame...
......

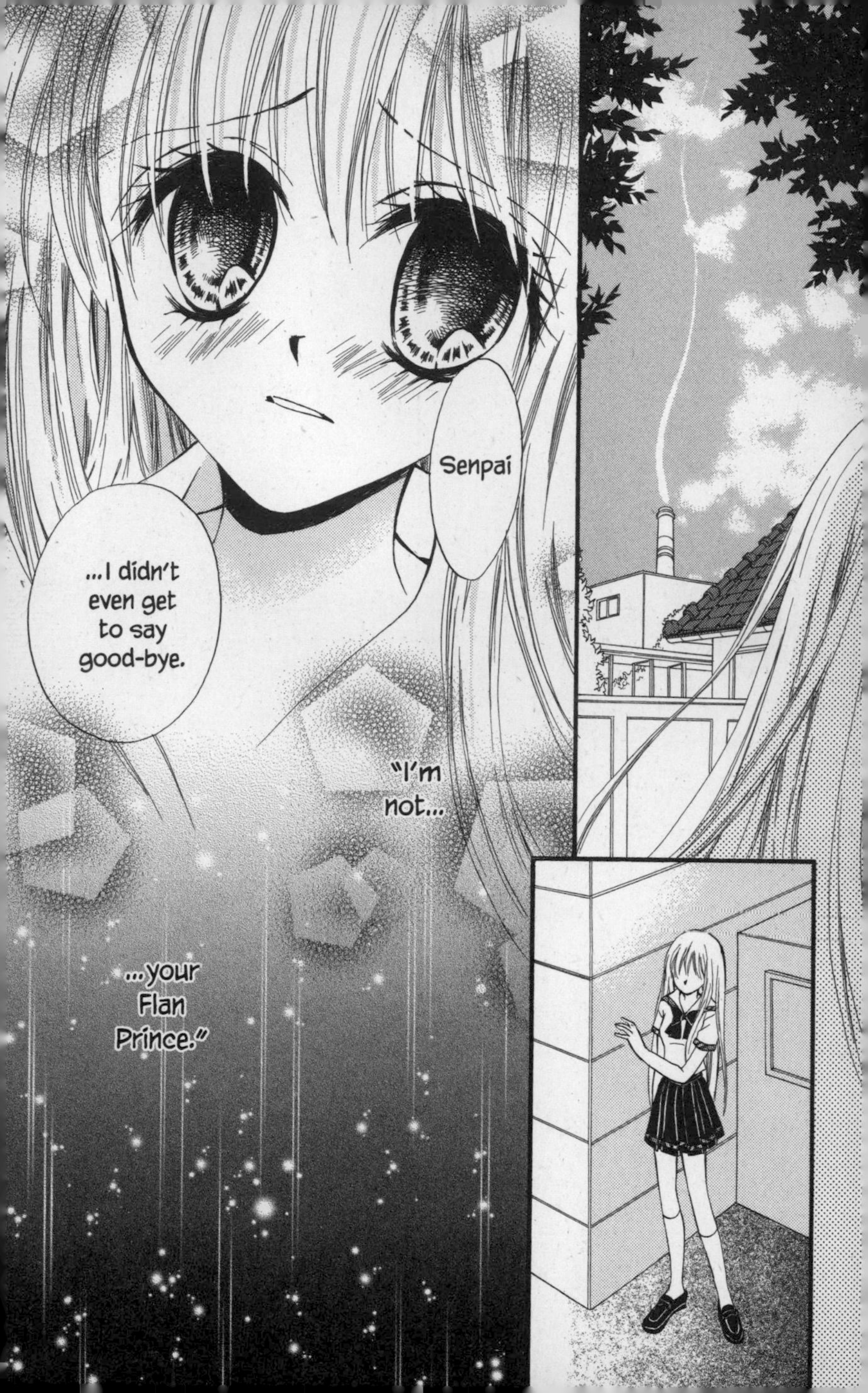
Senpai
...I didn't even get to say good-bye.
"I'm not...
...your Flan Prince."

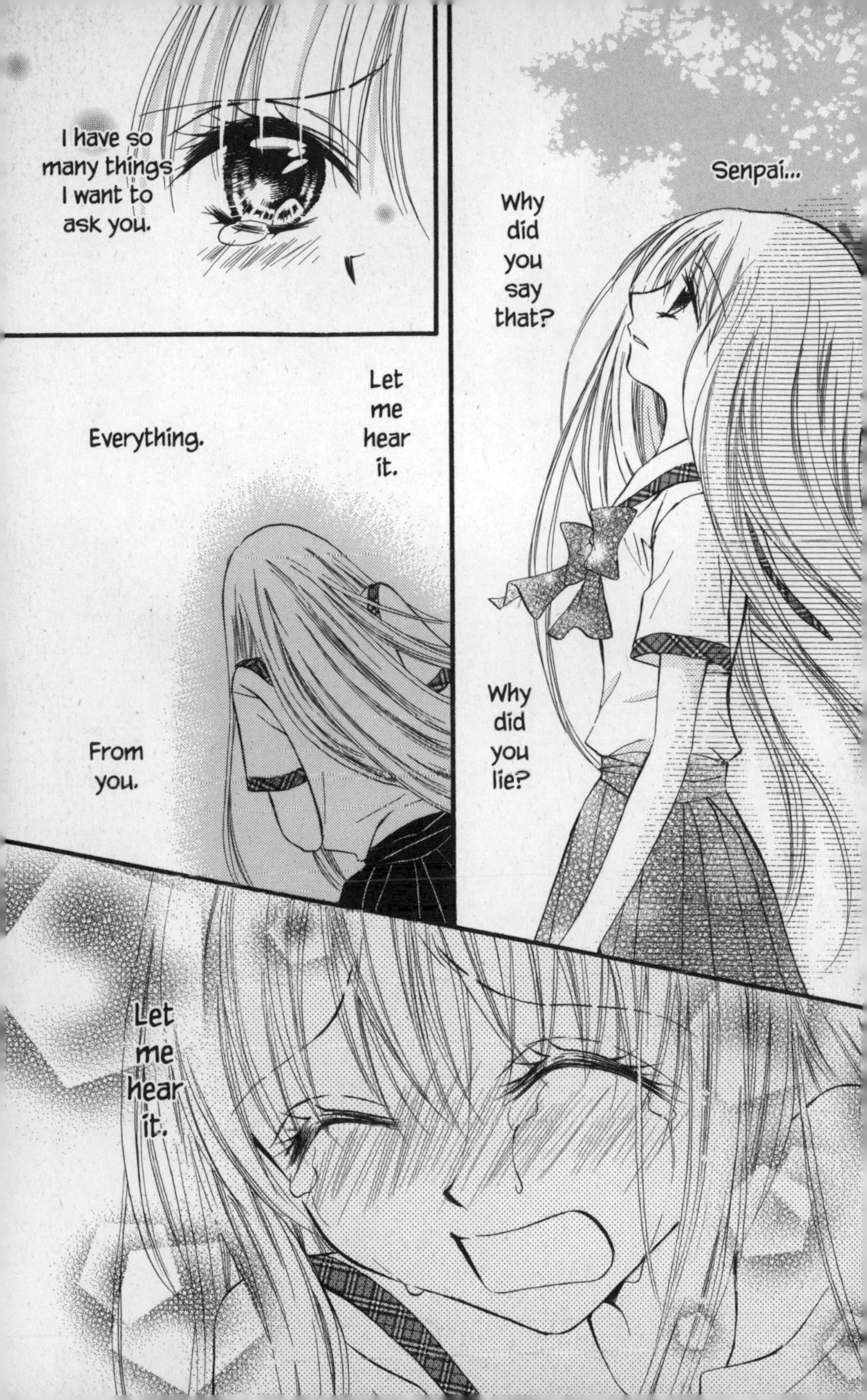
Senpai...
Why did you say that?
Why did you lie?
I have so many things I want to ask you.
Let me hear it.
Everything.
From you.
Let me hear it.

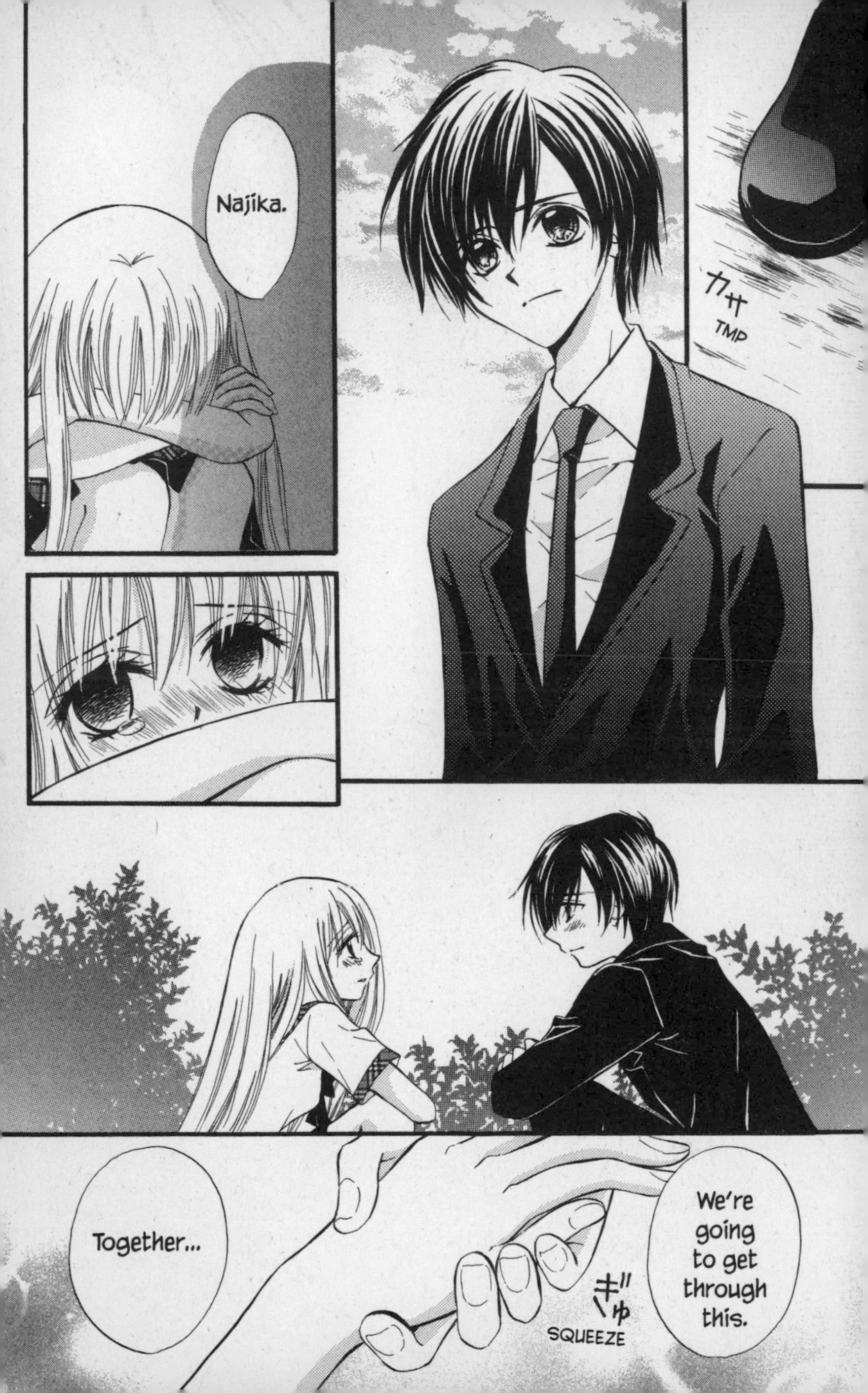
カサ
TMP
Najika.
We're going to get through this.
ギュ
SQUEEZE
Together...

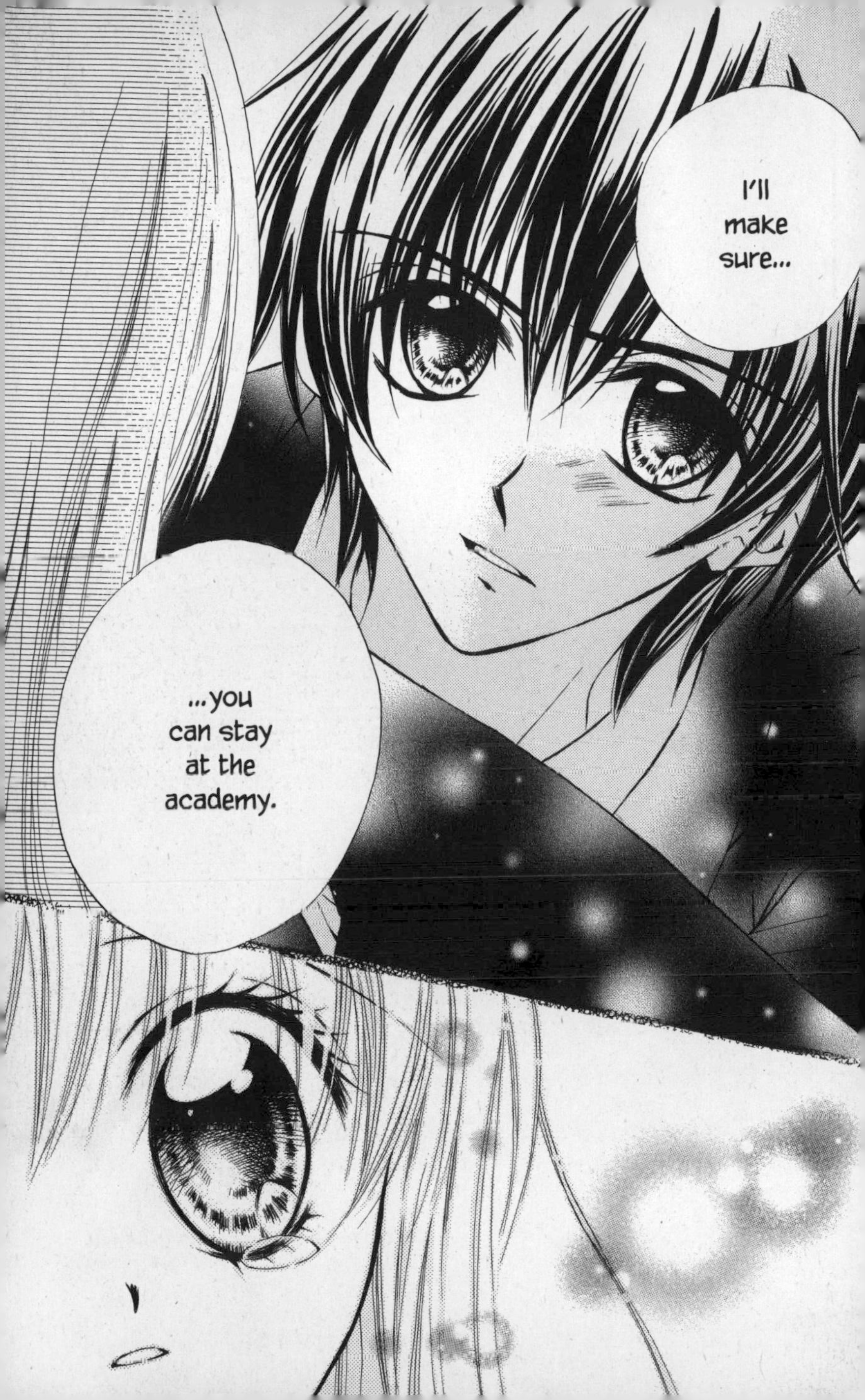
I'll make sure...
...you can stay at the academy.

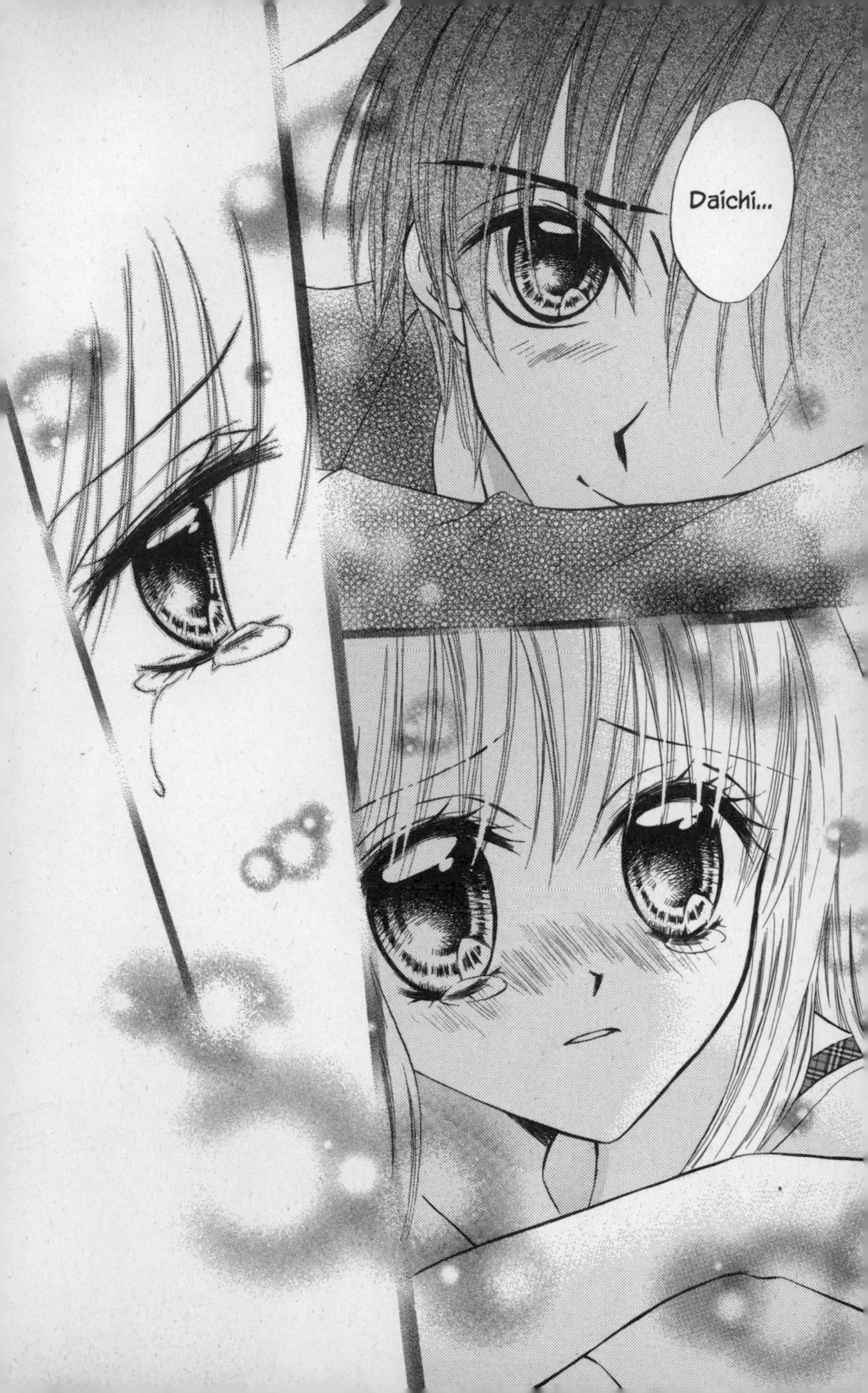
Daichi...

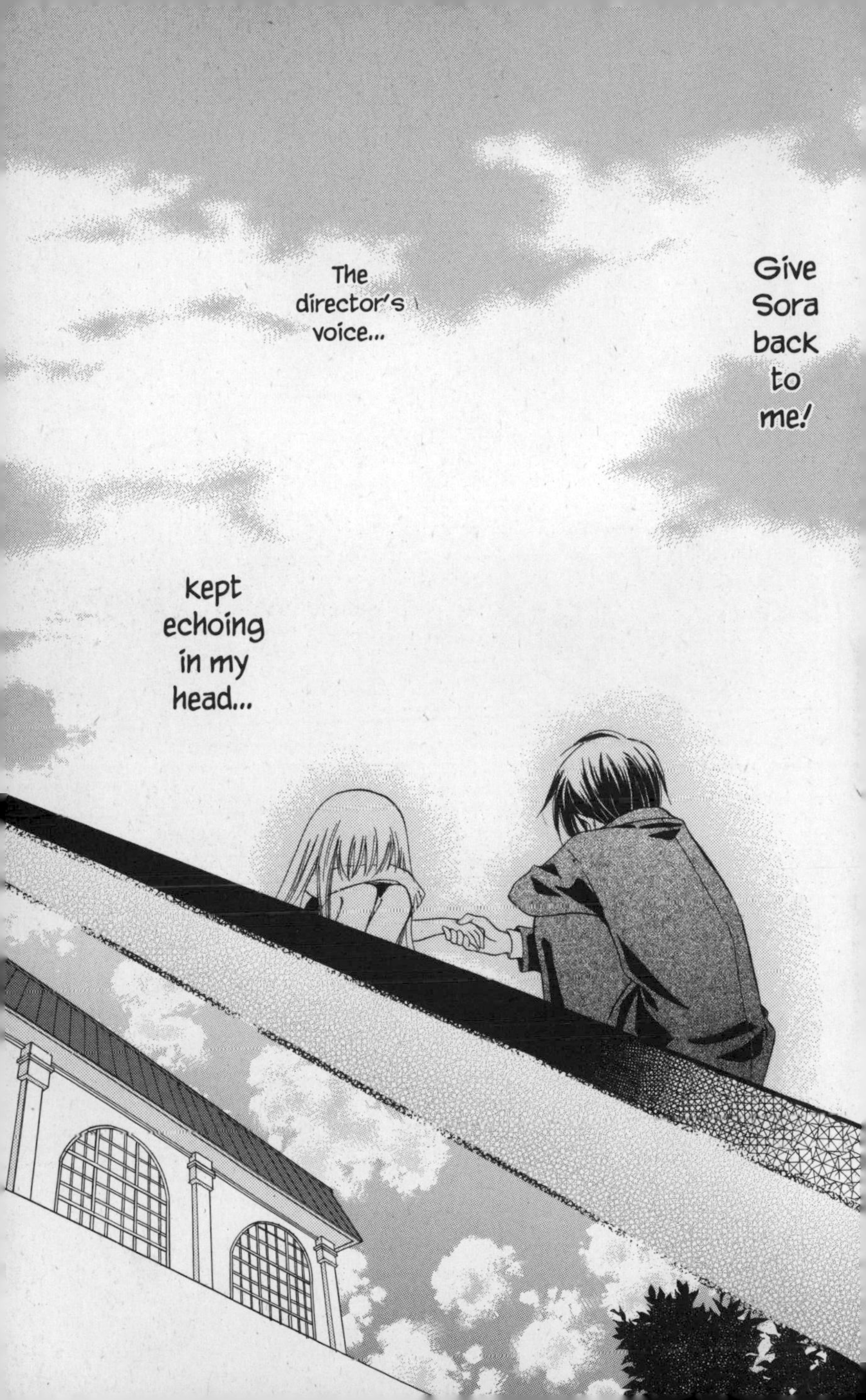
Give Sora back to me!
The director's voice...
kept echoing in my head...

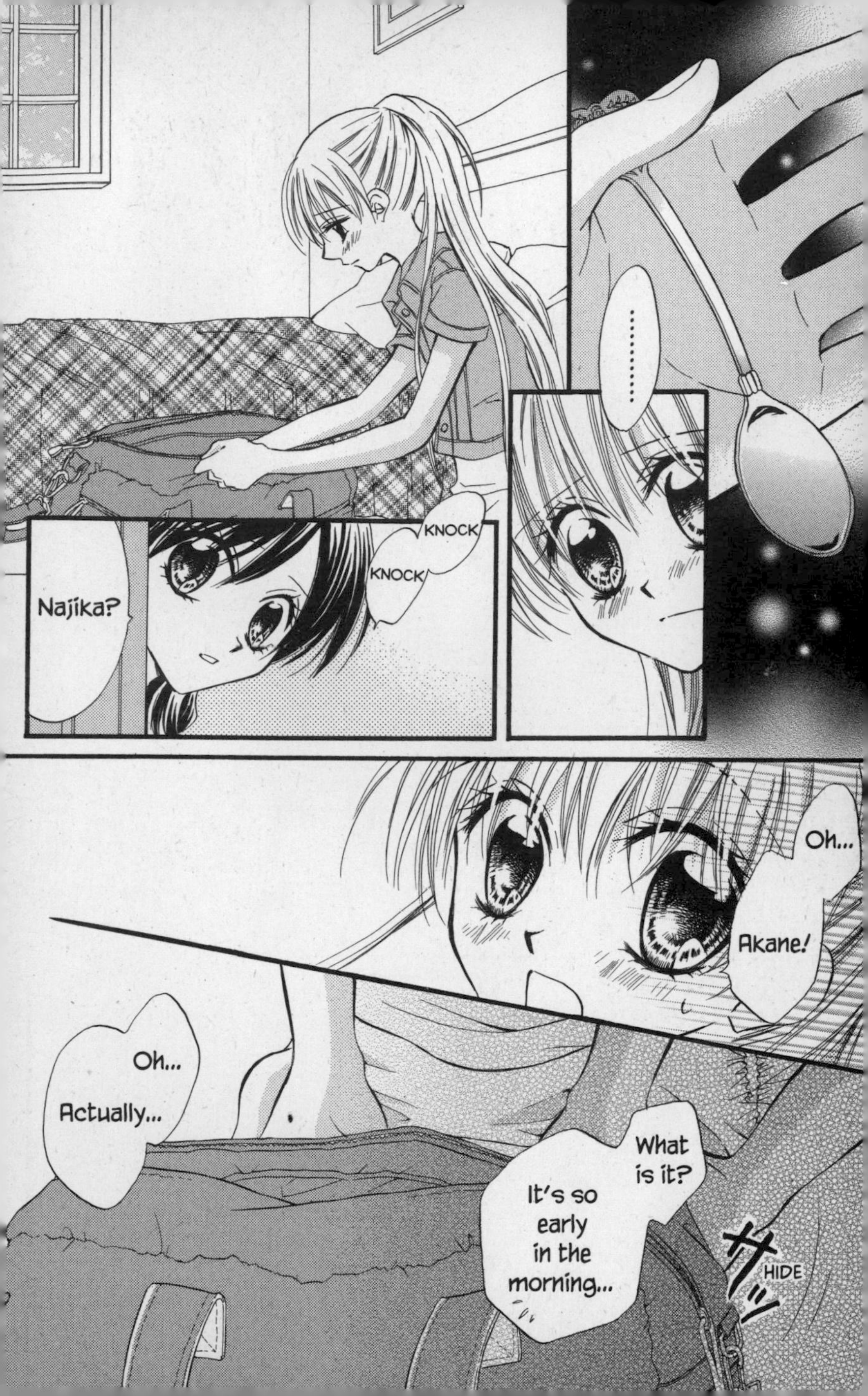
......
KNOCK
KNOCK
Najika?
Oh...
Akane!
What is it?
It's so early in the morning...
サッ
HIDE
Oh...
Actually...

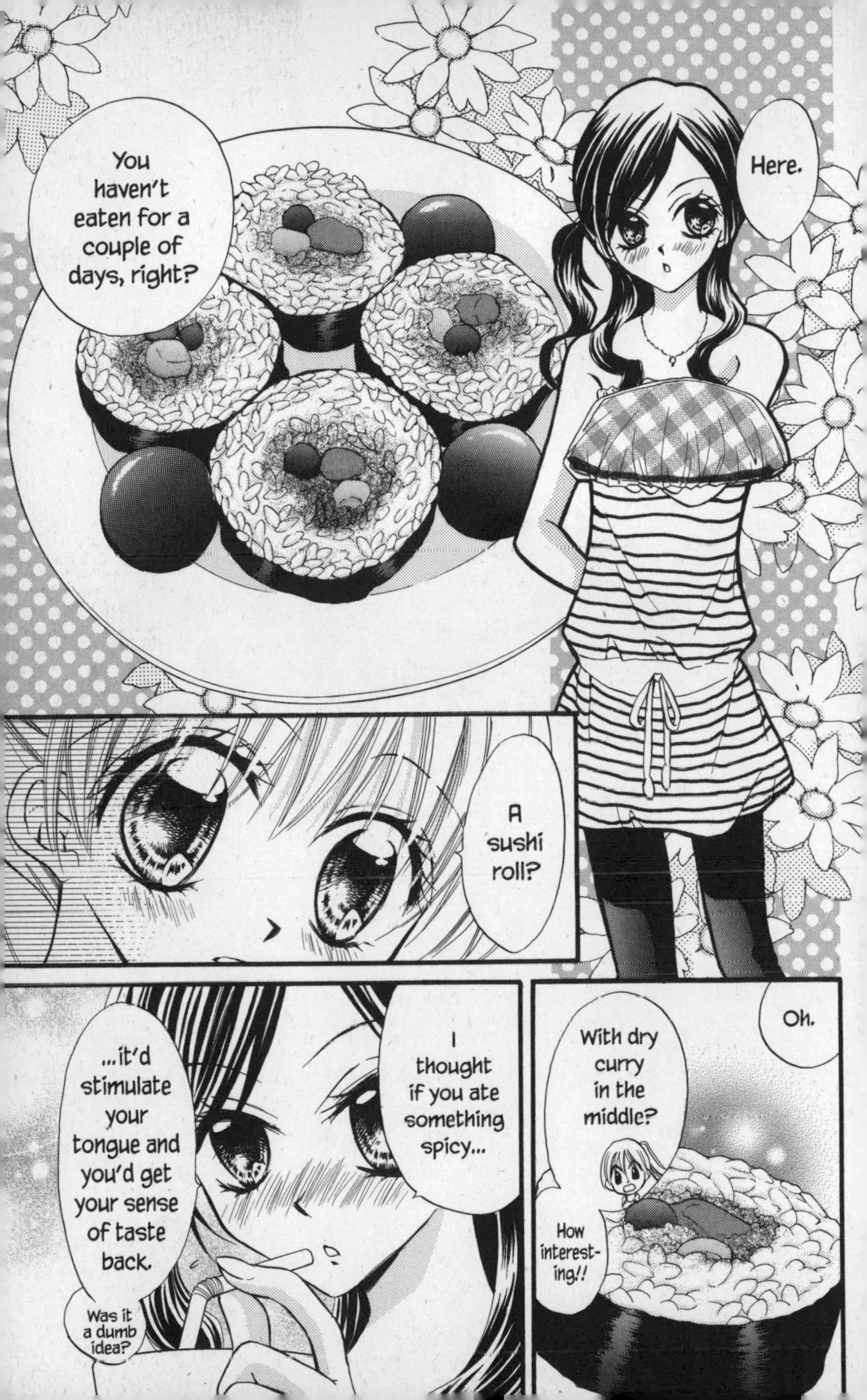
Here.
You haven't eaten for a couple of days, right?
A sushi roll?
Oh.
With dry curry in the middle?
How interest-ing!!
I thought if you ate something spicy...
...it'd stimulate your tongue and you'd get your sense of taste back.
Was it a dumb idea?

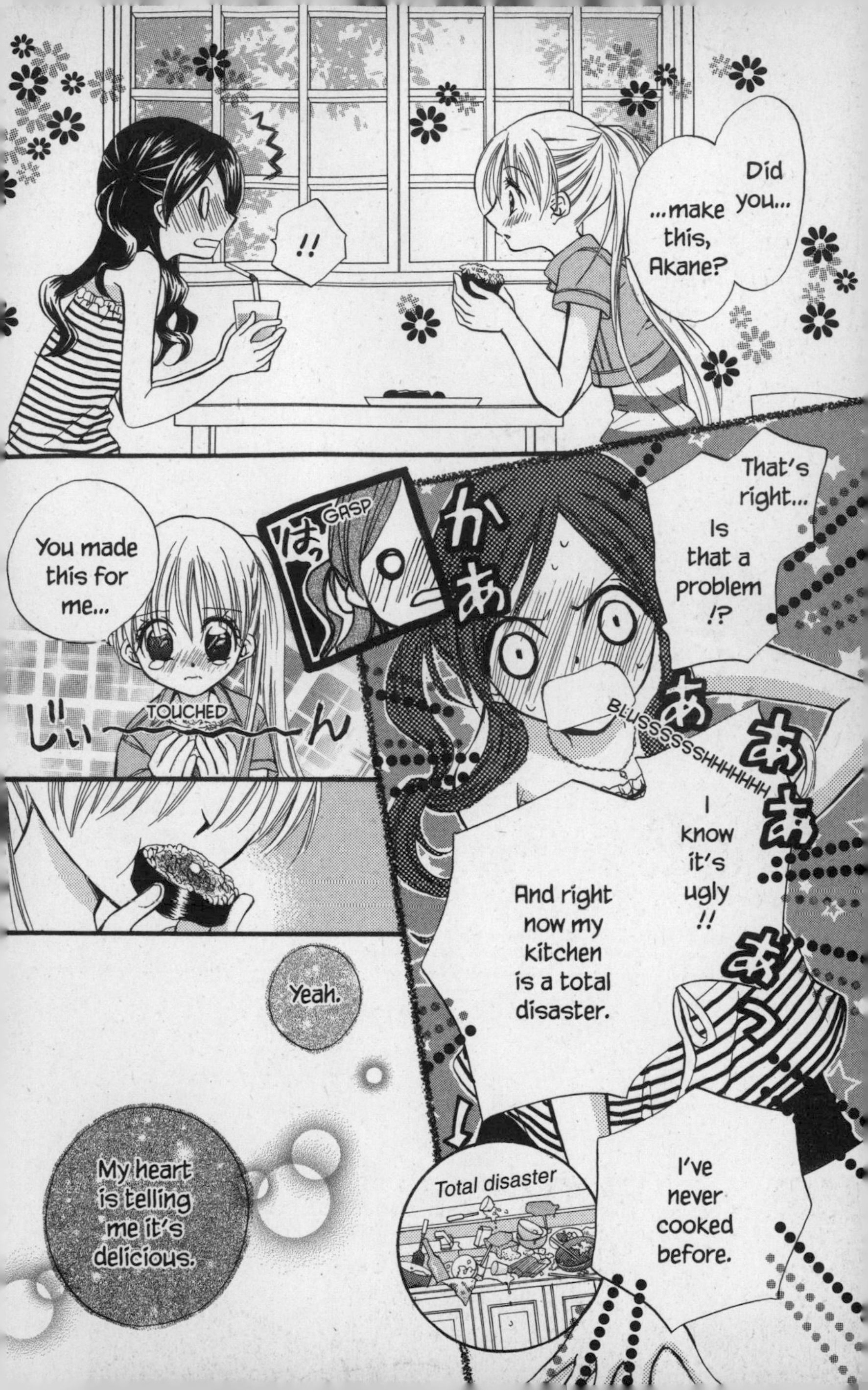
Did you... ...make this, Akane?
!!
はっ
GASP
That's right... Is that a problem!?
かぁぁぁぁっ
BLUSSSSSSHHHHHHH
I know it's ugly!!
And right now my kitchen is a total disaster.
I've never cooked before.
Total disaster
You made this for me...
じぃ~~ん
TOUCHED
Yeah.
My heart is telling me it's delicious.

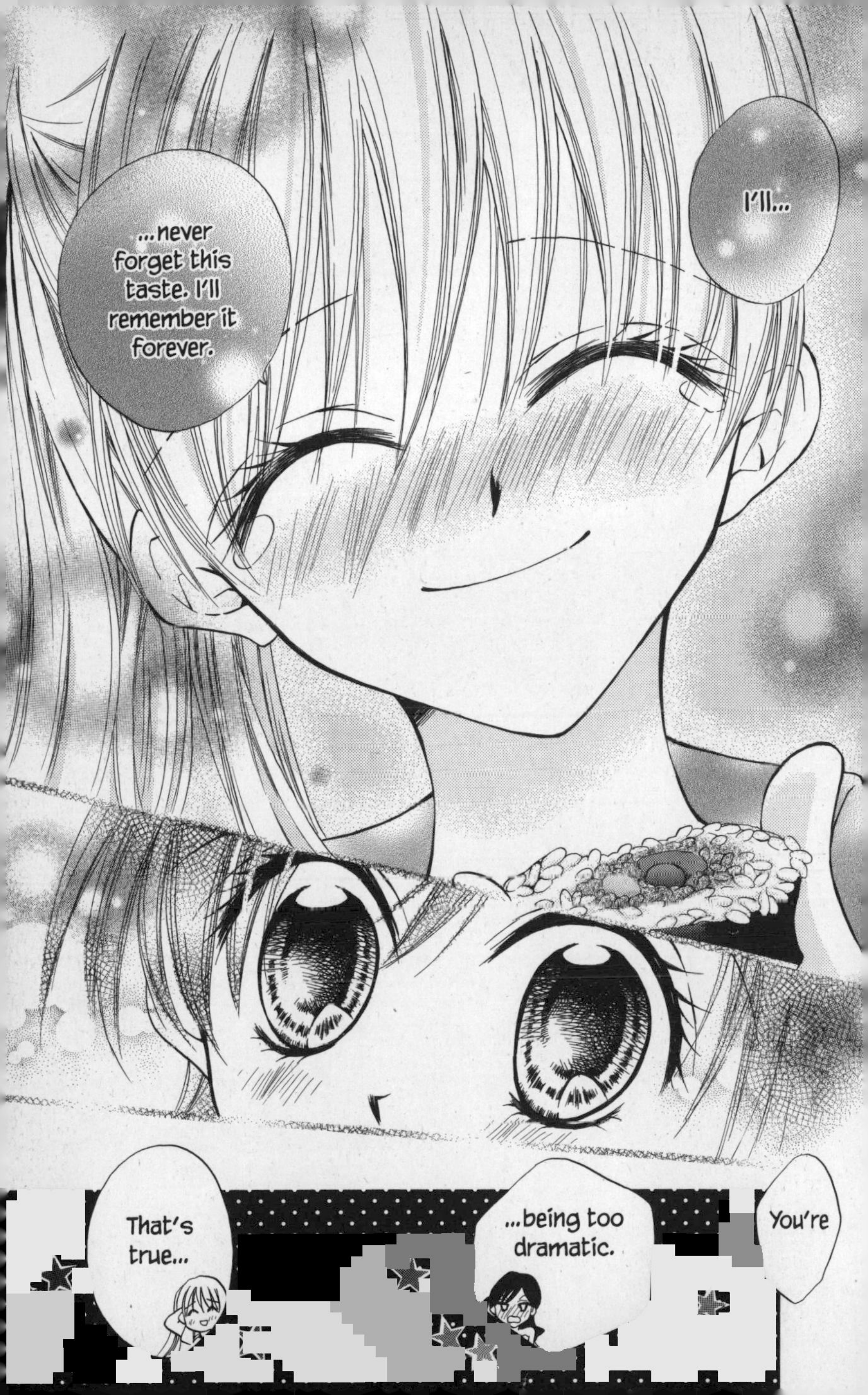
I'll...
...never forget this taste. I'll remember it forever.
You're
...being too dramatic.
That's true...

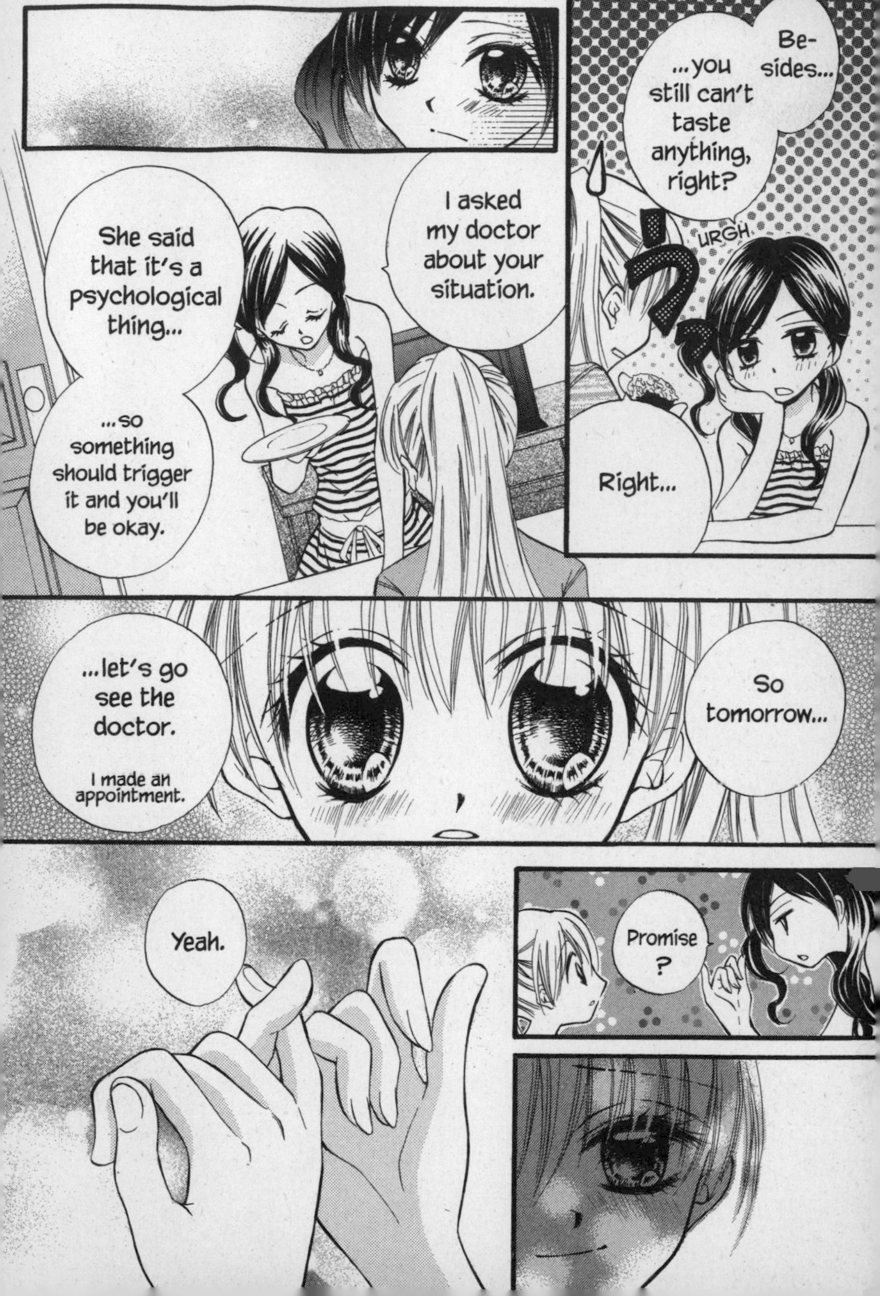
Be-sides...
...you still can't taste anything, right?
URGH
Right...
I asked my doctor about your situation.
She said that it's a psychological thing...
...so something should trigger it and you'll be okay.
So tomorrow...
...let's go see the doctor.
I made an appointment.
Promise?
Yeah.

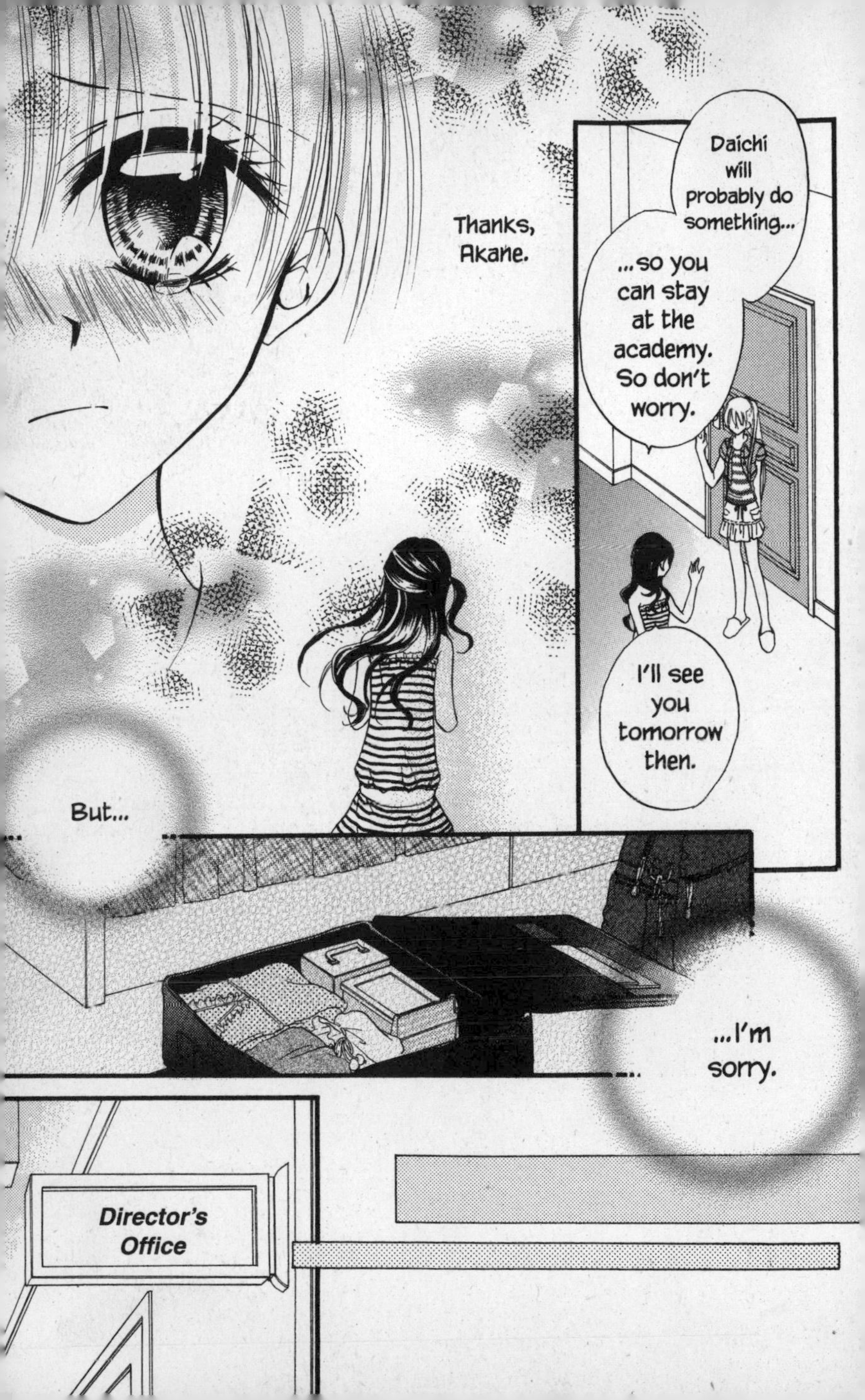
Daichi will probably do something...
...so you can stay at the academy. So don't worry.
I'll see you tomorrow then.
Thanks, Akane.
But...
...I'm sorry.
Director's Office

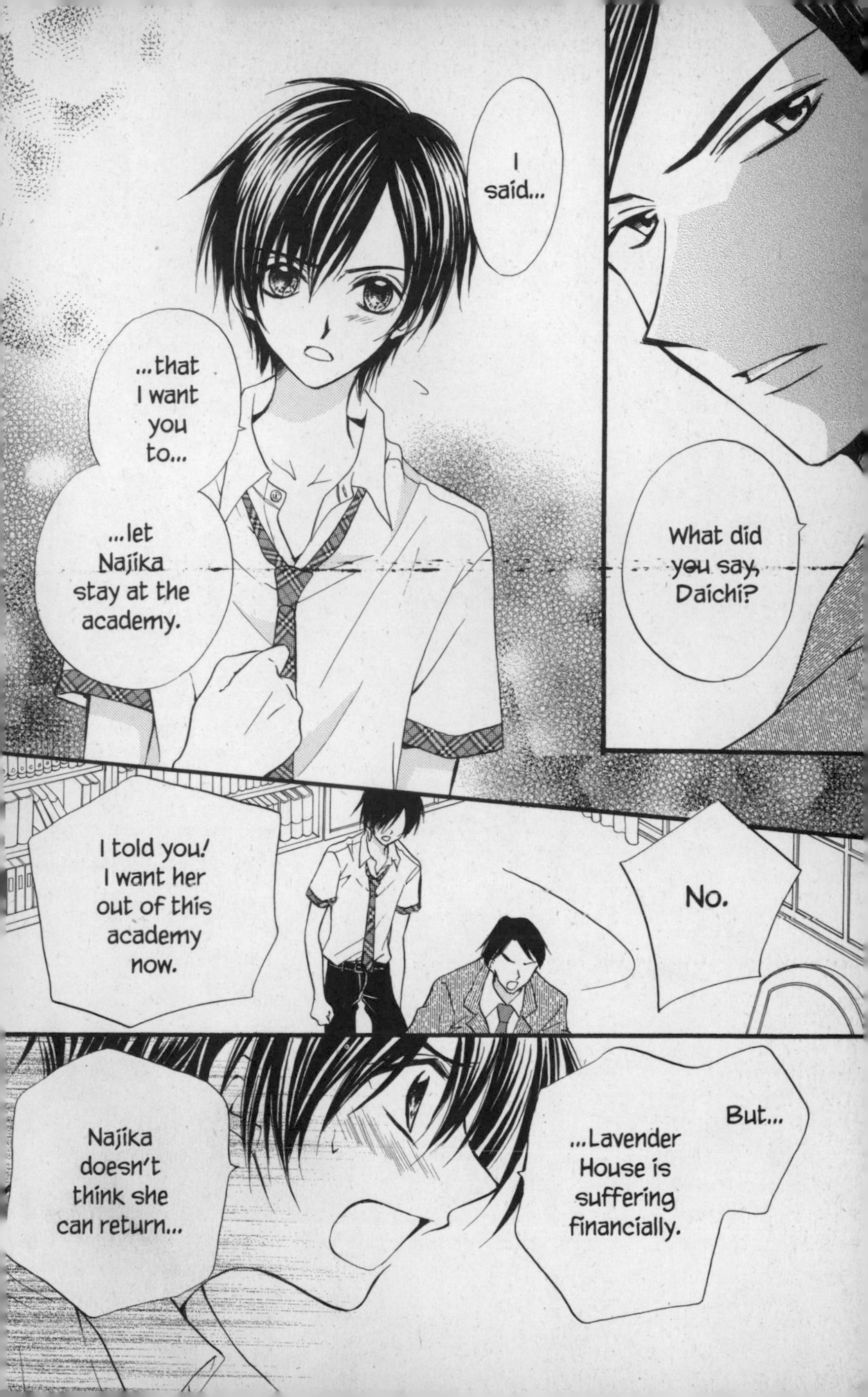
What did you say, Daichi?
I said...
...that I want you to...
...let Najika stay at the academy.
No.
I told you! I want her out of this academy now.
But...
...Lavender House is suffering financially.
Najika doesn't think she can return...

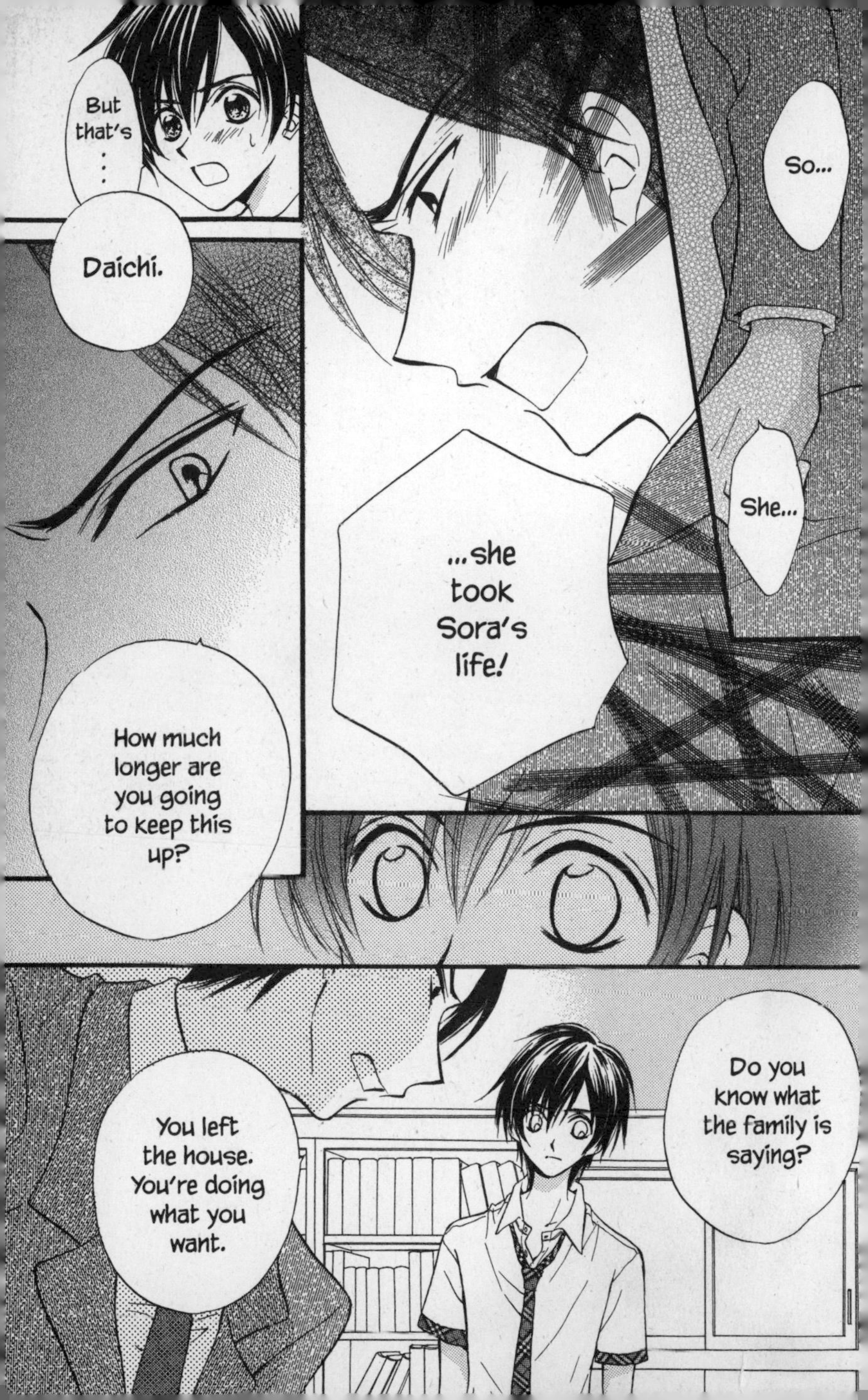
So...
She...
...she took Sora's life!
But that's . . .
Daichi.
How much longer are you going to keep this up?
Do you know what the family is saying?
You left the house. You're doing what you want.

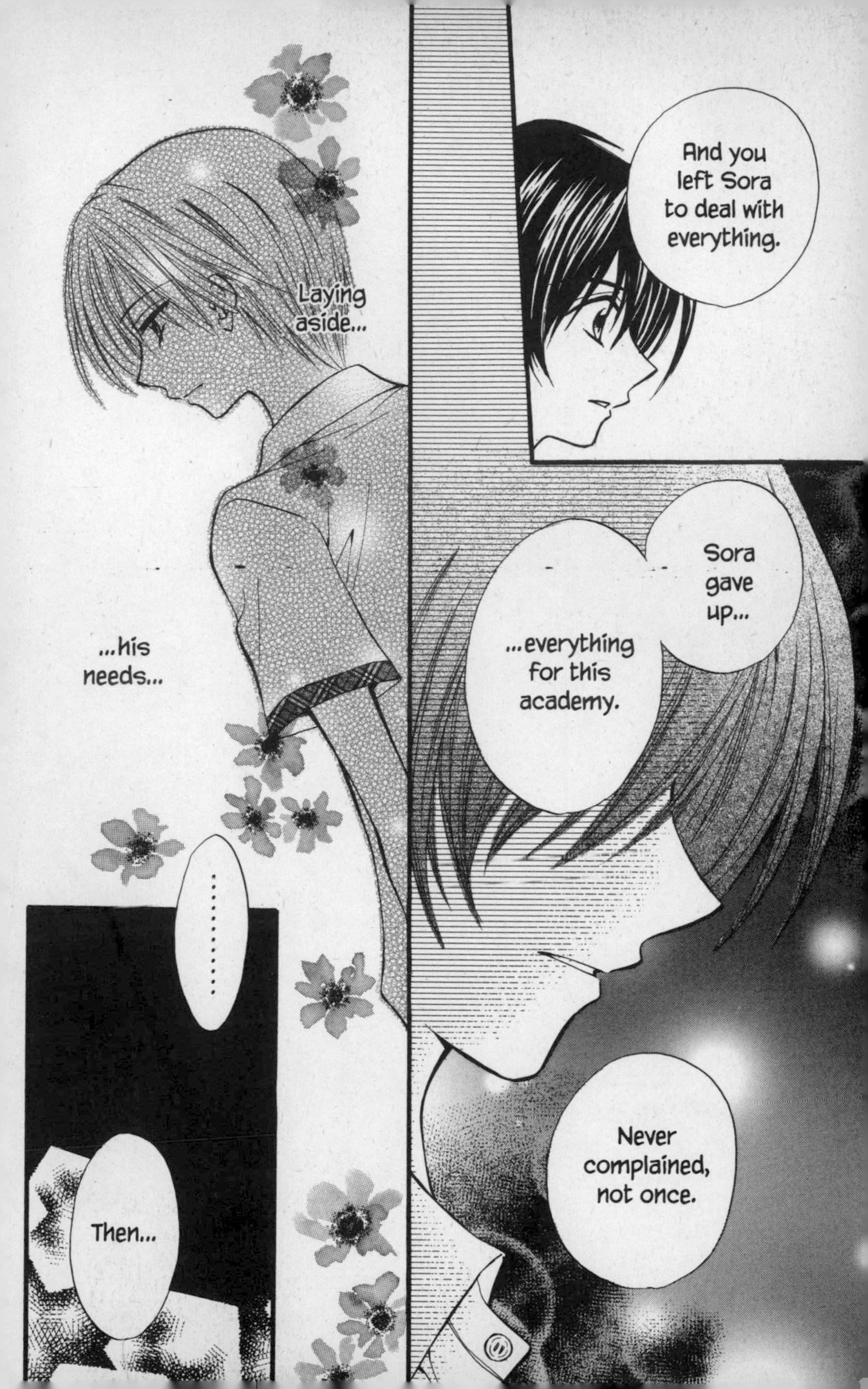
And you left Sora to deal with everything.
Sora gave up...
...everything for this academy.
Never complained, not once.
Laying aside...
...his needs...
......
Then...

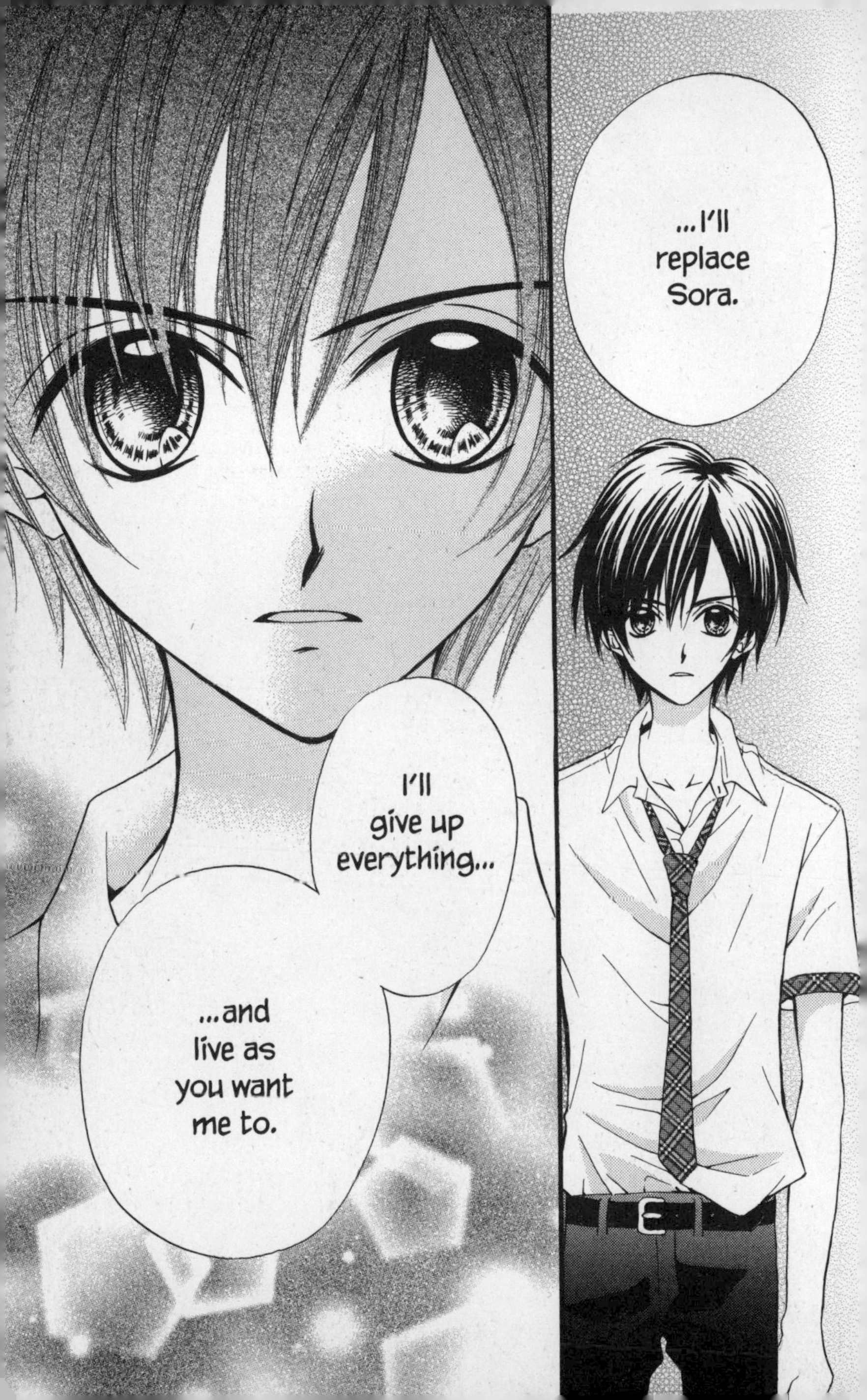
...I'll replace Sora.
I'll give up everything...
...and live as you want me to.

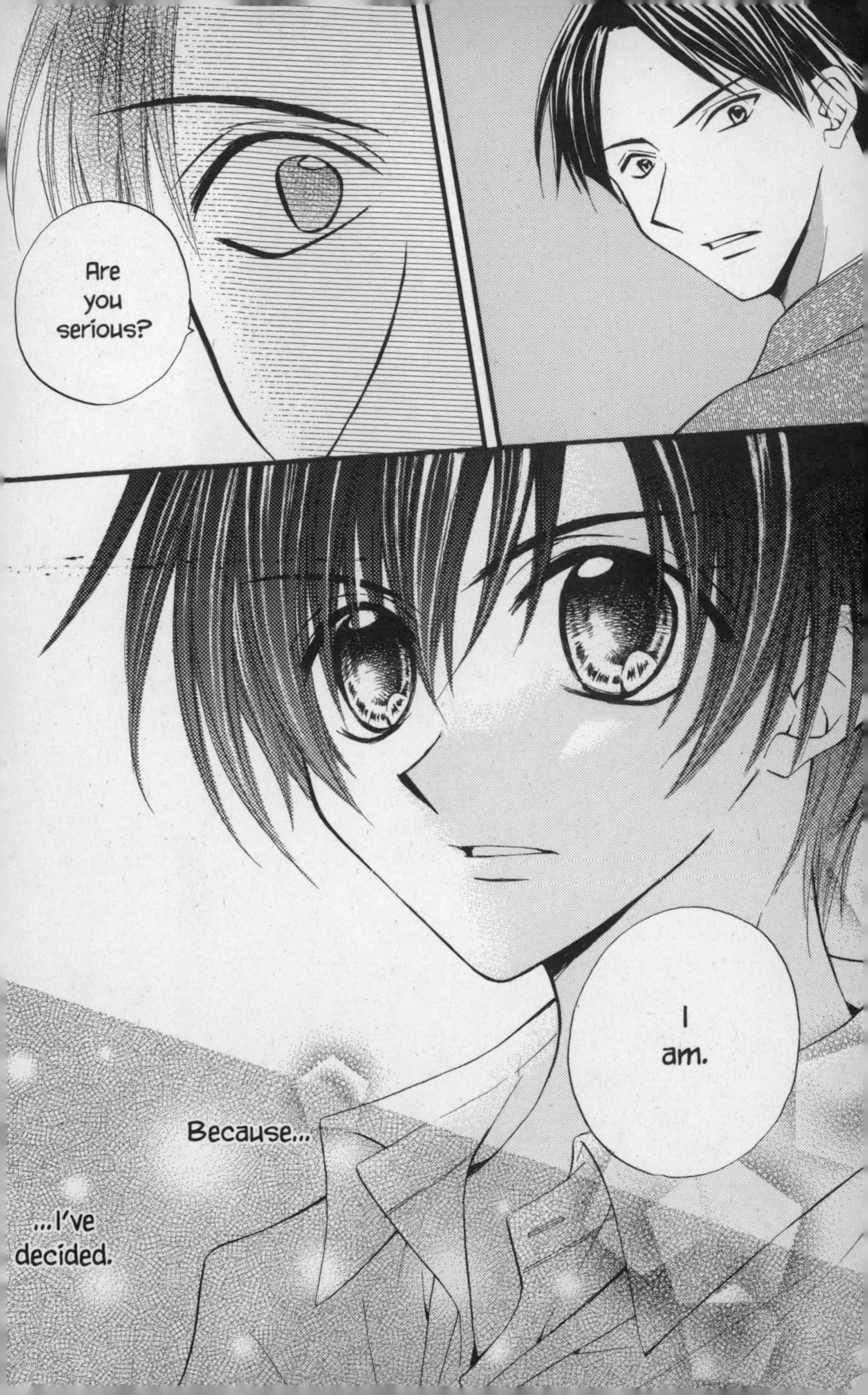
Are you serious?
I am.
Because...
...I've decided.

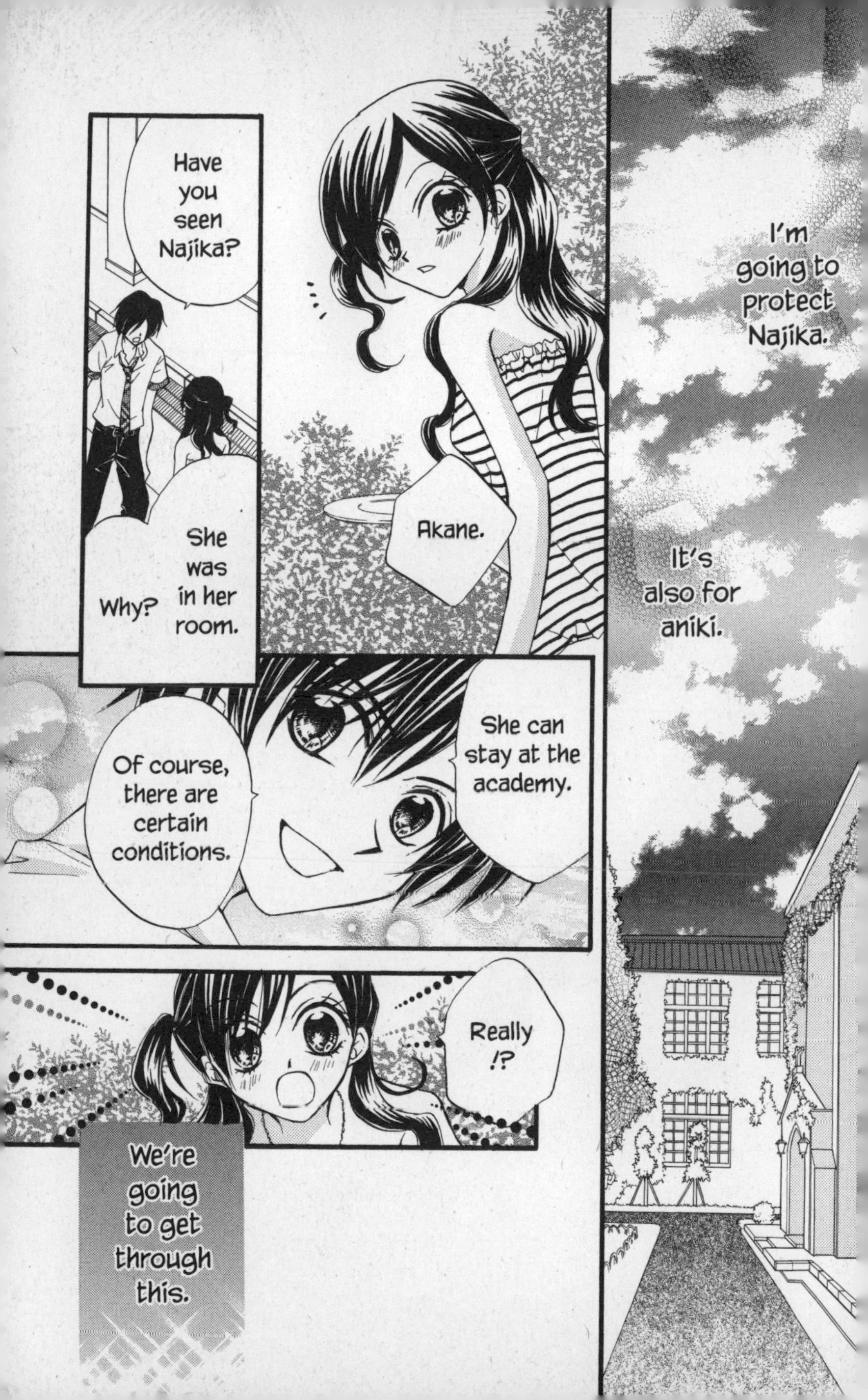
I'm going to protect Najika.
It's also for aniki.
Akane.
Have you seen Najika?
She was in her room.
Why?
She can stay at the academy.
Of course, there are certain conditions.
Really!?
We're going to get through this.

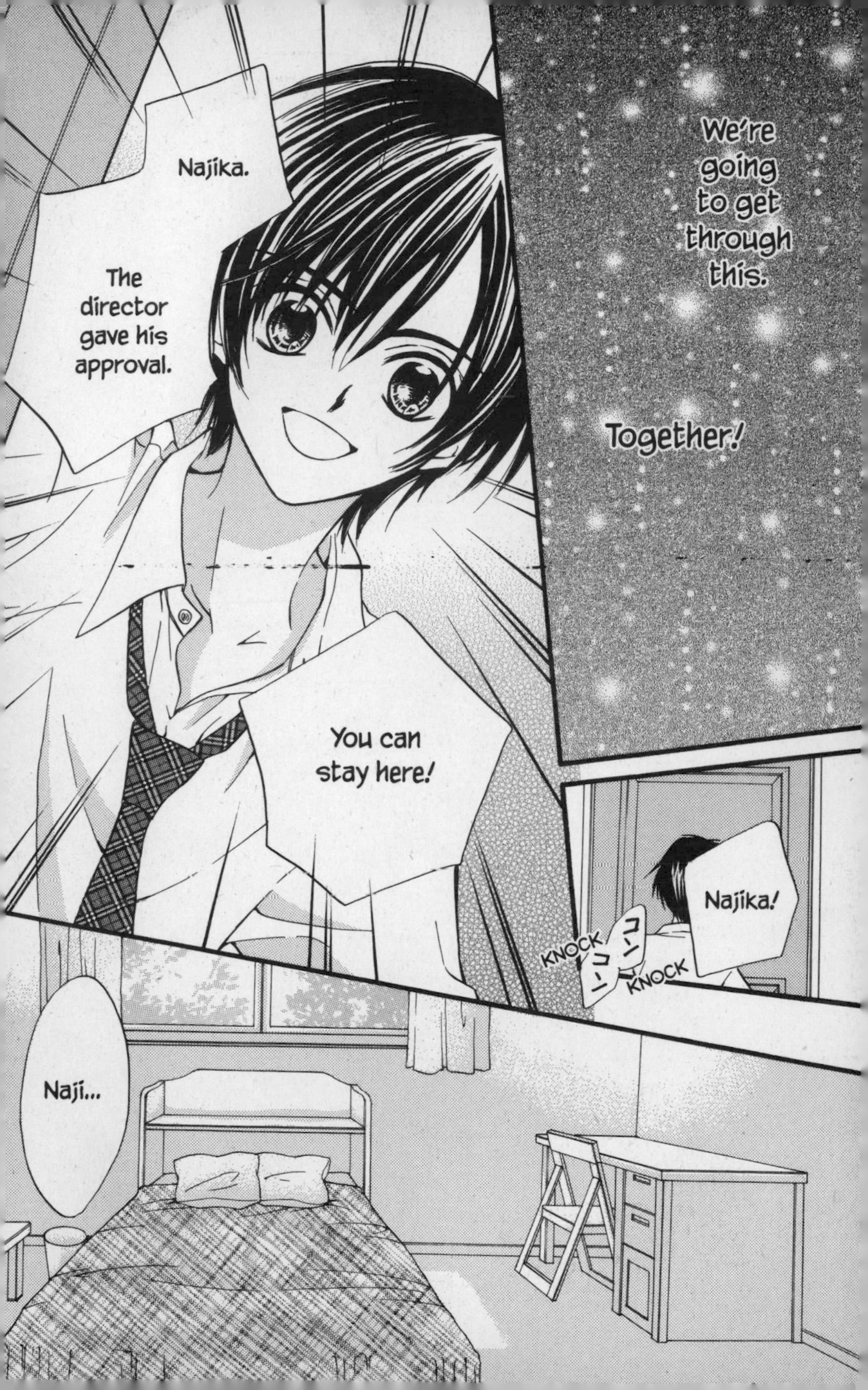
We're going to get through this.
Together!
Najika.
The director gave his approval.
You can stay here!
Najika!
KNOCK
KNOCK
Naji...

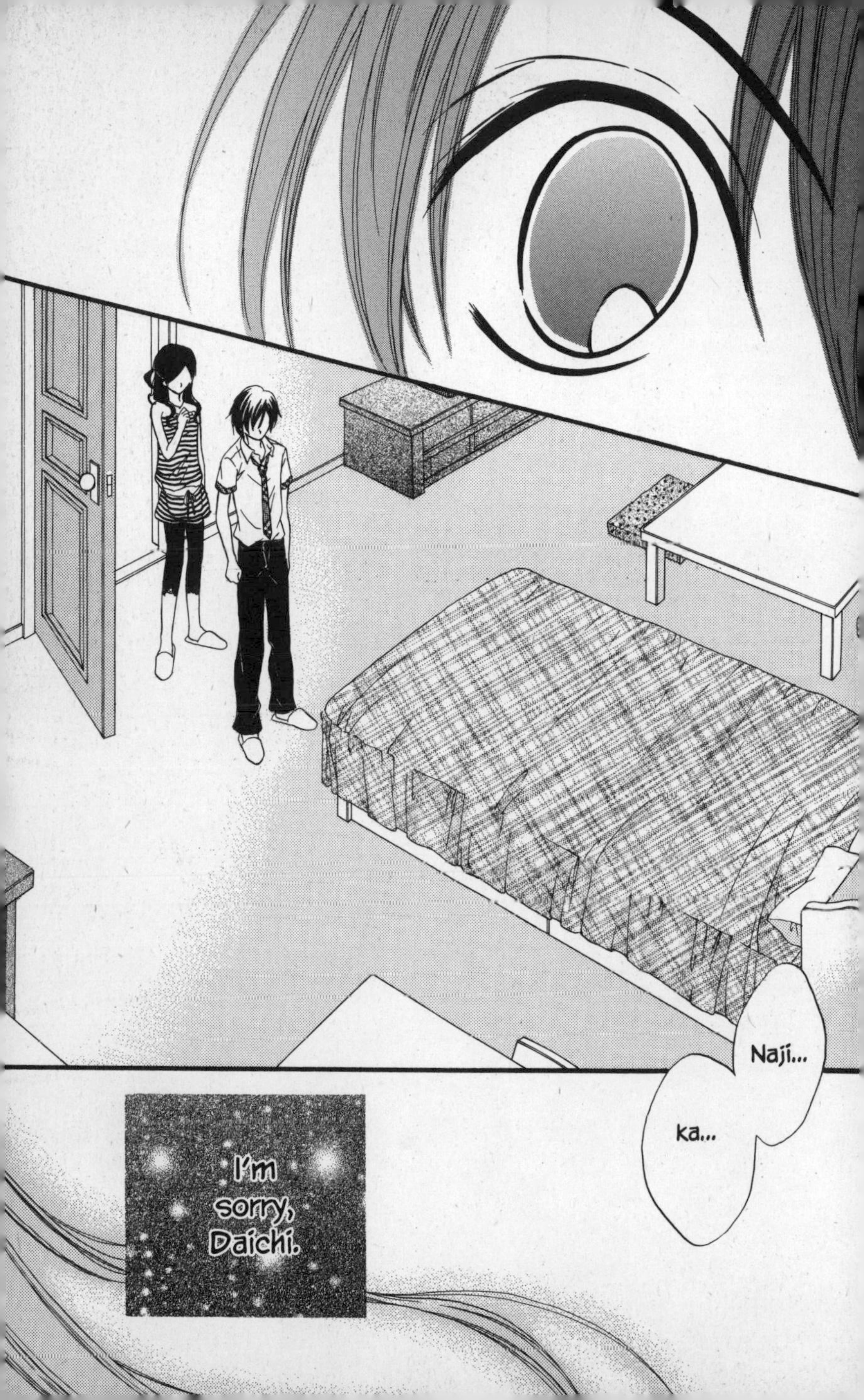
Naji...
ka...
I'm sorry, Daichi.

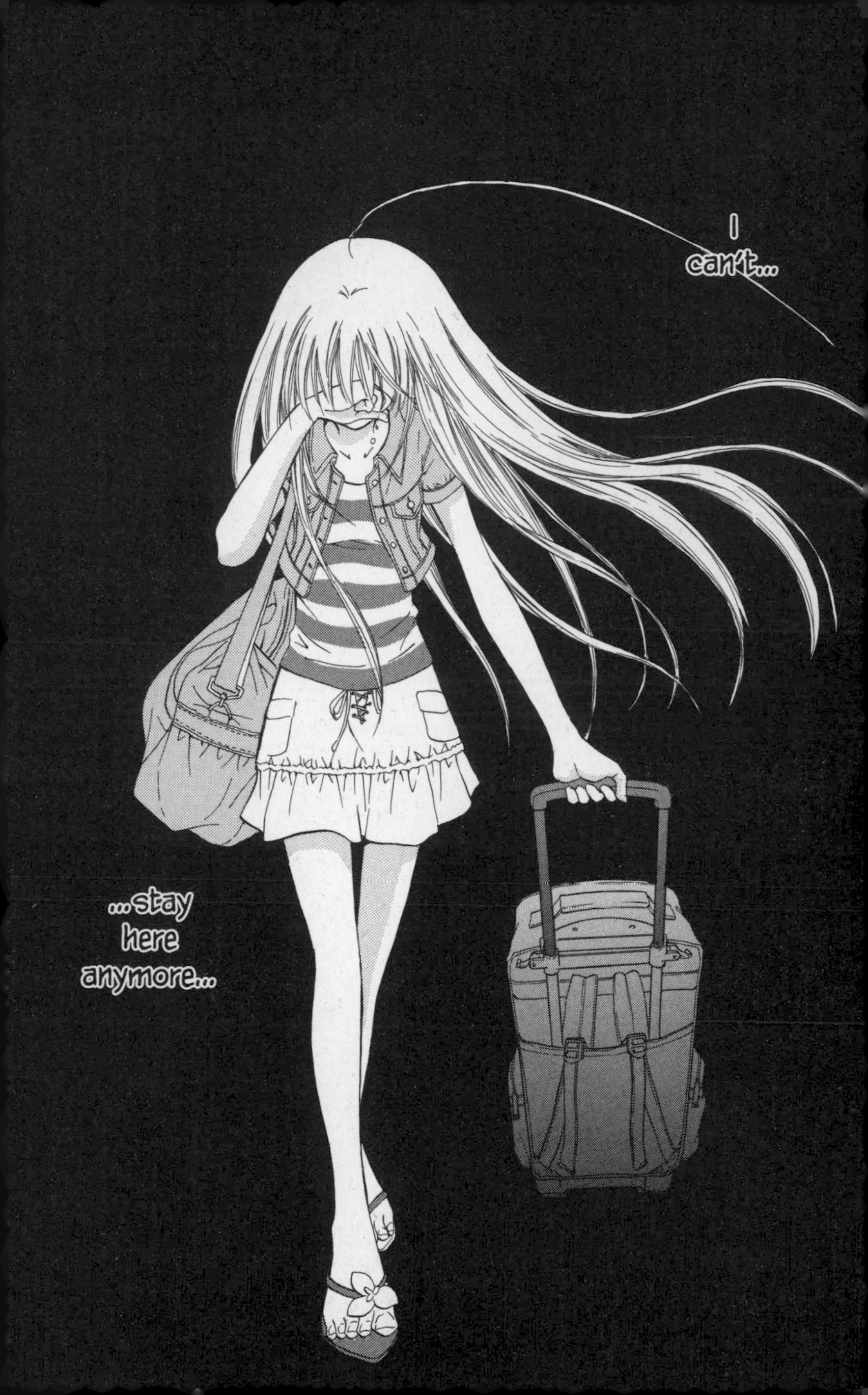
I can't...
...stay here anymore...

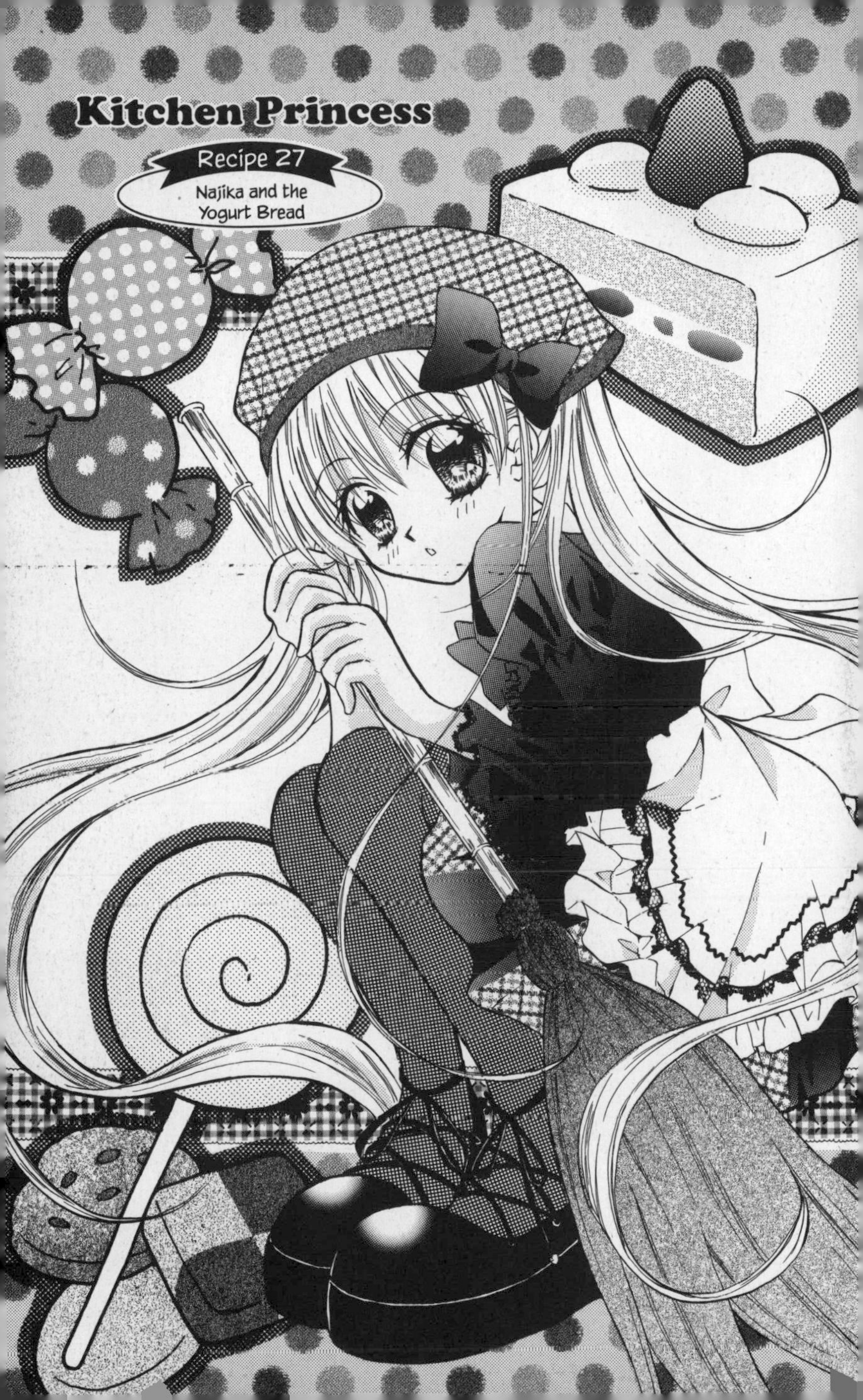
Kitchen Princess
Recipe 27
Najika and the Yogurt Bread

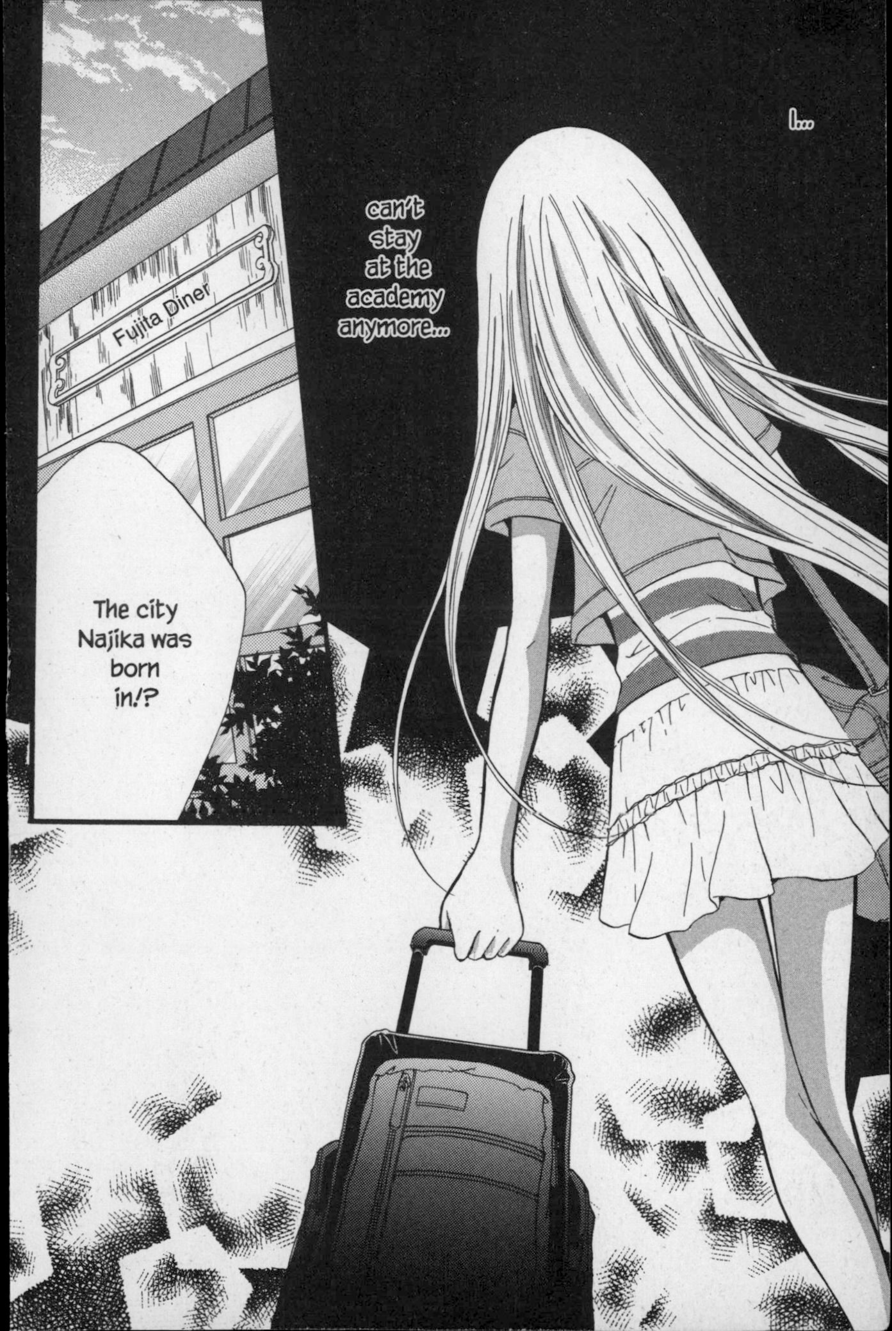
I...
can't stay at the academy anymore...
Fujita Diner
The city Najika was born in!?

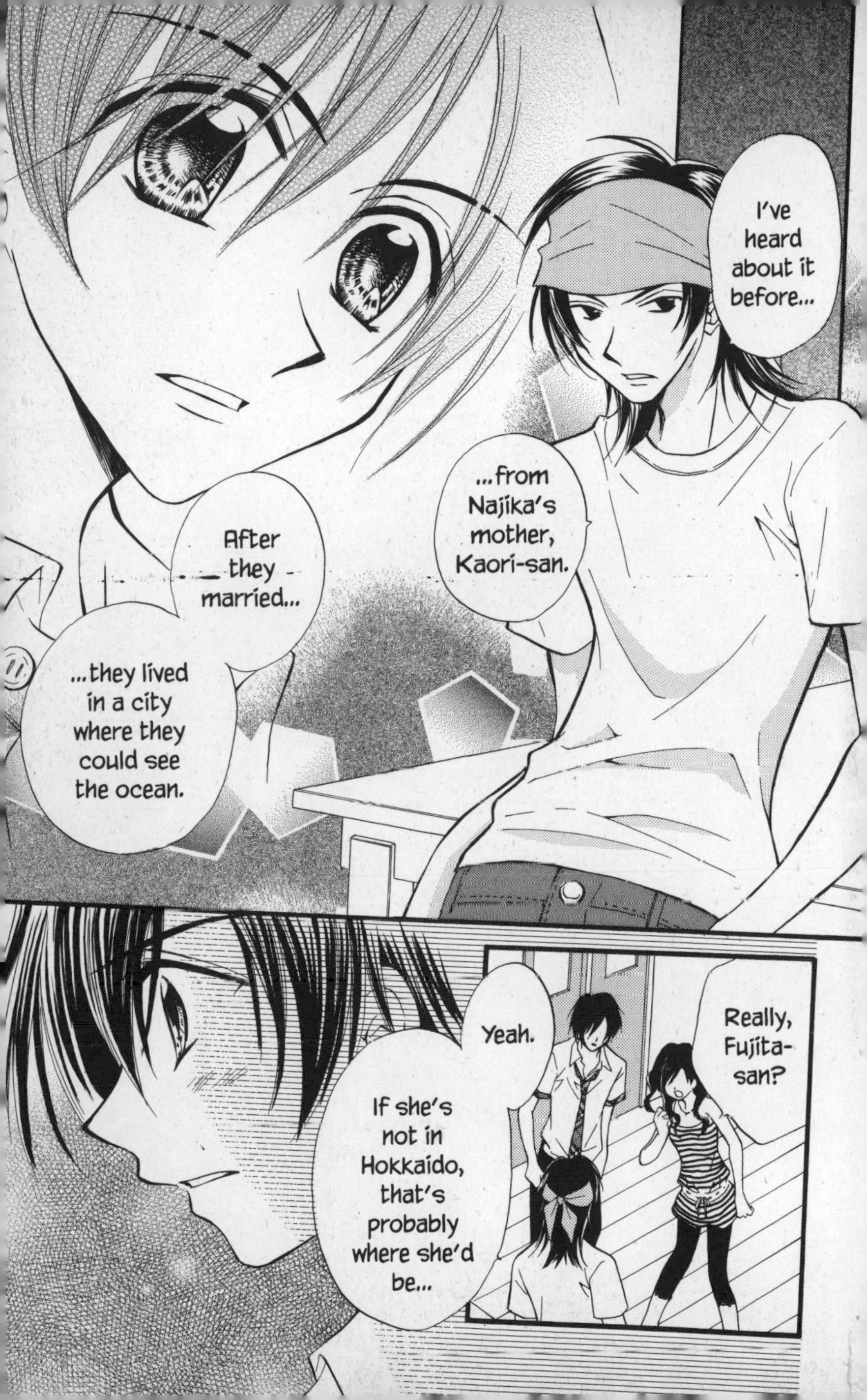
I've heard about it before...
...from Najika's mother, Kaori-san.
After they married...
...they lived in a city where they could see the ocean.
Really, Fujita-san?
Yeah.
If she's not in Hokkaido, that's probably where she'd be...

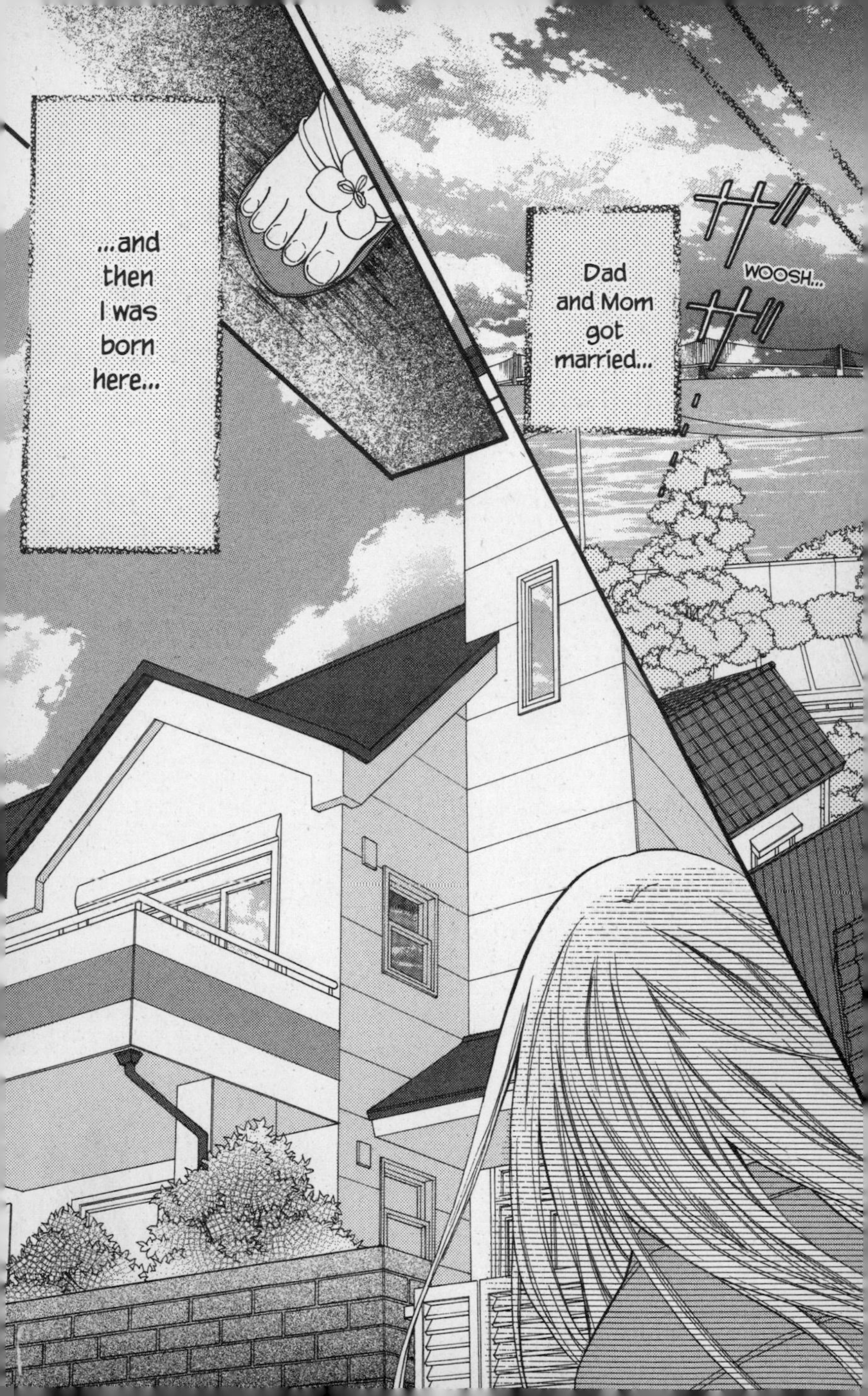
Dad and Mom got married...
WOOSH...
...and then I was born here...

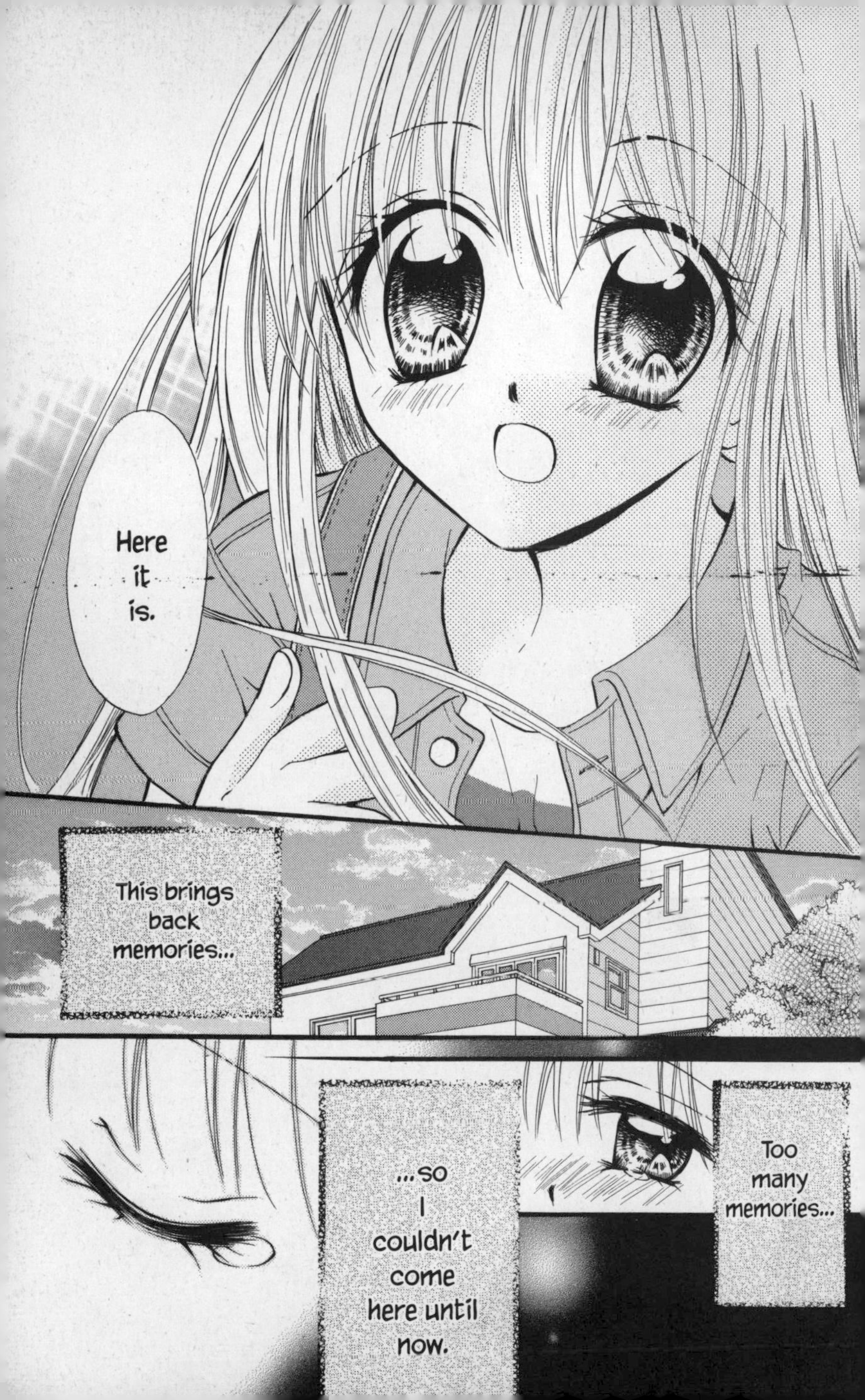
Here it is.
This brings back memories...
Too many memories...
...so I couldn't come here until now.

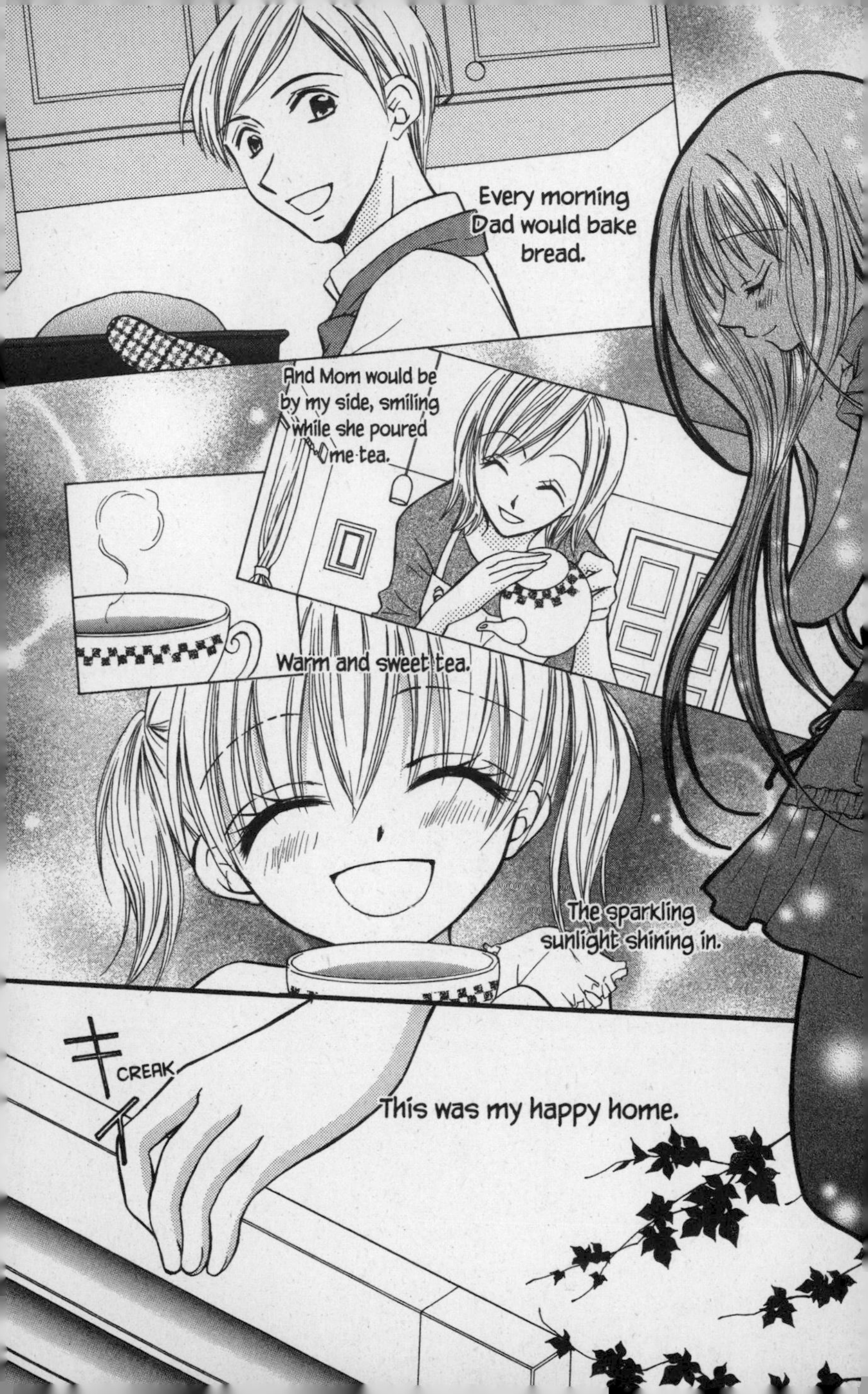
Every morning Dad would bake bread.
And Mom would be by my side, smiling while she poured me tea.
Warm and sweet tea.
The sparkling sunlight shining in.
CREAK
This was my happy home.

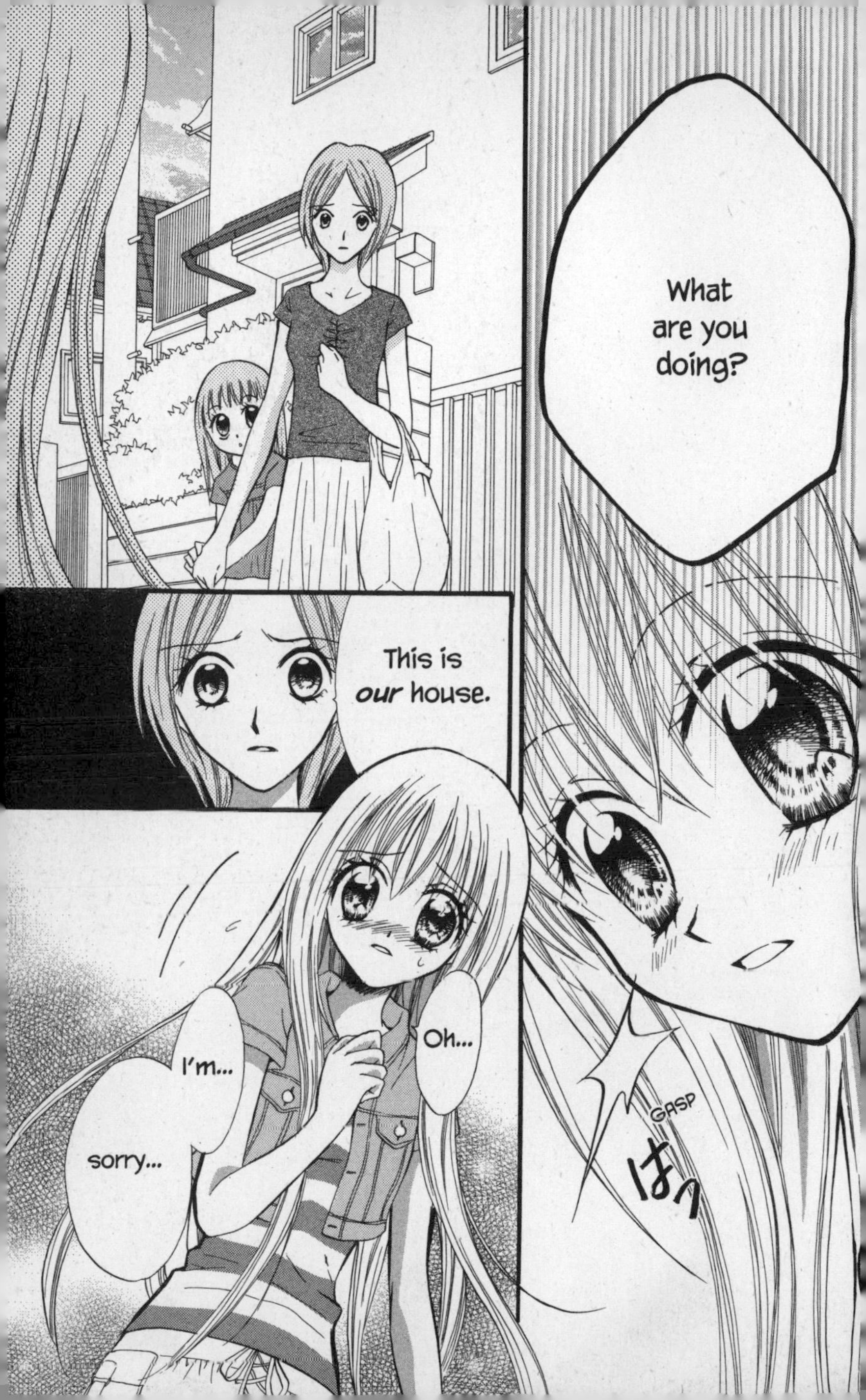
What are you doing?
GASP
はっ
This is *our* house.
Oh...
I'm...
sorry...

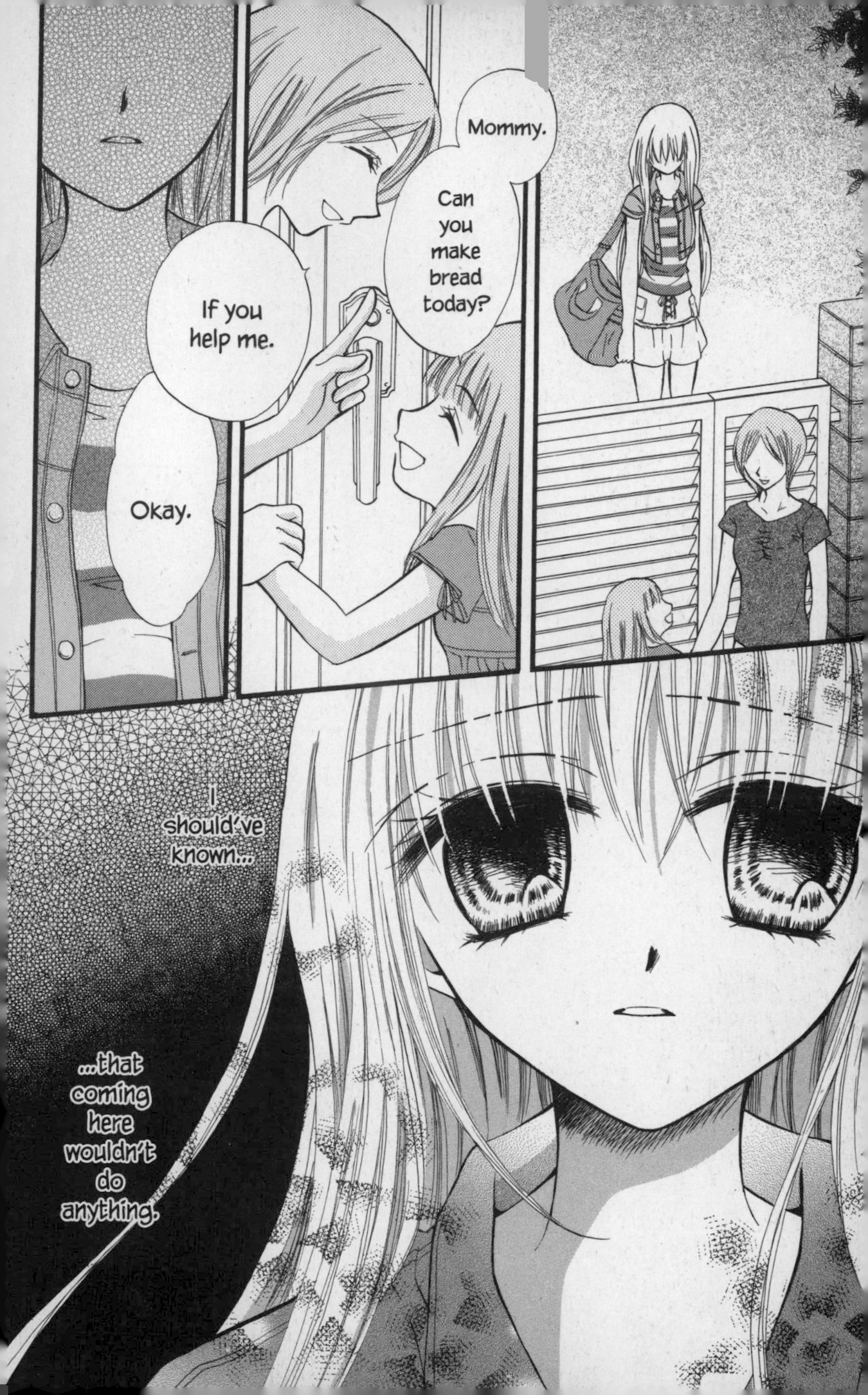
Mommy.
Can you make bread today?
If you help me.
Okay.
I should've known...
...that coming here wouldn't do anything.

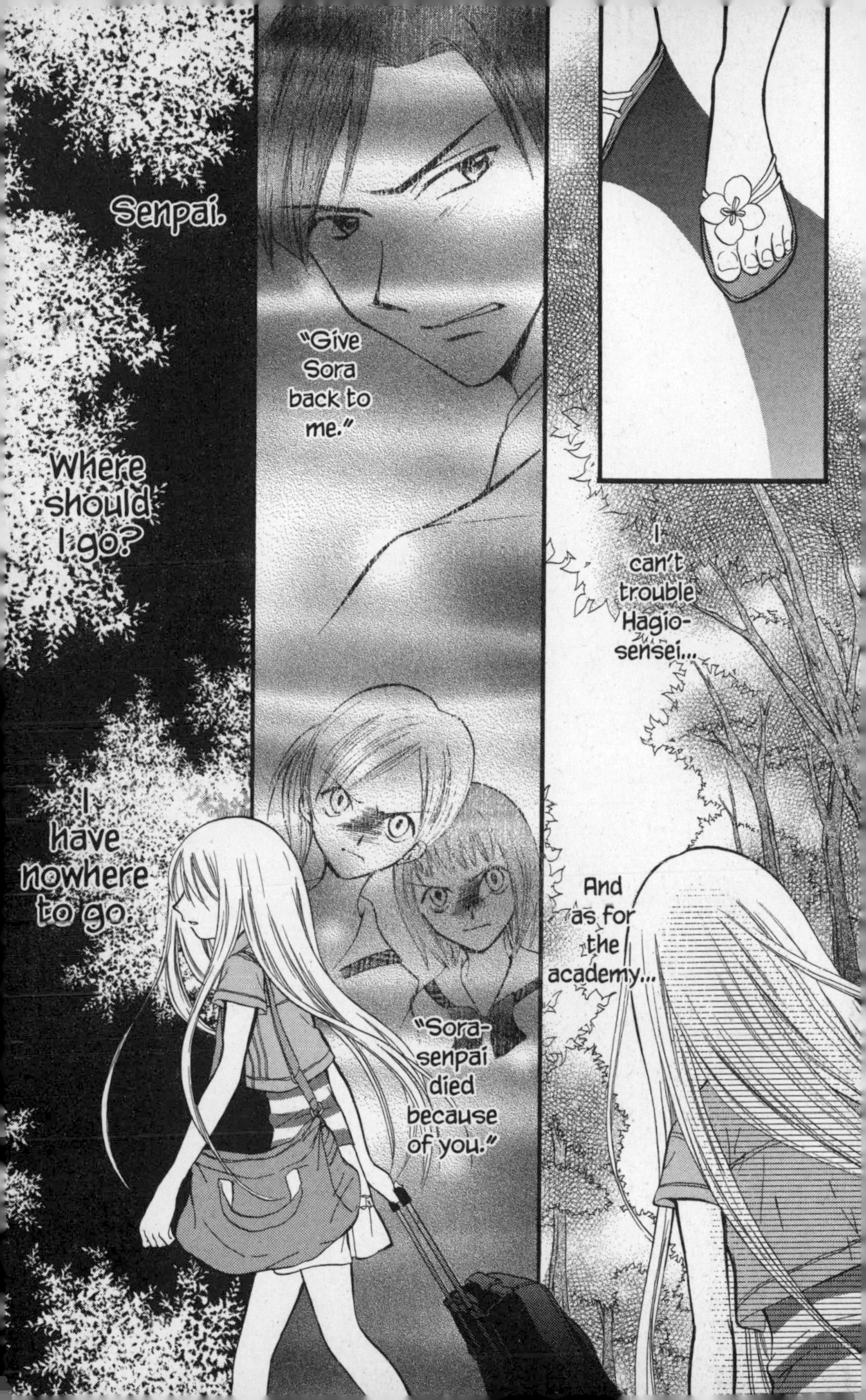
I can't trouble Hagio-sensei...
And as for the academy...
"Give Sora back to me."
"Sora-senpai died because of you."
Senpai.
Where should I go?
I have nowhere to go.

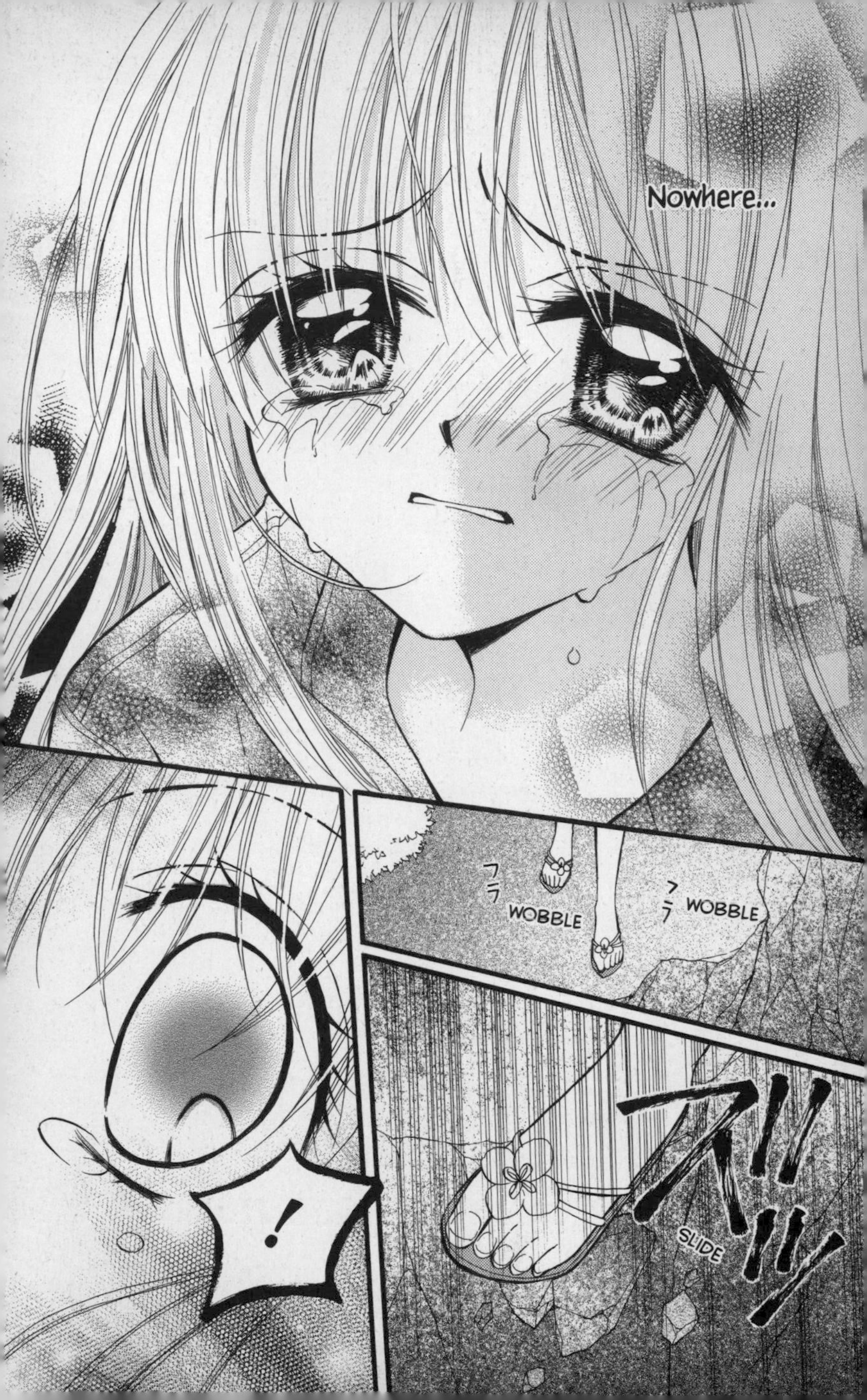
Nowhere...
フラ
WOBBLE
フラ
WOBBLE
!
SLIDE

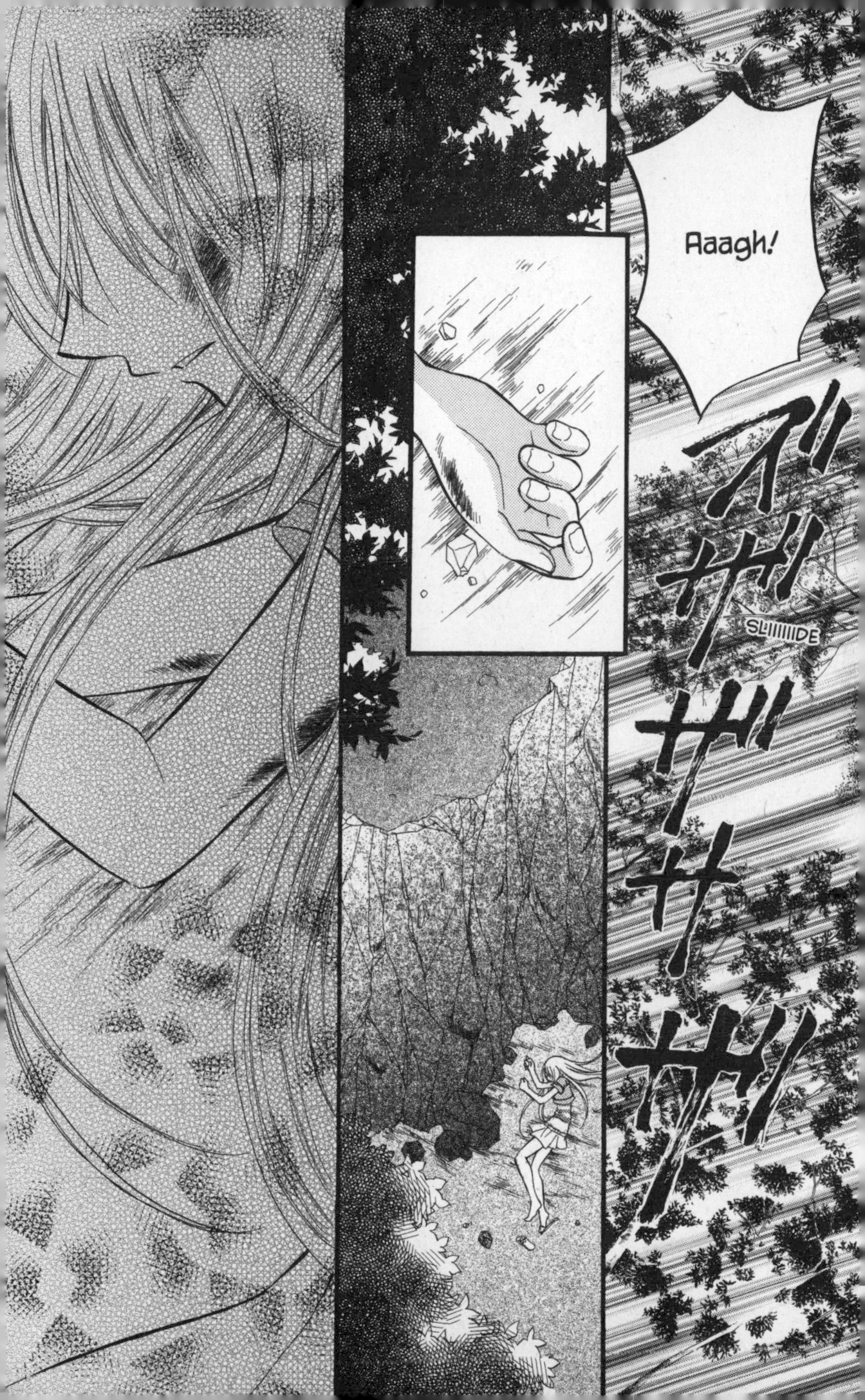
Aaagh!
ズザザザザ
SLIIIIIDE

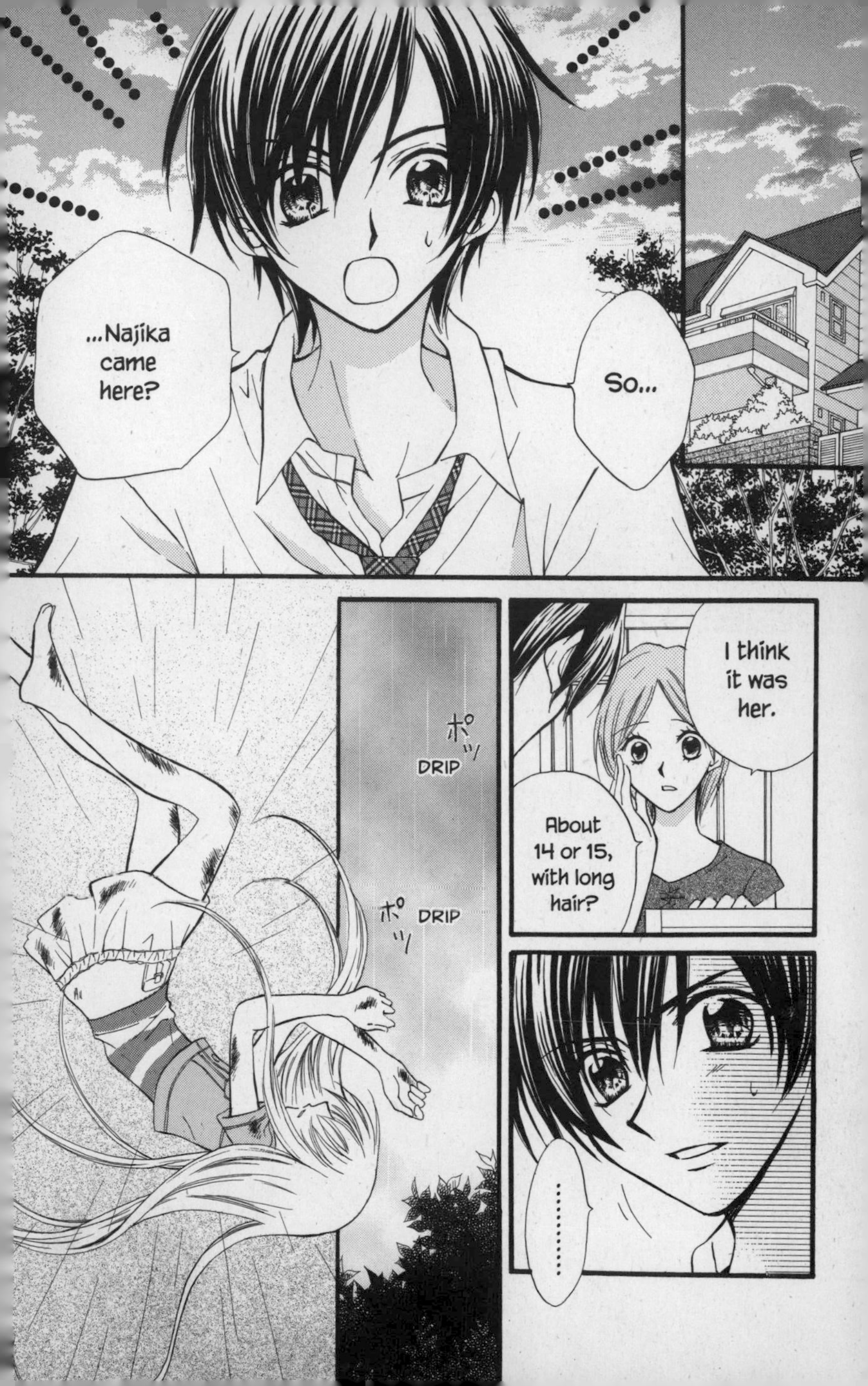
So...
...Najika came here?
I think it was her.
About 14 or 15, with long hair?
......
ポッ
DRIP
ポッ
DRIP

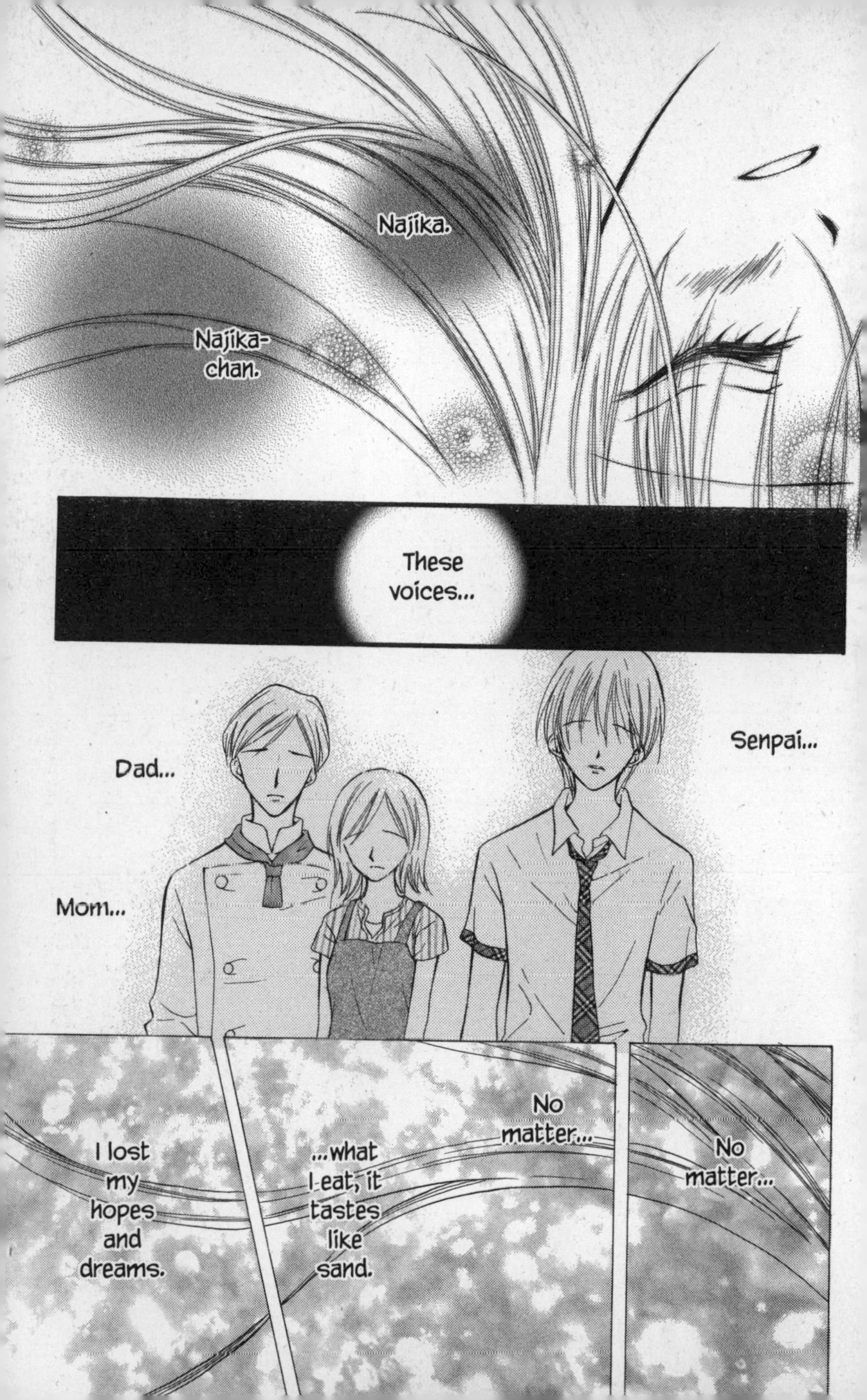
Najika.
Najika-chan.
These voices...
Senpai...
Dad...
Mom...
No matter...
No matter...
...what I eat, it tastes like sand.
I lost my hopes and dreams.

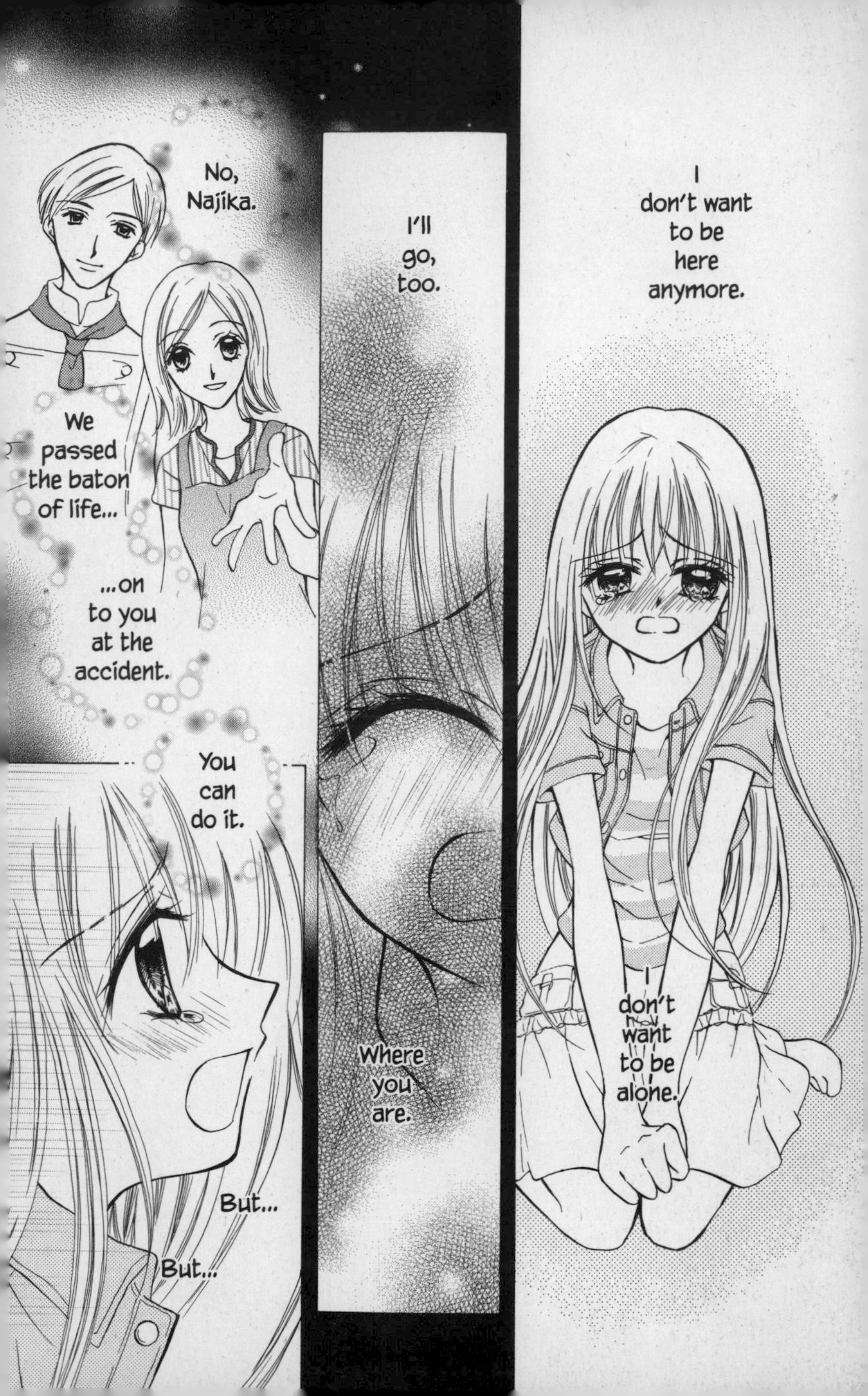
I don't want to be here anymore.
I don't want to be alone.
I'll go, too.
Where you are.
No, Najika.
We passed the baton of life...
...on to you at the accident.
You can do it.
But...
But...

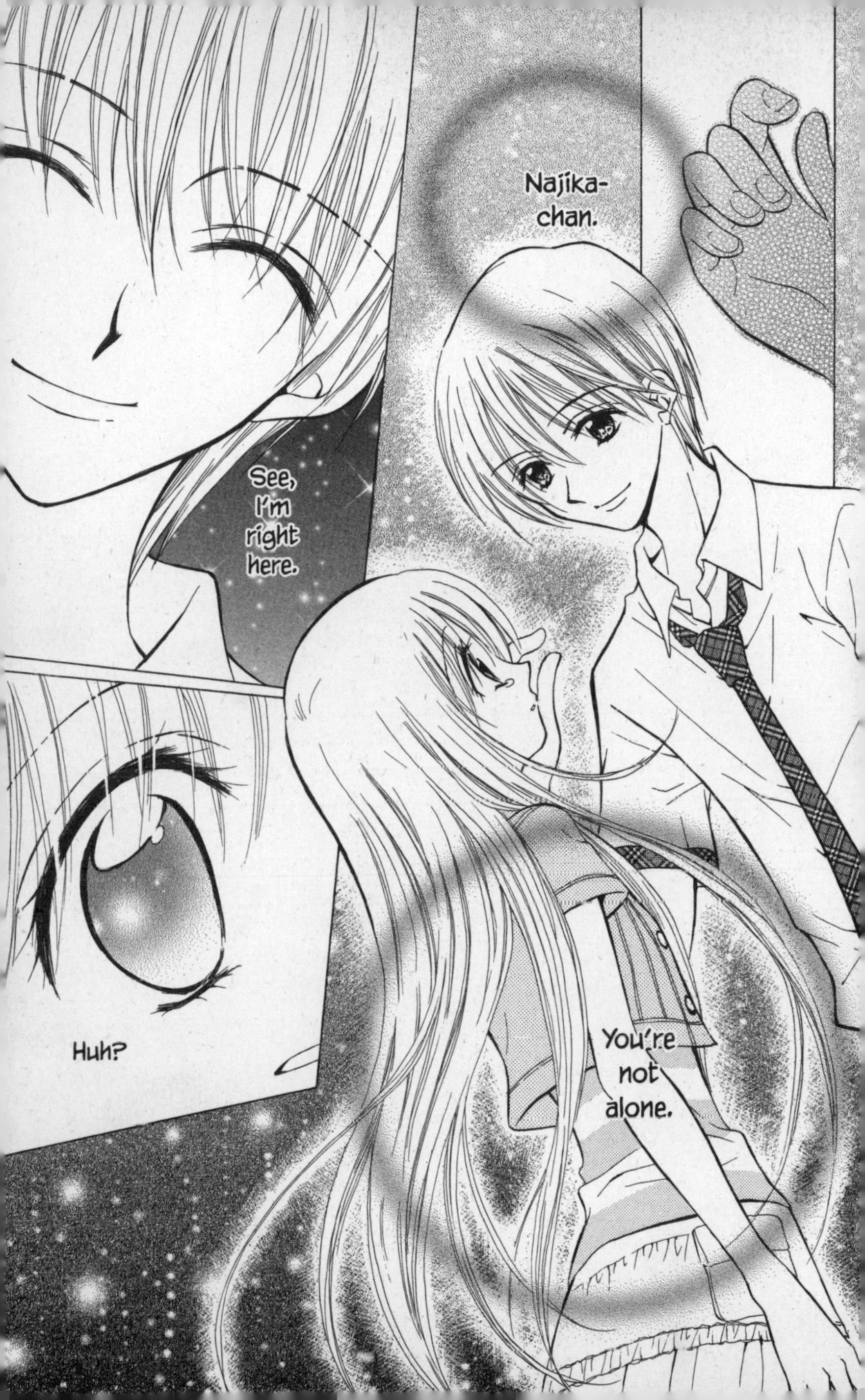

Najika-chan.
You're not alone.
See, I'm right here.
Huh?

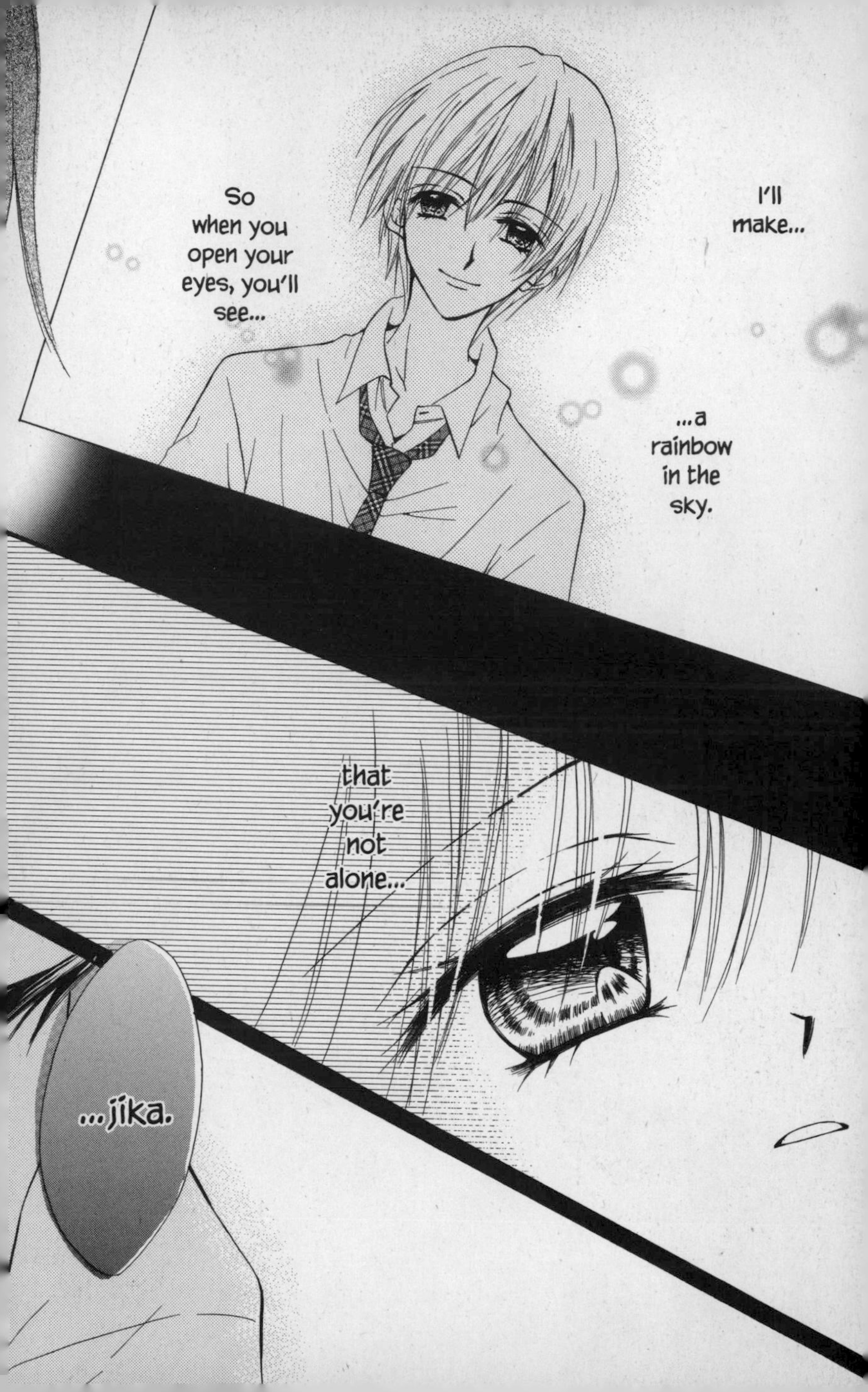
I'll make...
...a rainbow in the sky.
So when you open your eyes, you'll see...
that you're not alone...
...jika.

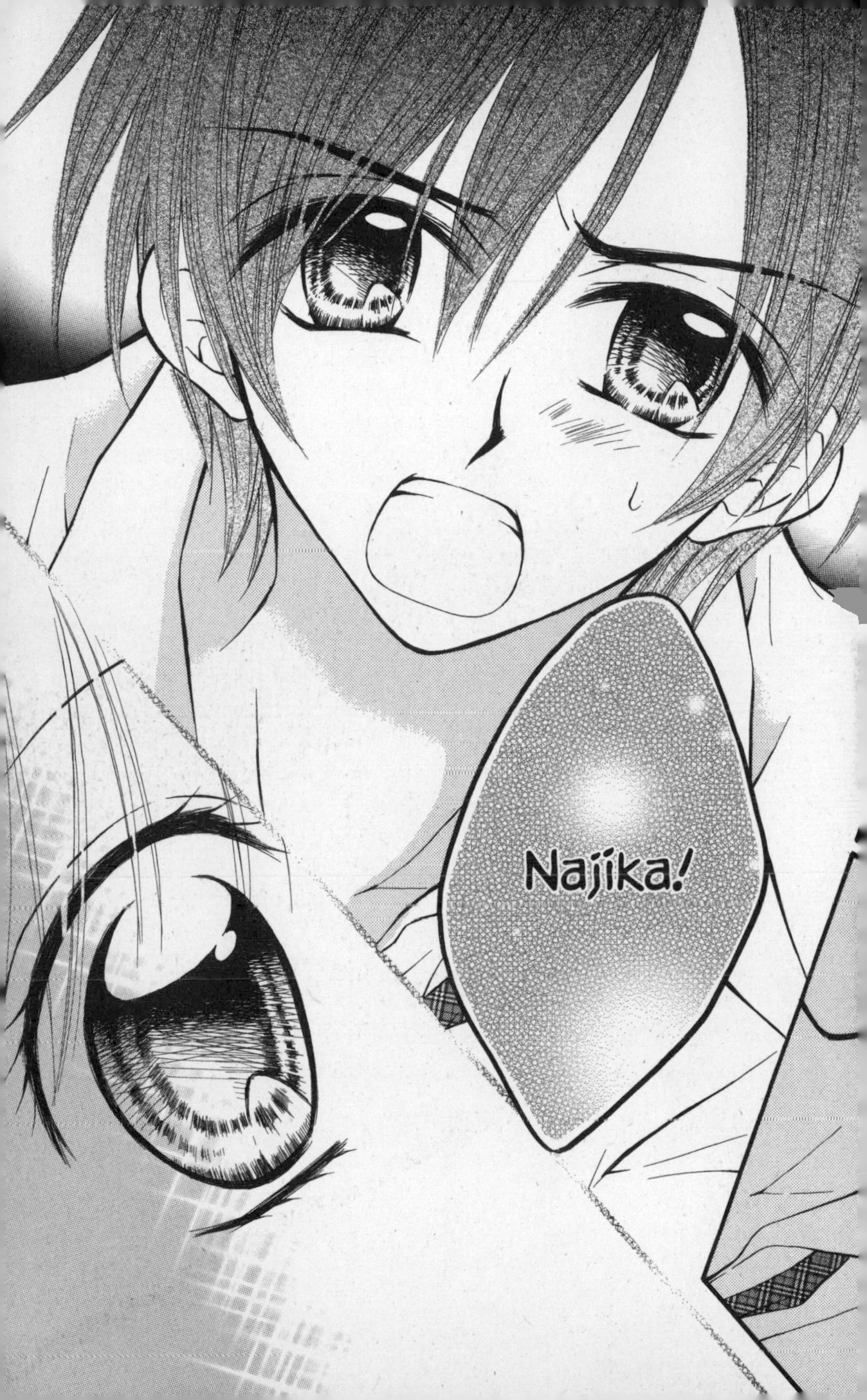
Najika!

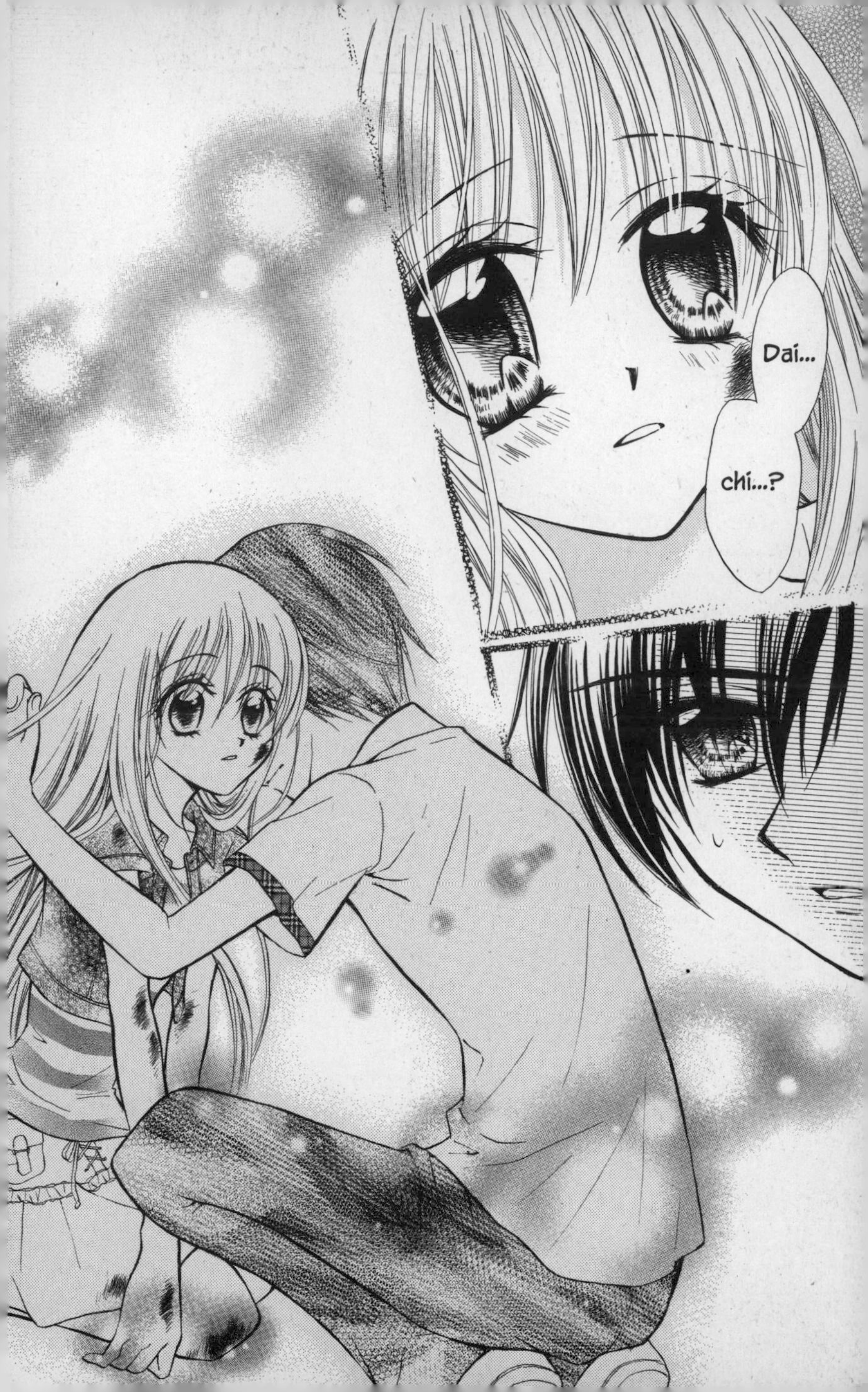
Dai...
chi...?

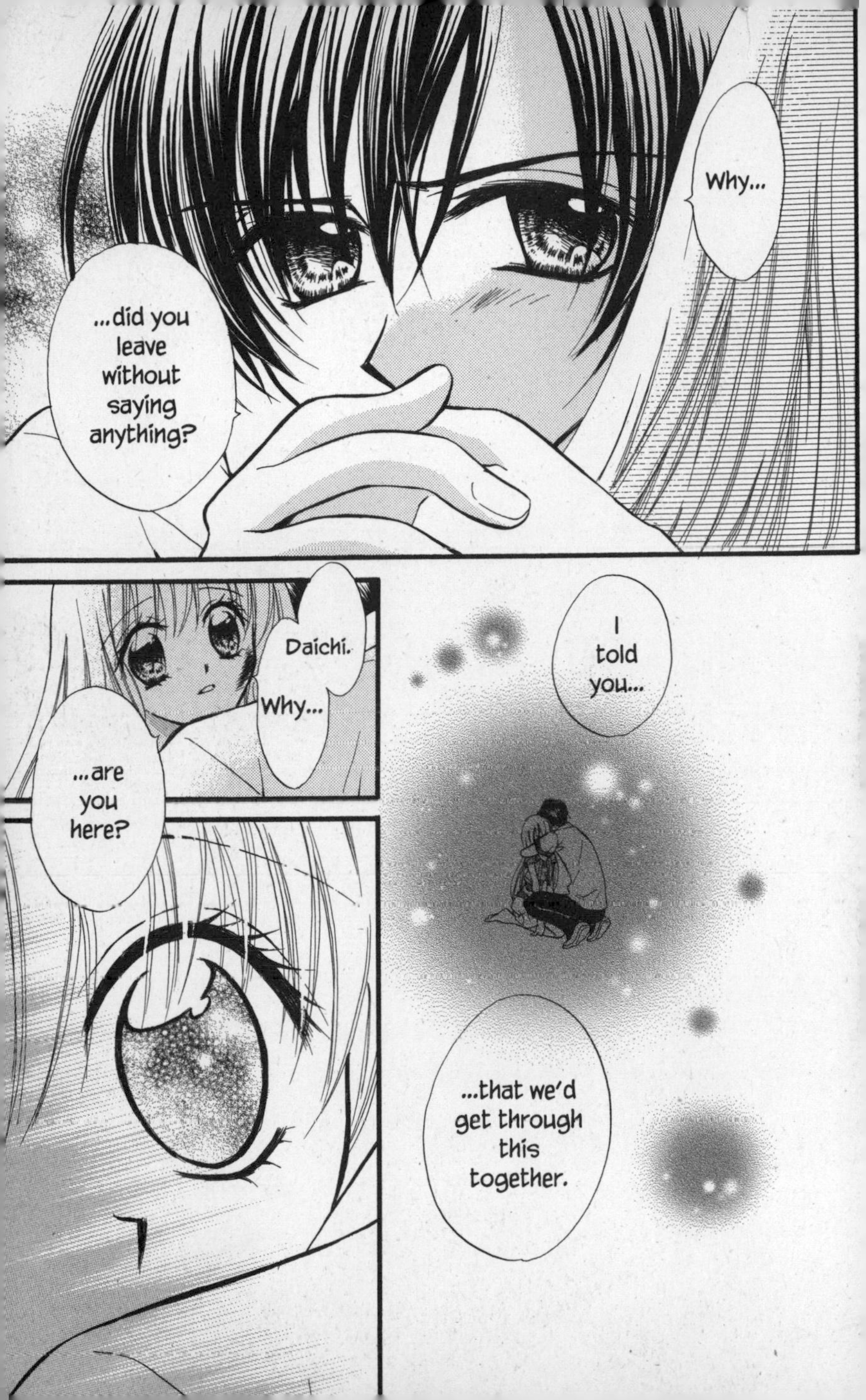
Why...
...did you leave without saying anything?
I told you...
...that we'd get through this together.
Daichi.
Why...
...are you here?

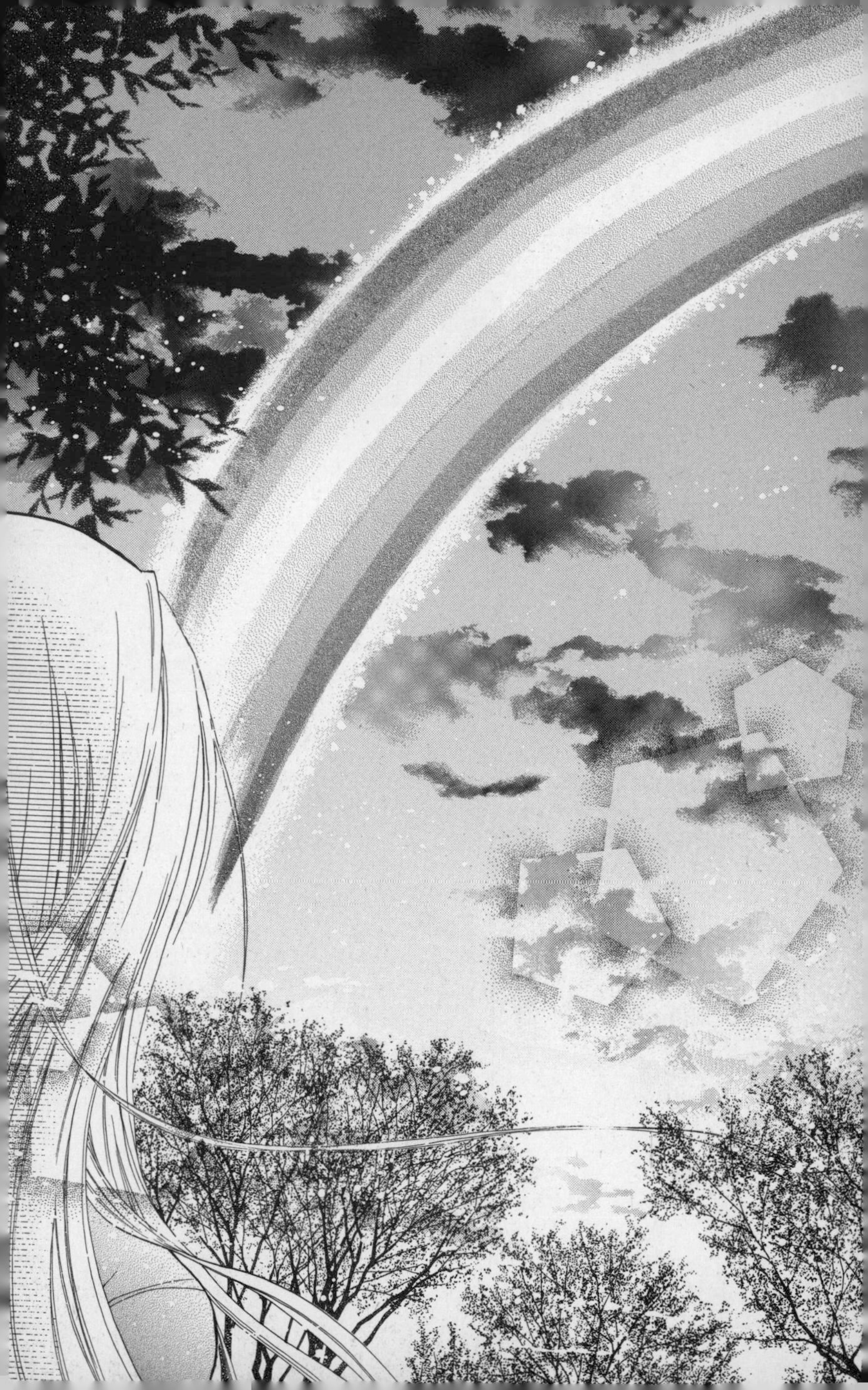

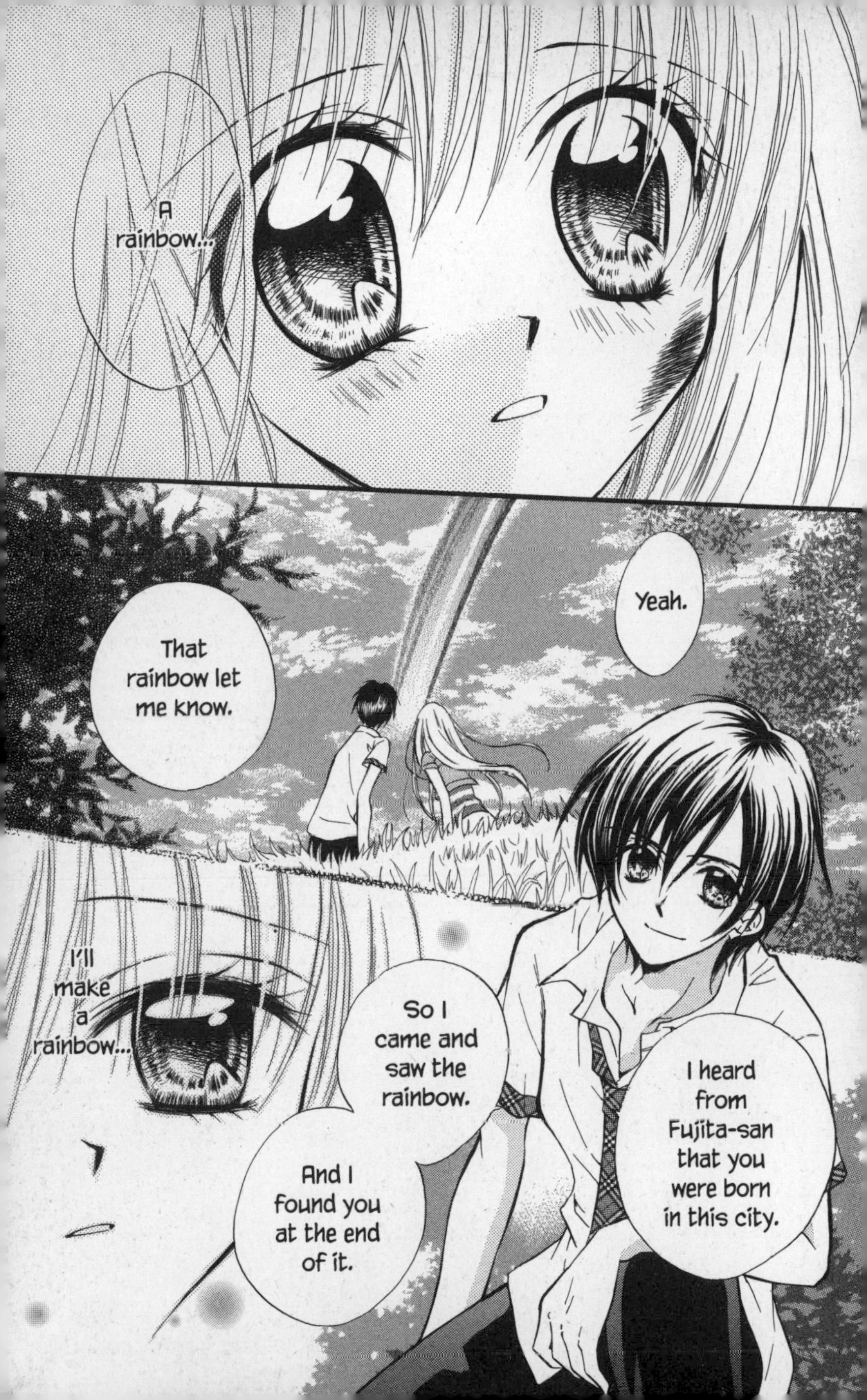
A rainbow...
Yeah.
That rainbow let me know.
I heard from Fujita-san that you were born in this city.
So I came and saw the rainbow.
And I found you at the end of it.
I'll make a rainbow...

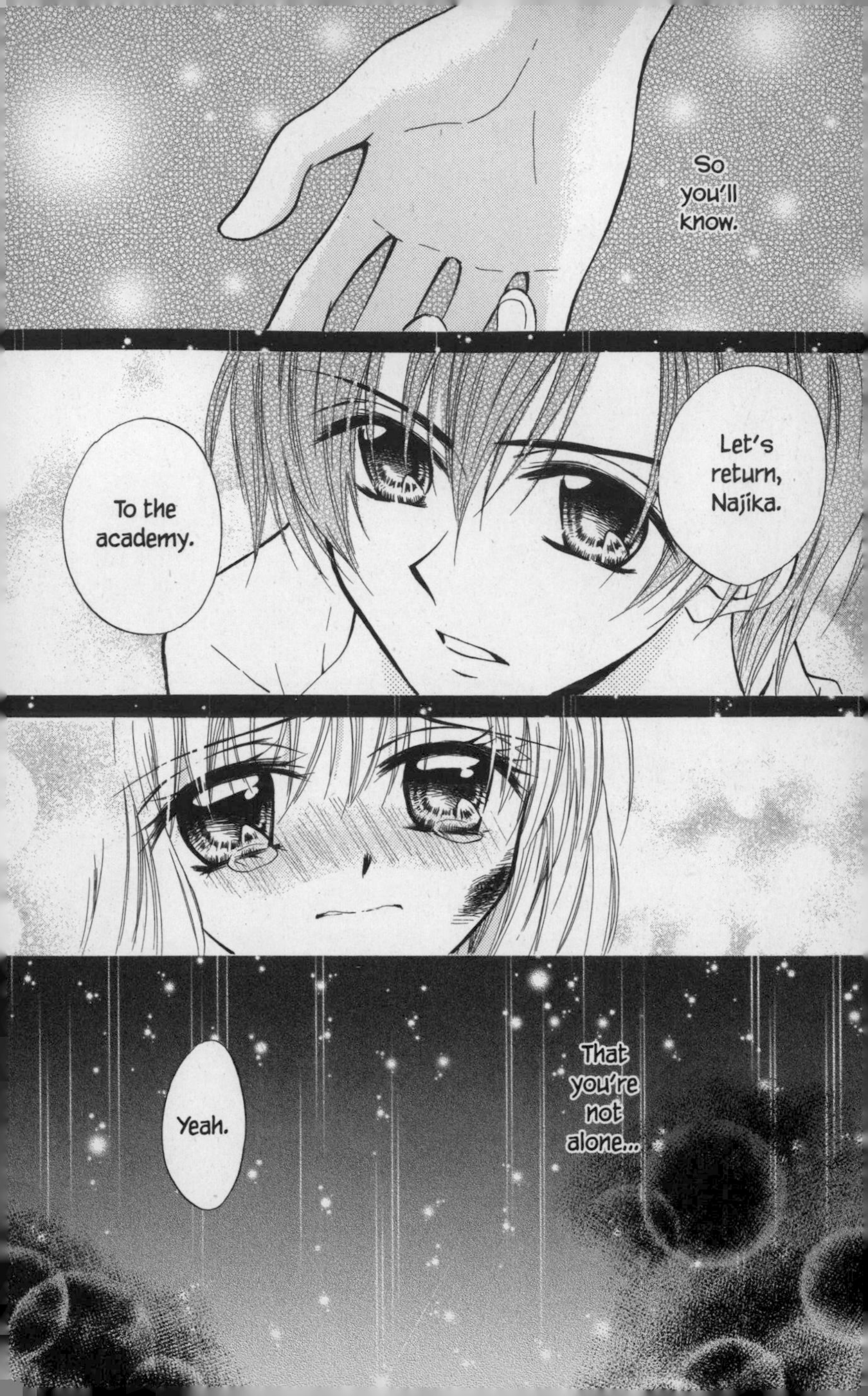
So you'll know.
Let's return, Najika.
To the academy.
That you're not alone...
Yeah.

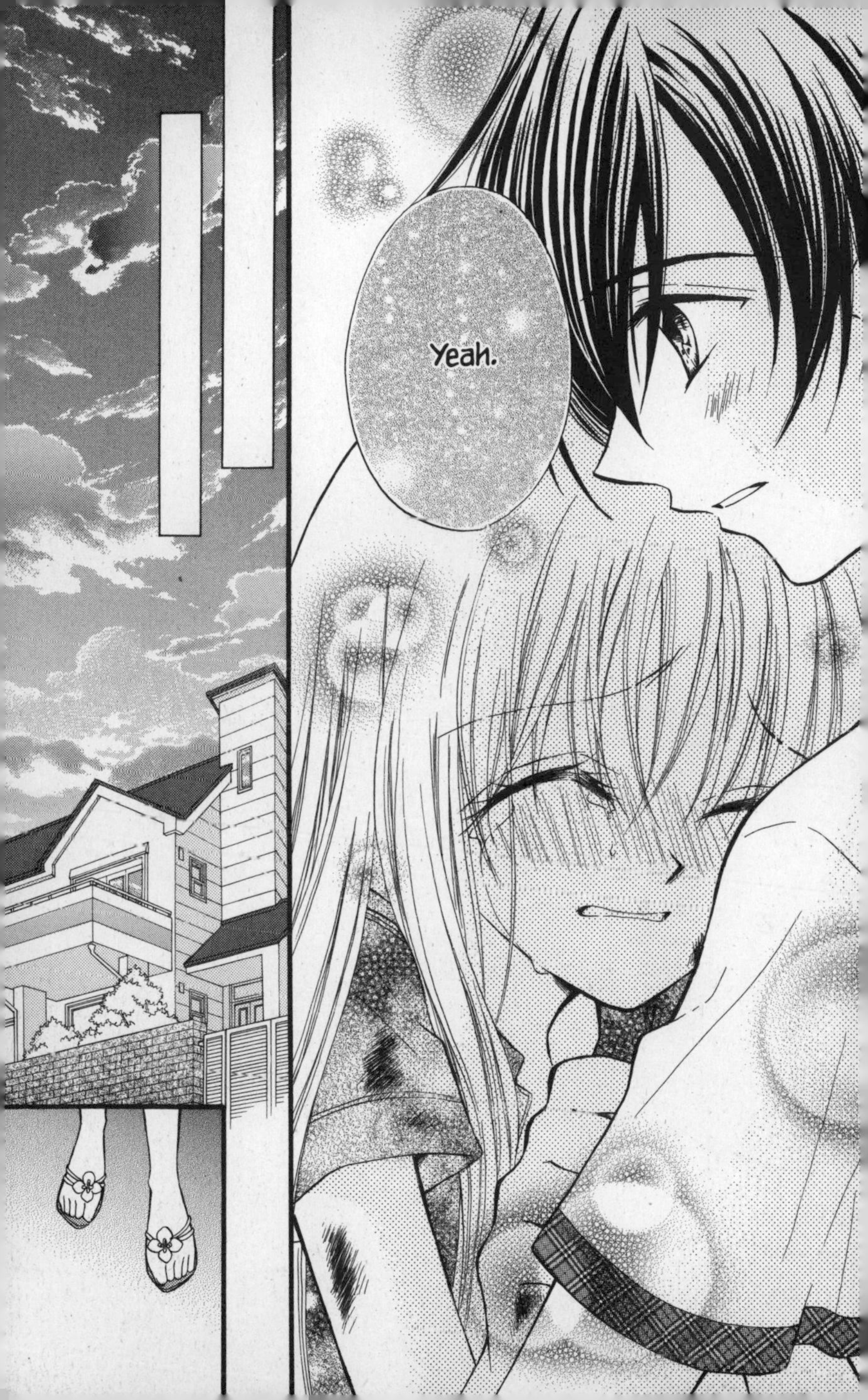
Yeah.

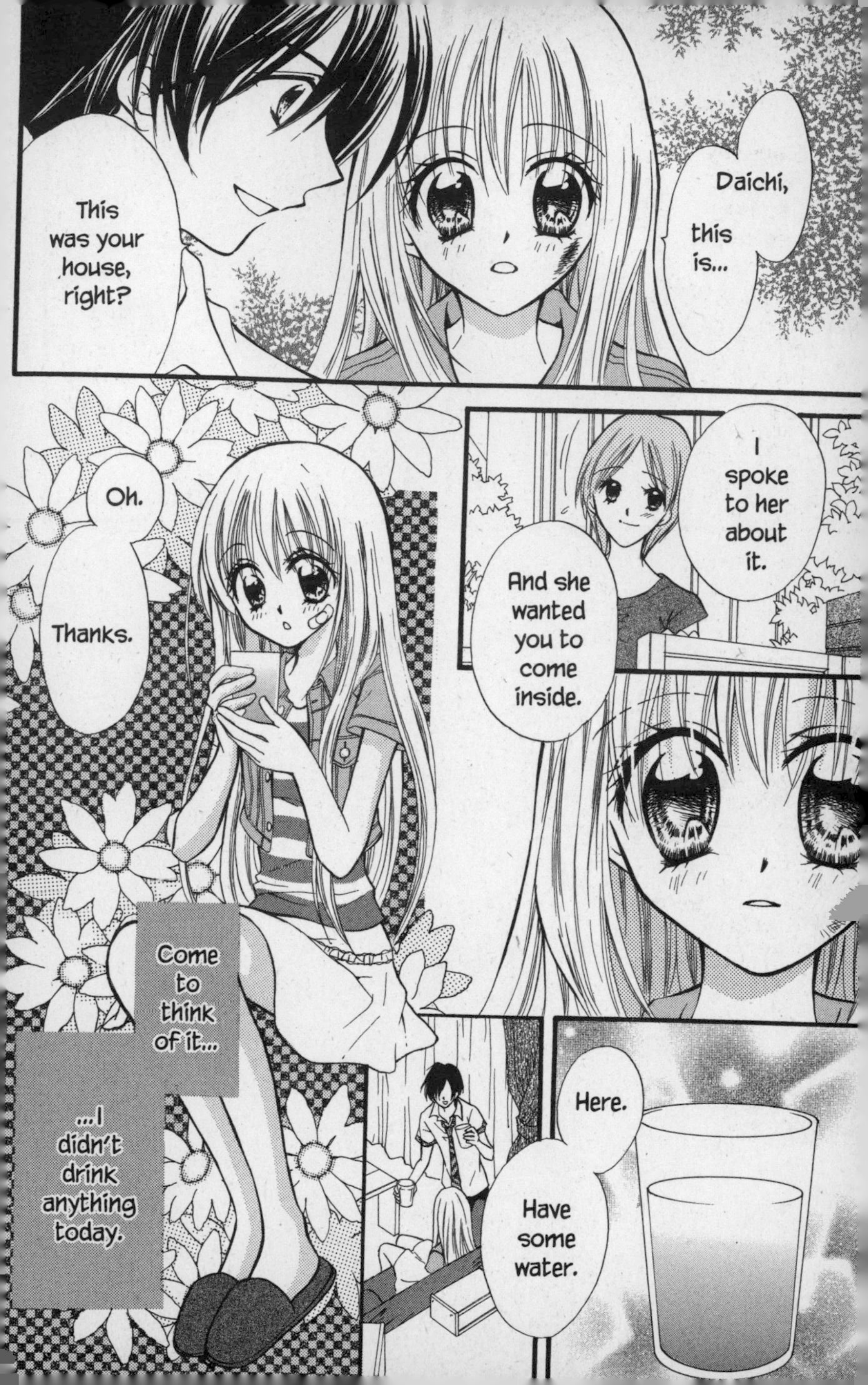
Daichi, this is...
This was your house, right?
I spoke to her about it.
And she wanted you to come inside.
Here.
Have some water.
Oh.
Thanks.
Come to think of it...
...I didn't drink anything today.

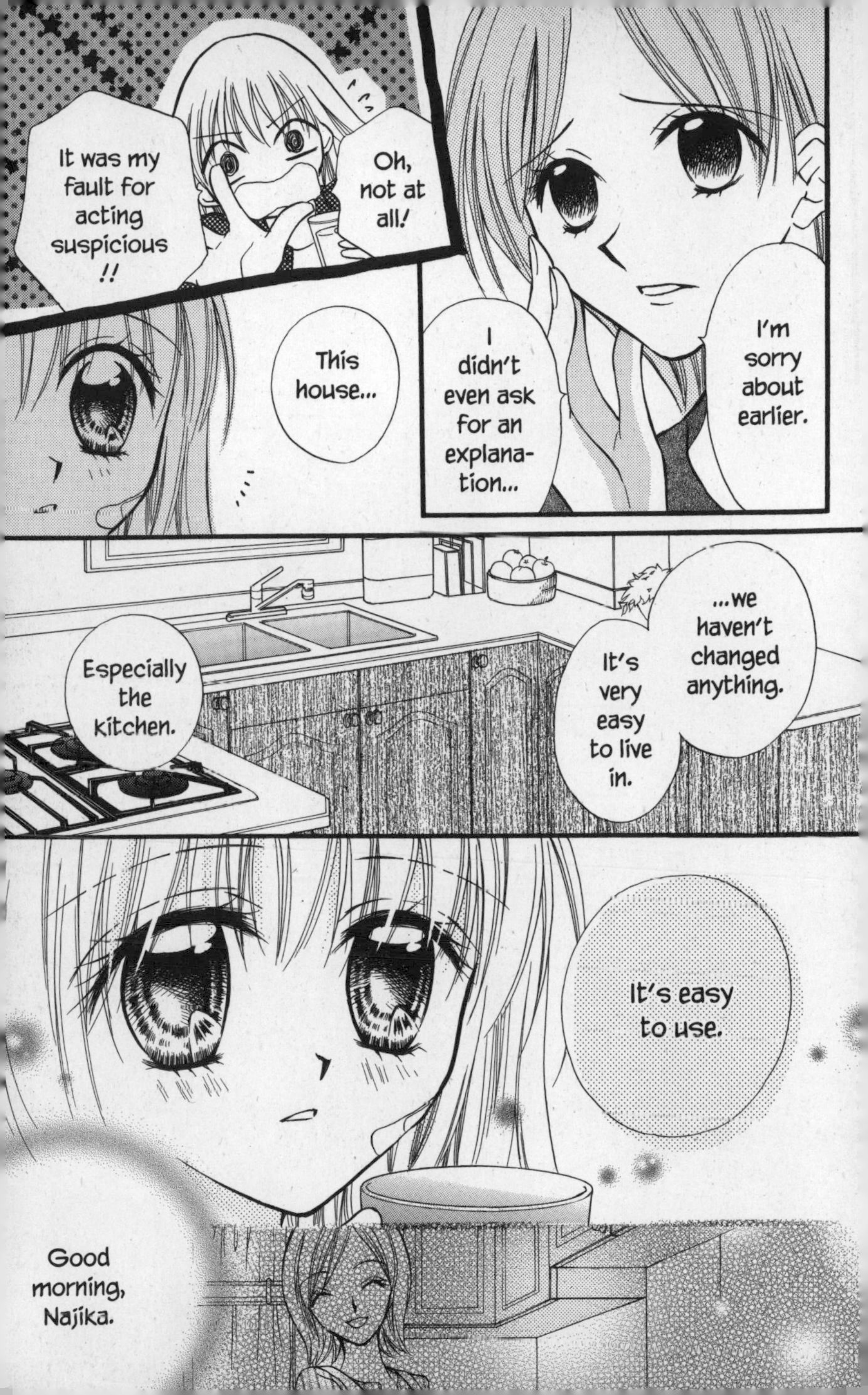

I'm sorry about earlier.
I didn't even ask for an explanation...
Oh, not at all!
It was my fault for acting suspicious!!
This house...
...we haven't changed anything.
It's very easy to live in.
Especially the kitchen.
It's easy to use.
Good morning, Najika.

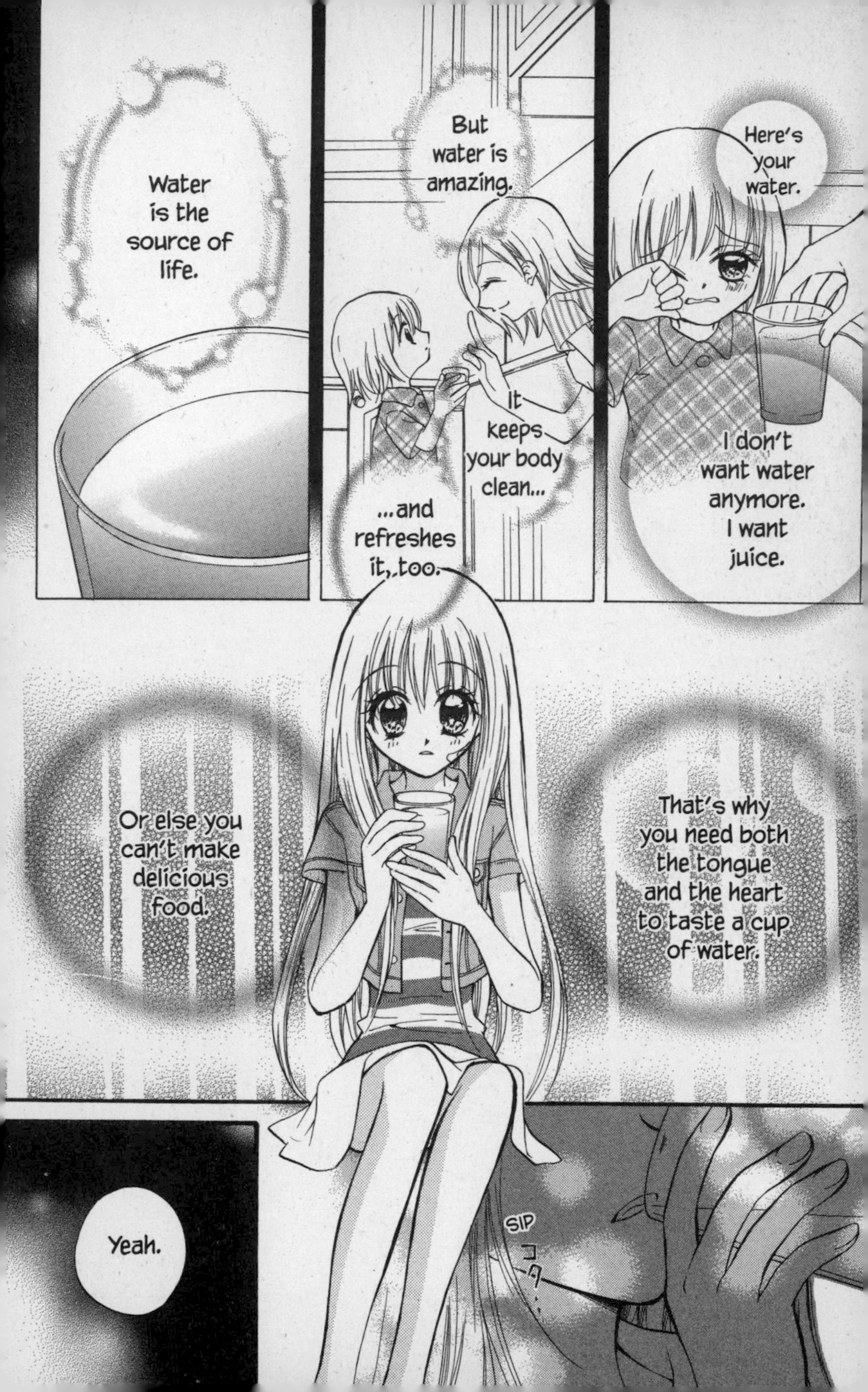
Here's your water.
I don't want water anymore. I want juice.
But water is amazing.
It keeps your body clean...
...and refreshes it, too.
Water is the source of life.
That's why you need both the tongue and the heart to taste a cup of water.
Or else you can't make delicious food.
SIP
Yeah.

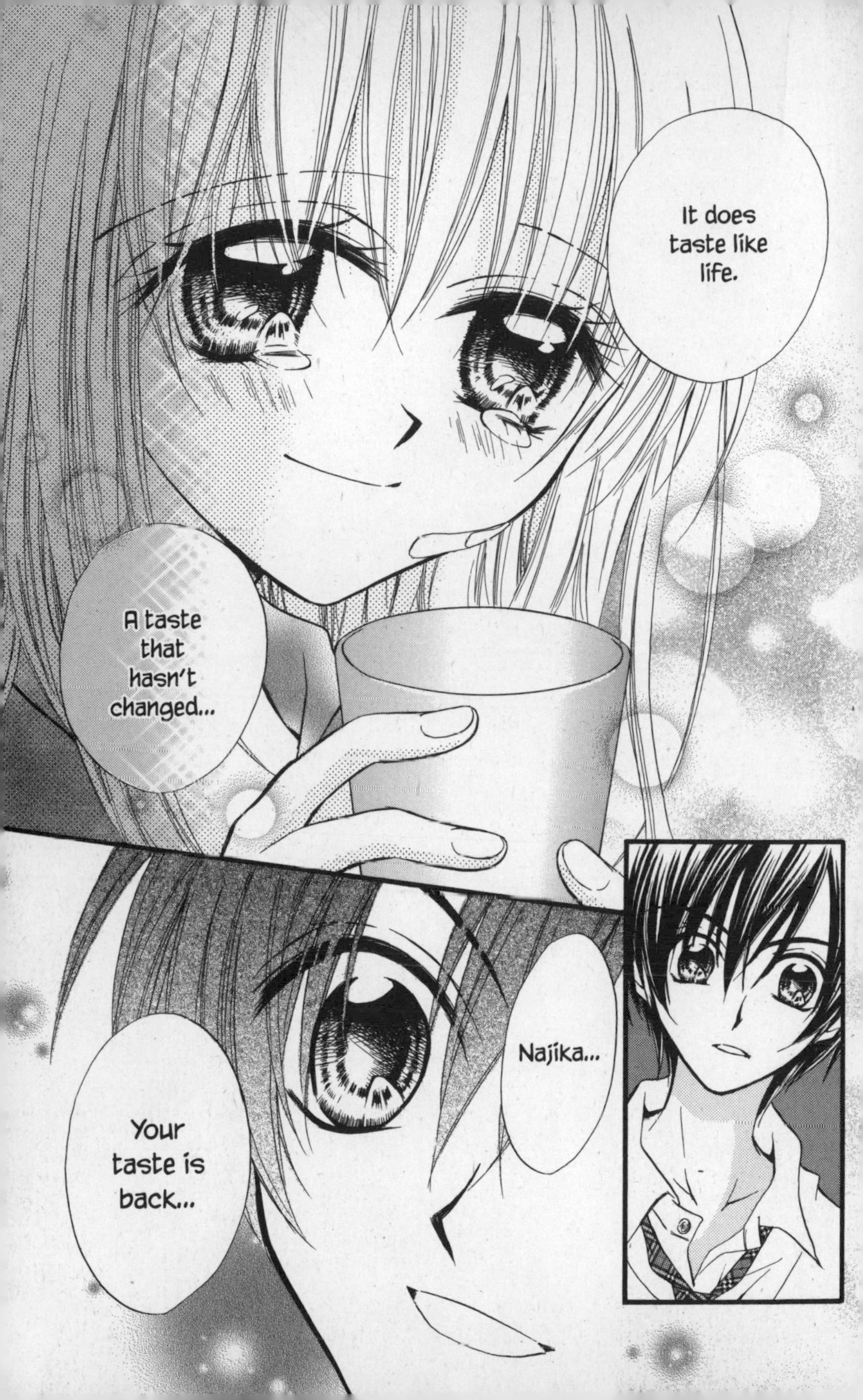
It does taste like life.
A taste that hasn't changed...
Najika...
Your taste is back...

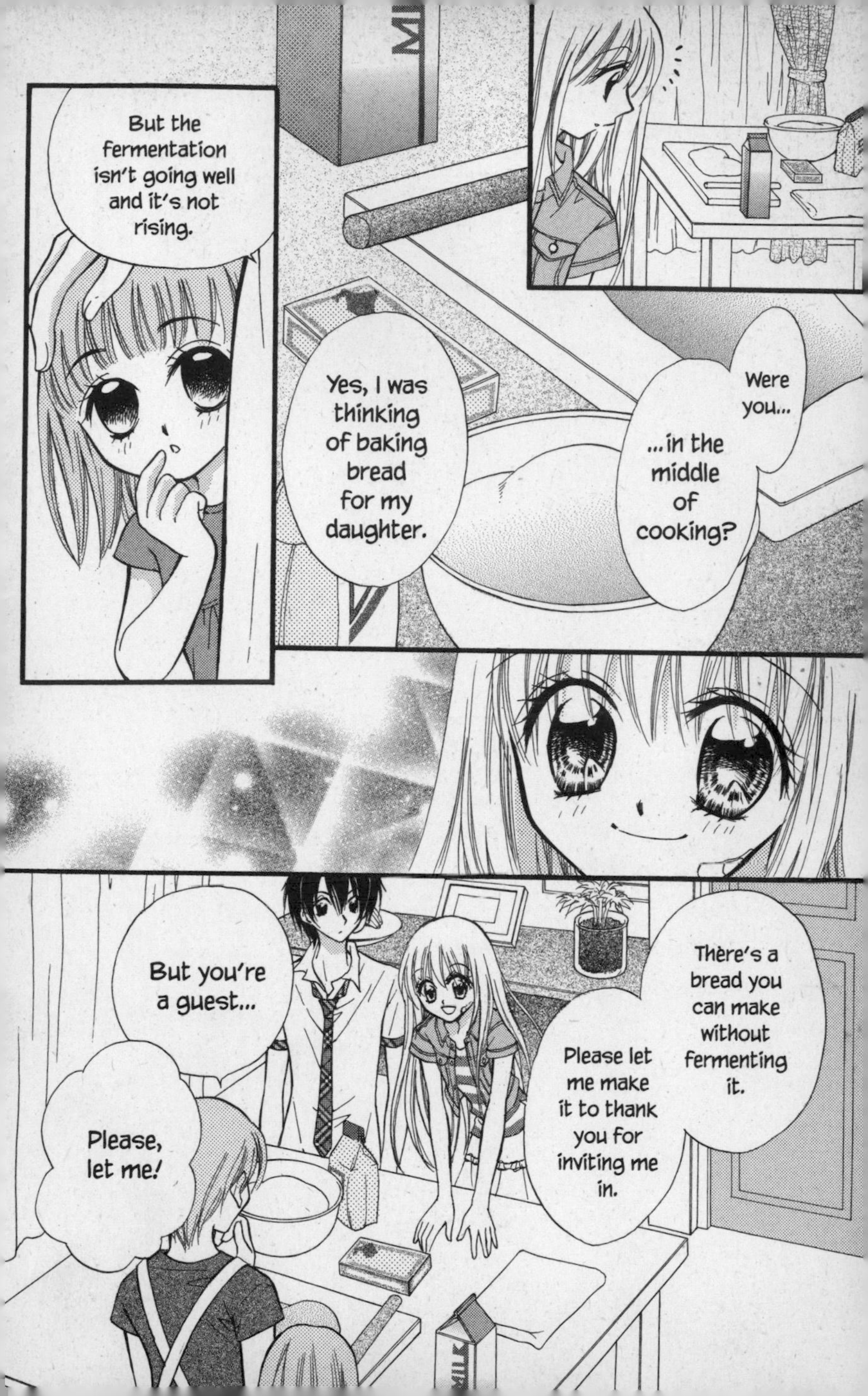
Were you...
...in the middle of cooking?
Yes, I was thinking of baking bread for my daughter.
But the fermentation isn't going well and it's not rising.
There's a bread you can make without fermenting it.
Please let me make it to thank you for inviting me in.
But you're a guest...
Please, let me!

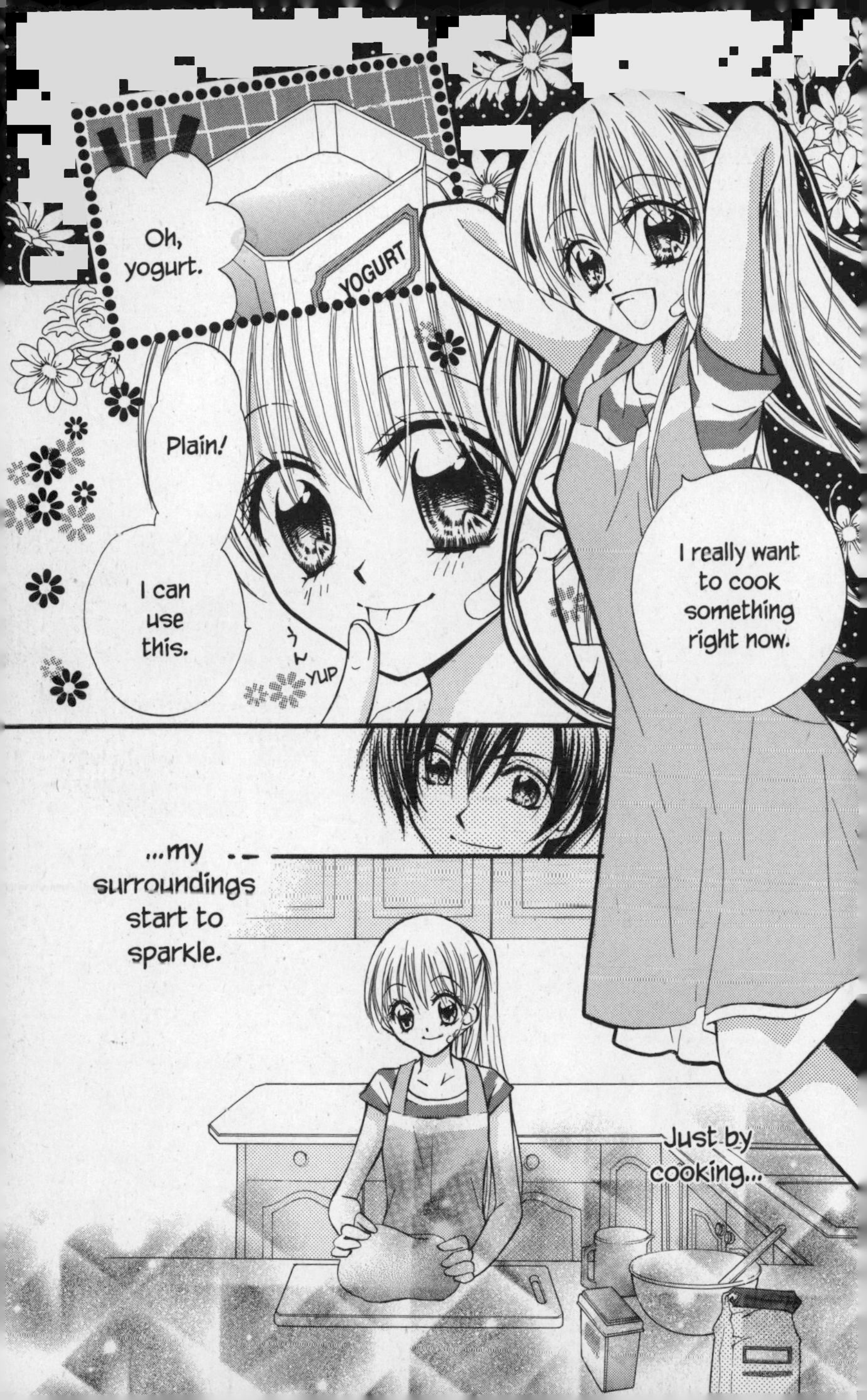
I really want to cook something right now.
YOGURT
Oh, yogurt.
Plain!
I can use this.
YUP
Just by cooking...
...my surroundings start to sparkle.

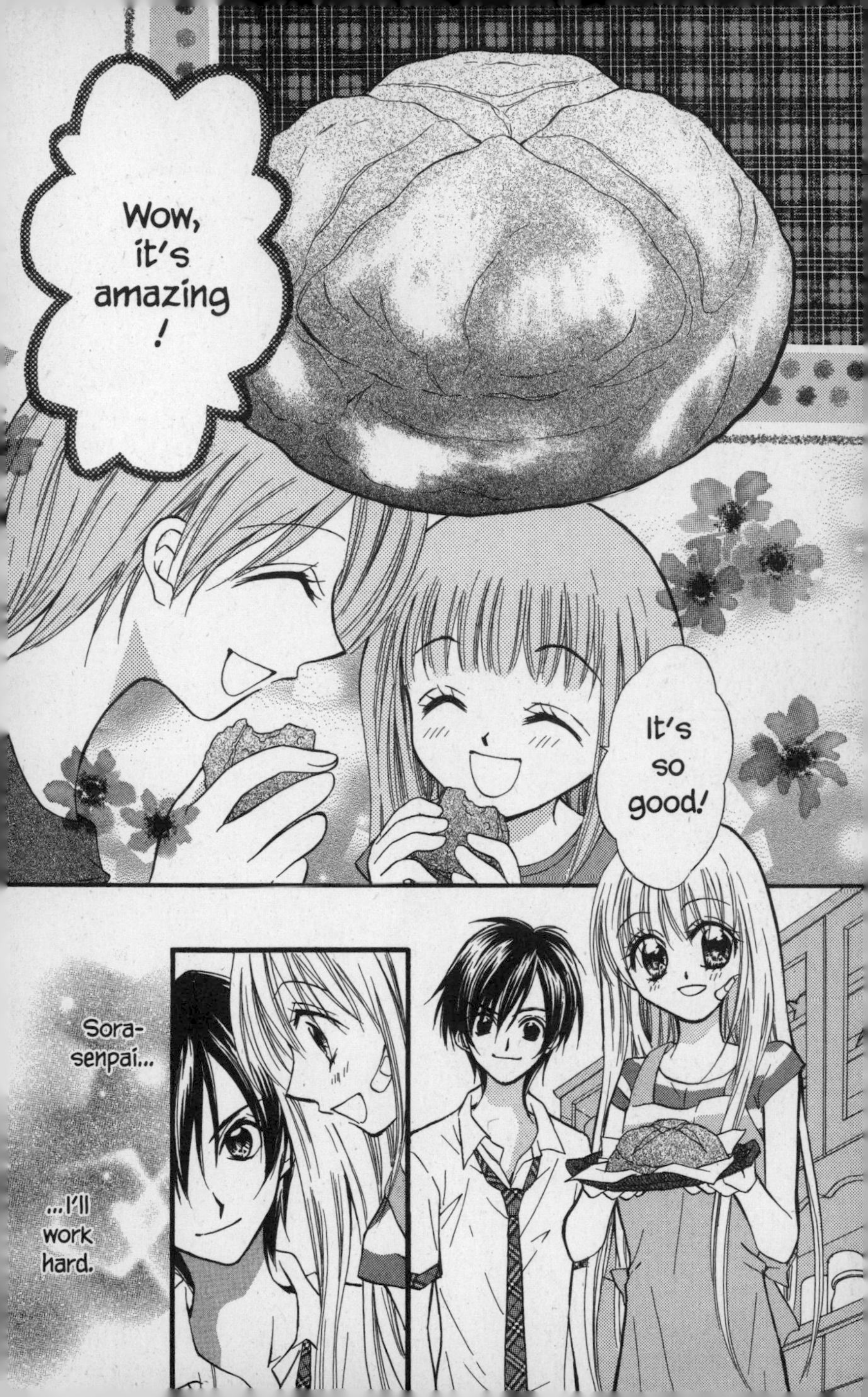
Wow, it's amazing!
It's so good!
Sora-senpai...
...I'll work hard.

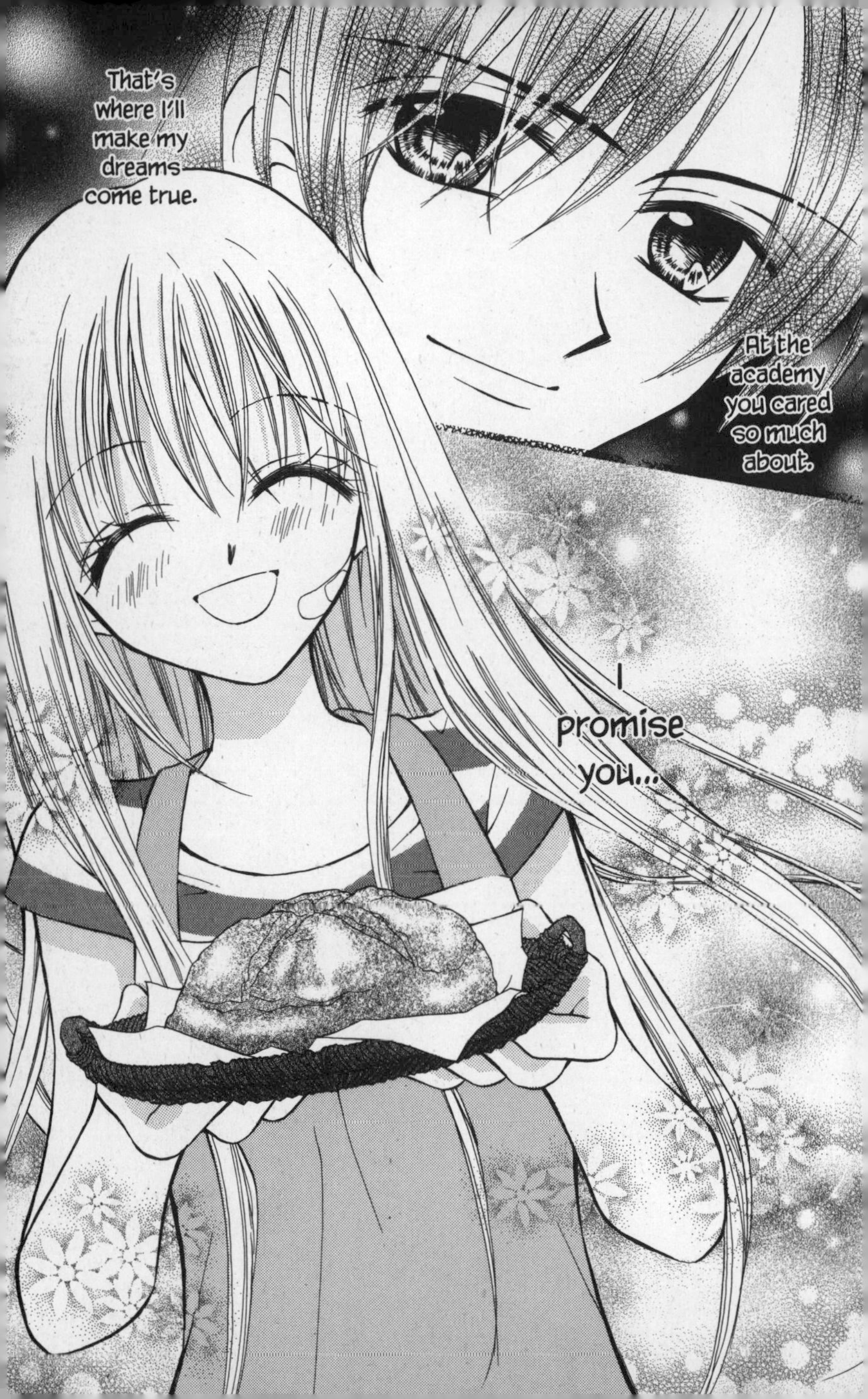
I promise you...
At the academy you cared so much about.
That's where I'll make my dreams come true.

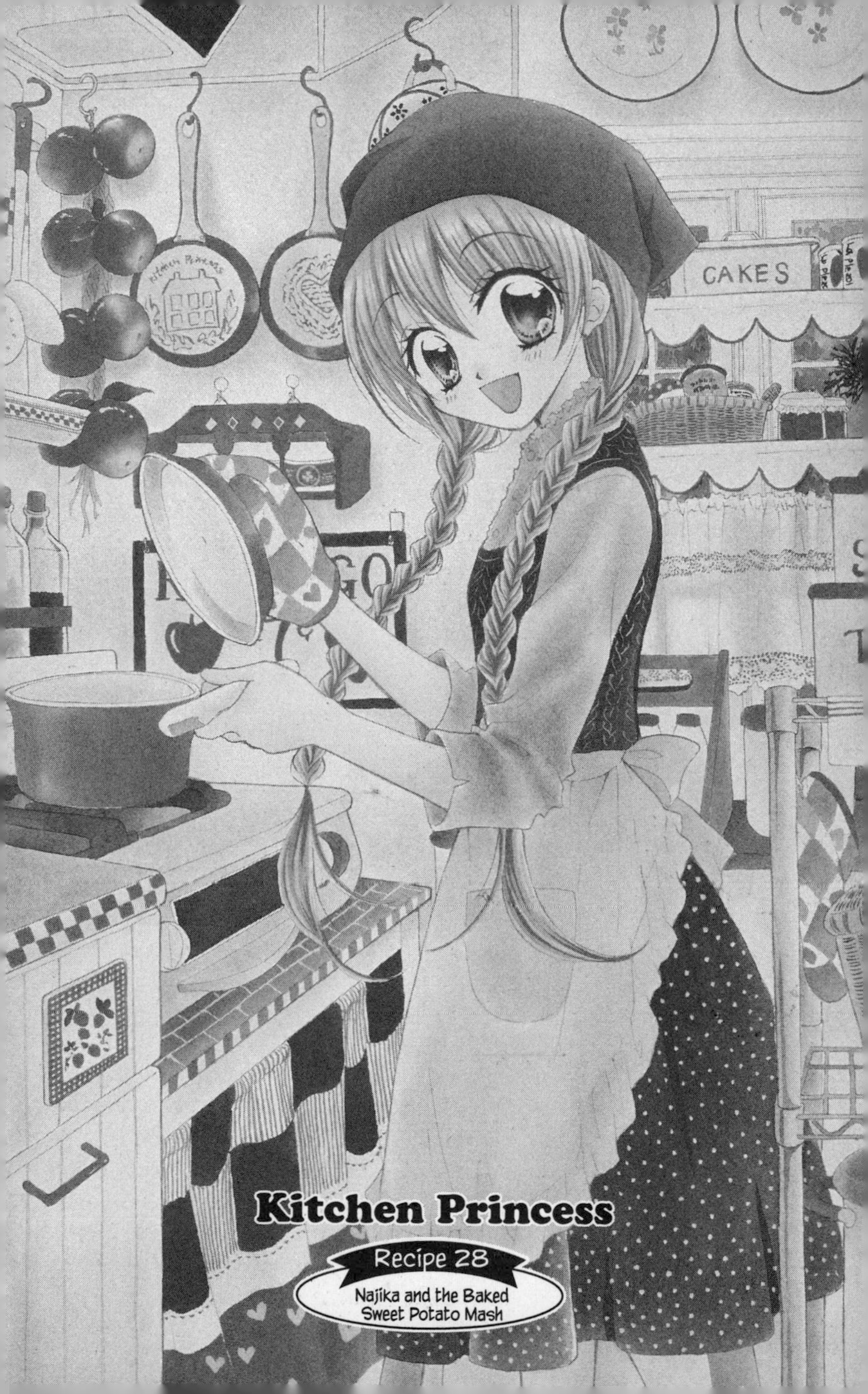
kitchen Princess
CAKES
Kitchen Princess
Recipe 28
Najika and the Baked Sweet Potato Mash

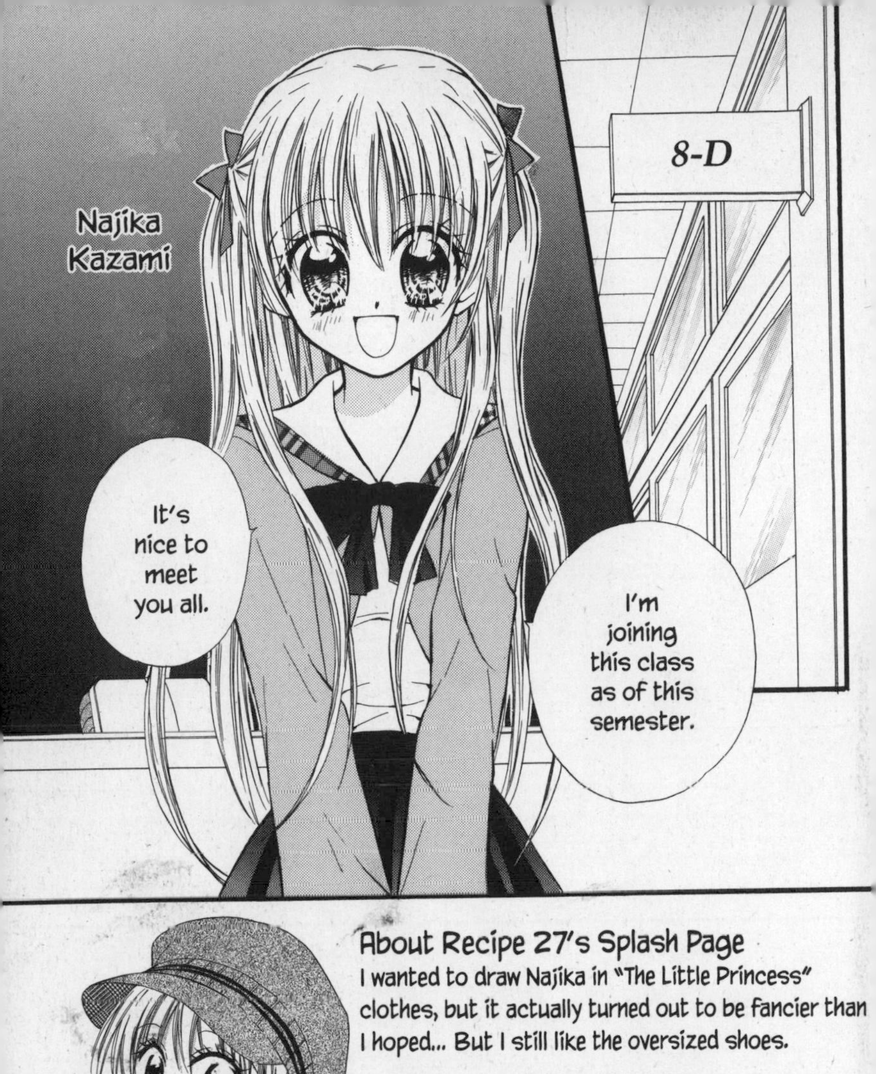
8-D
Najika Kazami
I'm joining this class as of this semester.
It's nice to meet you all.

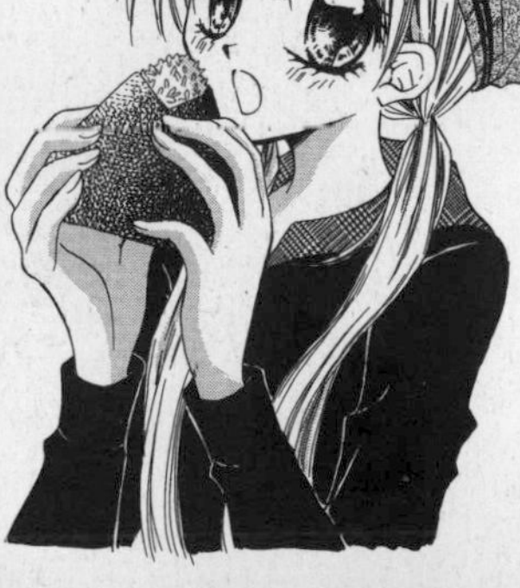

About Recipe 27's Splash Page

I wanted to draw Najika in "The Little Princess" clothes, but it actually turned out to be fancier than I hoped... But I still like the oversized shoes.

About Recipe 28's Splash Page

At the time I was drawing this I was considering moving. And I was thinking that my next kitchen would be country-style! And I kept thinking about the interior designs. That thought was what affected the splash page. I drew everything by hand myself. It was well received by the editors and thus became the cover of this volume.

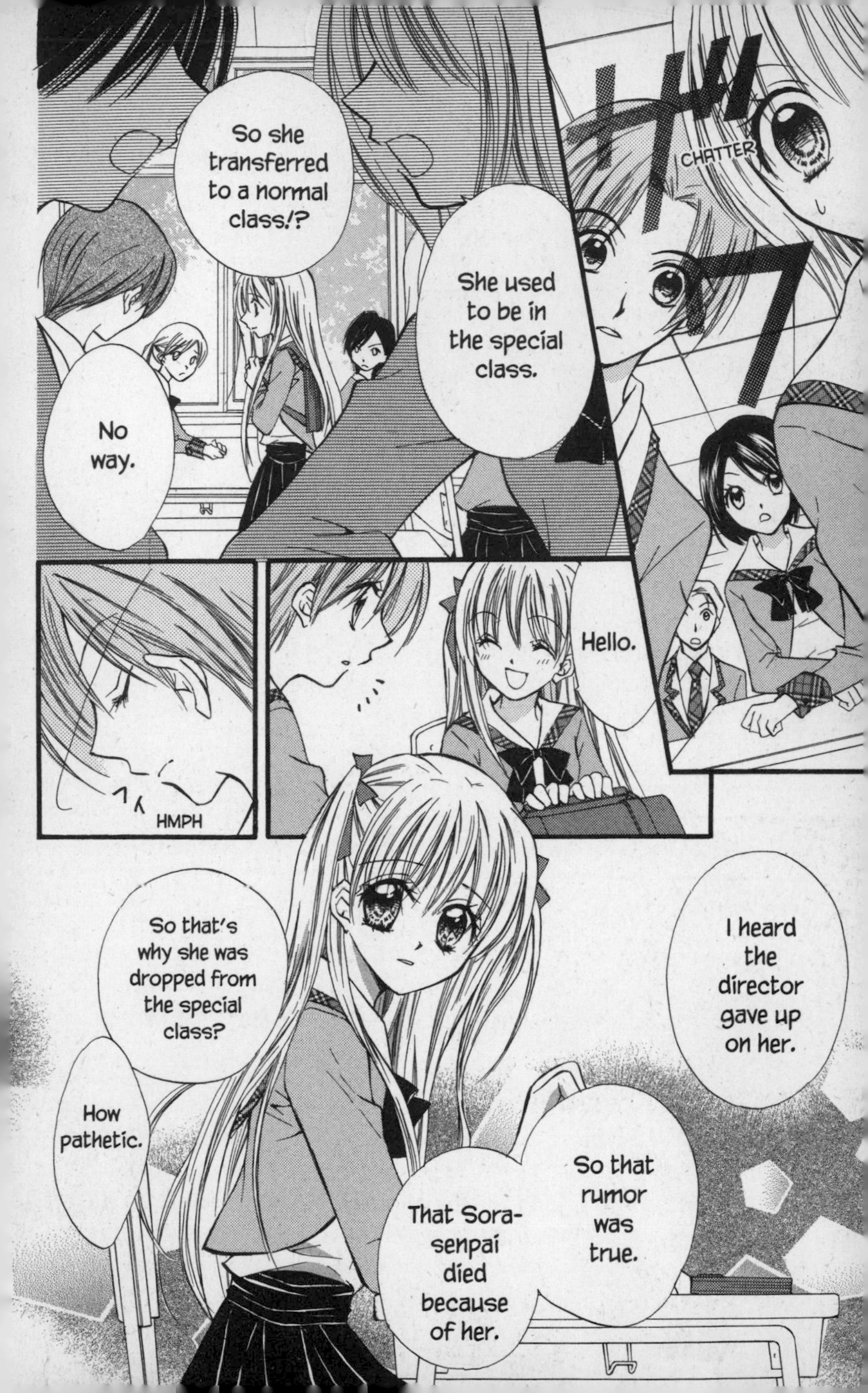
CHATTER
So she transferred to a normal class!?
She used to be in the special class.
No way.
Hello.
HMPH
I heard the director gave up on her.
So that's why she was dropped from the special class?
How pathetic.
So that rumor was true.
That Sora-senpai died because of her.

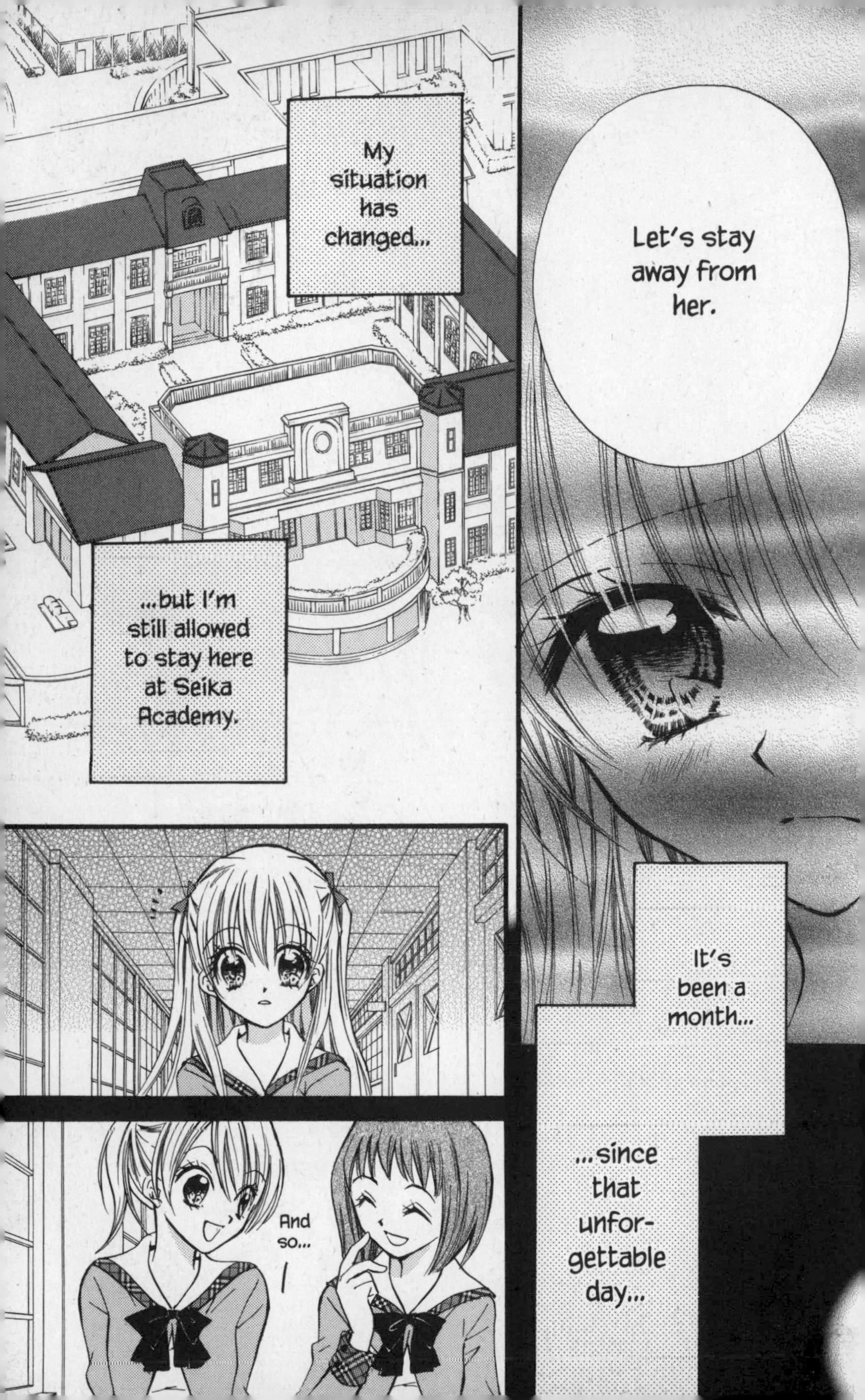
Let's stay away from her.
It's been a month...
...since that unforgettable day...
My situation has changed...
...but I'm still allowed to stay here at Seika Academy.
And so...

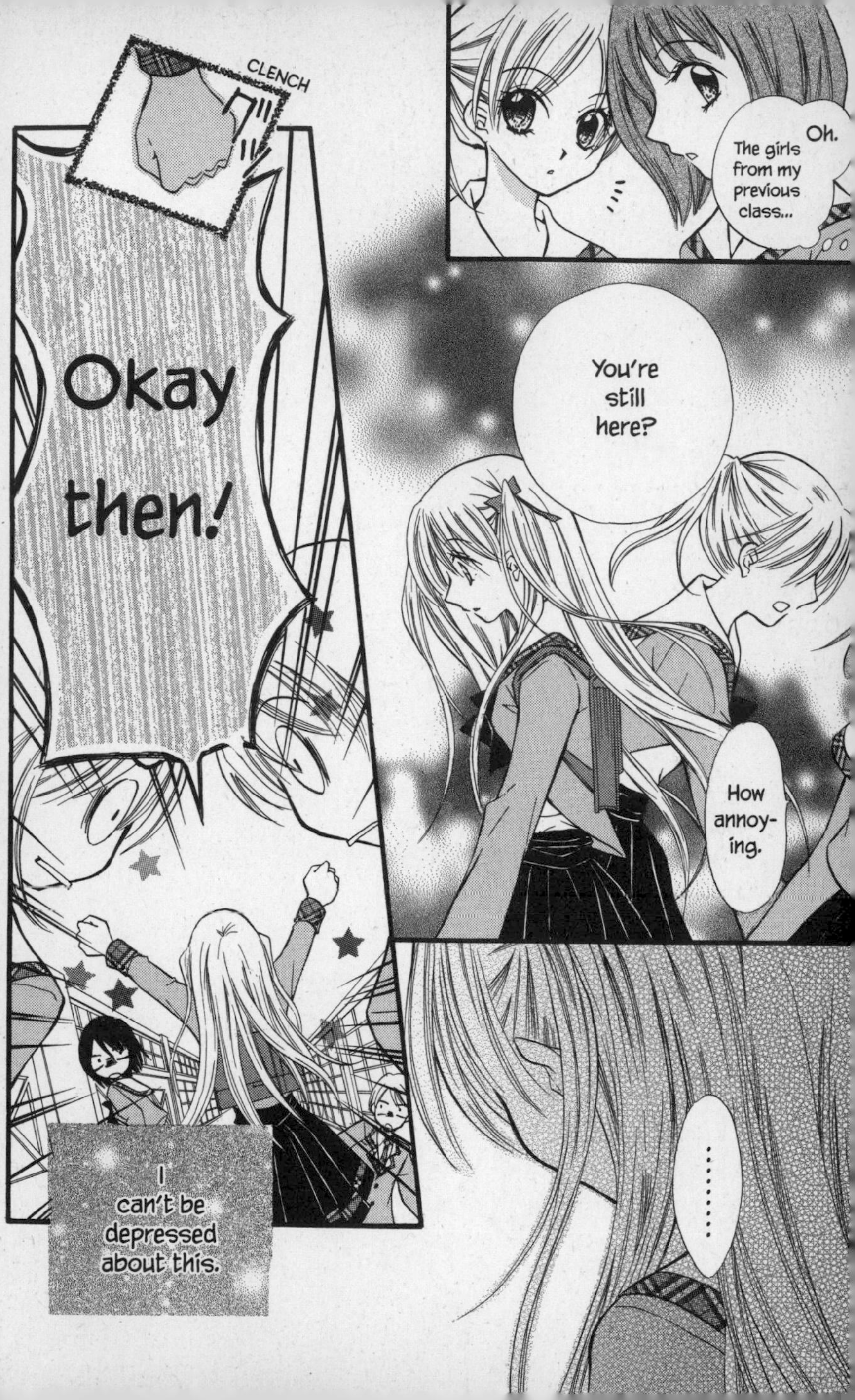
Oh.
The girls from my previous class...
...
You're still here?
How annoying.
....
CLENCH
Okay then!
I can't be depressed about this.

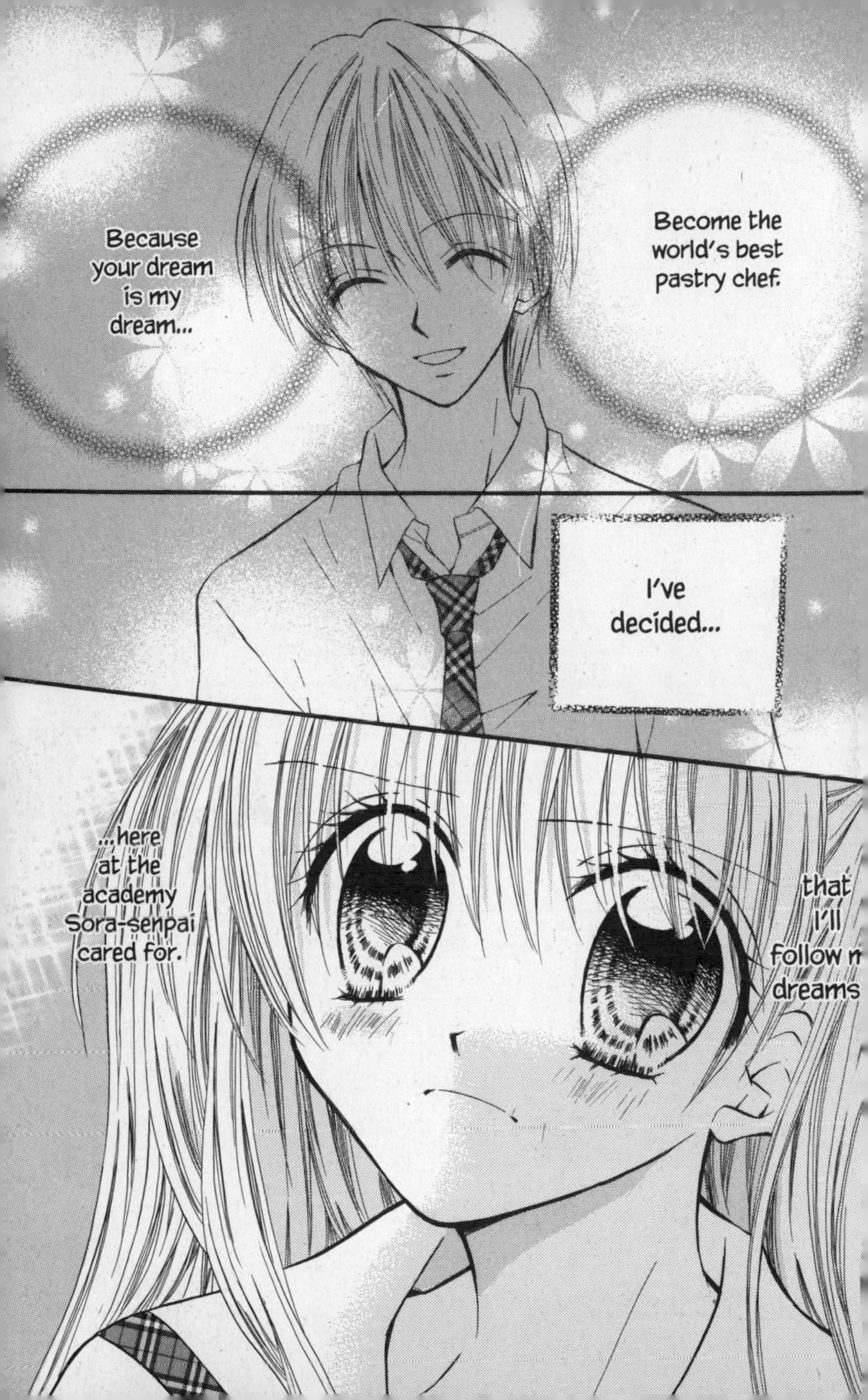
Become the world's best pastry chef.
Because your dream is my dream...
I've decided...
that I'll follow m dreams
...here at the academy Sora-senpai cared for.

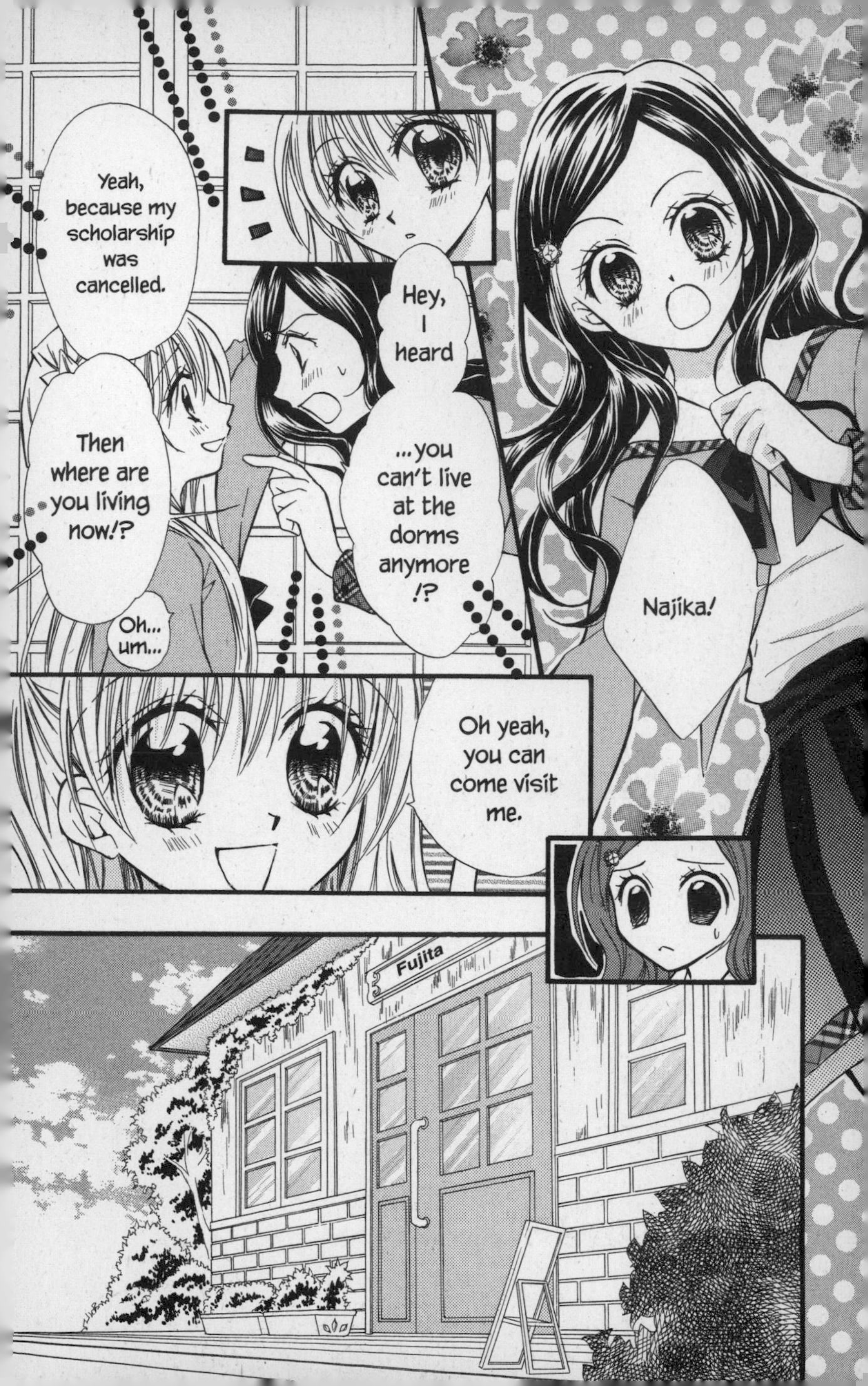
Najika!
Hey, I heard
...you can't live at the dorms anymore!?
Yeah, because my scholarship was cancelled.
Then where are you living now!?
Oh... um...
Oh yeah, you can come visit me.
Fujita

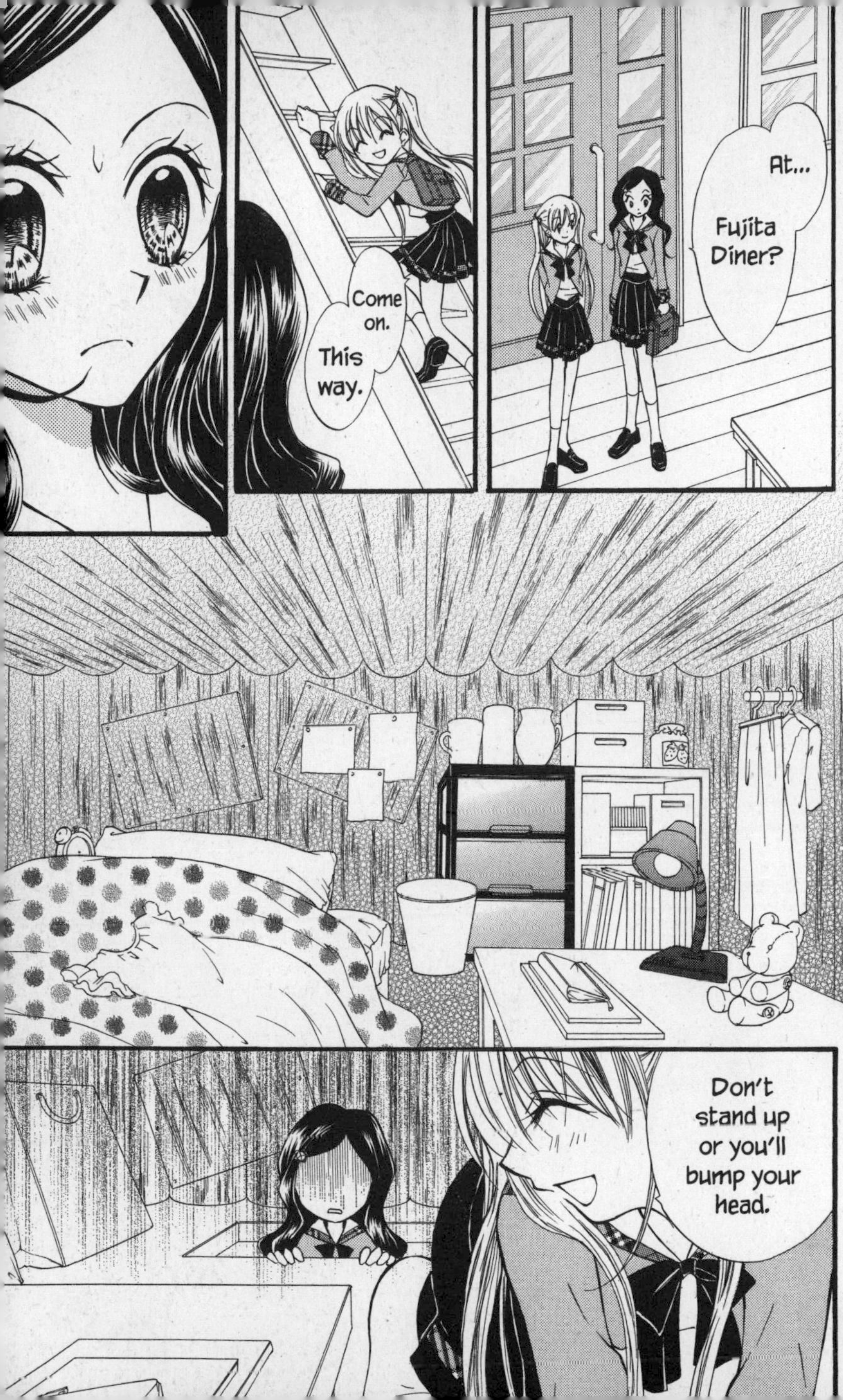
At... Fujita Diner?
Come on. This way.
Don't stand up or you'll bump your head.

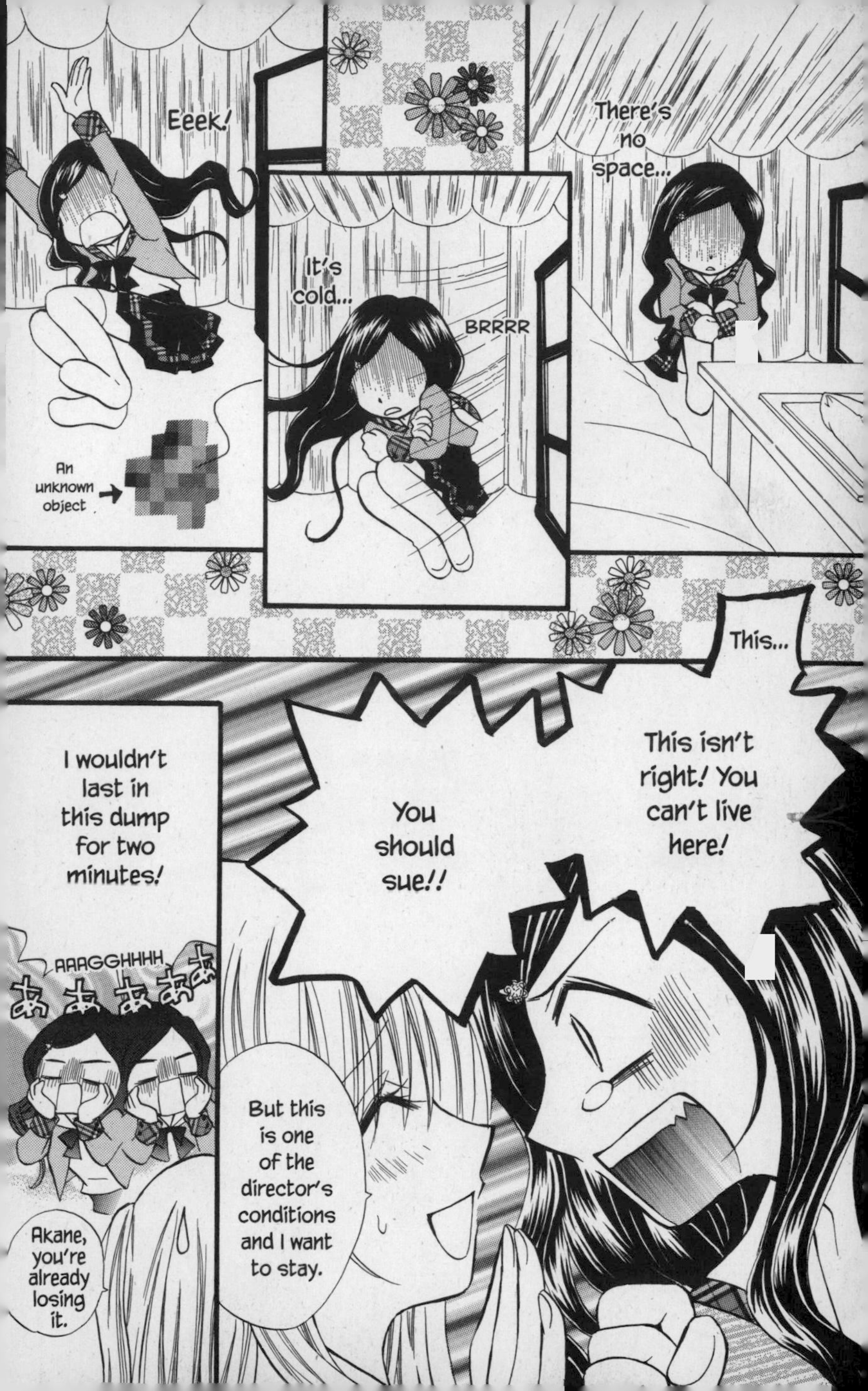
There's no space...
It's cold...
BRRRR
Eeek!
An unknown object
This...
This isn't right! You can't live here!
You should sue!!
But this is one of the director's conditions and I want to stay.
I wouldn't last in this dump for two minutes!
AAAGGHHH
ああああ
Akane, you're already losing it.

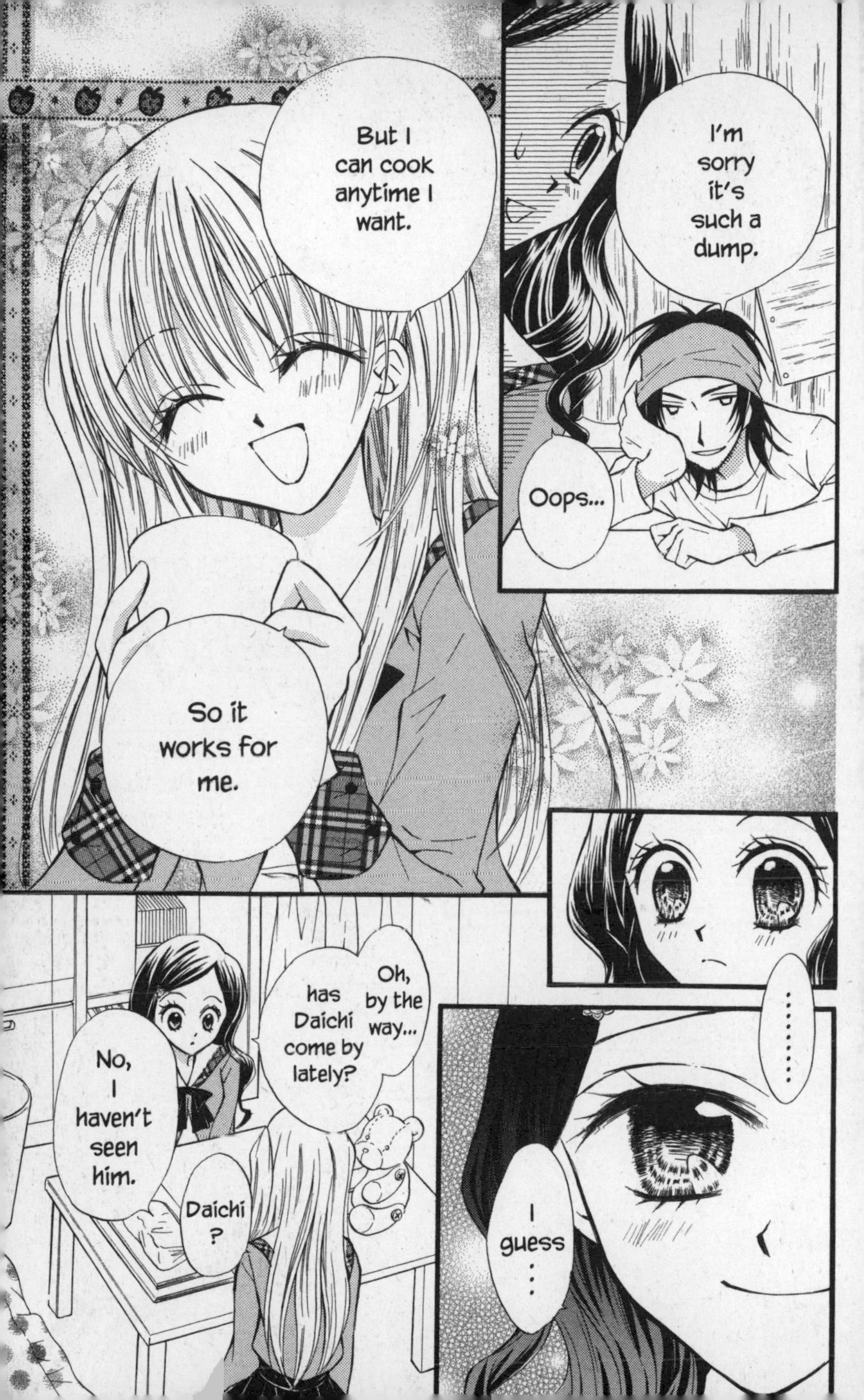
I'm sorry it's such a dump.
Oops...
But I can cook anytime I want.
So it works for me.
....
I guess...
Oh, by the way...
has Daichi come by lately?
No, I haven't seen him.
Daichi?

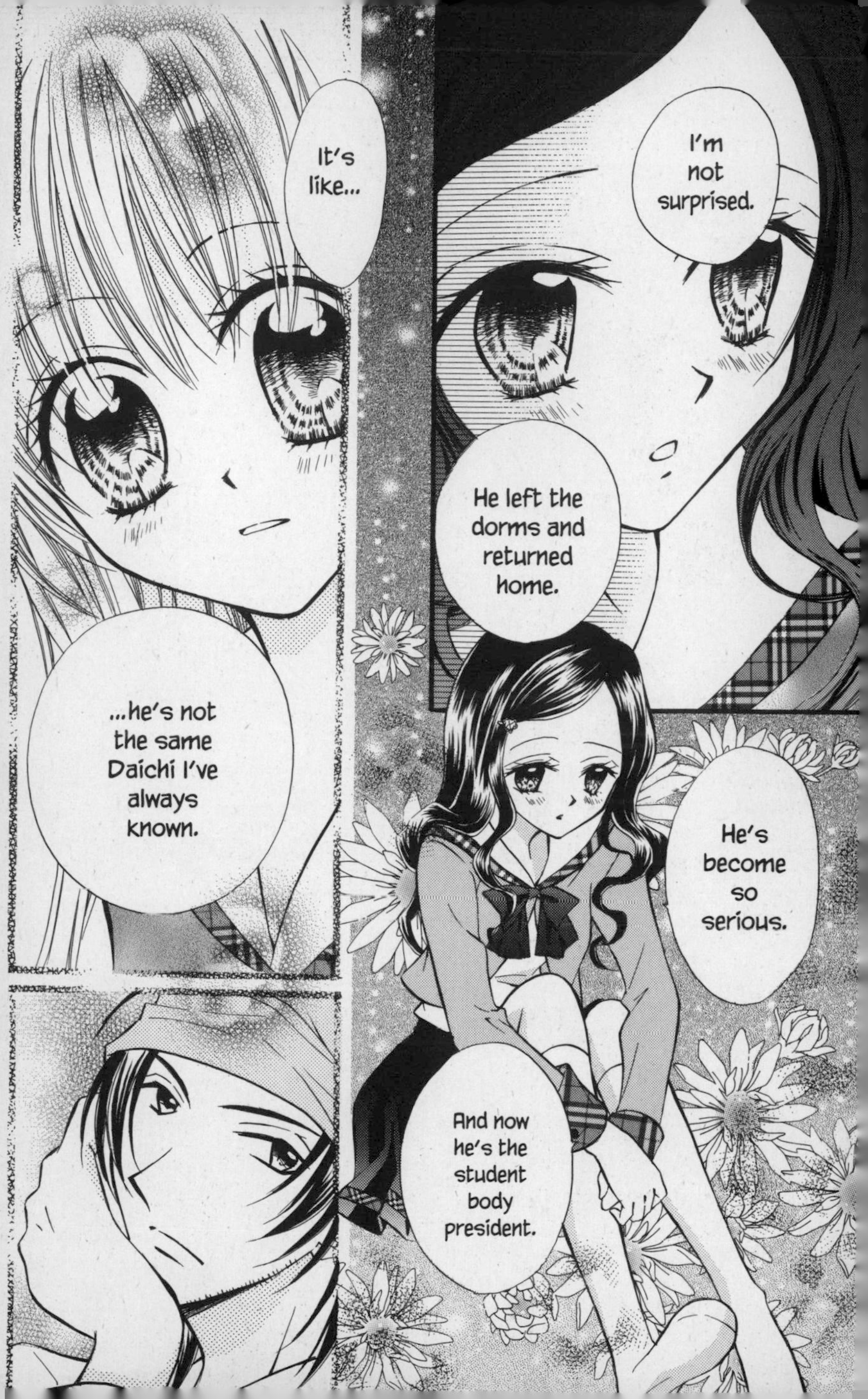
I'm not surprised.
He left the dorms and returned home.
He's become so serious.
And now he's the student body president.
It's like...
...he's not the same Daichi I've always known.

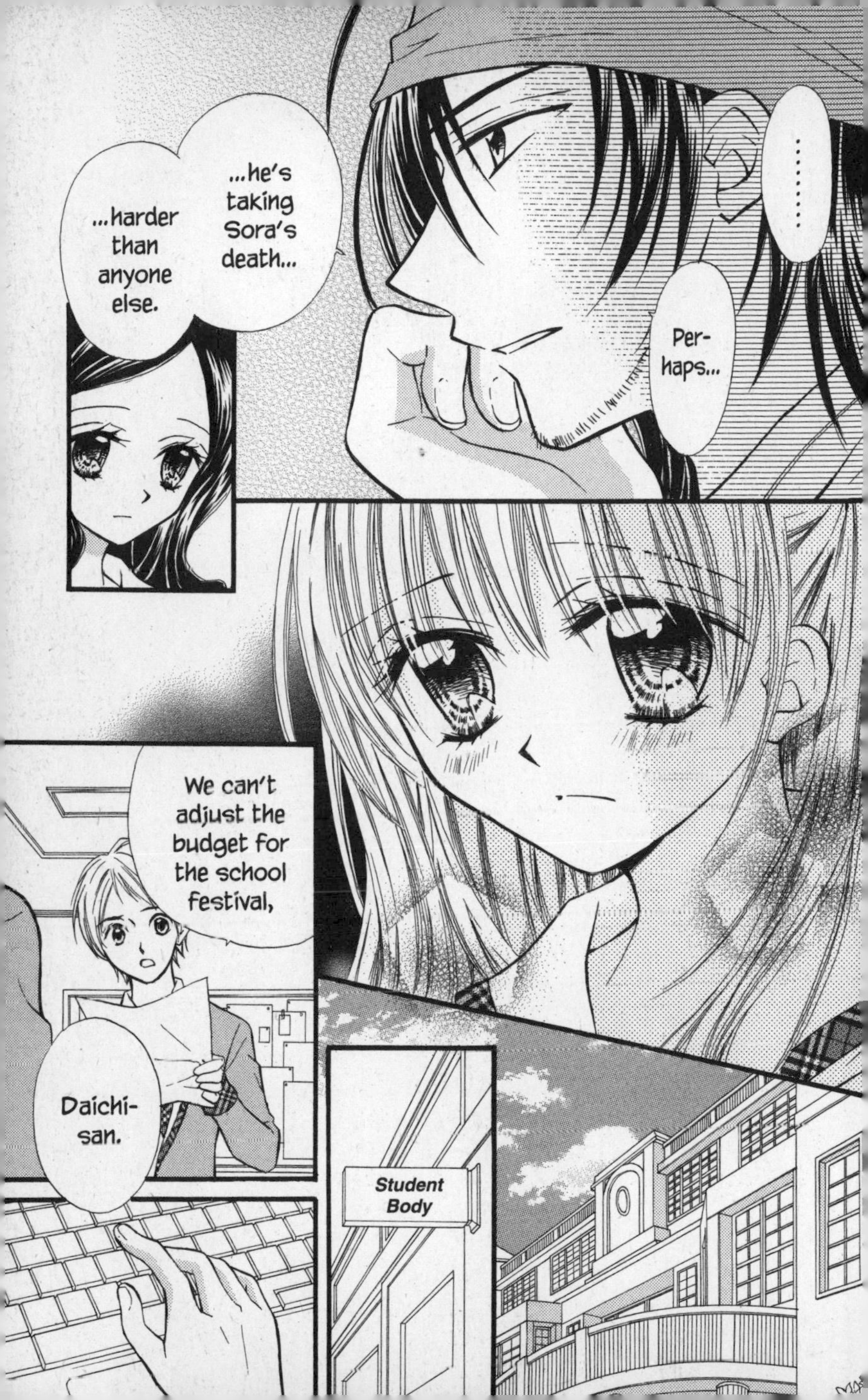
......
Per-haps...
...he's taking Sora's death...
...harder than anyone else.
Student Body
We can't adjust the budget for the school festival,
Daichi-san.

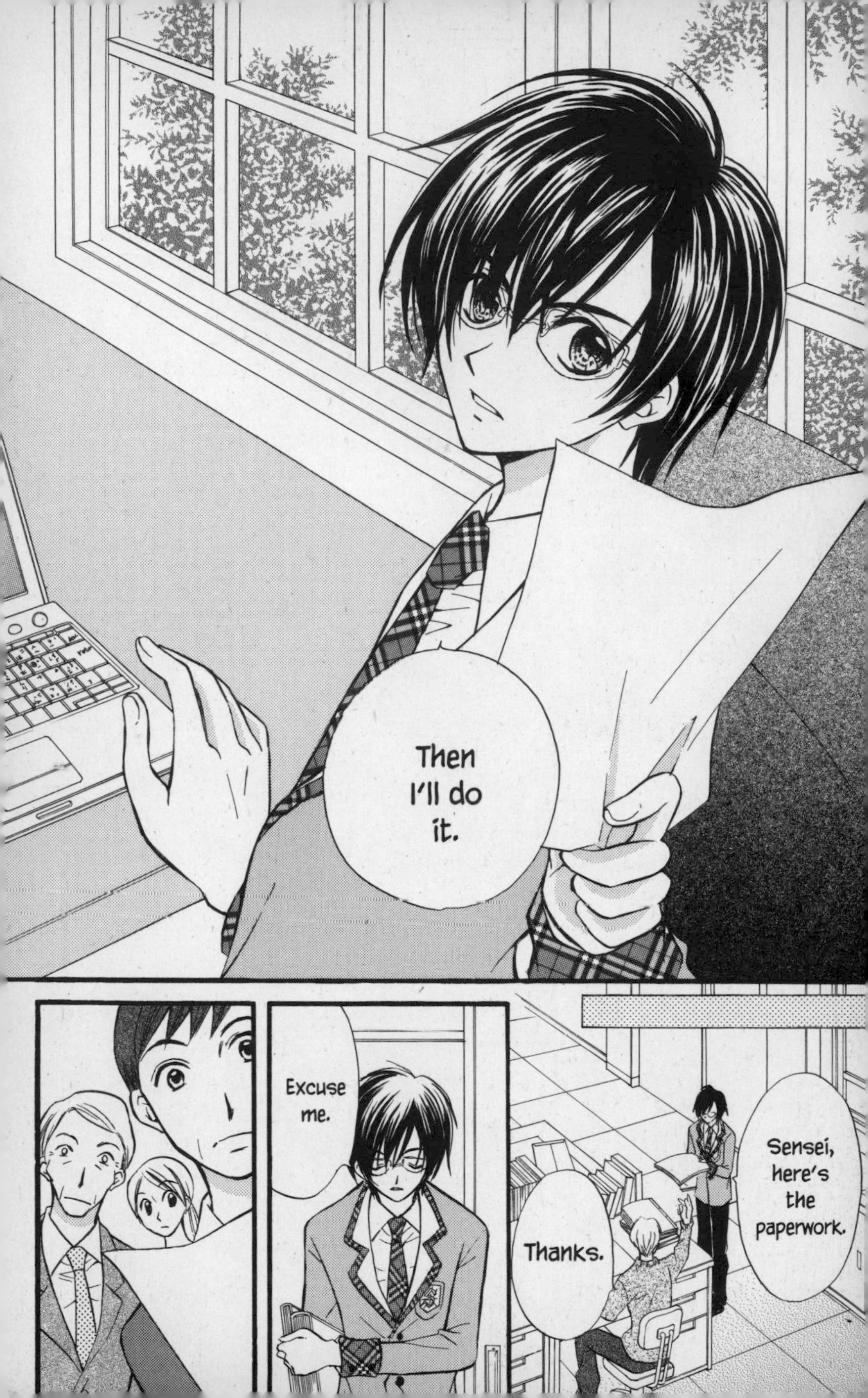
Then I'll do it.
Sensei, here's the paperwork.
Thanks.
Excuse me.

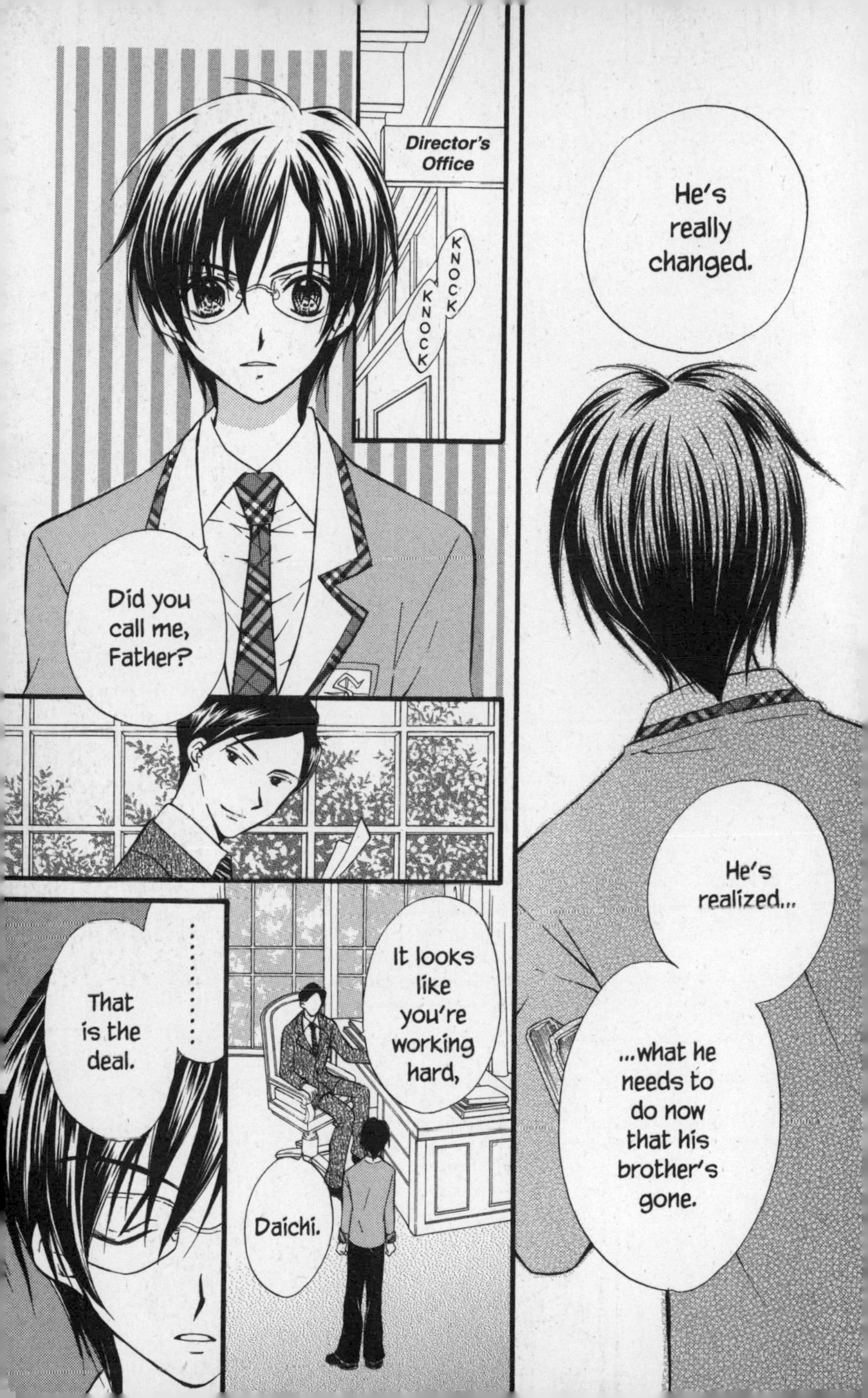

He's really changed.
He's realized...
...what he needs to do now that his brother's gone.
Director's Office
KNOCK
KNOCK
Did you call me, Father?
It looks like you're working hard,
Daichi.
......
That is the deal.

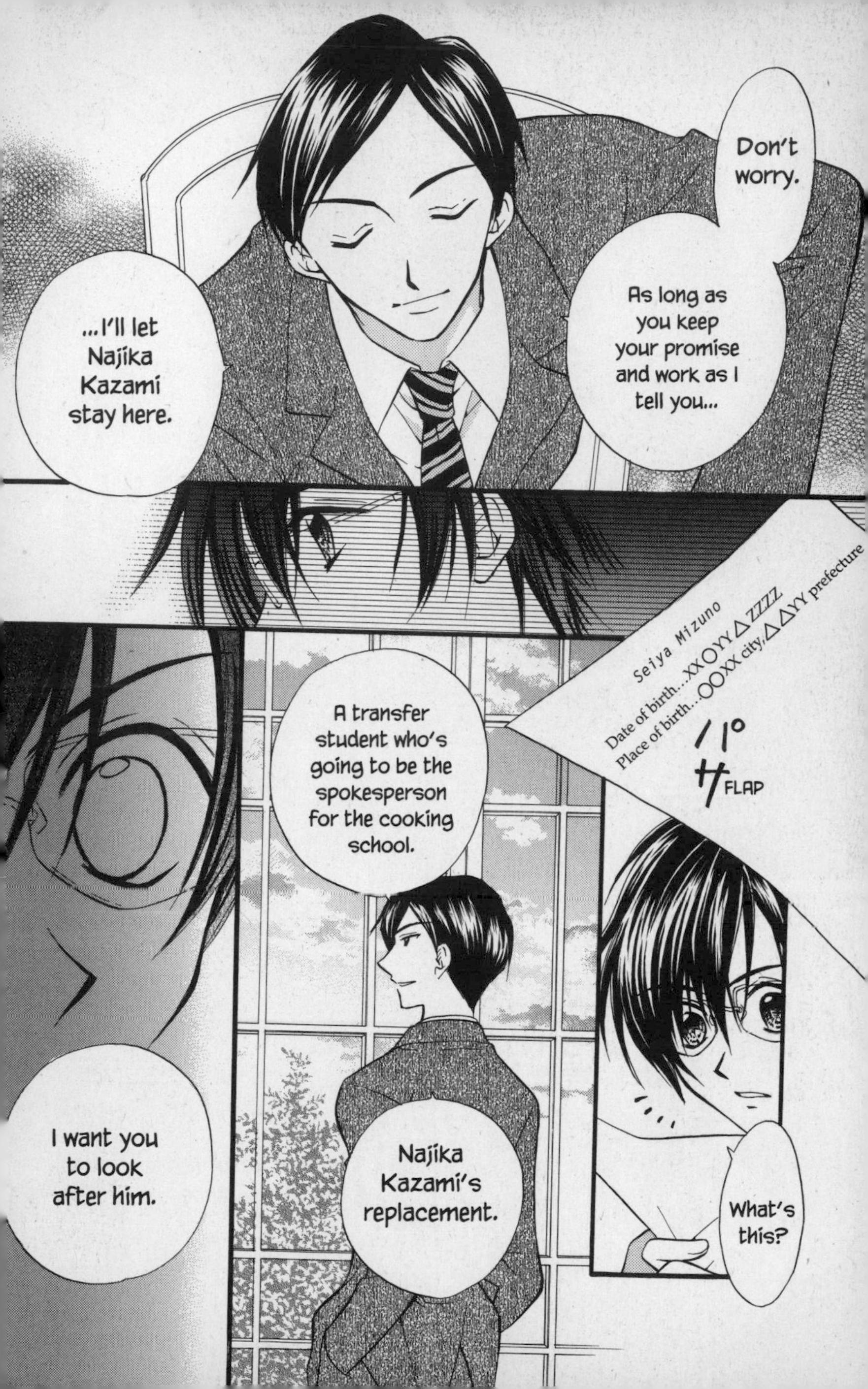
Don't worry.
As long as you keep your promise and work as I tell you...
...I'll let Najika Kazami stay here.
Seiya Mizuno
Date of birth...XX○YY△ZZZ
Place of birth...○○XX city,△△YY prefecture
FLAP
What's this?
A transfer student who's going to be the spokesperson for the cooking school.
Najika Kazami's replacement.
I want you to look after him.

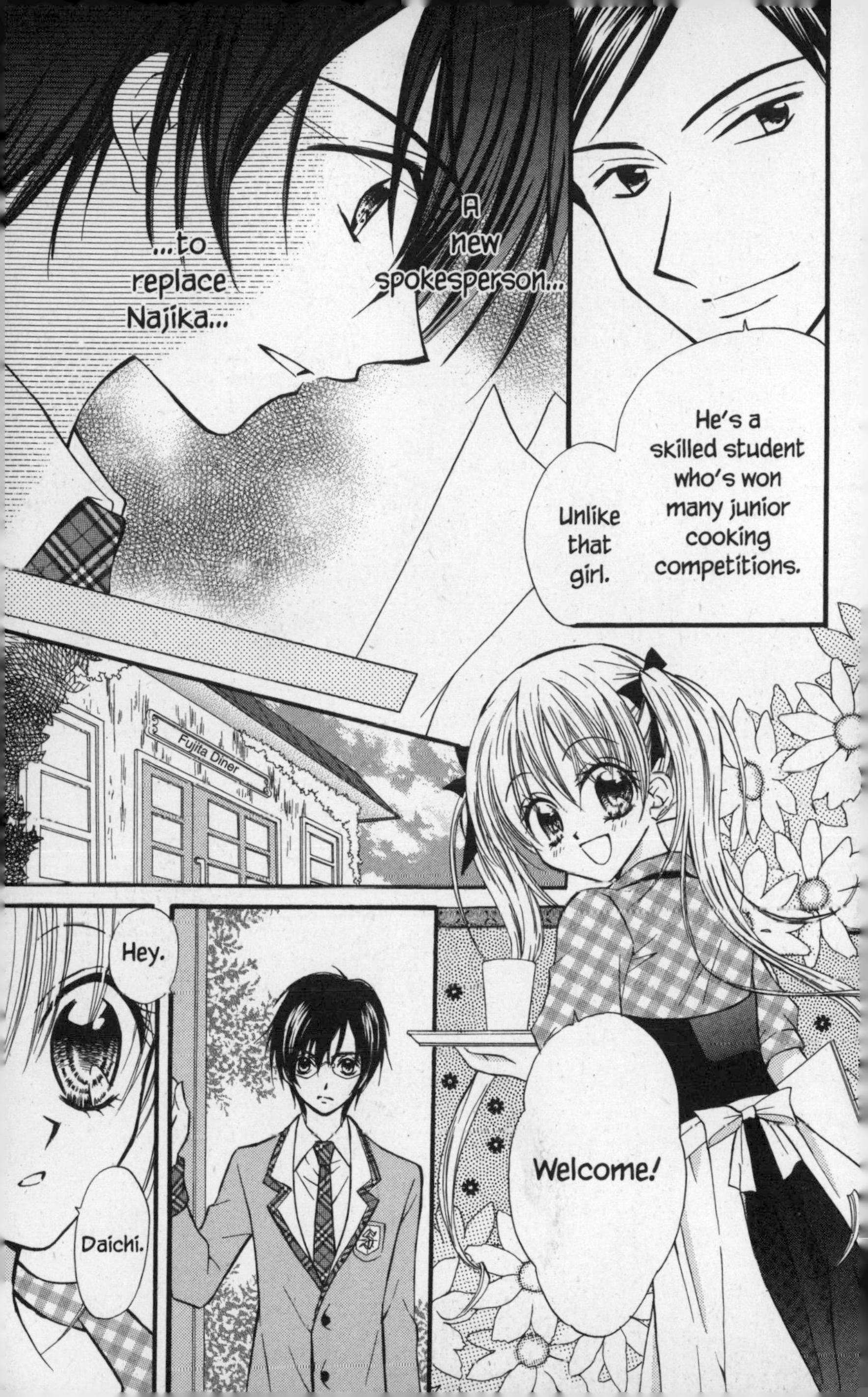
He's a skilled student who's won many junior cooking competitions.
Unlike that girl.
A new spokesperson...
...to replace Najika...
Fujita Diner
Welcome!
Hey.
Daichi.

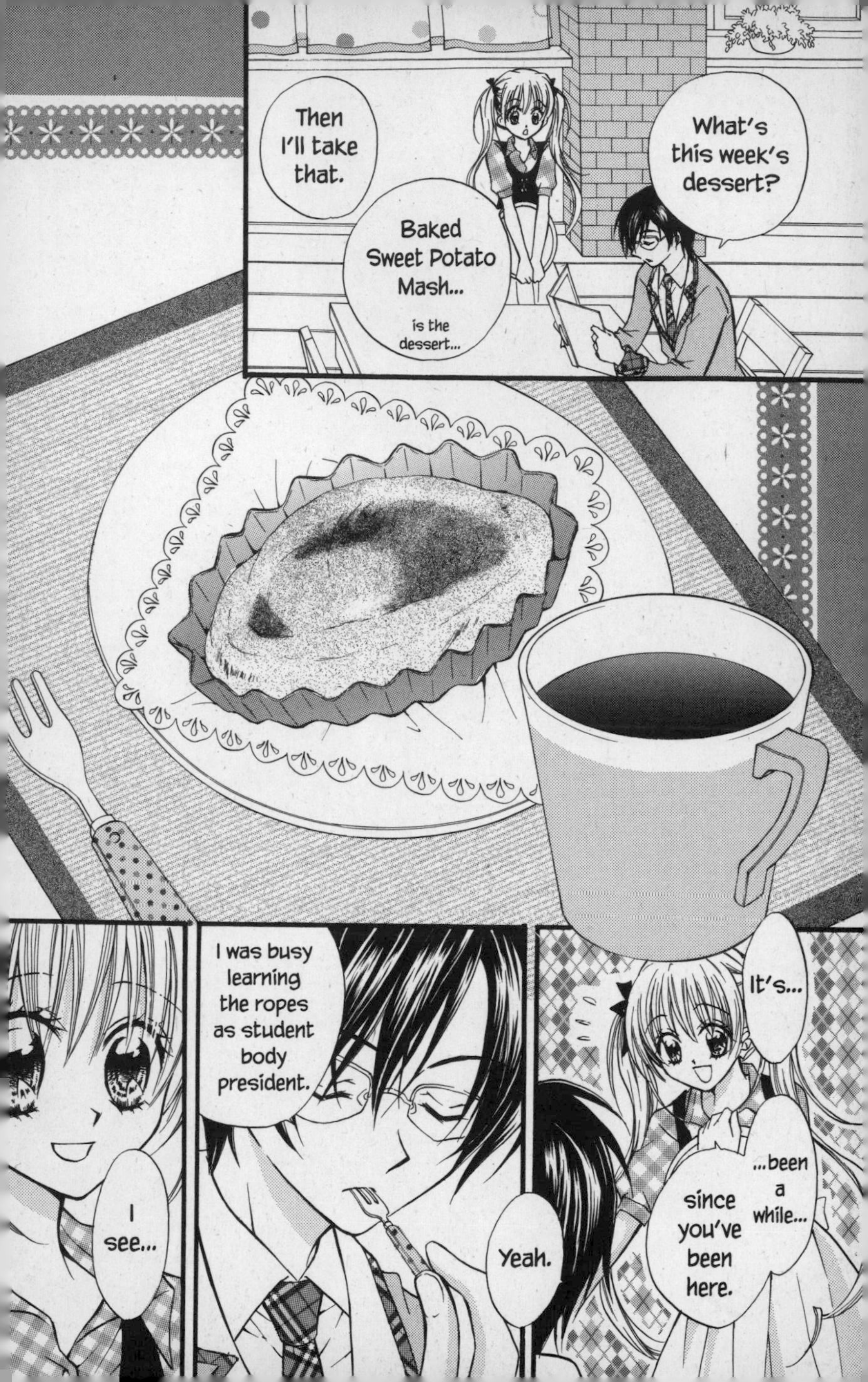
What's this week's dessert?
Baked Sweet Potato Mash...
is the dessert...
Then I'll take that.
It's...
...been a while...
since you've been here.
Yeah.
I was busy learning the ropes as student body president.
I see...

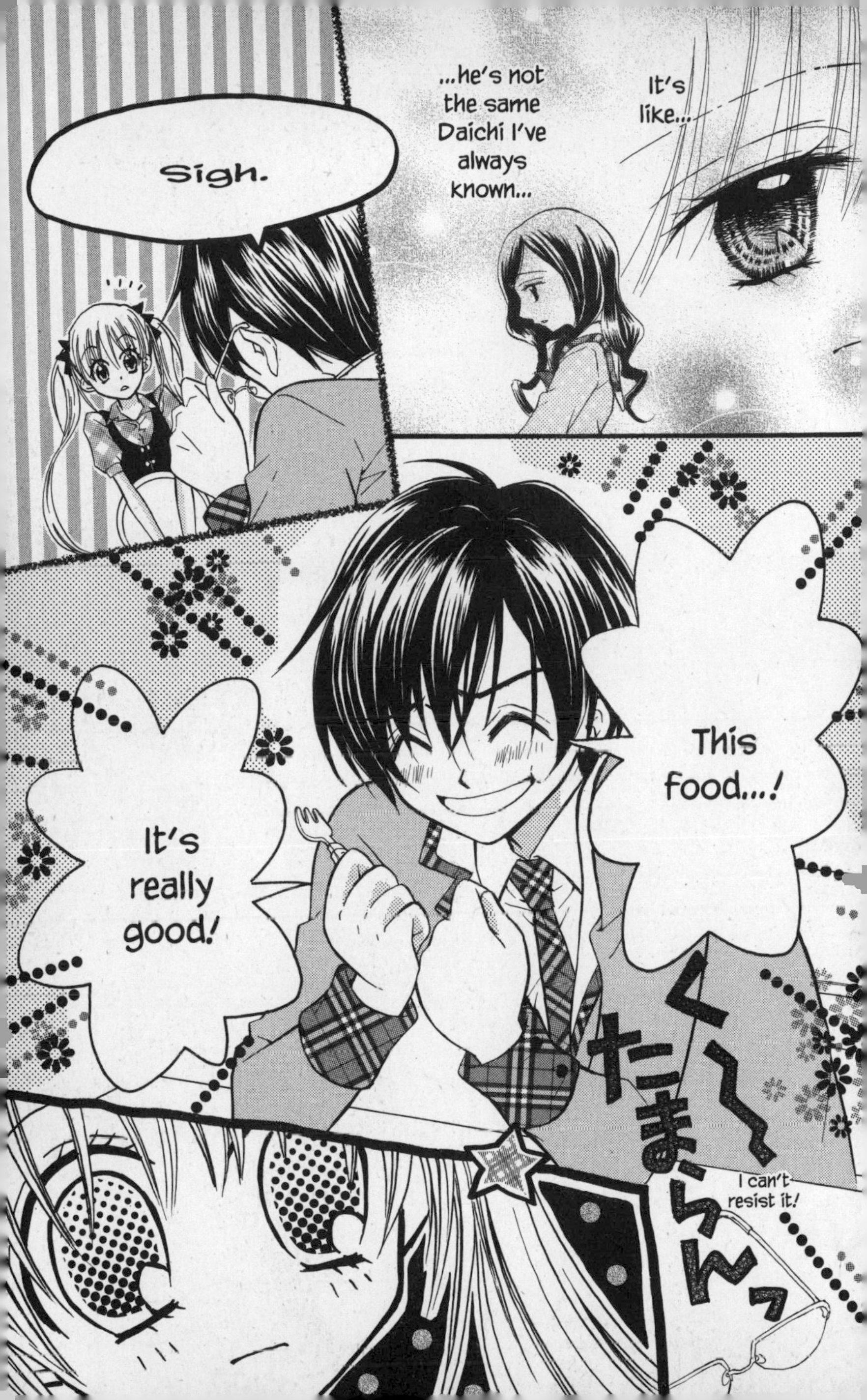
It's like...
...he's not the same Daichi I've always known...
Sigh.
This food...!
It's really good!
く〜〜
たまらんっ
I can't resist it!

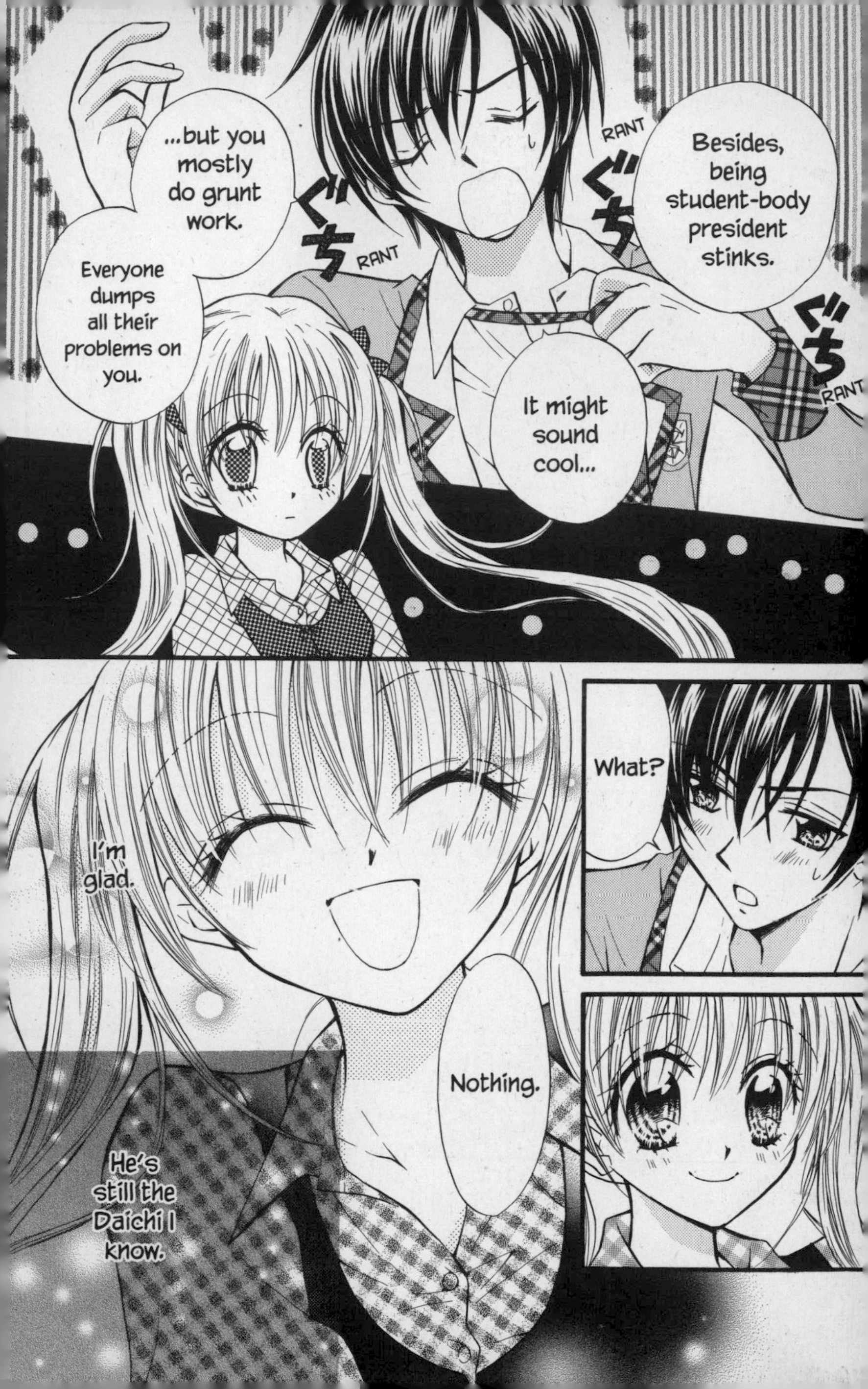

Besides, being student-body president stinks.
ぐち RANT
ぐち RANT
ぐち RANT
It might sound cool...
...but you mostly do grunt work.
Everyone dumps all their problems on you.
What?
Nothing.
I'm glad.
He's still the Daichi I know.

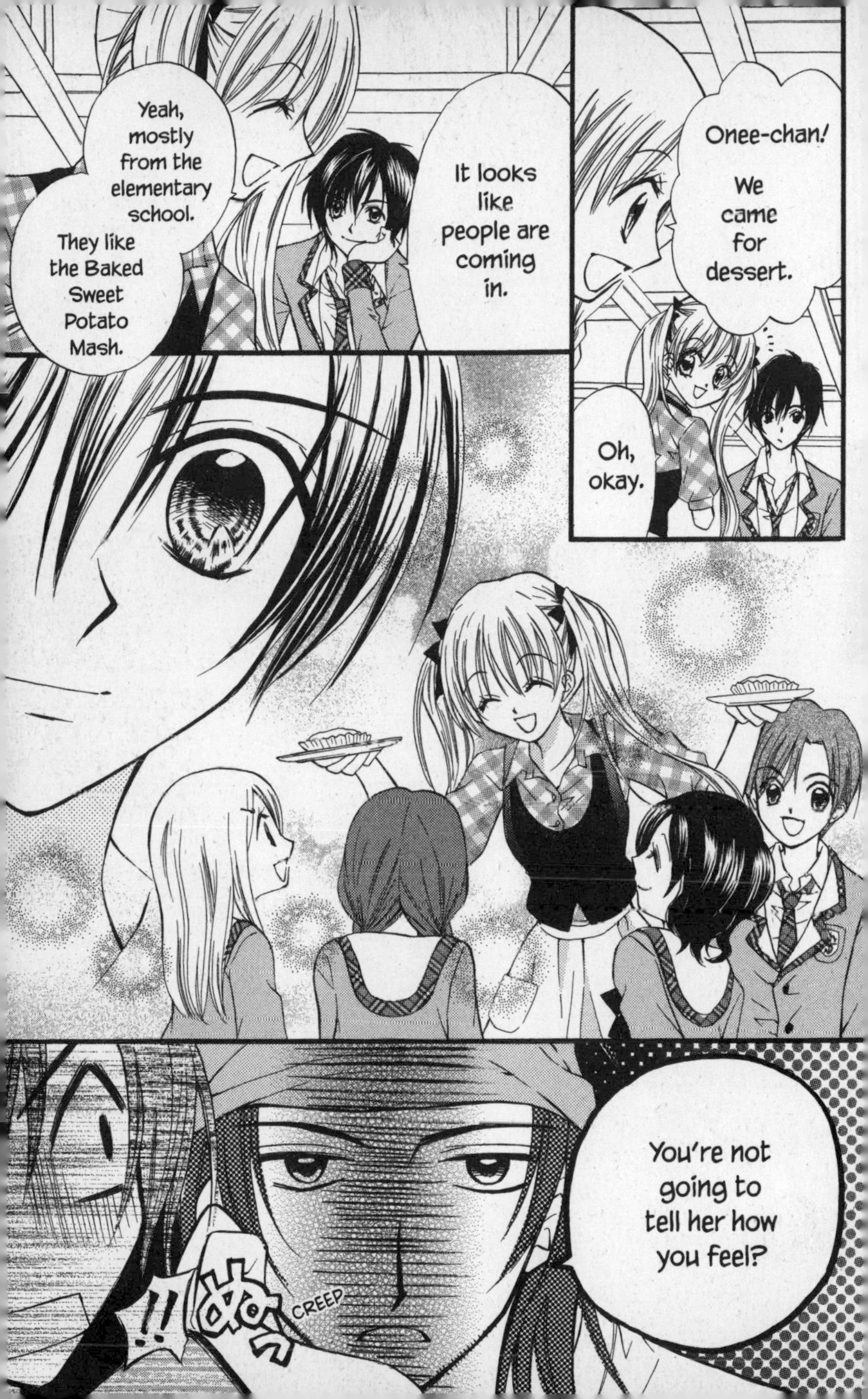
Onee-chan! We came for dessert.
Oh, okay.
It looks like people are coming in.
Yeah, mostly from the elementary school.
They like the Baked Sweet Potato Mash.
You're not going to tell her how you feel?
CREEP
!!

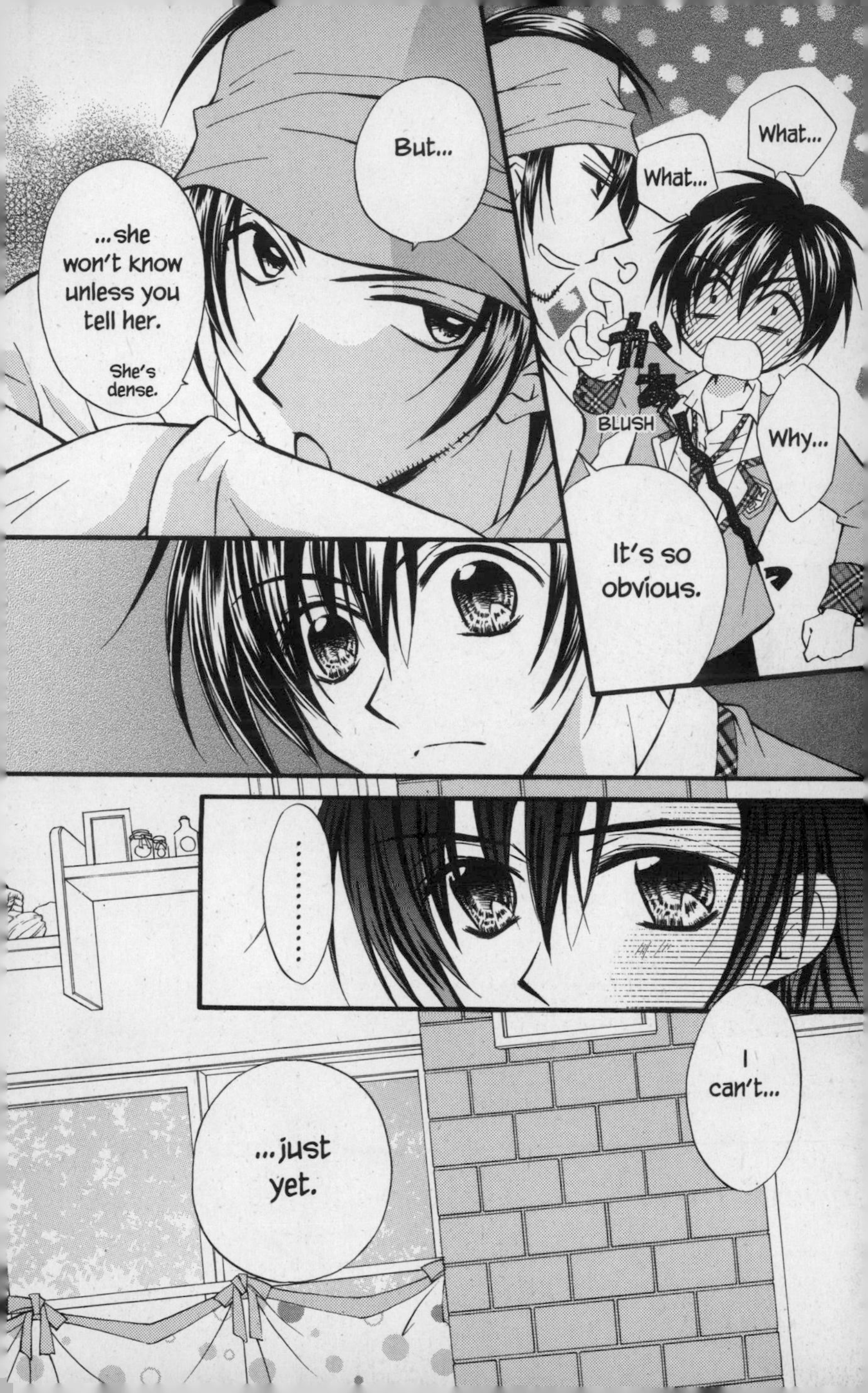
What...
What...
BLUSH
Why...
It's so obvious.
But...
...she won't know unless you tell her.
She's dense.
......
I can't...
...just yet.

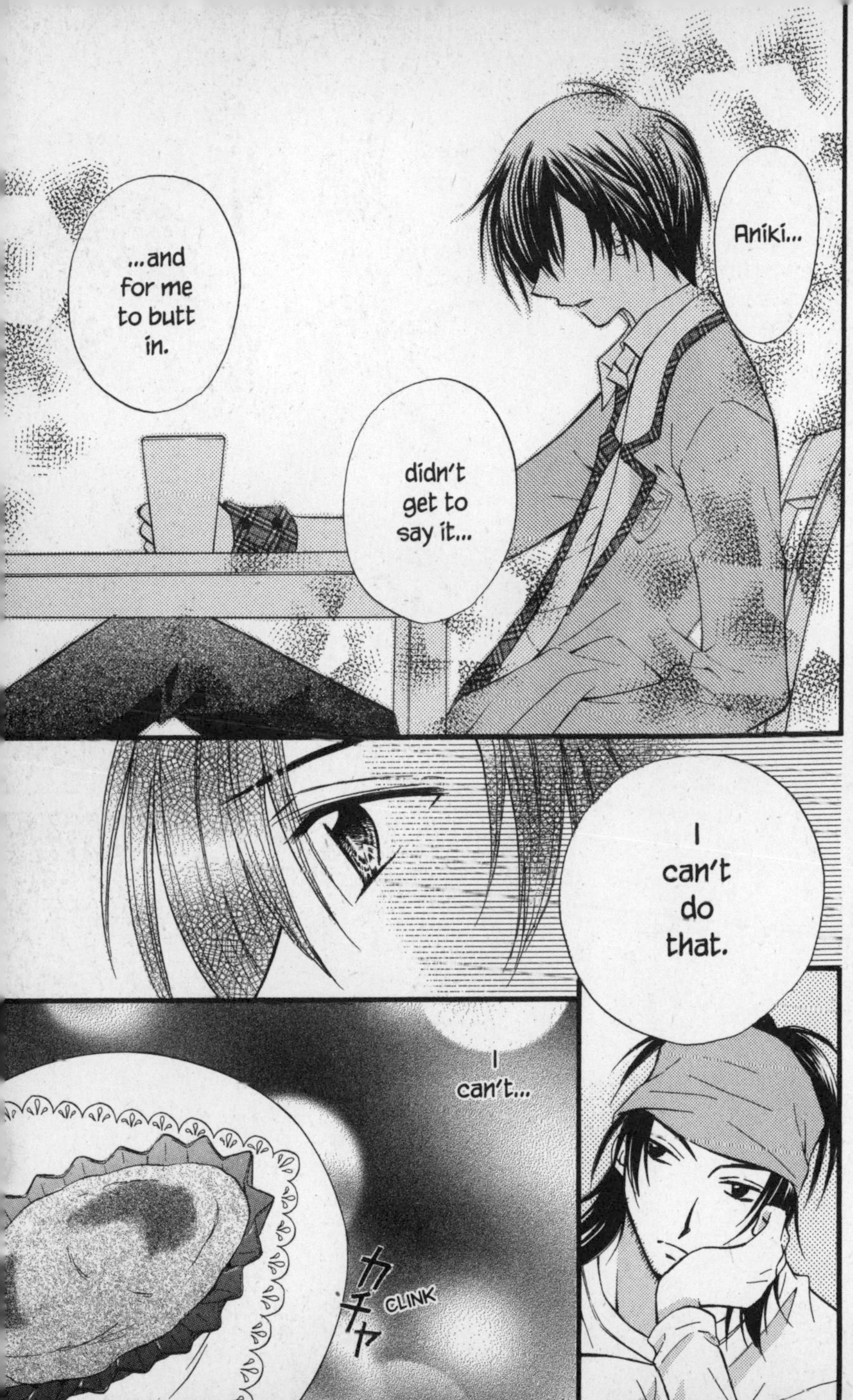
Aniki...
didn't get to say it...
...and for me to butt in.
I can't do that.
I can't...
カチャ
CLINK

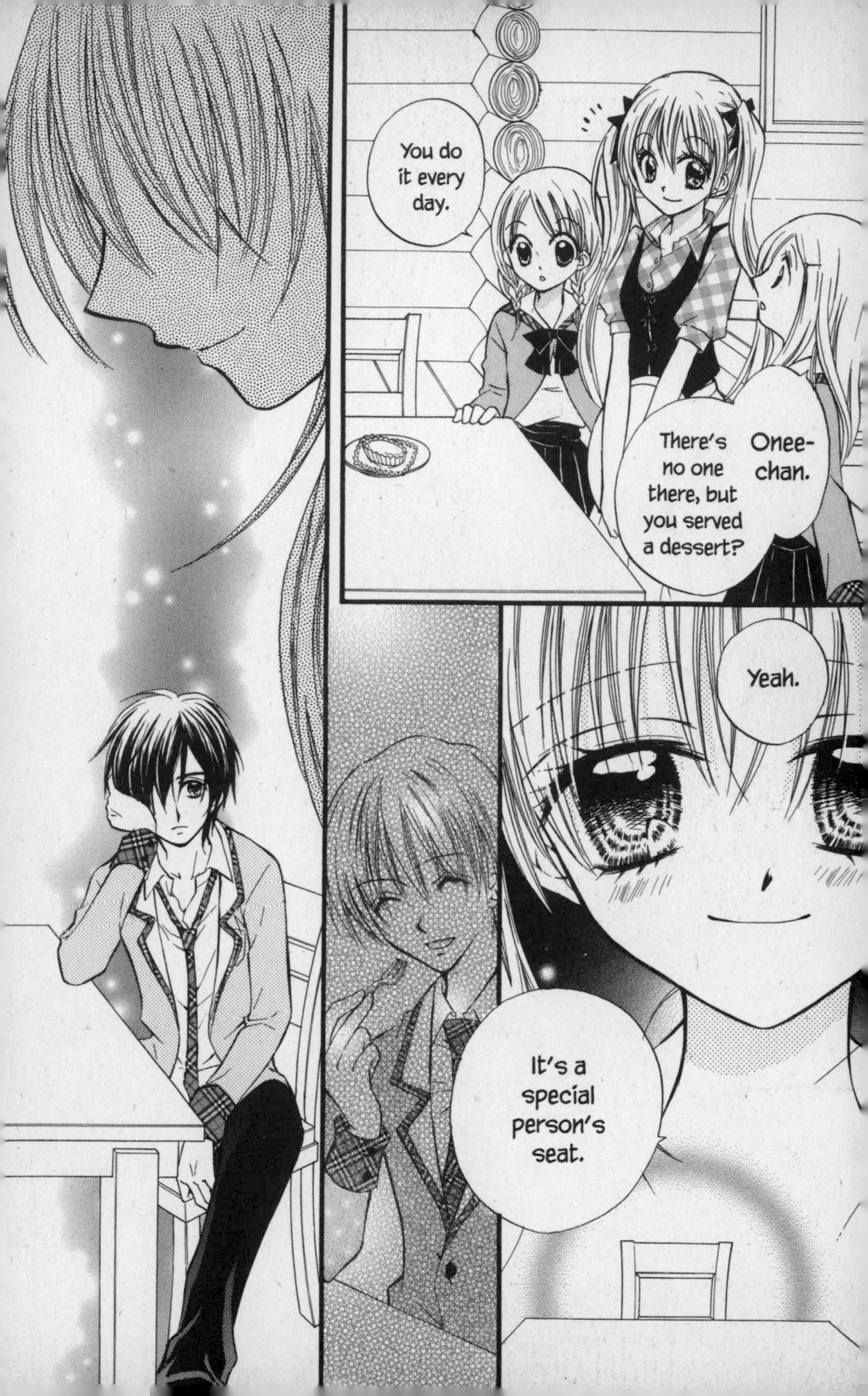
Onee-chan.
There's no one there, but you served a dessert?
You do it every day.
Yeah.
It's a special person's seat.

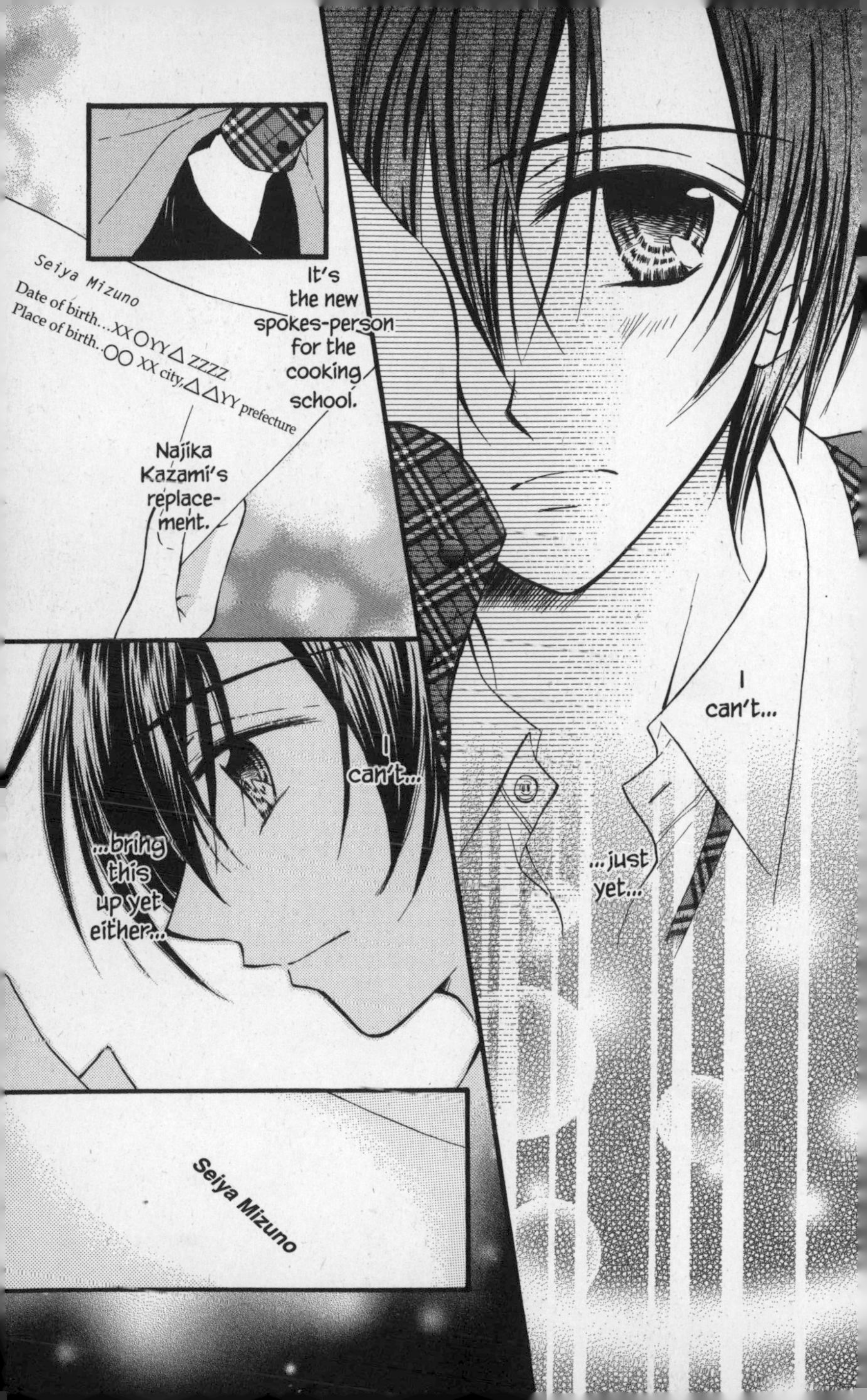

I can't...
...just yet...
Seiya Mizuno
Date of birth…XX〇YY△ZZZZ
Place of birth..〇〇 XX city,△△YY prefecture
It's the new spokes-person for the cooking school.
Najika Kazami's replace-ment.
I can't...
...bring this up yet either...
Seiya Mizuno

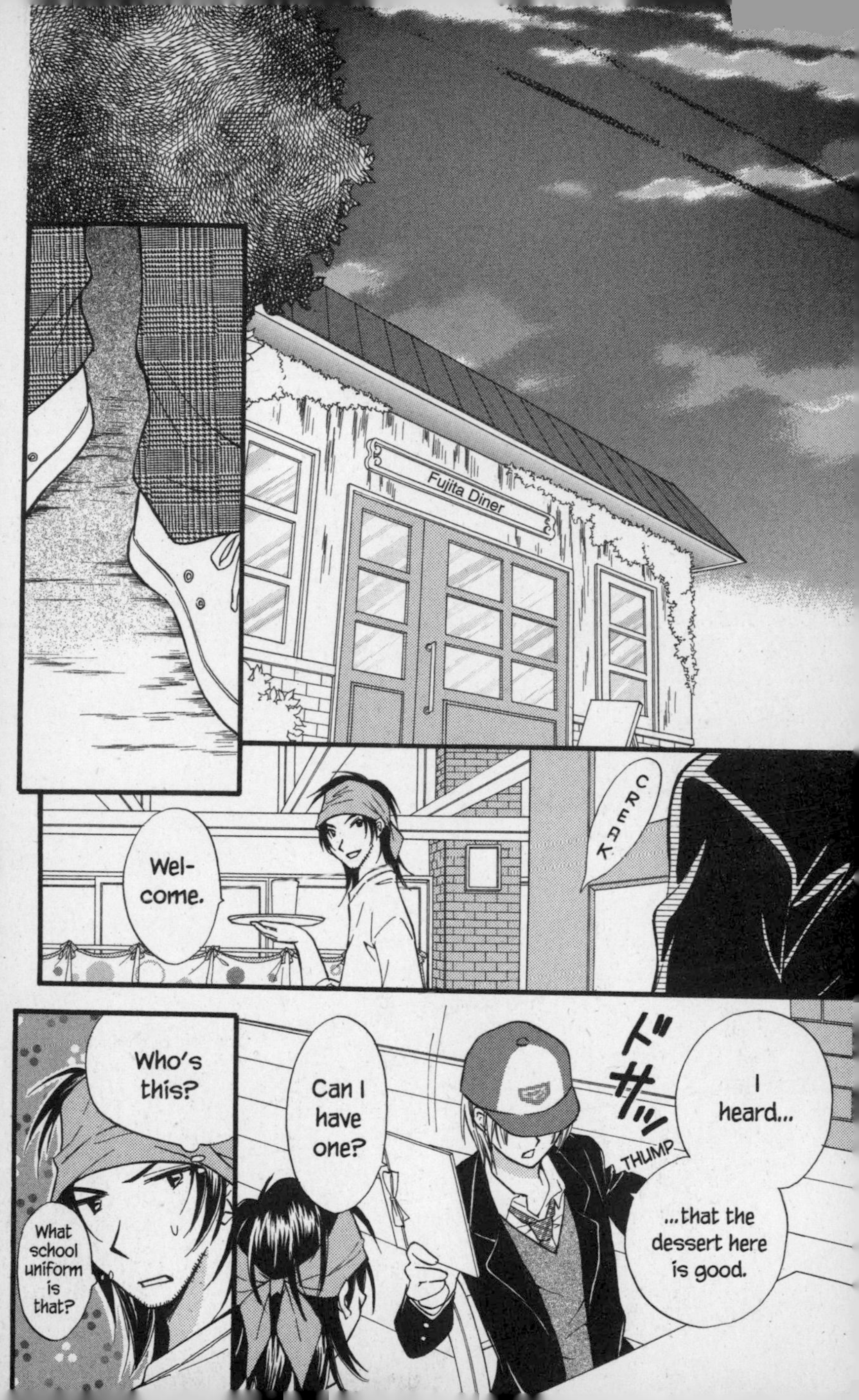
Fujita Diner
CREAK
Wel-come.
ドザッ
THUMP
I heard...
...that the dessert here is good.
Can I have one?
Who's this?
What school uniform is that?

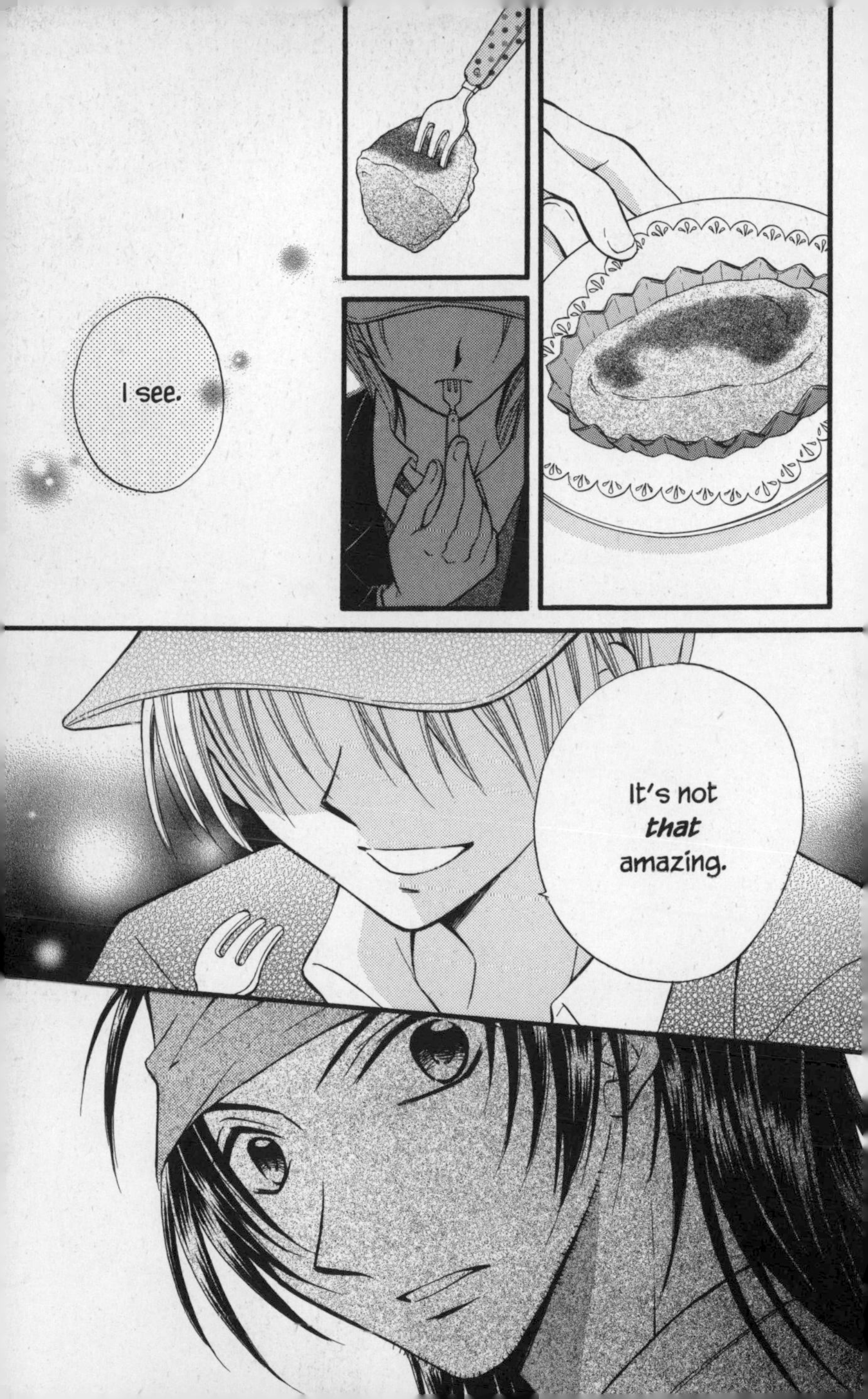
I see.
It's not *that* amazing.

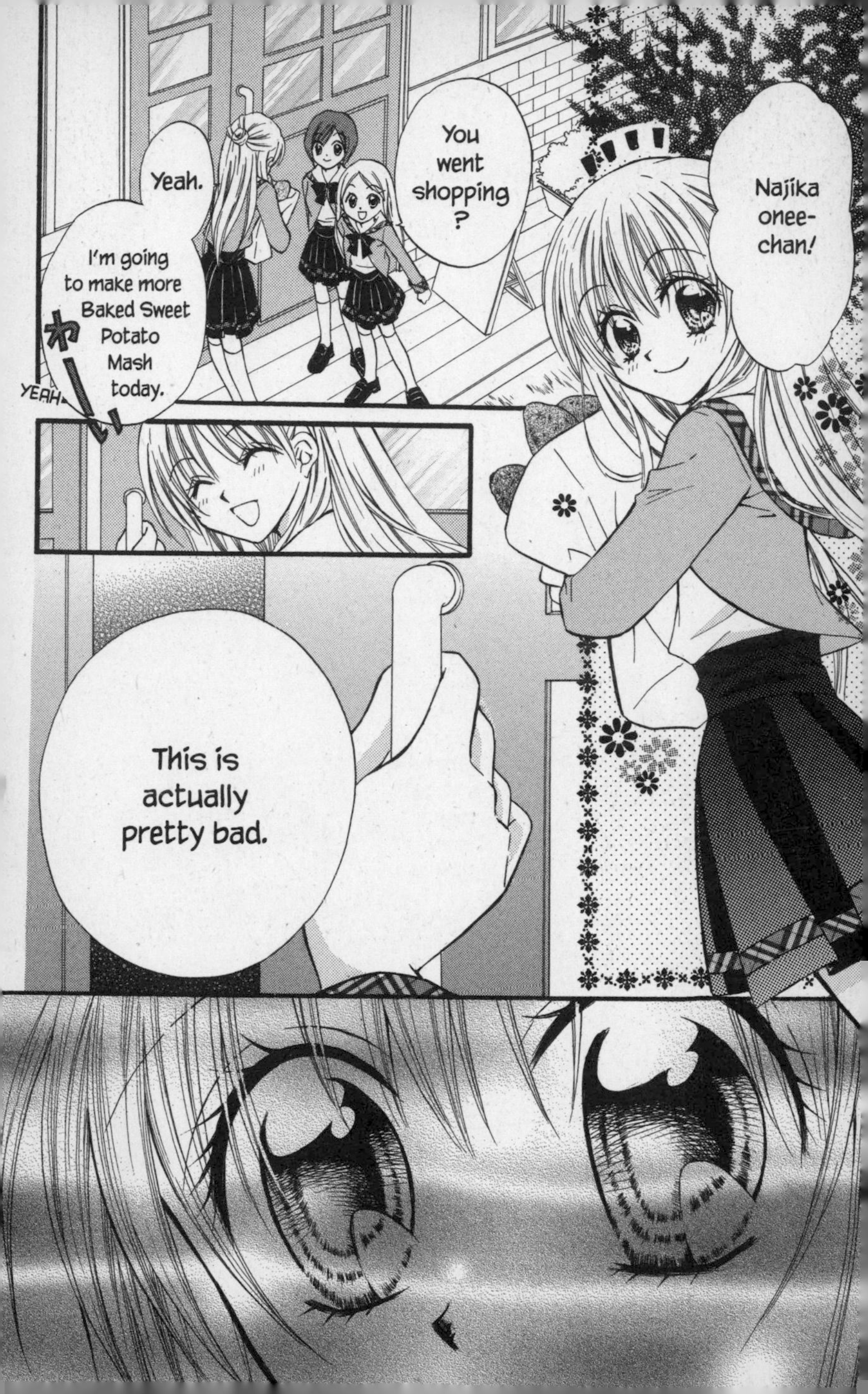
Najika onee-chan!
You went shopping?
Yeah.
I'm going to make more Baked Sweet Potato Mash today.
YEAH
This is actually pretty bad.

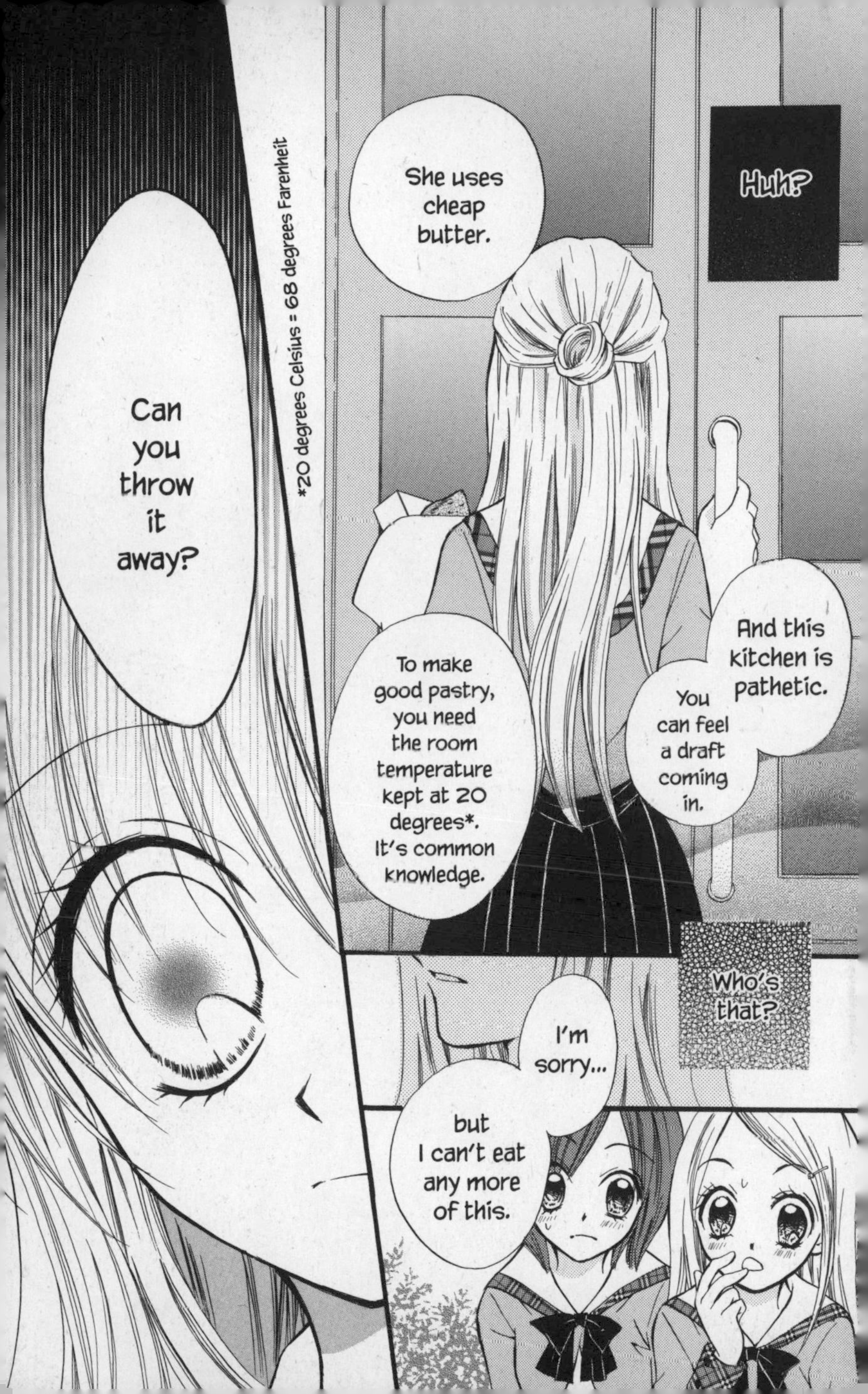
Huh?
She uses cheap butter.
And this kitchen is pathetic.
You can feel a draft coming in.
To make good pastry, you need the room temperature kept at 20 degrees*. It's common knowledge.
Who's that?
I'm sorry...
but I can't eat any more of this.
Can you throw it away?

*20 degrees Celsius = 68 degrees Farenheit

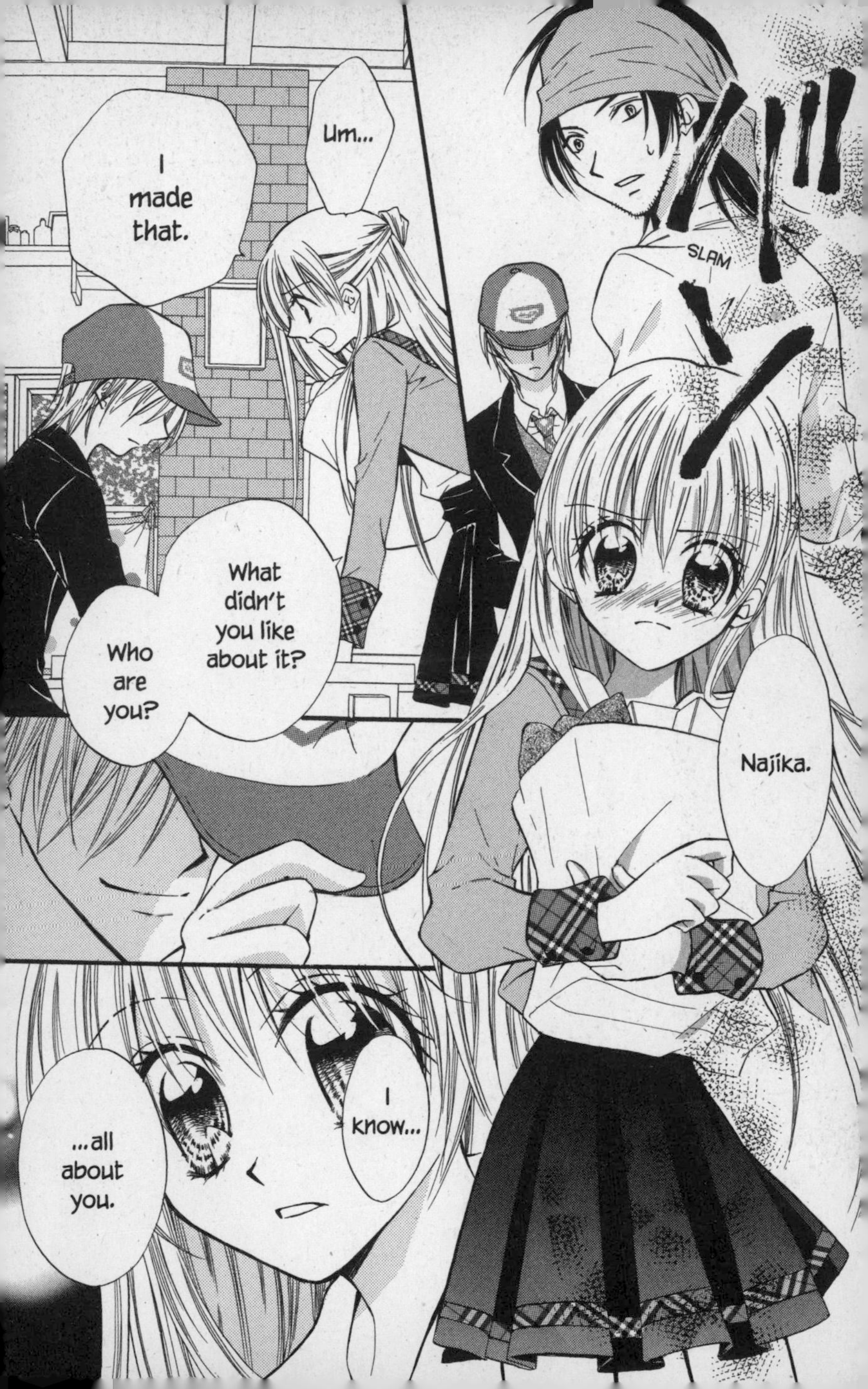
SLAM
Najika.
Um...
I made that.
What didn't you like about it?
Who are you?
I know...
...all about you.

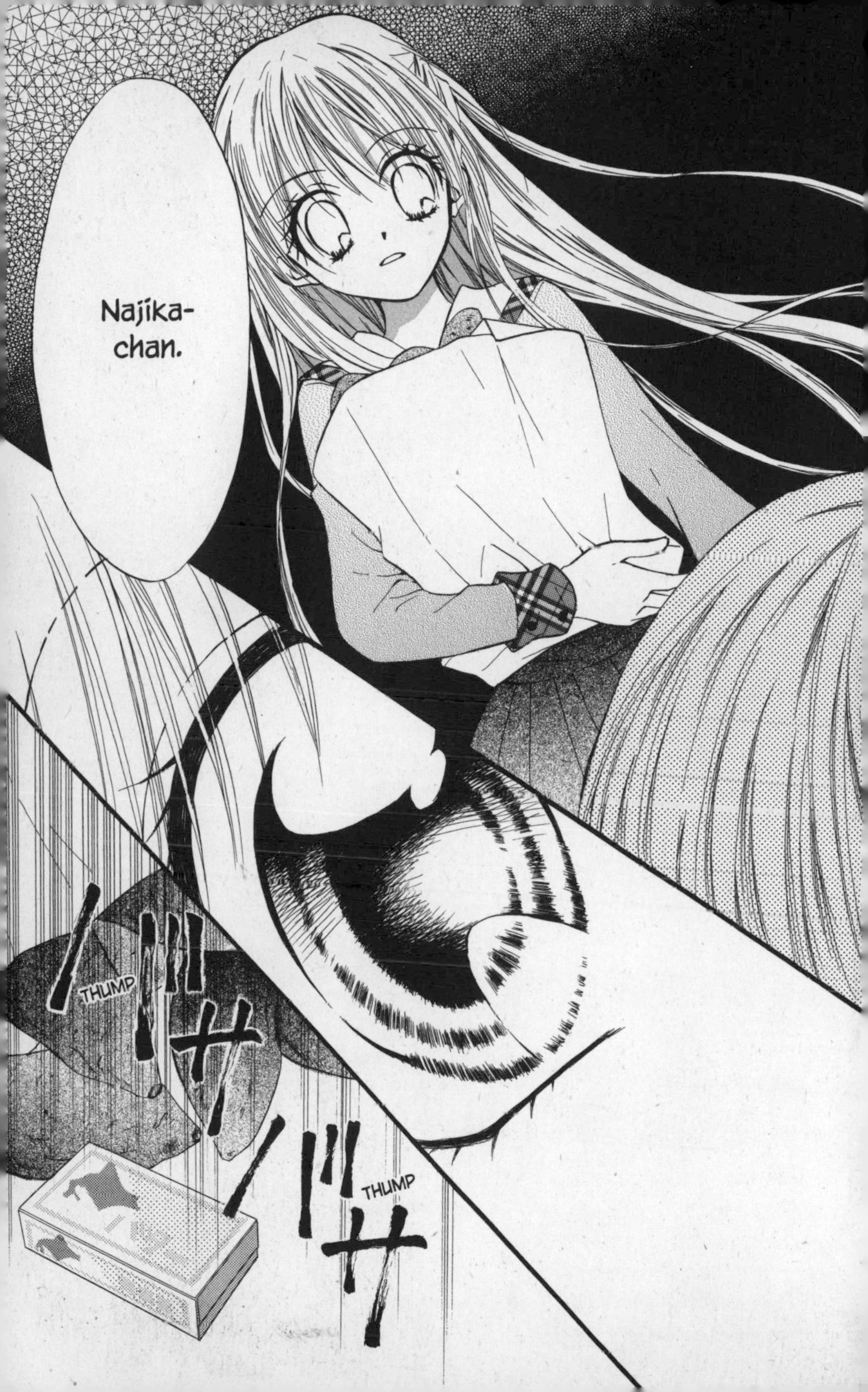
Najika-
chan.
THUMP
THUMP

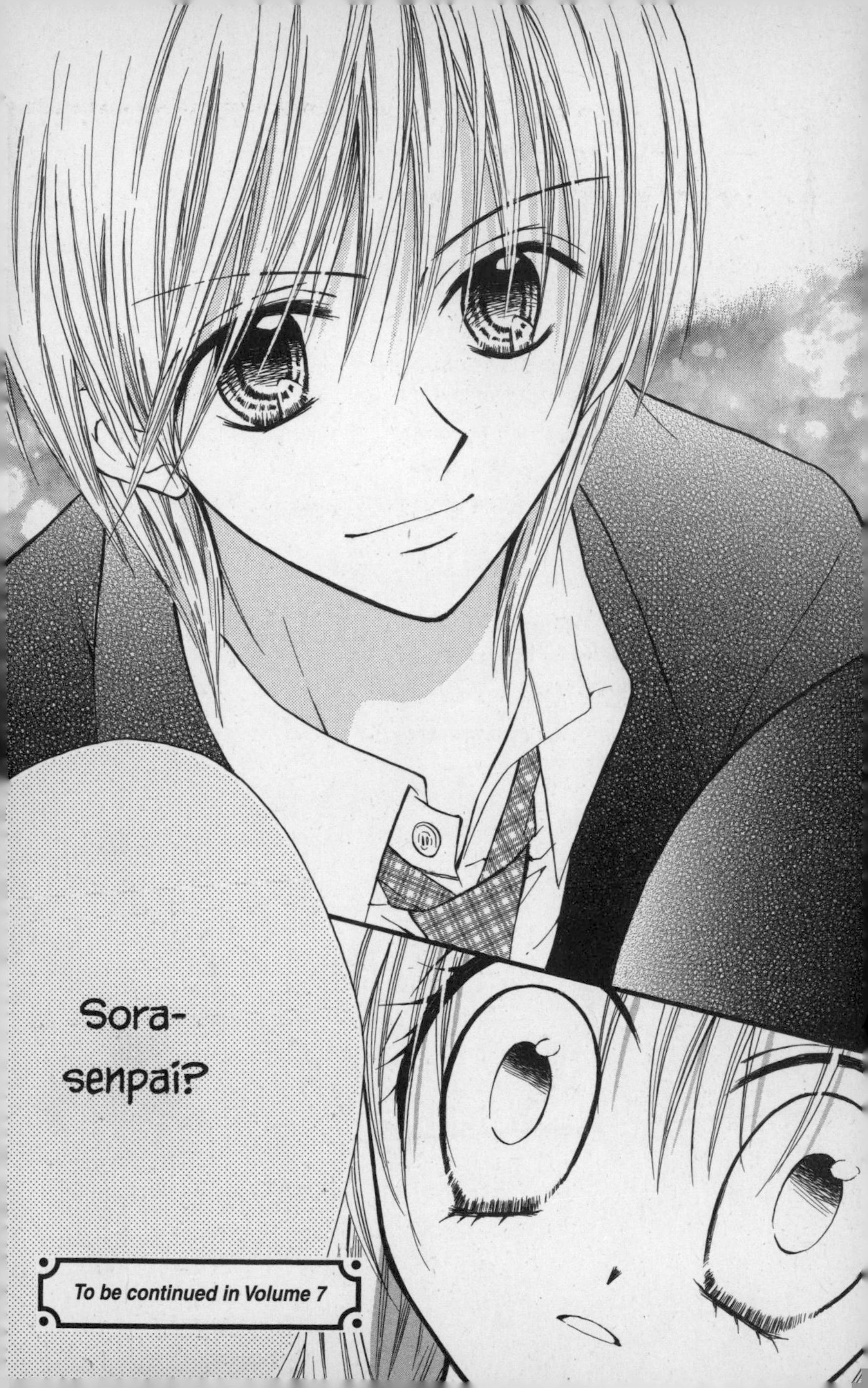
Sora-senpai?
To be continued in Volume 7

Thank you

I cried a lot with Najika in this volume.

I once saw this show on TV. They had surveyed elementary school kids and I was surprised by the results. Over 60% of the kids believed that people who die will somehow come back.

So I prayed that I could depict what it's like for someone to pass away while working on this volume.

Please look out for Najika. She went through some tough times and grew up a little.

And also, it would be great if I saw you in Volume 7!!

✿Thank you very much ★

Shobayashi-sama
Yamada-sama & Miyuki-sensei & Kishimoto-sama
Shirasawa-sama

❀ Comments and ❀
fan letters

Del Rey Manga
Natsumi Ando
1745 Broadway,
18th Floor
New York, NY 10019

Kitchen Princess

From the Writer

Hello! This is the writer and recipe person, Miyuki Kobayashi.

Thank you for always writing to me!

While I got many letters congratulating me for the Kodansha Award (Thank you! I was so happy.) I also got many letters saying, "No way Sora died!" "Make him come back!" "Stupid writer!" with tears and objections. I'm very sorry!! My apologies to the Sora fans. I can't apologize enough. Waah (crying)!

But just as I wrote in the previous volume, this was decided before the series started. But I did get attached to Sora as I progressed, and I'm very sad that I can't write about Sora anymore... That is why the following special story is about Sora! And I would like to write more about Sora, so if you have any requests, I'd like to hear them!

Finally, I want to thank Natsumi Ando-sensei, our editor Kishimoto-san, Saito-san from the editorial team, and Matsumoto, the editor in chief. Thank you very much! I will see you in Volume 7!

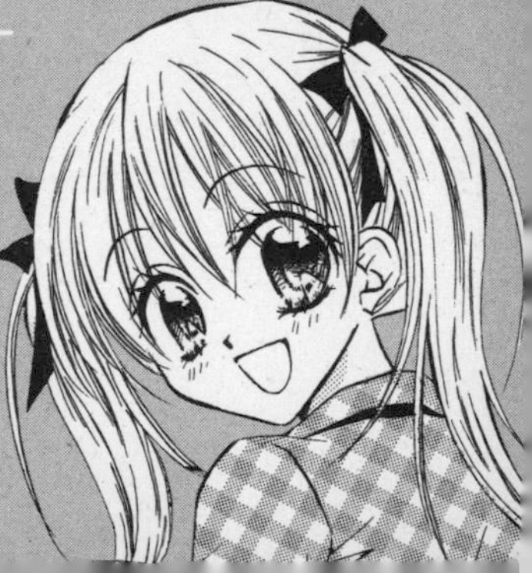

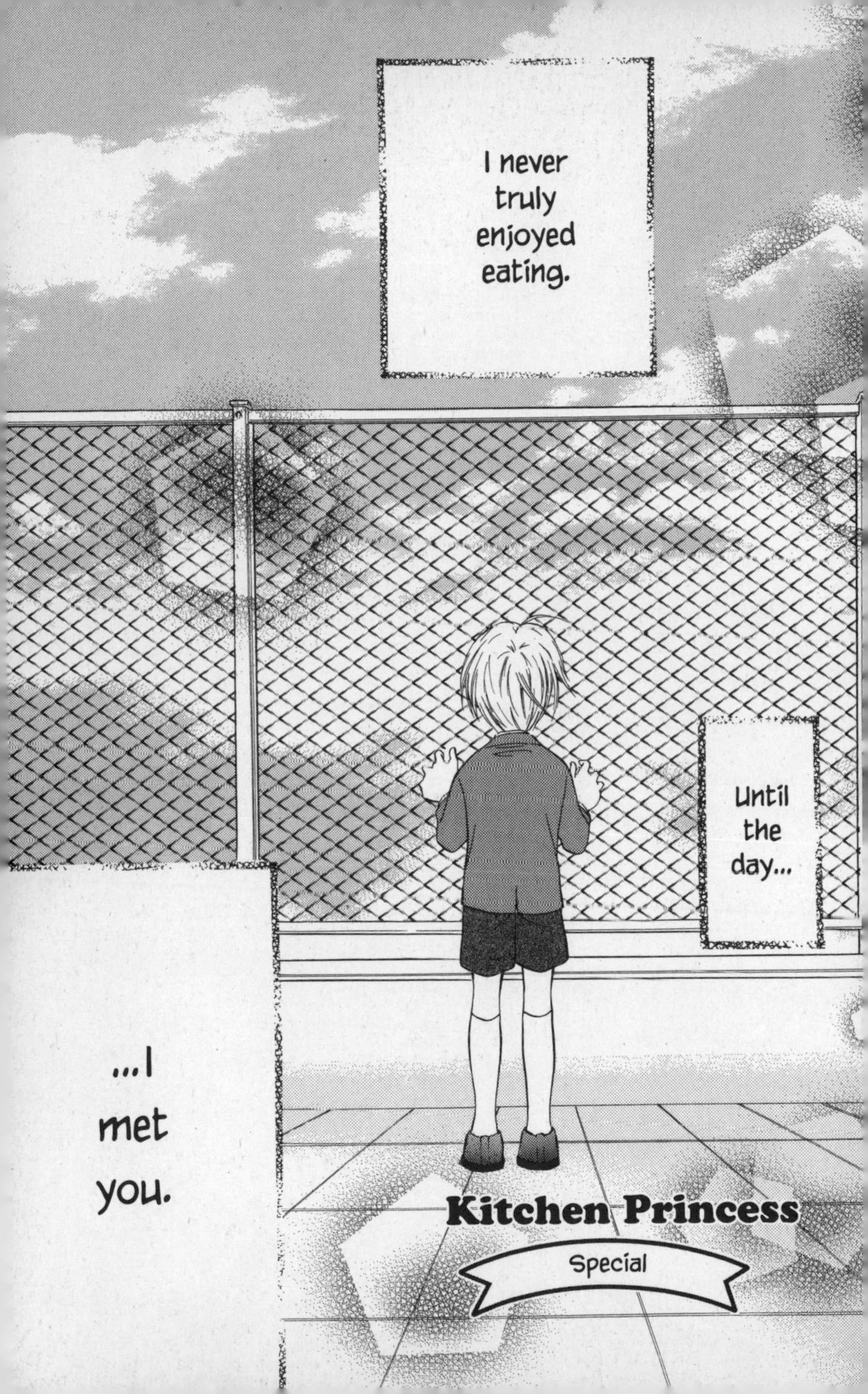
I never truly enjoyed eating.
Until the day...
...I met you.
Kitchen Princess
Special

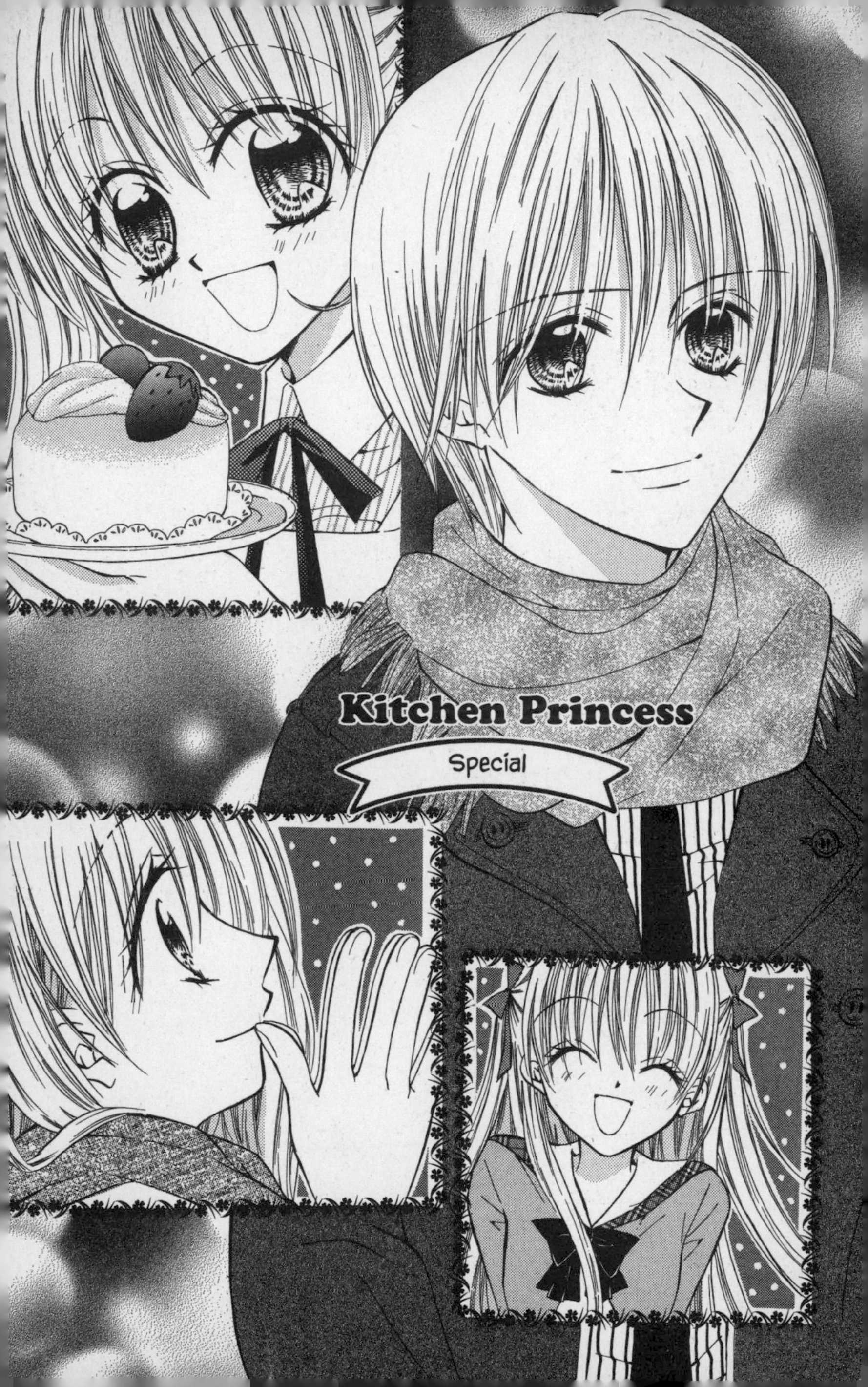
Kitchen Princess
Special

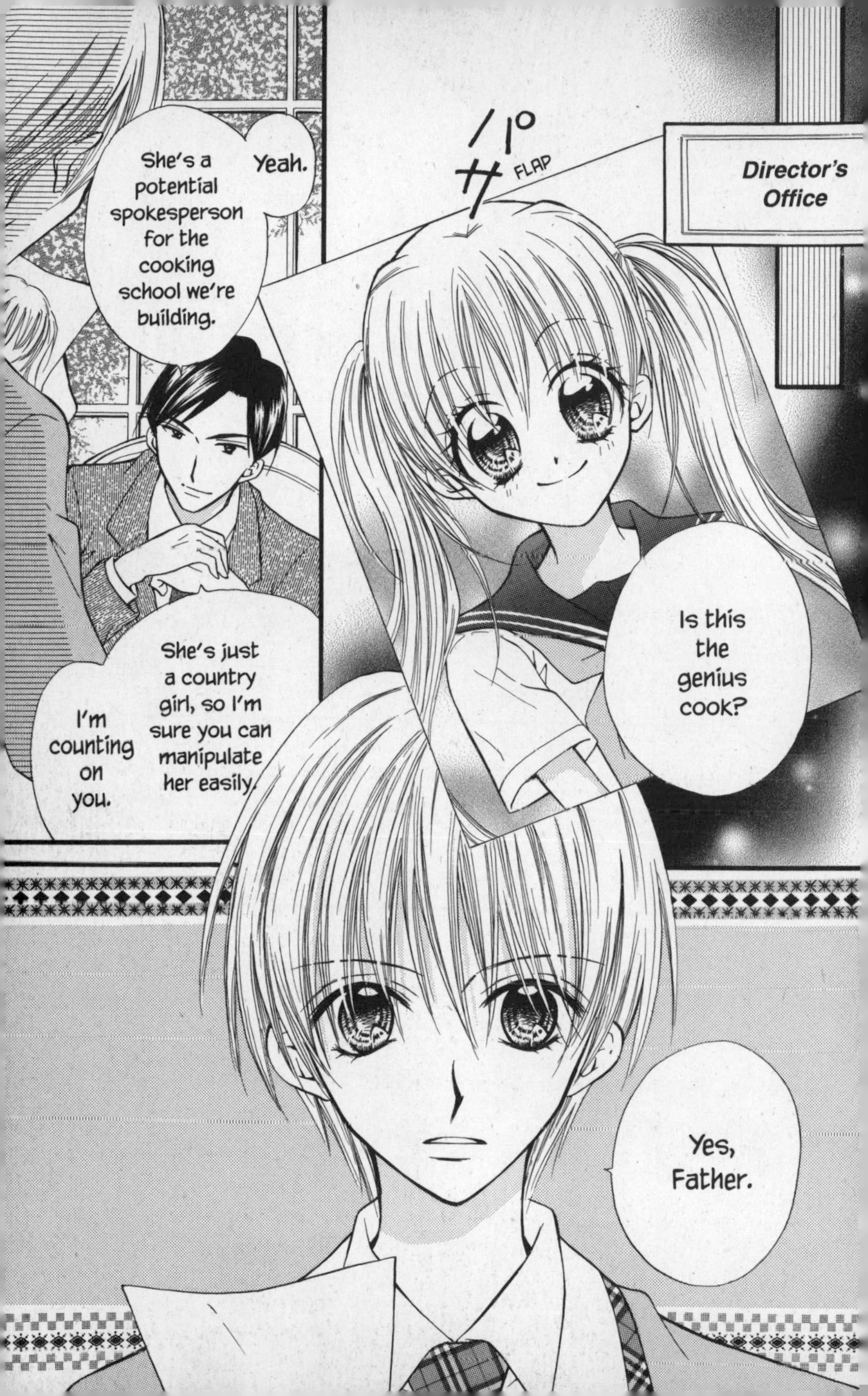
Director's Office
パサ FLAP
Is this the genius cook?
Yeah.
She's a potential spokesperson for the cooking school we're building.
She's just a country girl, so I'm sure you can manipulate her easily.
I'm counting on you.
Yes, Father.

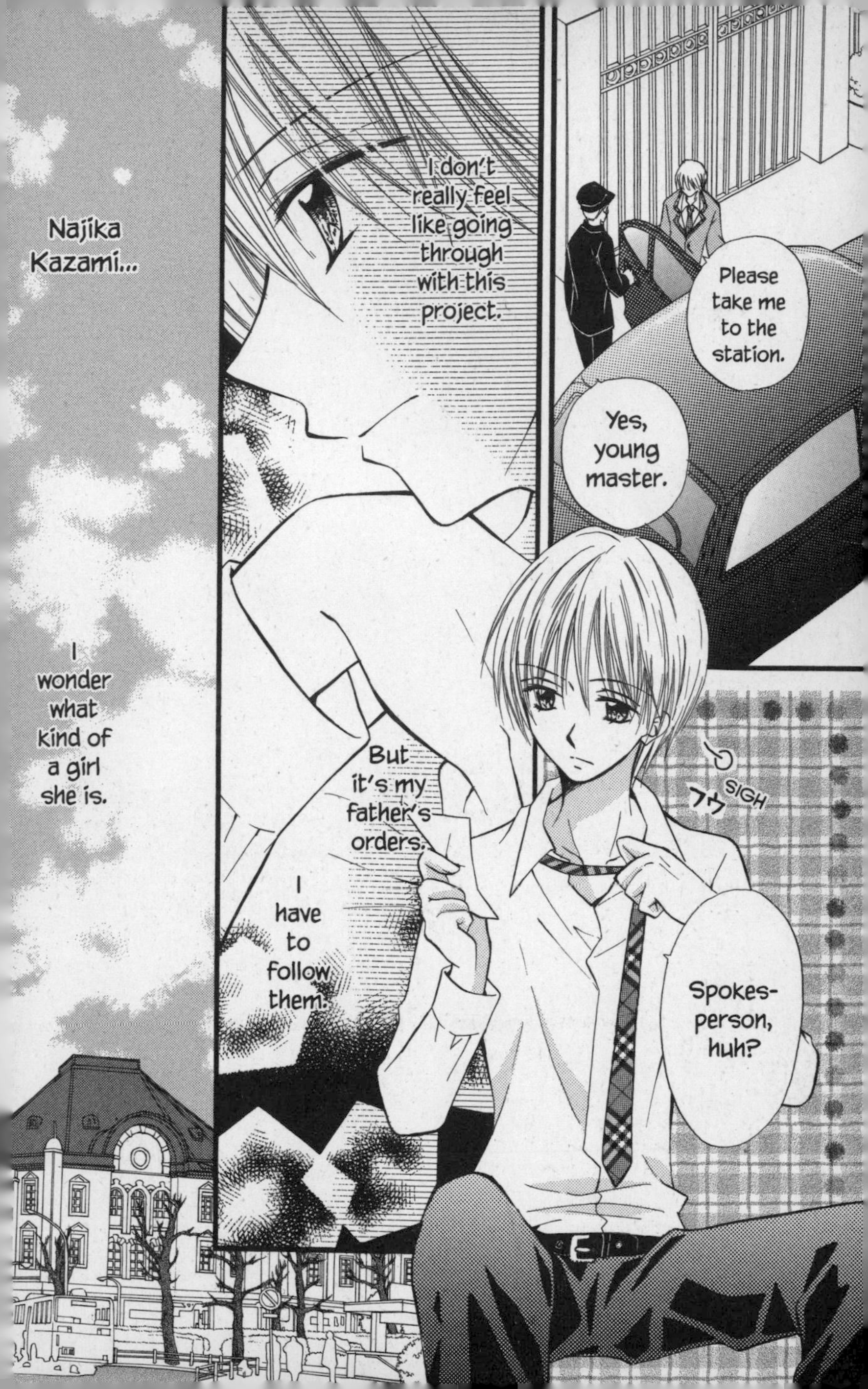
Please take me to the station.
Yes, young master.
フウ SIGH
Spokes-person, huh?
I don't really feel like going through with this project.
But it's my father's orders.
I have to follow them.
Najika Kazami...
I wonder what kind of a girl she is.

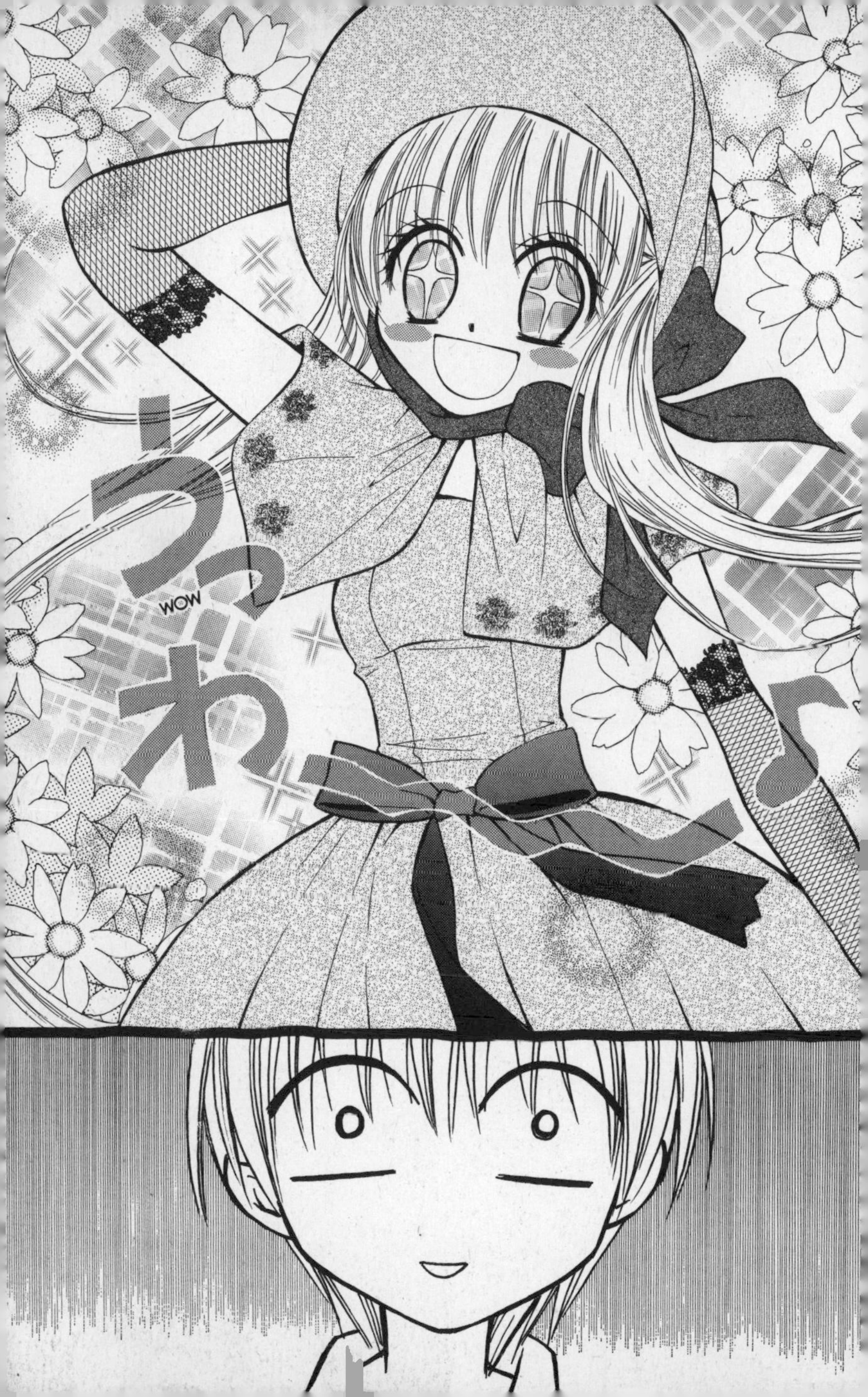
うわ〜♪
WOW

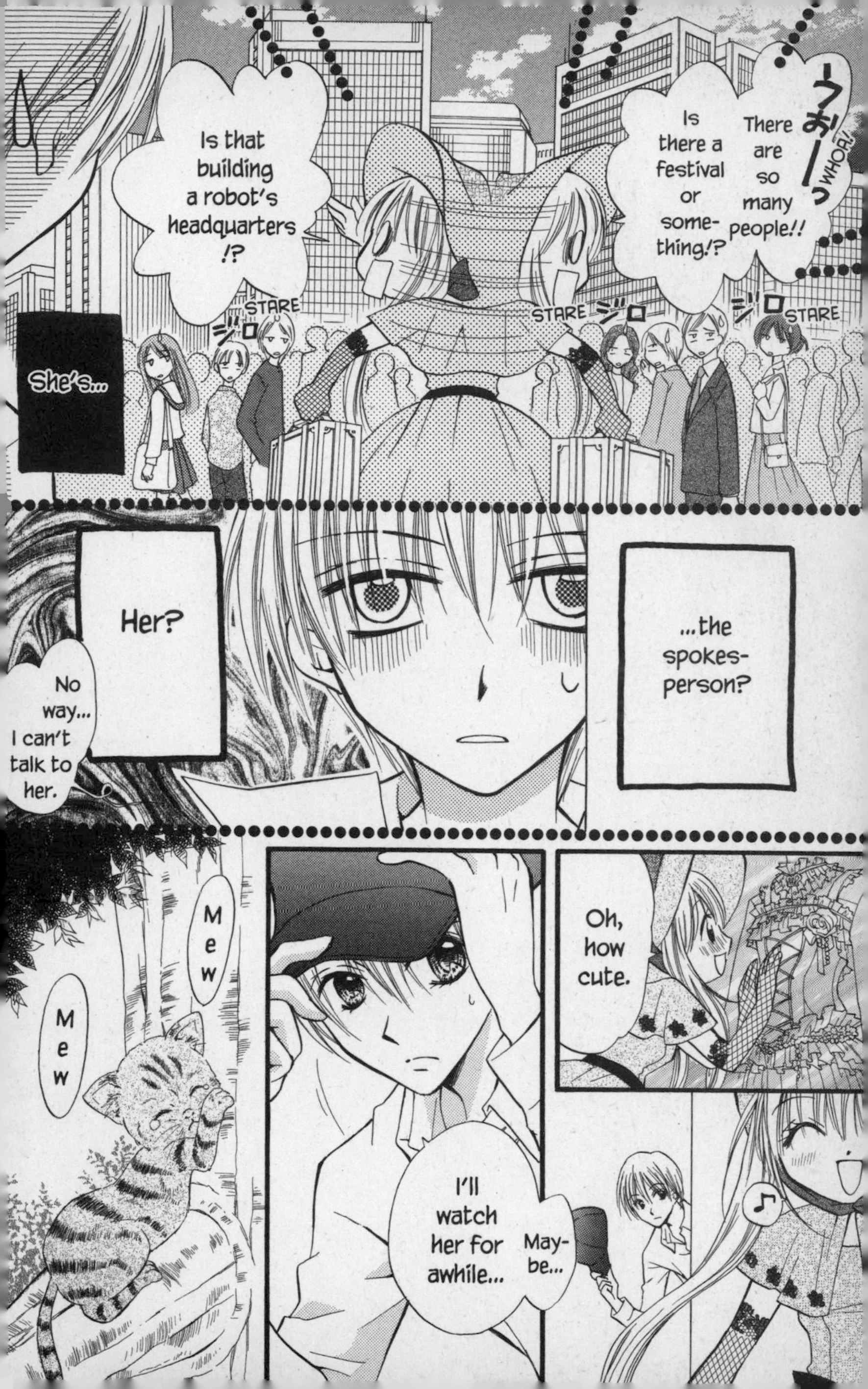
うおーっ WHOA!
There are so many people!!
Is there a festival or something!?
Is that building a robot's headquarters!?
ジロ STARE
STARE ジロ
ジロ STARE
She's...
...the spokes-person?
Her?
No way... I can't talk to her.
Oh, how cute.
♪
I'll watch her for awhile...
May-be...
Mew
Mew

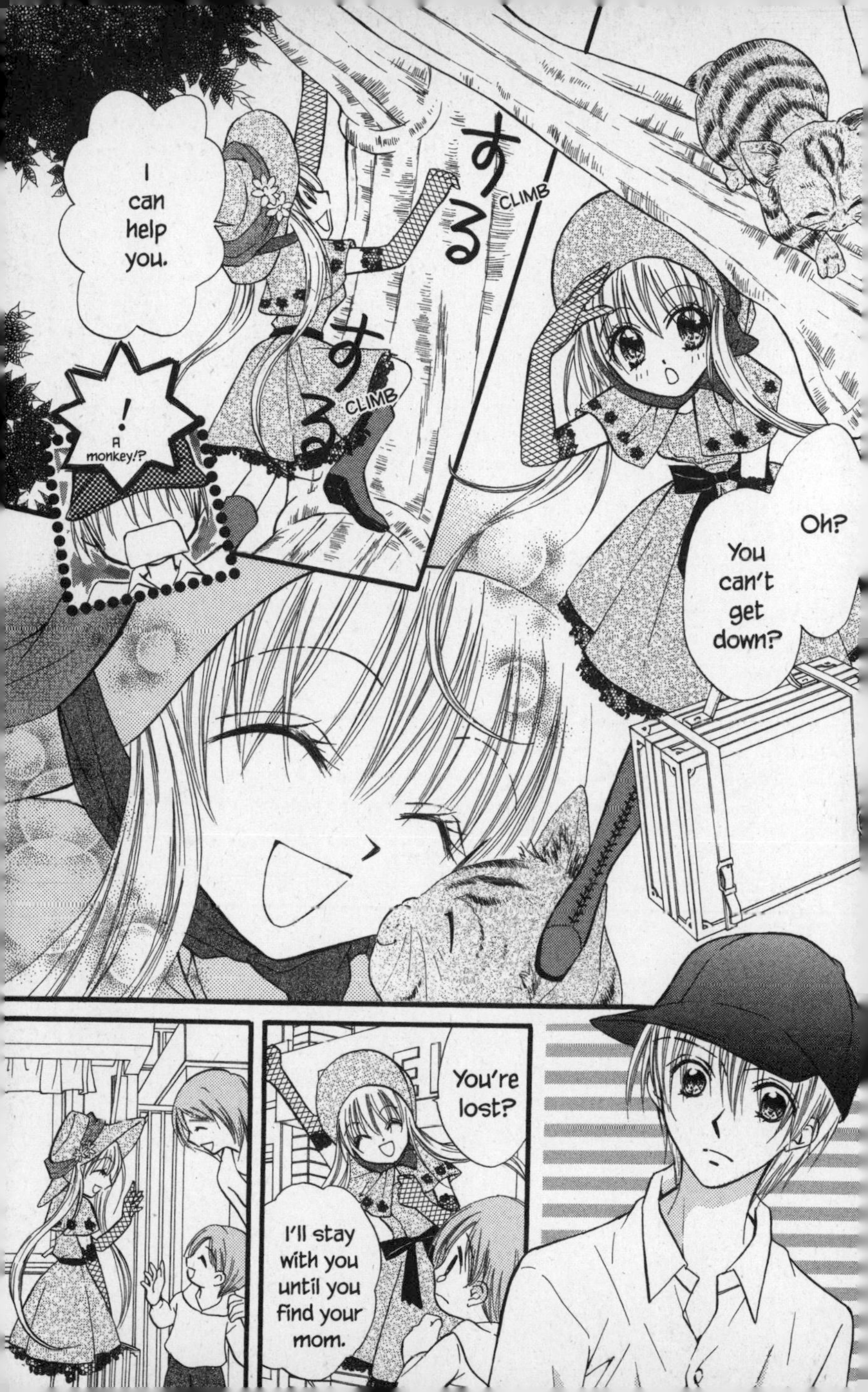
Oh? You can't get down?
するする
CLIMB
CLIMB
I can help you.
! A monkey!?
You're lost?
I'll stay with you until you find your mom.

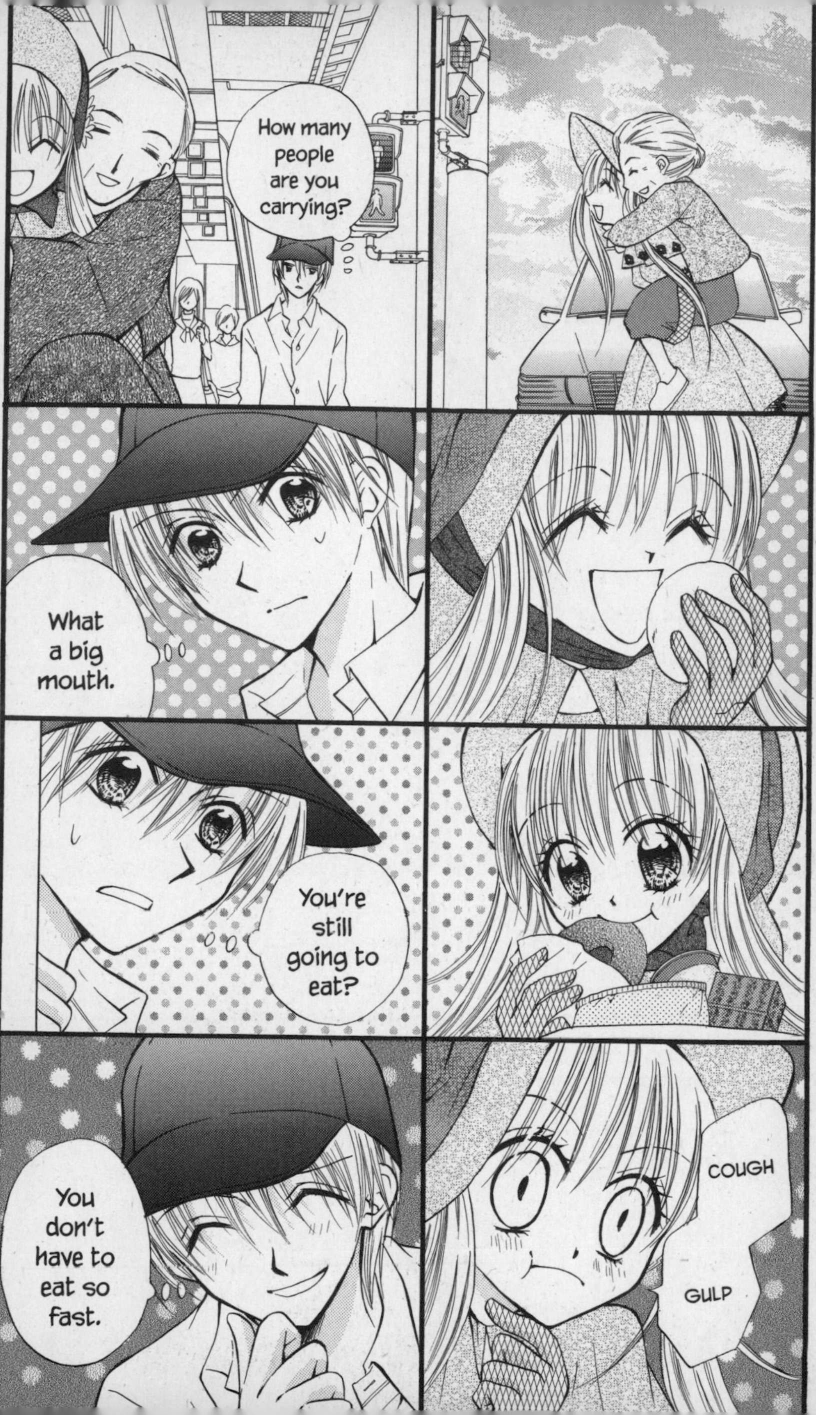
How many people are you carrying?
What a big mouth.
You're still going to eat?
COUGH
GULP
You don't have to eat so fast.

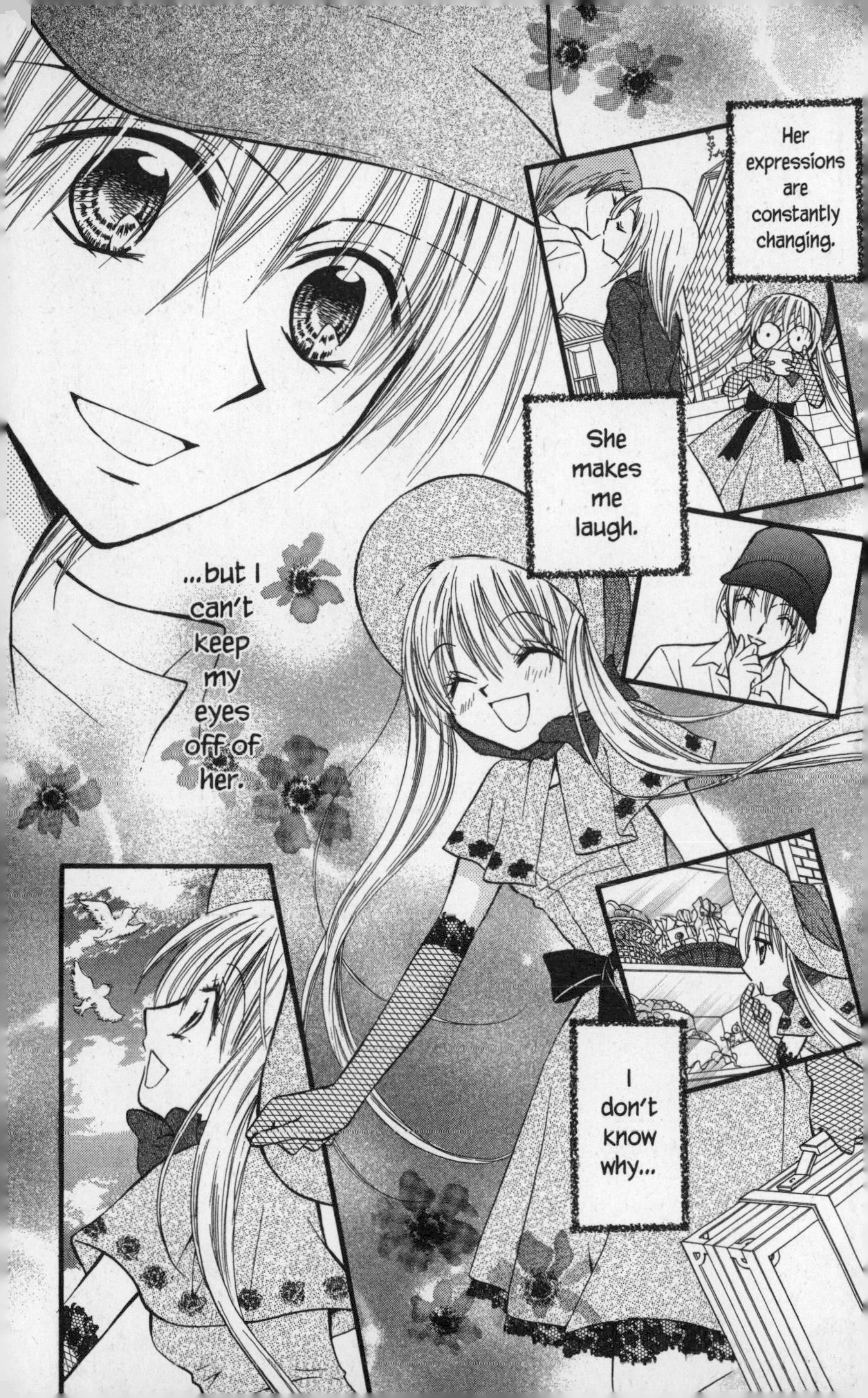
Her expressions are constantly changing.
She makes me laugh.
...but I can't keep my eyes off of her.
I don't know why...

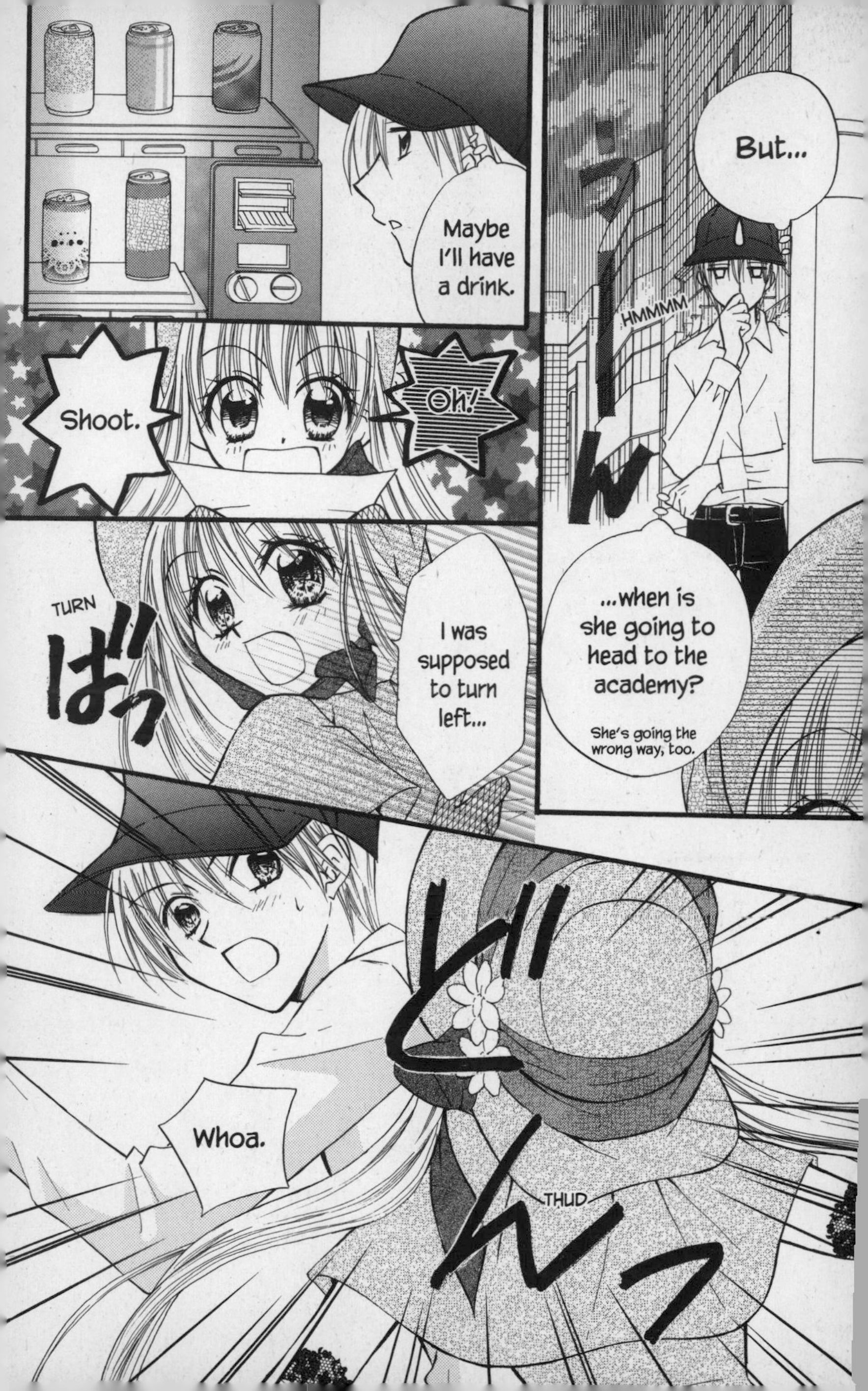
But...
HMMMM
...when is she going to head to the academy?
She's going the wrong way, too.
Maybe I'll have a drink.
Oh!
Shoot.
TURN
ばっ
I was supposed to turn left...
Whoa.
THUD

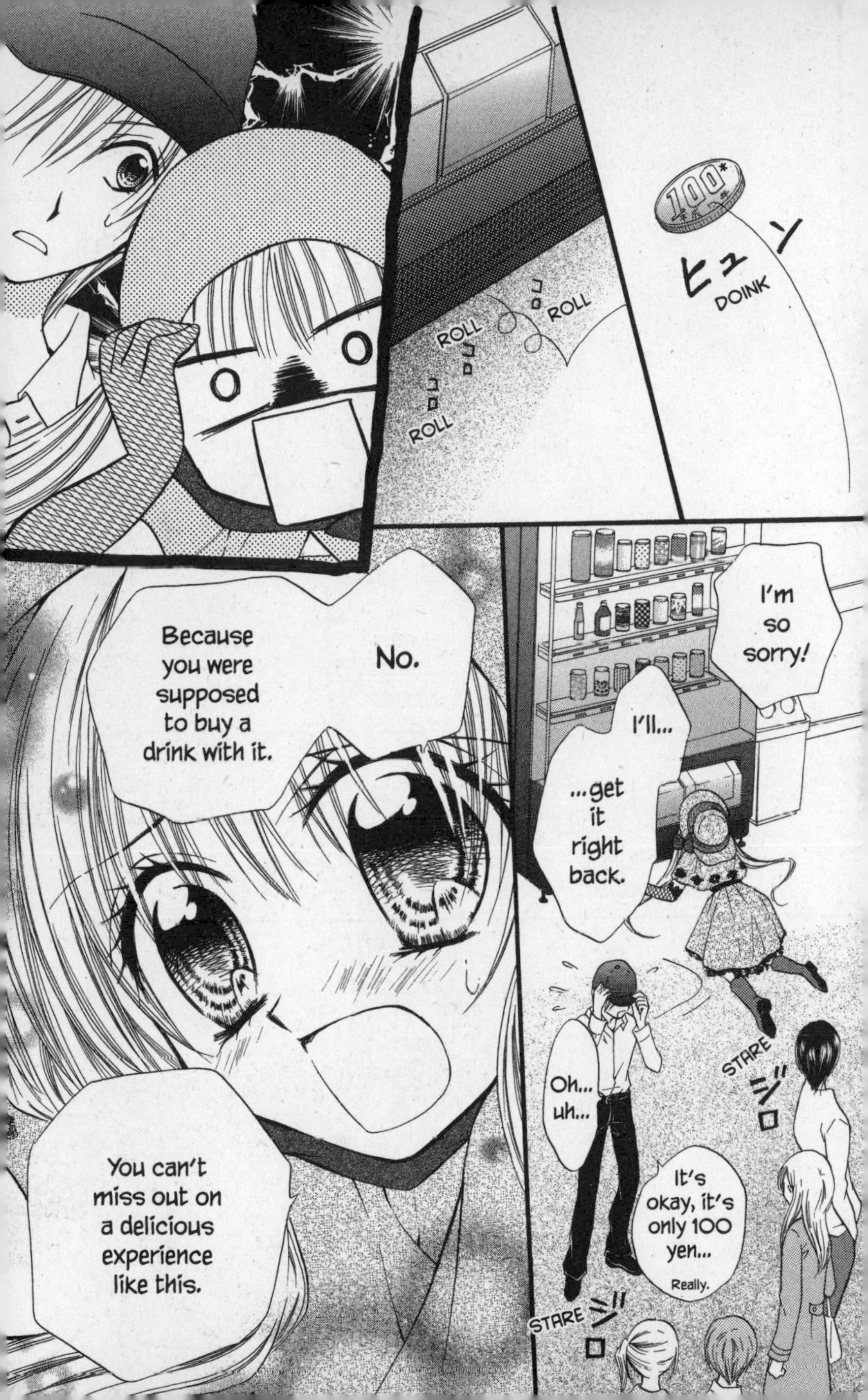
100*
ヒュン
DOINK
コロ ROLL
コロ ROLL
コロ ROLL
I'm so sorry!
I'll...
...get it right back.
Oh... uh...
STARE ジロ
It's okay, it's only 100 yen...
Really.
STARE ジロ
No.
Because you were supposed to buy a drink with it.
You can't miss out on a delicious experience like this.

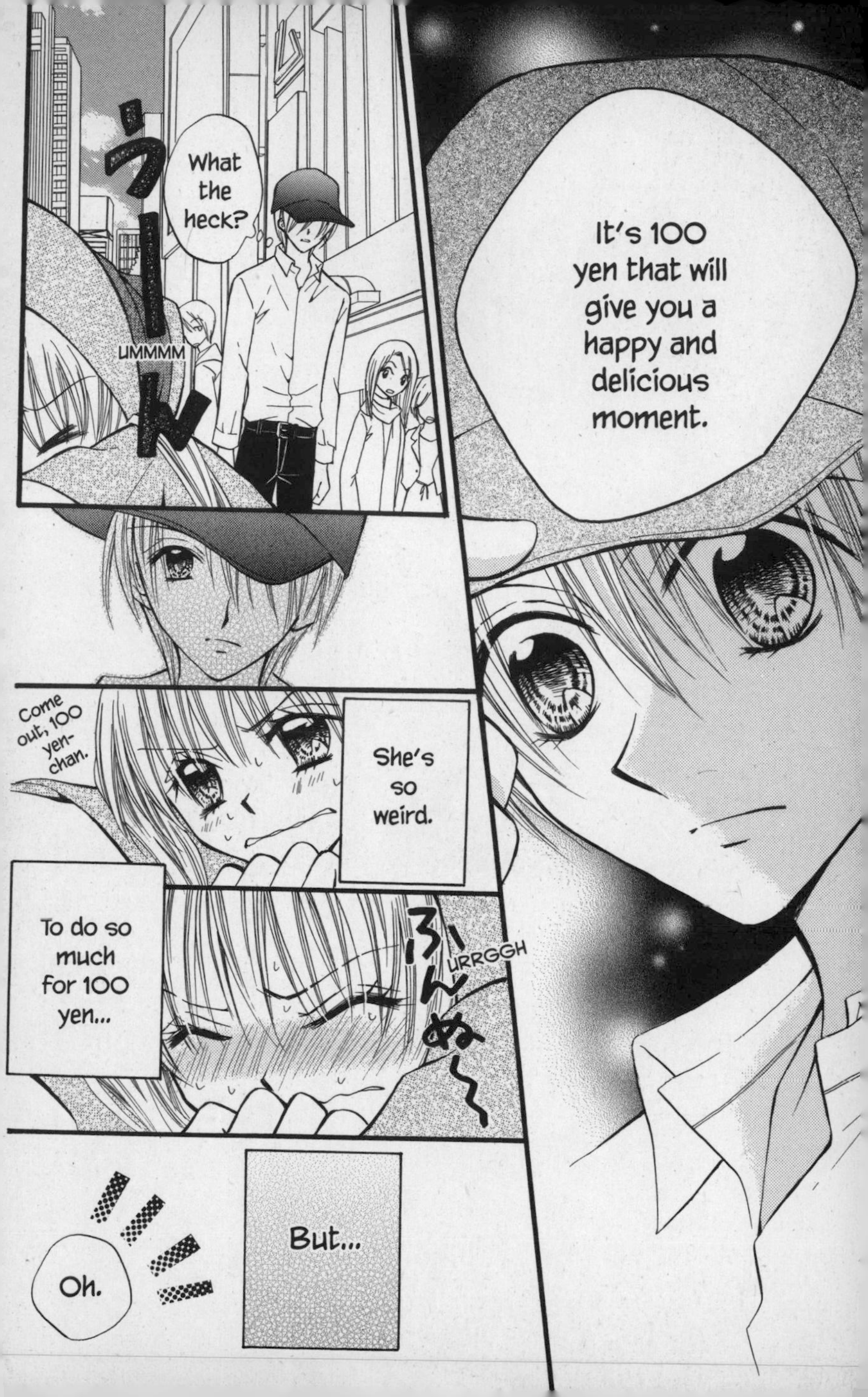

It's 100 yen that will give you a happy and delicious moment.
What the heck?
うーーん
UMMMM
She's so weird.
Come out, 100 yen-chan.
ふんぬ〜〜
URRGGH
To do so much for 100 yen...
But...
Oh.

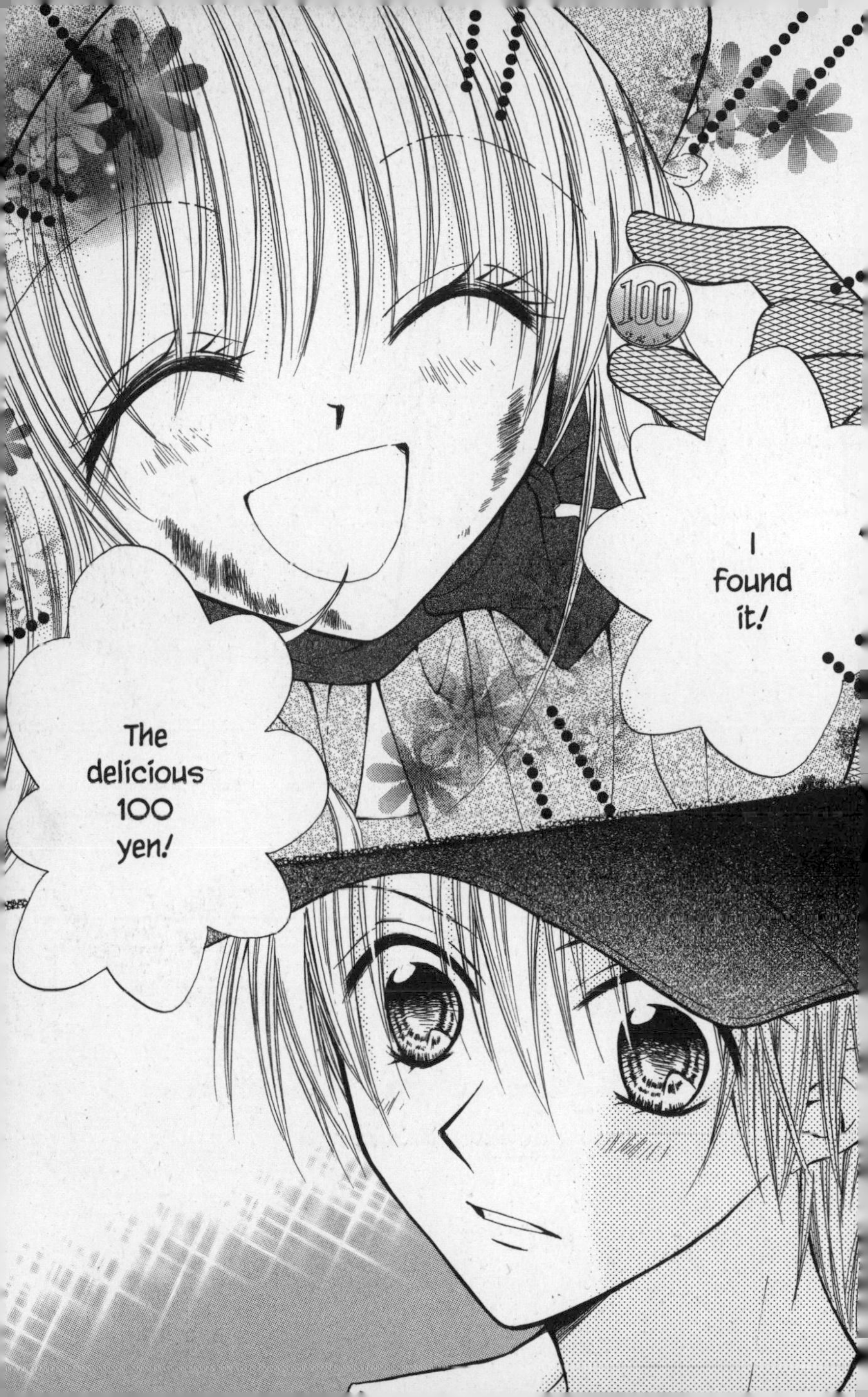
I found it!
The delicious 100 yen!

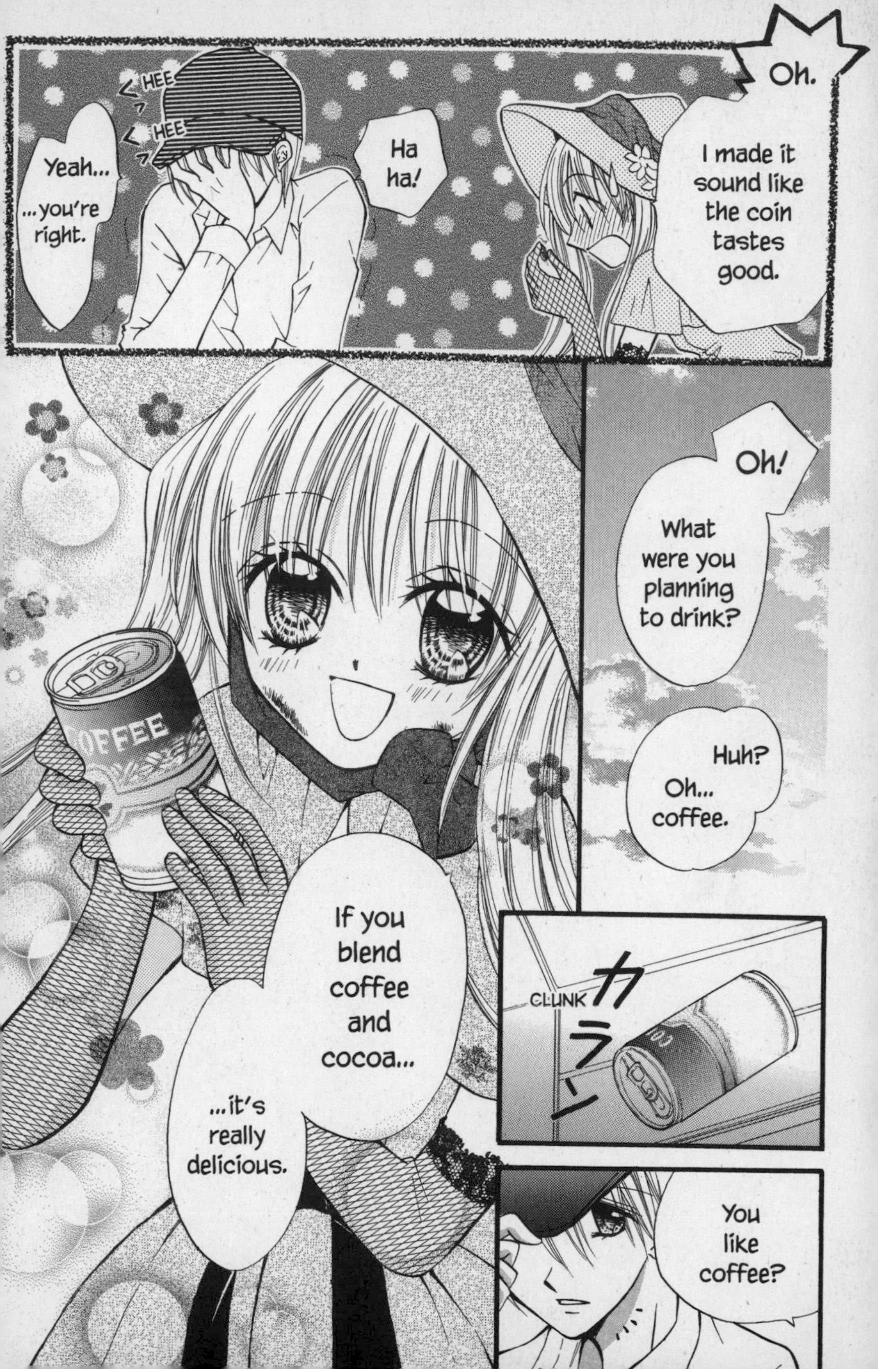

Oh.
I made it sound like the coin tastes good.
Ha ha!
HEE HEE
Yeah... ...you're right.
Oh!
What were you planning to drink?
Huh? Oh... coffee.
CLUNK
カラーン
You like coffee?
COFFEE
If you blend coffee and cocoa...
...it's really delicious.

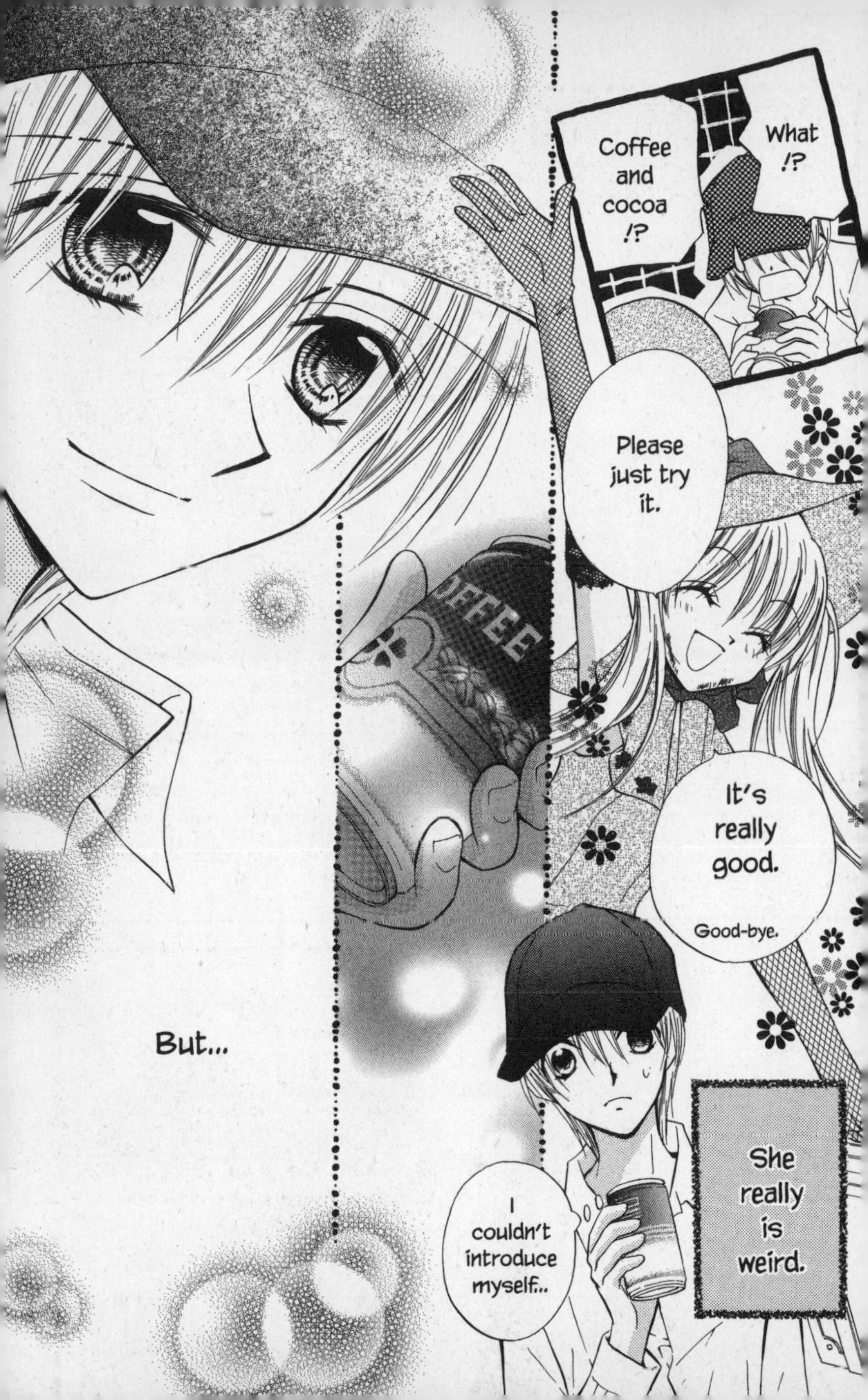

What !?
Coffee and cocoa !?
Please just try it.
It's really good.
Good-bye.
She really is weird.
I couldn't introduce myself...
But...

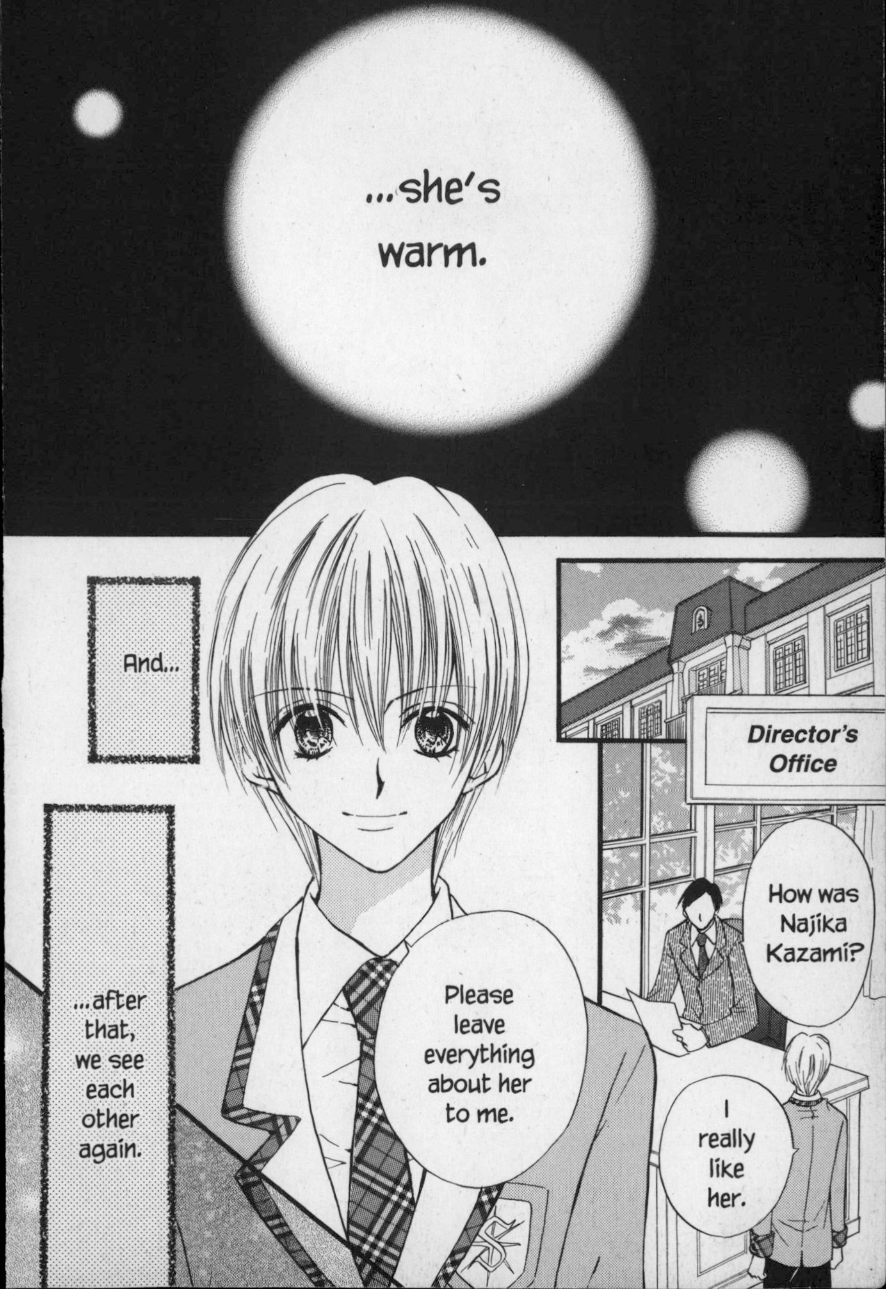
...she's warm.
Director's Office
How was Najika Kazami?
I really like her.
Please leave everything about her to me.
And...
...after that, we see each other again.

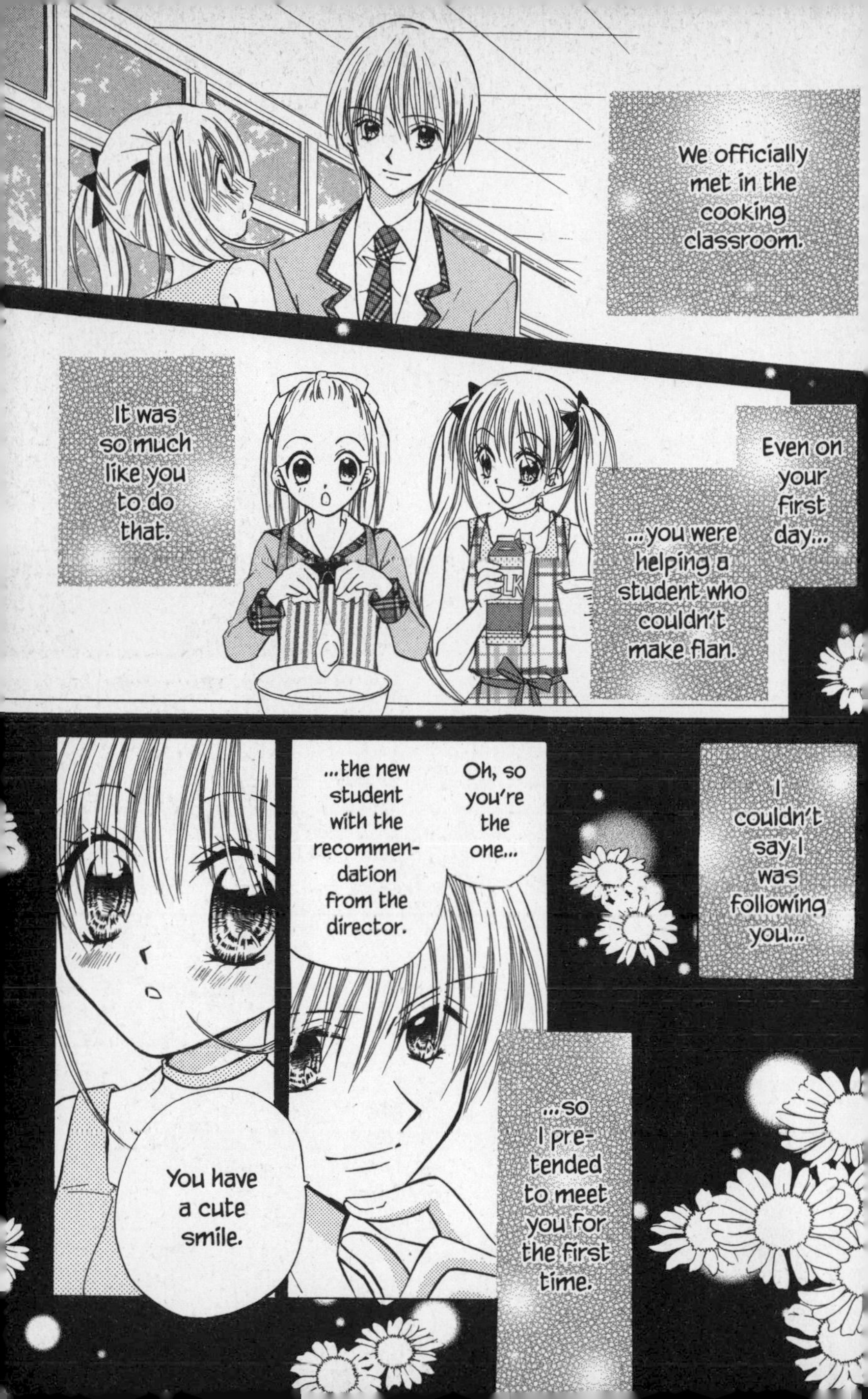
We officially met in the cooking classroom.
Even on your first day...
...you were helping a student who couldn't make flan.
It was so much like you to do that.
I couldn't say I was following you...
Oh, so you're the one...
...the new student with the recommendation from the director.
...so I pretended to meet you for the first time.
You have a cute smile.

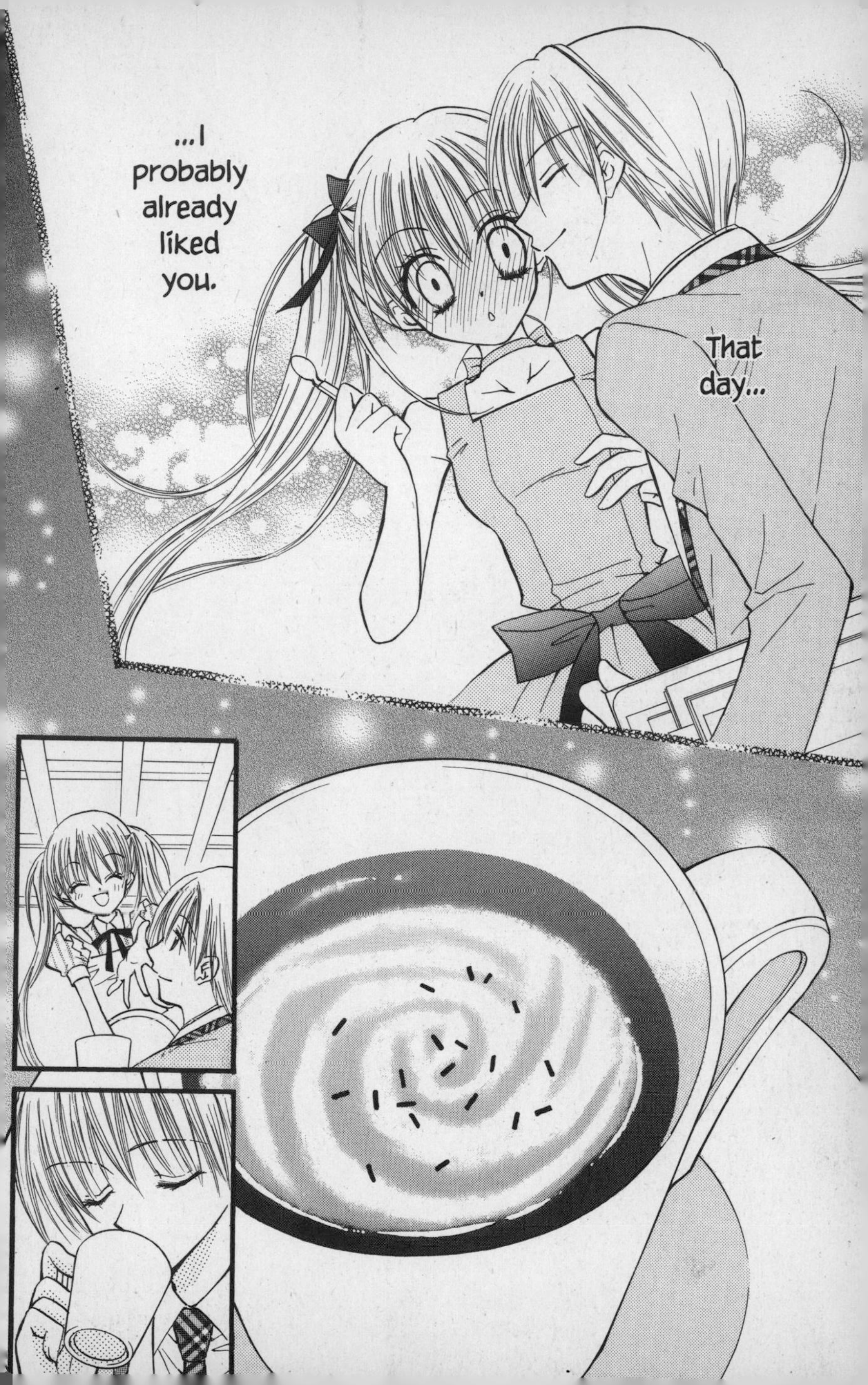
That day...
...I probably already liked you.

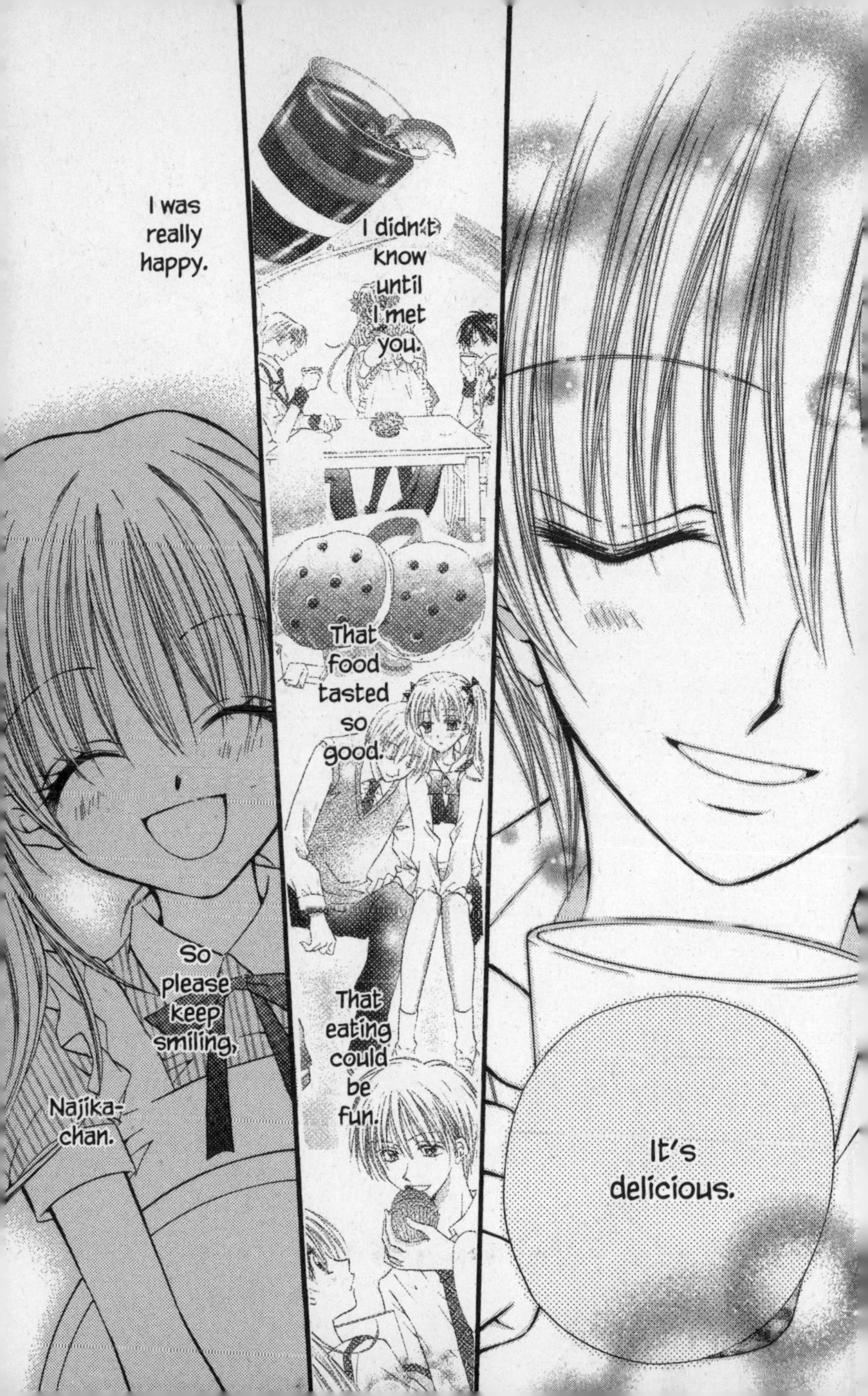
It's delicious.
I didn't know until I met you.
That food tasted so good.
That eating could be fun.
I was really happy.
So please keep smiling,
Najika-chan.

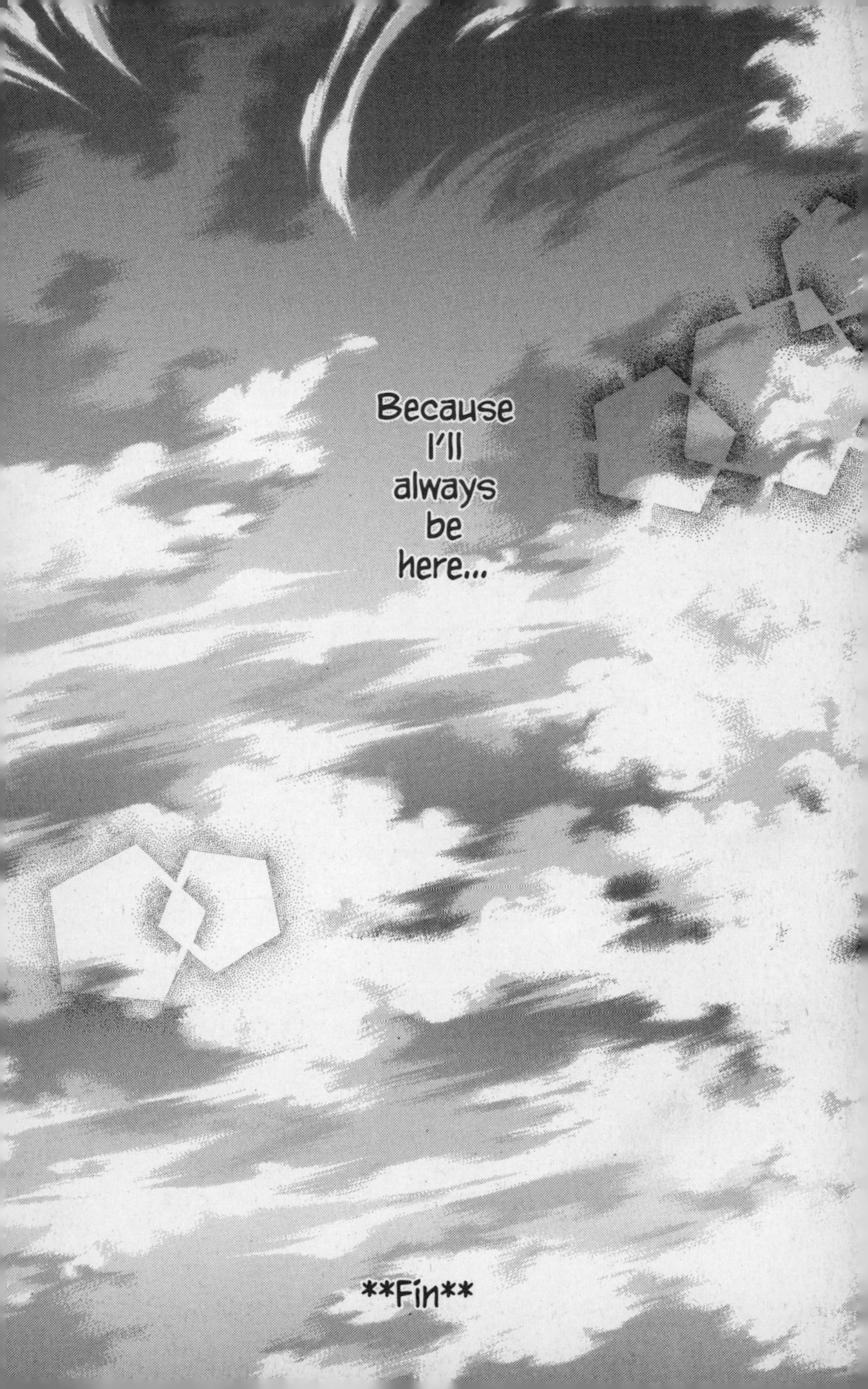
Because I'll always be here...
Fin

[redacted]

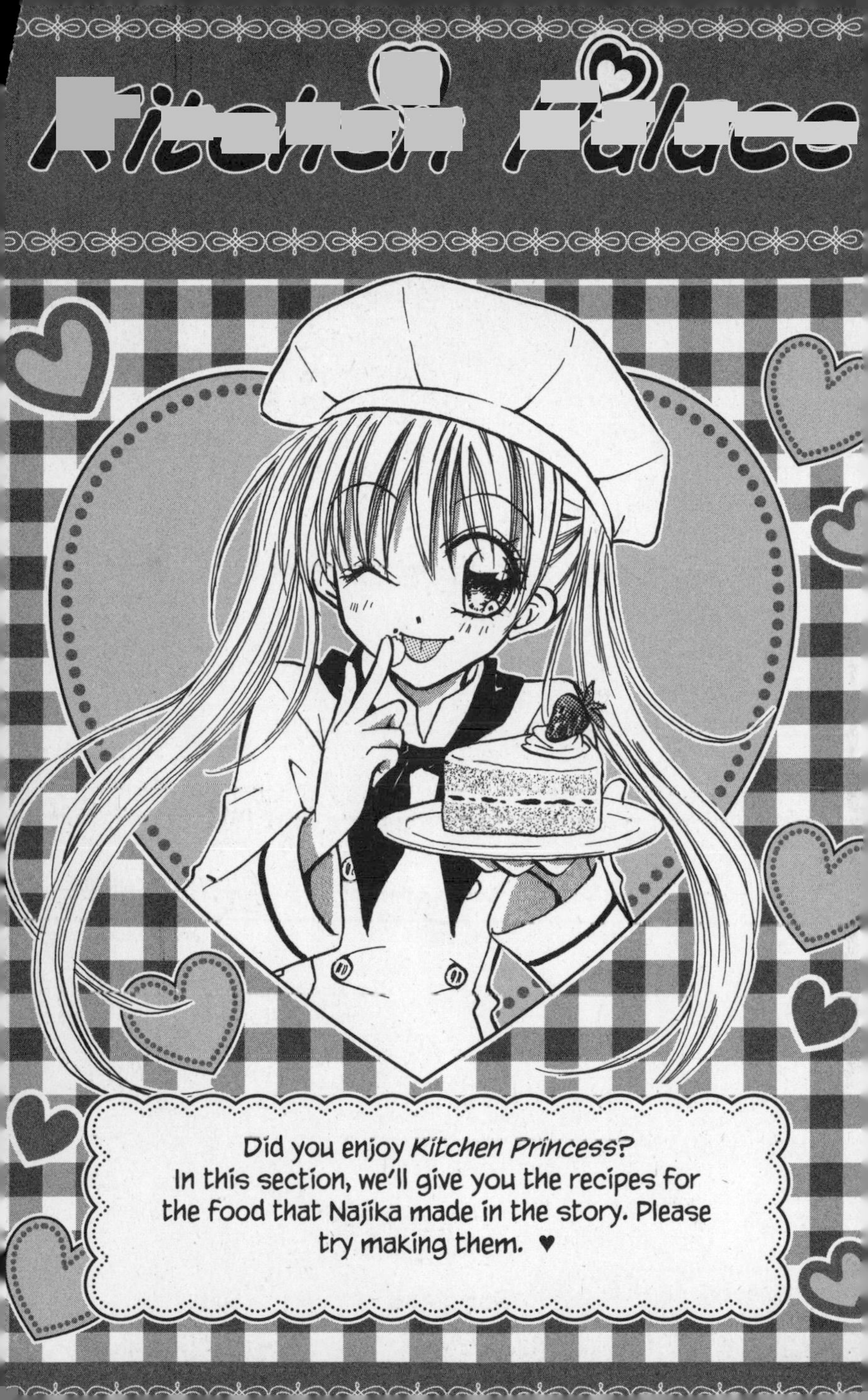

Did you enjoy *Kitchen Princess*?
In this section, we'll give you the recipes for the food that Najika made in the story. Please try making them. ♥

Tomato Bruschetta

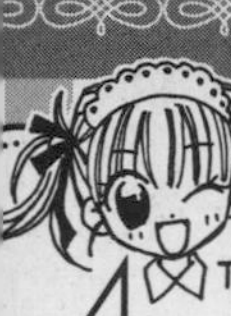

Tip from Najika.

Bruschetta means "to scorch and toast" in Italian. It's a light appetizer popular in Italy!

Tomato Bruschetta

1 tomato, 2 teaspoons of olive oil (extra virgin will smell better), salt and pepper to taste, 5 or 6 slices of French bread (it can be thinly sliced white sandwich bread, too), 1 clove of garlic, and basil (optional)

How to Make

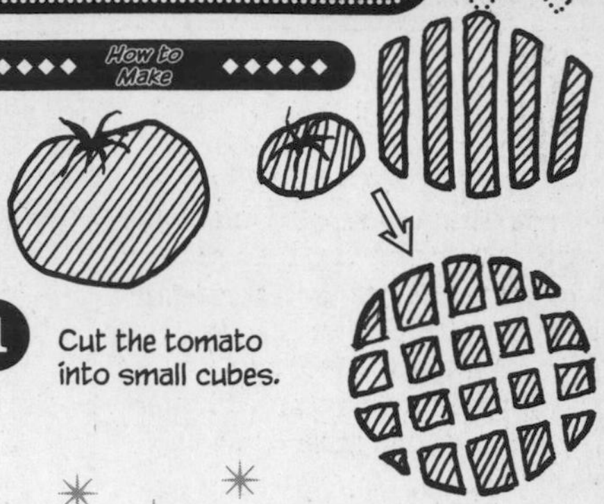

1 Cut the tomato into small cubes.

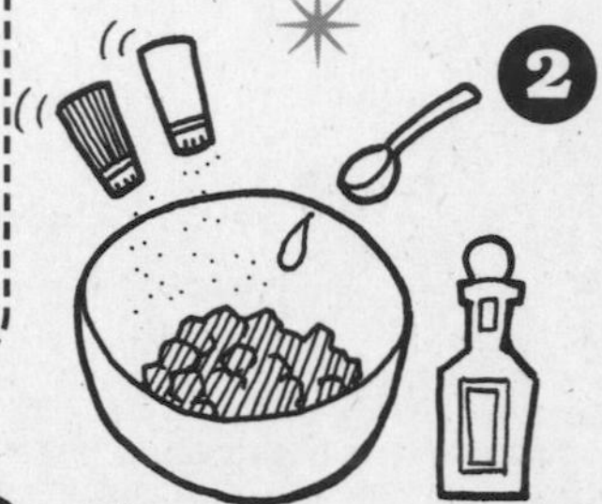

2 Put the tomato pieces, olive oil, salt, and pepper in a bowl and mix well. Let it sit for a bit so the taste will sink in.

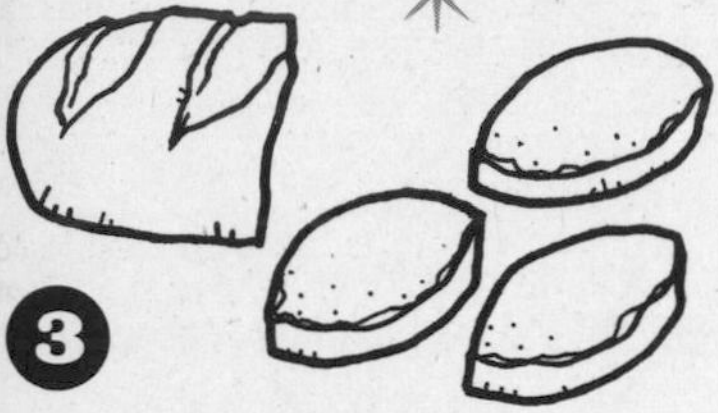

3 Slice the bread thinly and toast the slices until golden brown.

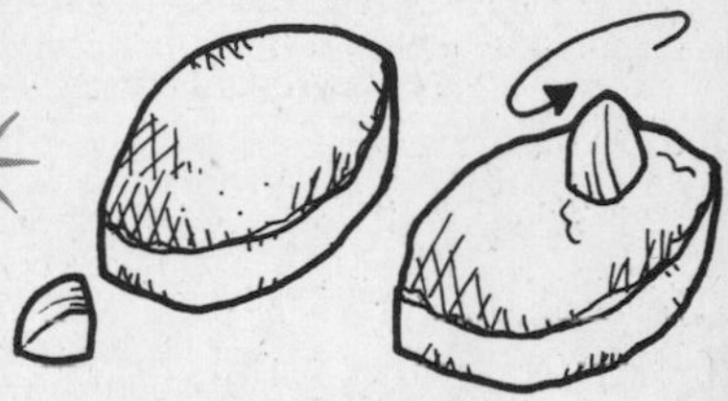

4 Cut the garlic in half and rub the cut side all over the bread.

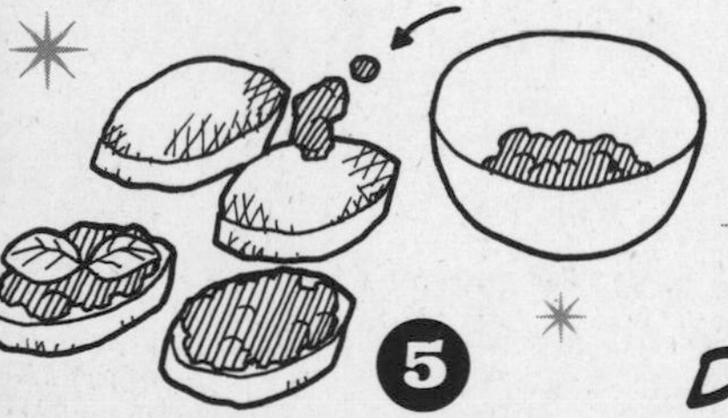

5 Place a spoonful of the mixture from step 2 onto the bread from step 4 and serve. Top it with chopped basil if you like.

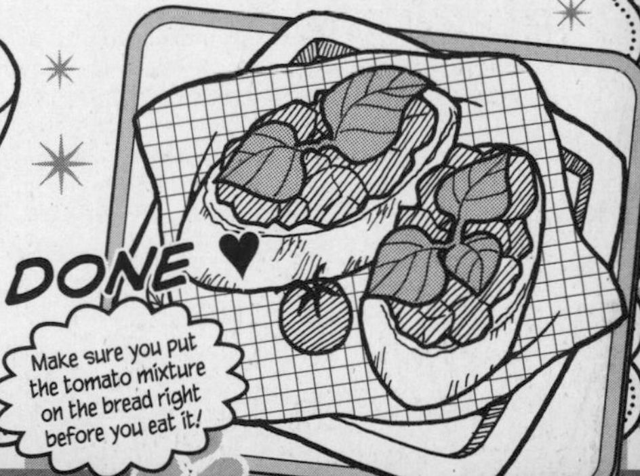
DONE ♥
Make sure you put the tomato mixture on the bread right before you eat it!

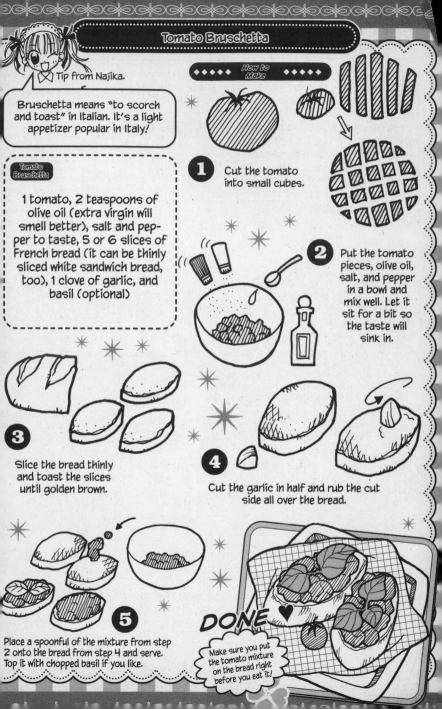

Flan Cake

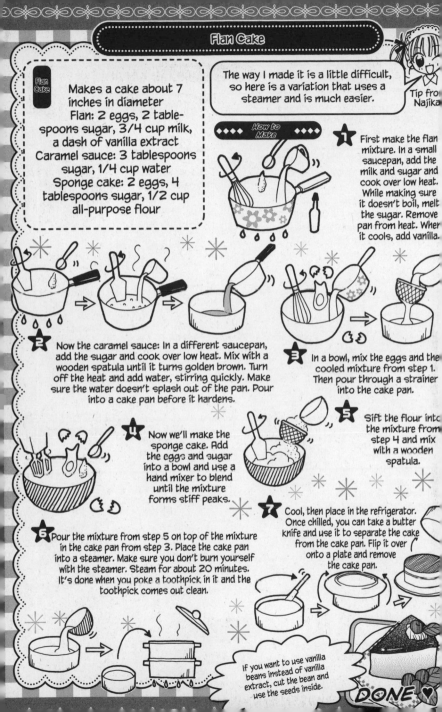

Makes a cake about 7 inches in diameter
Flan: 2 eggs, 2 tablespoons sugar, 3/4 cup milk, a dash of vanilla extract
Caramel sauce: 3 tablespoons sugar, 1/4 cup water
Sponge cake: 2 eggs, 4 tablespoons sugar, 1/2 cup all-purpose flour

The way I made it is a little difficult, so here is a variation that uses a steamer and is much easier.

Tip from Najika

How to Make

1 First make the flan mixture. In a small saucepan, add the milk and sugar and cook over low heat. While making sure it doesn't boil, melt the sugar. Remove pan from heat. When it cools, add vanilla.

2 Now the caramel sauce: In a different saucepan, add the sugar and cook over low heat. Mix with a wooden spatula until it turns golden brown. Turn off the heat and add water, stirring quickly. Make sure the water doesn't splash out of the pan. Pour into a cake pan before it hardens.

3 In a bowl, mix the eggs and the cooled mixture from step 1. Then pour through a strainer into the cake pan.

4 Now we'll make the sponge cake. Add the eggs and sugar into a bowl and use a hand mixer to blend until the mixture forms stiff peaks.

5 Sift the flour into the mixture from step 4 and mix with a wooden spatula.

6 Pour the mixture from step 5 on top of the mixture in the cake pan from step 3. Place the cake pan into a steamer. Make sure you don't burn yourself with the steamer. Steam for about 20 minutes. It's done when you poke a toothpick in it and the toothpick comes out clean.

7 Cool, then place in the refrigerator. Once chilled, you can take a butter knife and use it to separate the cake from the cake pan. Flip it over onto a plate and remove the cake pan.

If you want to use vanilla beans instead of vanilla extract, cut the bean and use the seeds inside.

DONE♡

Curry Roll

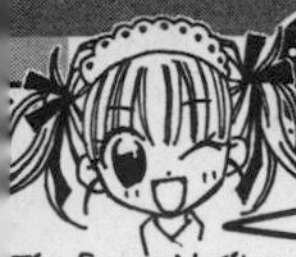

Tip from Najika.

This is like an Indian-style sushi roll ♥ But use plain white rice instead of sushi rice (rice with vinegar in it).

Curry Roll Makes about 2 rolls

Dry curry: onion, 1/4 cup of mixed vegetables, 1/4 lb. minced beef, 1 tablespoon vegetable oil, 1 tablespoon curry powder, 1 tablespoon ketchup, salt and pepper to taste

Roll: 4 cups of rice, 2 sheets of seaweed squares (called sushi nori)

How to Make

1. Cut the onion into small pieces. Heat up a frying pan and add vegetable oil. Stir-fry the onion over medium heat. Mixed vegetables should be thawed to room temperature.

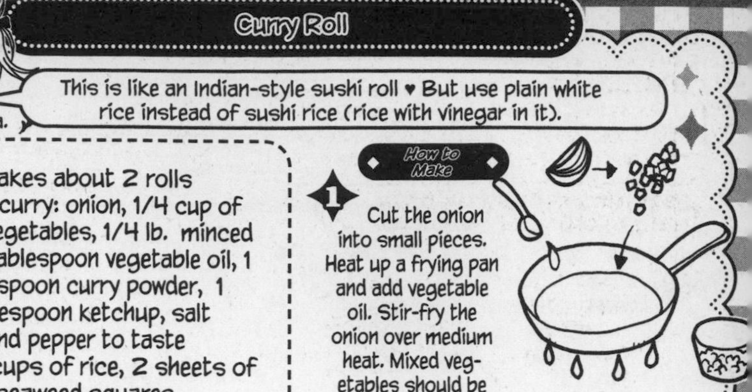

2. Add the minced beef and the mixed vegetables into the onions from step 1 and stir-fry.

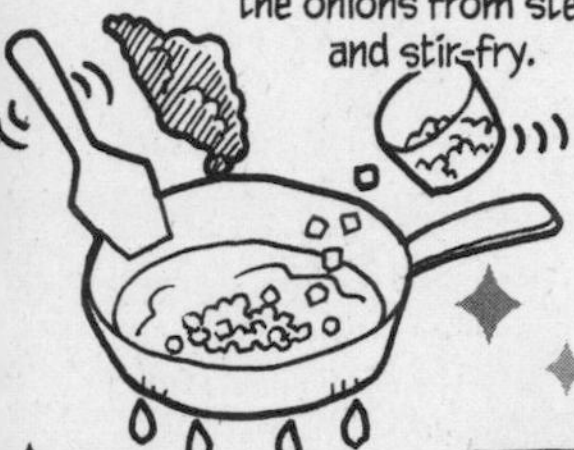

3. When the minced meat is well done and separated, add curry powder, ketchup, salt, and pepper. Remove from heat and cool.

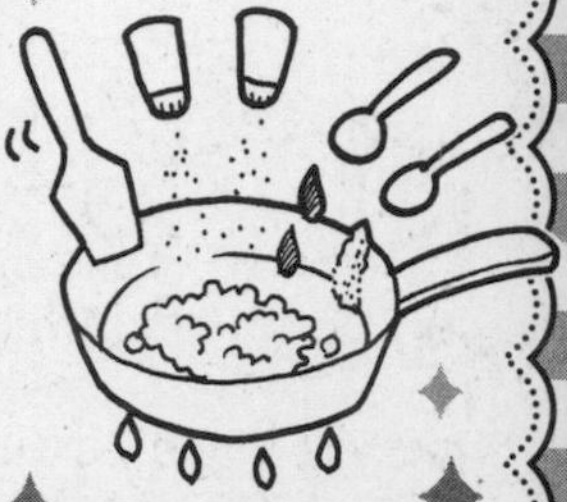

4. Place the seaweed sheet on a bamboo sushi-roll mat. Leave about 1 inch at the top open and place 2 small bowls worth of rice on the seaweed sheet.

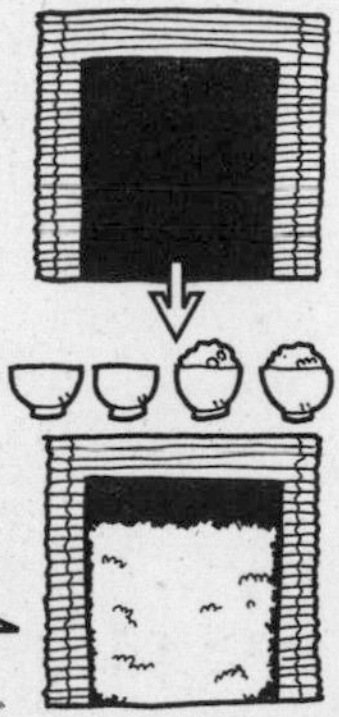

Make sure the shiny side of the seaweed sheet is facing down!

5. In the middle of the rice, place half of the mixture from step 3 and roll it into a sushi roll! Make another one just like it.

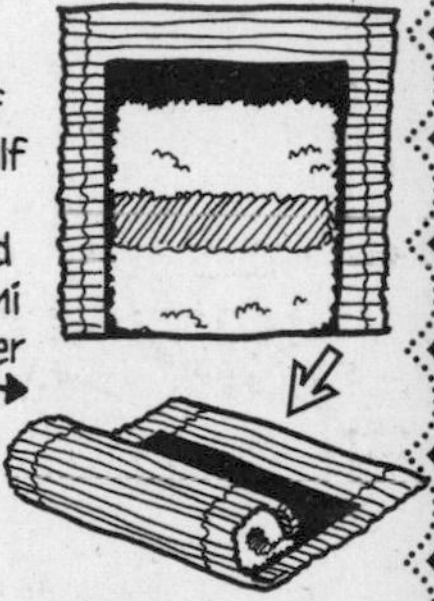

6. Use a knife to cut the roll into 5 or 6 equal-size pieces. If you wipe the knife with a wet towel after each cut, the slices will come out clean.

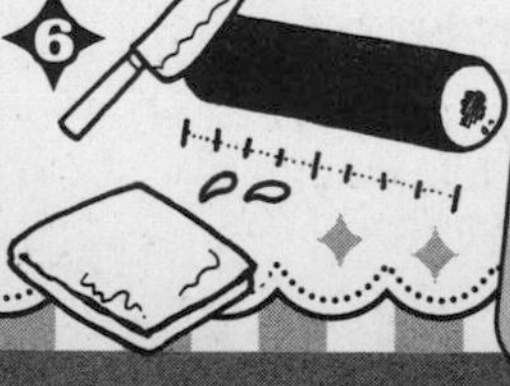

DONE ♥

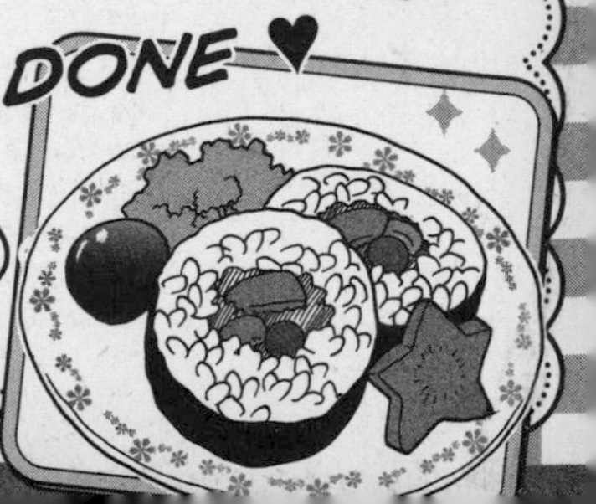

Yogurt Bread

Tip from Najika.

This is an easy bread to make because you don't need yeast to ferment and because you don't have to knead the bread either.

Yogurt Bread

Makes one loaf of round bread about 5 inches in diameter
1 1/2 cups all-purpose flour, 1 tablespoon baking powder, 1 teaspoon salt, 1/3 cup plain yogurt, 1/4 cup milk, 1 tablespoon sugar

How to Make

1 Sift flour, baking powder, and salt into a bowl.

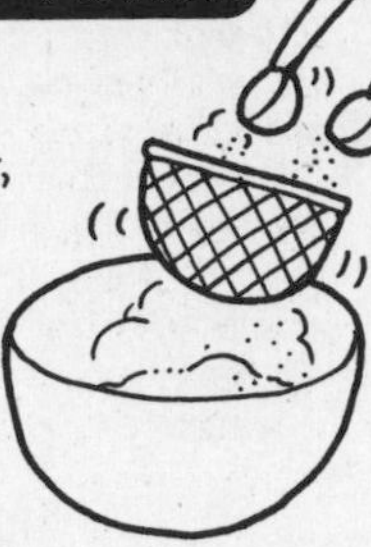

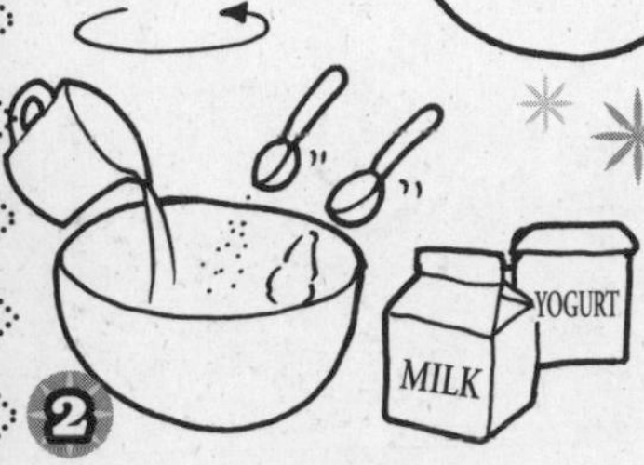
YOGURT
MILK

2 Add plain yogurt and sugar to the mix from step 1 and stir in the milk.

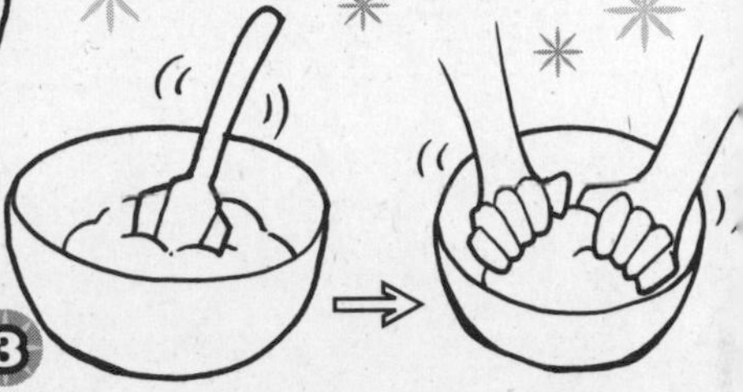

3 Use a rubber spatula to mix. When the dough hardens, put some flour on your hands and form it into a round shape. If the dough is crumbly, you can add a little bit more milk to soften it.

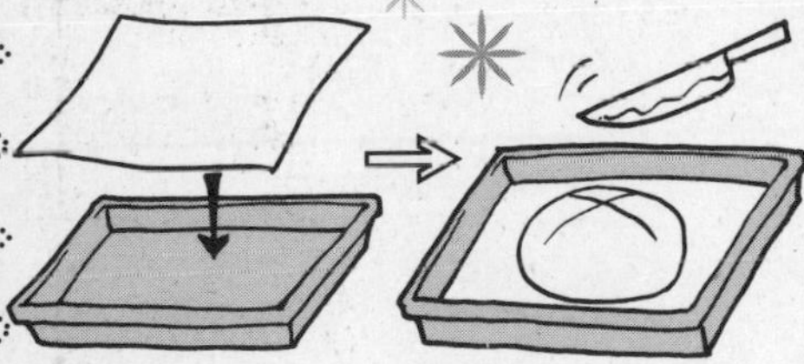

4 Put waxed paper on a cooking pan and place the dough from step 3 on top of it. Use a knife to slit a cross on top of the bread. The bread will cook better this way.

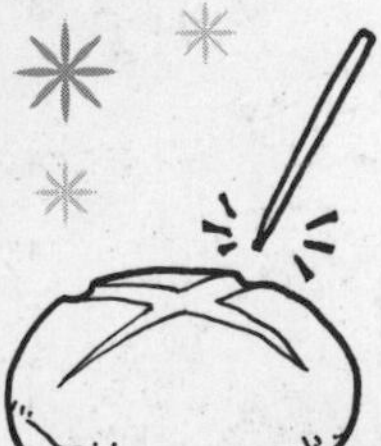

5 Bake for 25 to 30 minutes at 190 degrees (approx. 375° F). It's done when you poke it with a toothpick and the toothpick comes out clean! Let it cool, then slice.

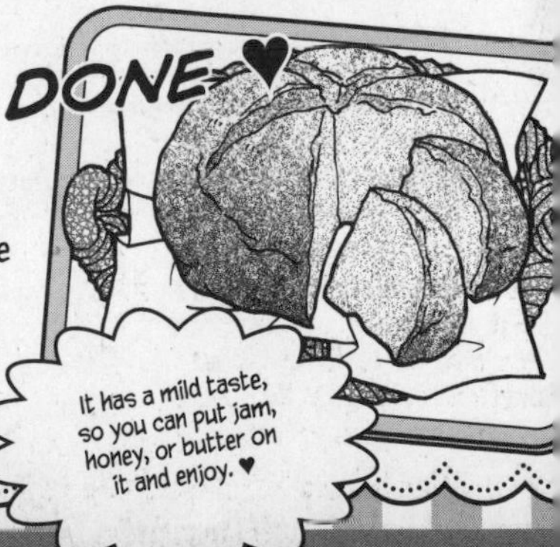
DONE♥
It has a mild taste, so you can put jam, honey, or butter on it and enjoy. ♥

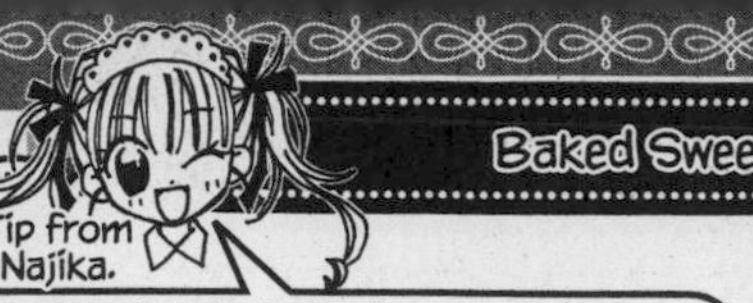

Tip from Najika.

Baked Sweet Potato Mash

Sweet potatoes have lots of fiber and vitamin C. ♥ This is a very healthy snack!

Baked Sweet Potato Mash

Makes 4 foil cups about 3 inches wide
1 large sweet potato (about 2/3 lb.), 2 tablespoons sugar, 2 tablespoons milk, 2 tablespoons butter, 1 egg (to add color when baking)

How to Make

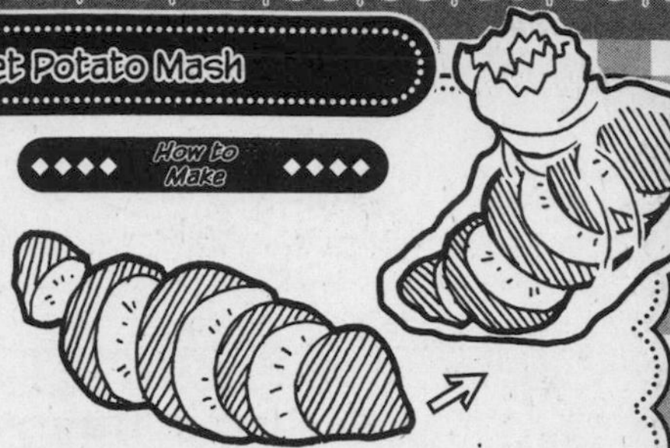

1 Wash the sweet potato and slice it into small pieces. Wrap in plastic wrap and microwave for 6 minutes. It's ready when a toothpick goes in easily. You can use a steamer if you'd like, too.

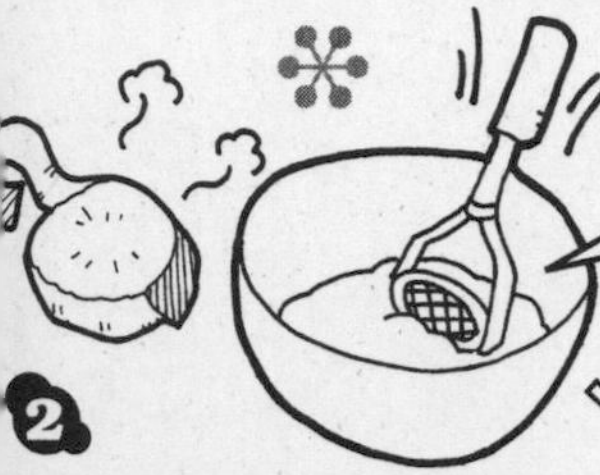

2 Peel off the skin while it's hot. Make sure you don't burn yourself. You can peel it easier if you dip your hands often in a bowl filled with cold water. Mash the potato in a bowl while it's still hot. Add butter that has been melted and cooled to room temperature. Add sugar. Mix well.

If you want to make it softer, you can puree the sweet potatoes after you mash them.

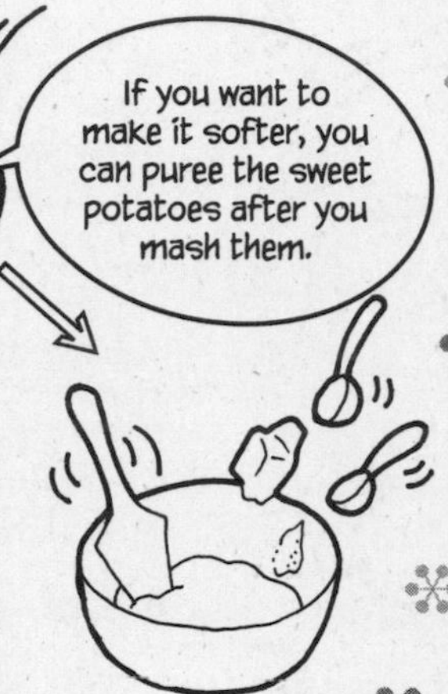

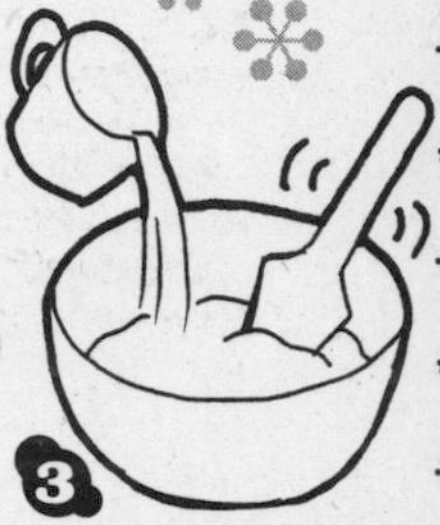

3 Add milk to the mix from step 2 and stir.

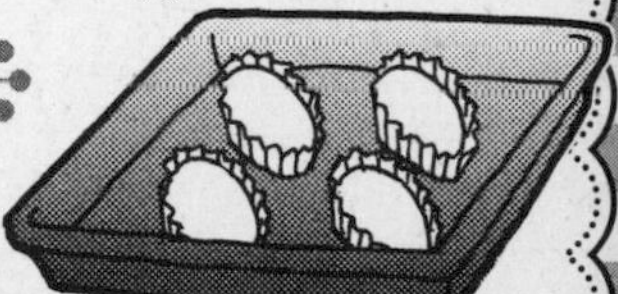

4 Pour the mix from step 3 into tinfoil cups. Whisk egg and brush on the surface to make it brown when baked.

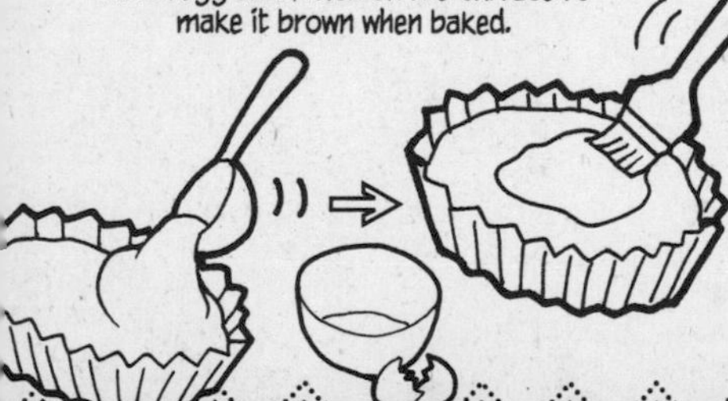

5 Bake in the oven for 5 minutes in 250 degrees (approx. 480° F). It's done when the top is a nice golden brown! You can even make it in a toaster oven!

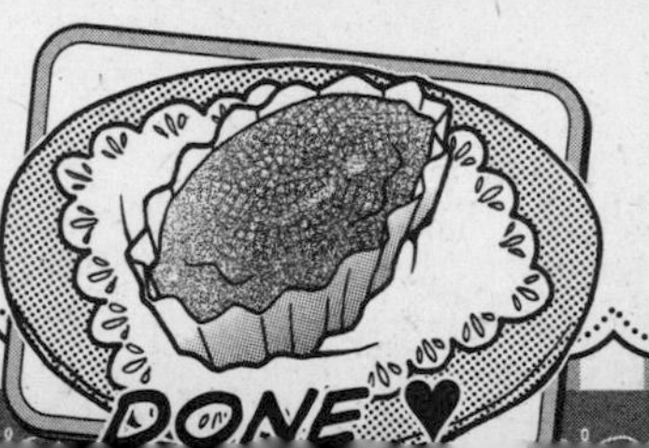
DONE♥

Café Au Chocolat

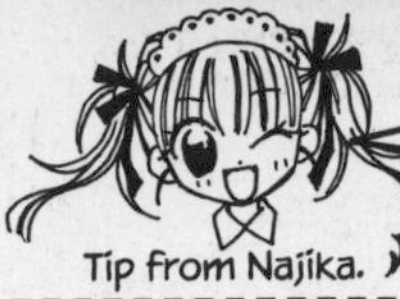

This is recommended for coffee lovers like Sora-senpai. ♡

Tip from Najika.

Café Au Chocolat

Makes 1 serving
1 cup of coffee, 1 tablespoon unsweetened cocoa, 1 to 2 teaspoons sugar (depends on your taste), milk, some unsweetened cocoa (for decoration)

How to Make

1 Put coffee in a mug. You can use instant coffee. While it's hot, add cocoa and sugar and stir.

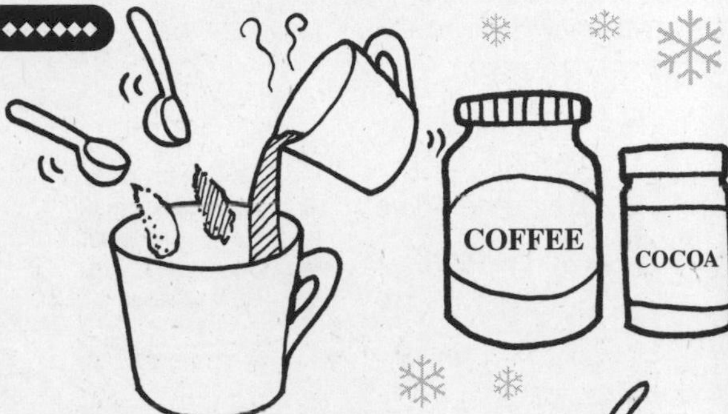

COFFEE
COCOA

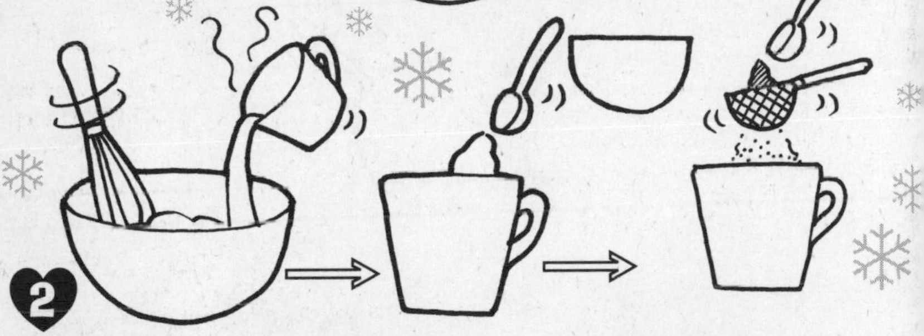

2 Warm the milk and place in a bowl. Whisk it until it's foamy. Pour on top of the coffee from step 1. Make sure you gently pour it in so the foam doesn't disappear. Sift some cocoa on the foam and you're done!

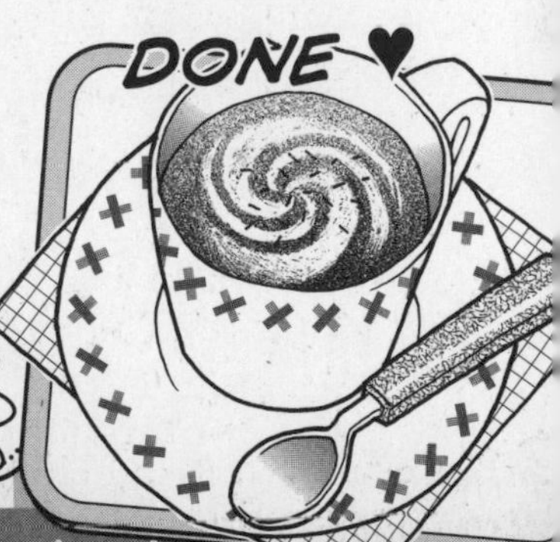

DONE ♥

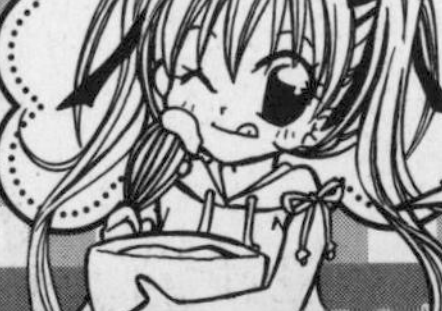

You can put marshmallows or whipped cream on the coffee, too!

About the Creator

Natsumi Ando

  She was born January 27th in Aichi prefecture. She won the 19th
Nakayoshi Rookie Award in 1994 and debuted as a manga artist. The
title she drew was *Headstrong Cinderella*. Her other known works are
Zodiac P.I., Wild Heart, and others. Her hobbies include reading,
watching movies, and eating delicious food.

Translation Notes

Japanese is a tricky language for most Westerners, and translation is often more art than science. For your edification and reading pleasure, here are notes on some of the places where we could have gone in a different direction in our translation of the work, or where a Japanese cultural reference is used.

Kasumin, author's note

Kasumin is a housewife with four children who is now famous for her boxed lunches that feature characters and celebrities. She started making interesting and funny lunches because her teenage son never thanked her for making lunch every day—and eating cartoon character–themed lunches is embarrassing for a high school boy. She currently has a recipe book out, too, entitled *Ai no Gag Bento (Funny Boxed Lunch of Love)*.

Bento, author's note

Bento is the term for "boxed lunch" in Japanese. It usually includes rice, a side dish of meat or fish, vegetables, and either a pickled dish or dessert.

Hokkaido, page 3

Hokkaido is located in the northern part of Japan. It is the second largest island and the biggest prefecture.

Aniki, page 10

Aniki is a term for "older brother," usually used by boys (or girls who are tomboys) in their younger teens. It is less honorific than "onii-chan" and "onii-san."

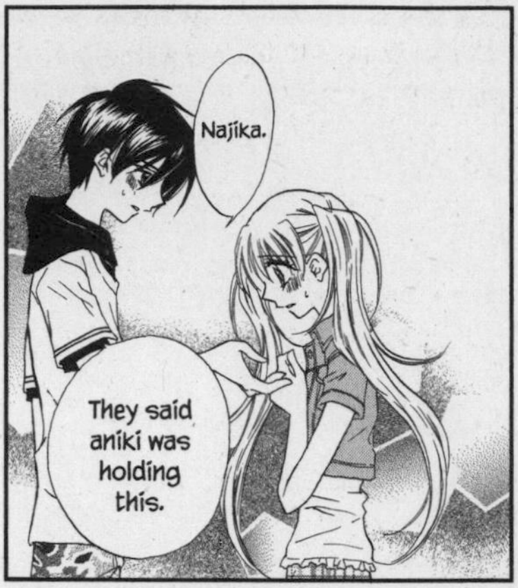
Najika.
They said aniki was holding this.

Dry curry, page 87

The term *dry curry* is used in Japan to indicate a stir-fried mixture of curry powder, some kind of meat (usually chicken, pork, or beef), and vegetables such as onions and carrots.

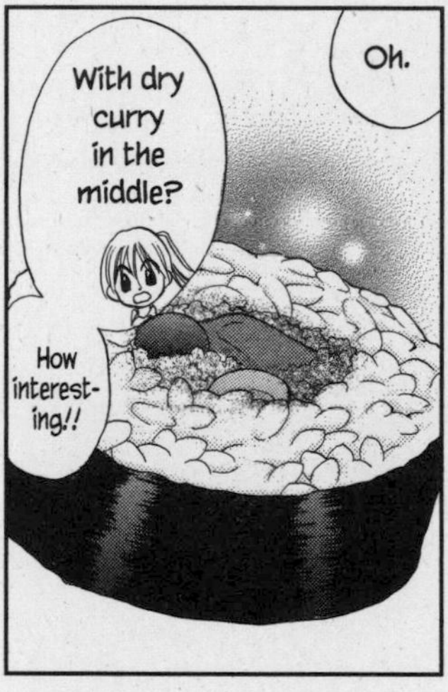
Oh.
With dry curry in the middle?
How interest-ing!!

Preview of Volume 7

We are pleased to present you a preview from the volume 7 of *Kitchen Princess*. Please check our website (www.delreymanga.com) to see when this volume will be available in English. For now you'll have to make do with Japanese!

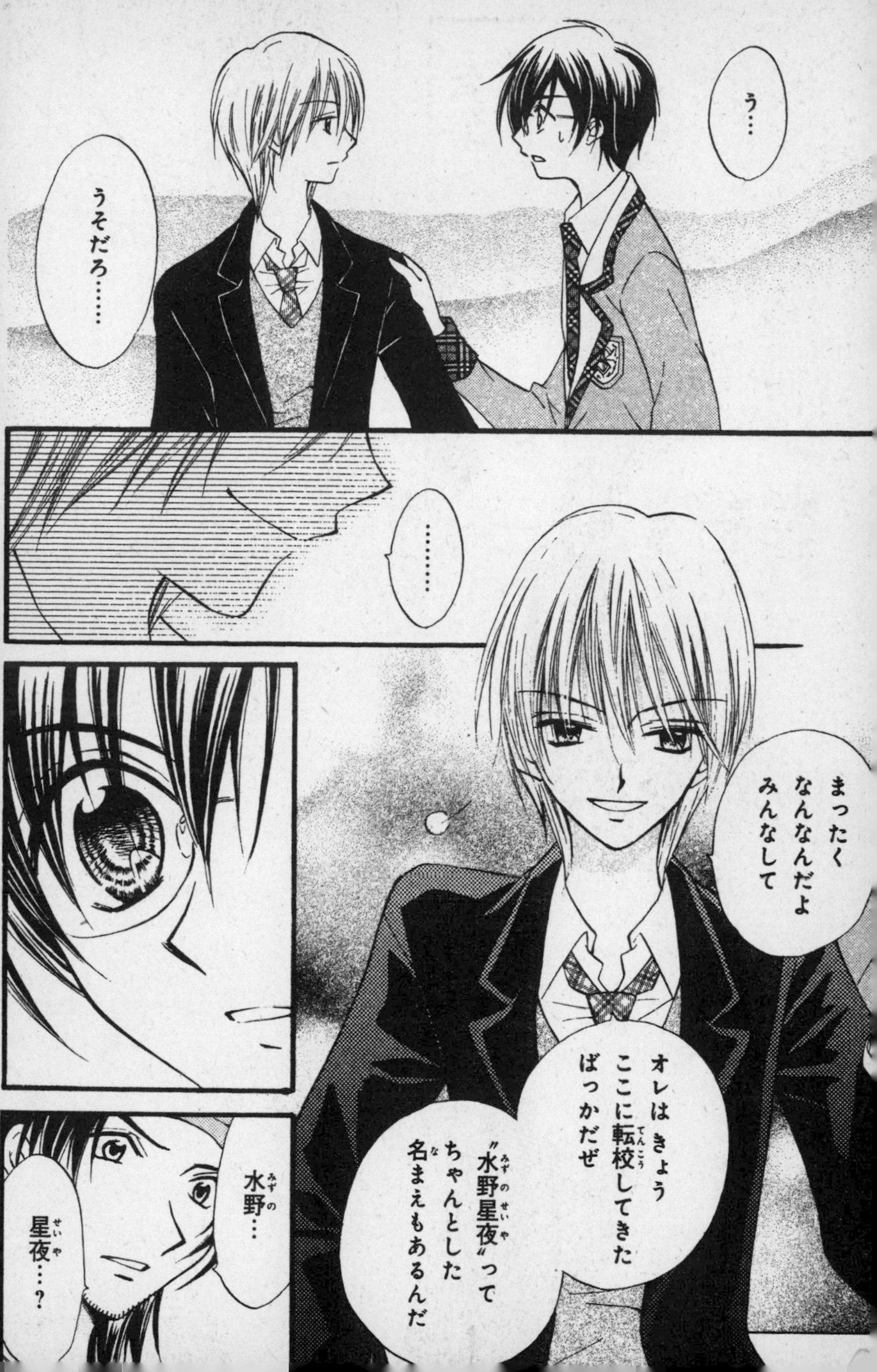
う…
うそだろ……
………
まったく なんなんだよ みんなして
オレは きょう ここに転校してきた ばっかだぜ
〝水野星夜〟って ちゃんとした 名まえもあるんだ
水野…
星夜…？

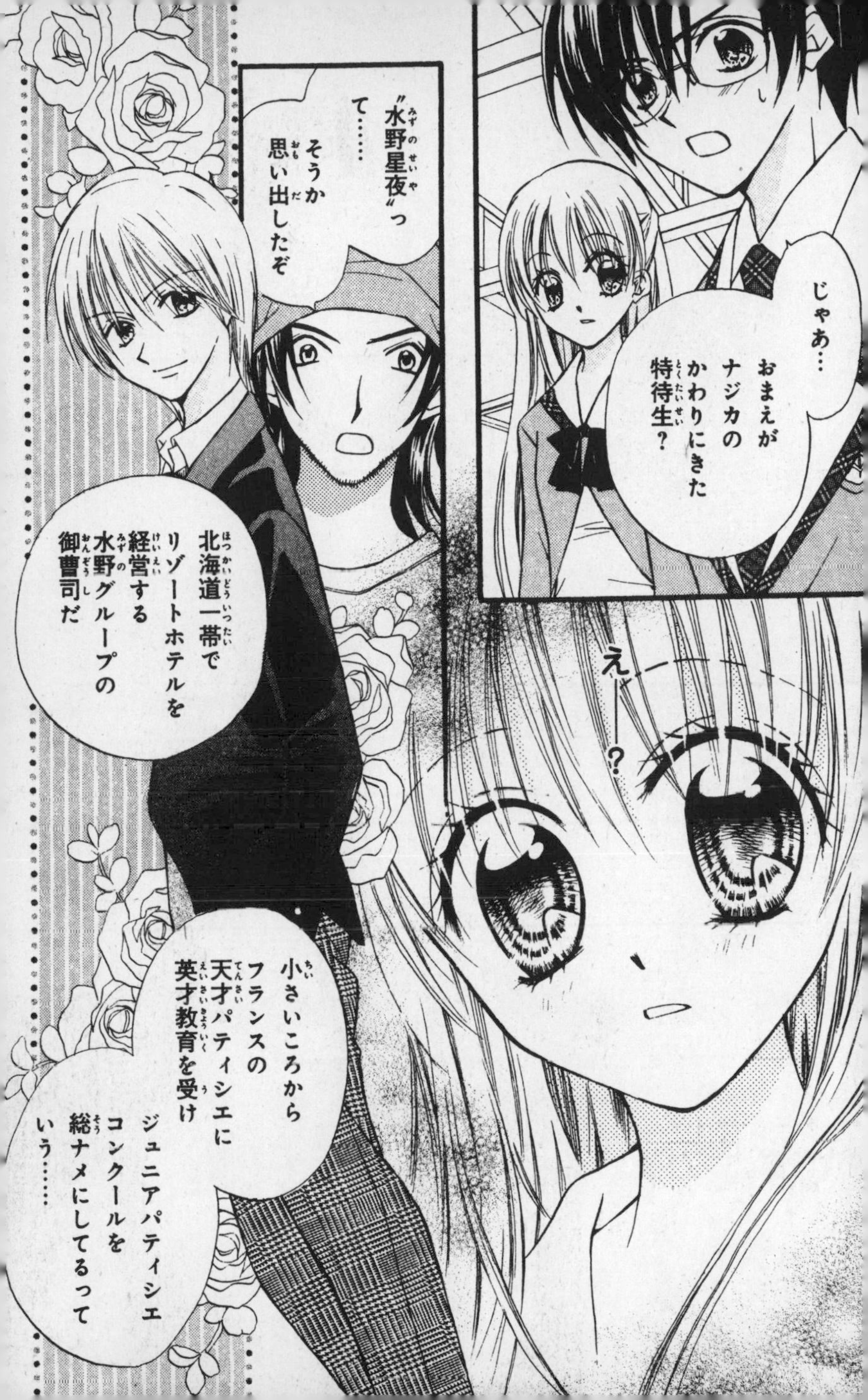
じゃあ…
おまえがナジカのかわりにきた特待生?
え——?
“水野星夜”って……
そうか思い出したぞ
北海道一帯でリゾートホテルを経営する水野グループの御曹司だ
小さいころからフランスの天才パティシエに英才教育を受け
ジュニアパティシエコンクールを総ナメにしてるっていう……

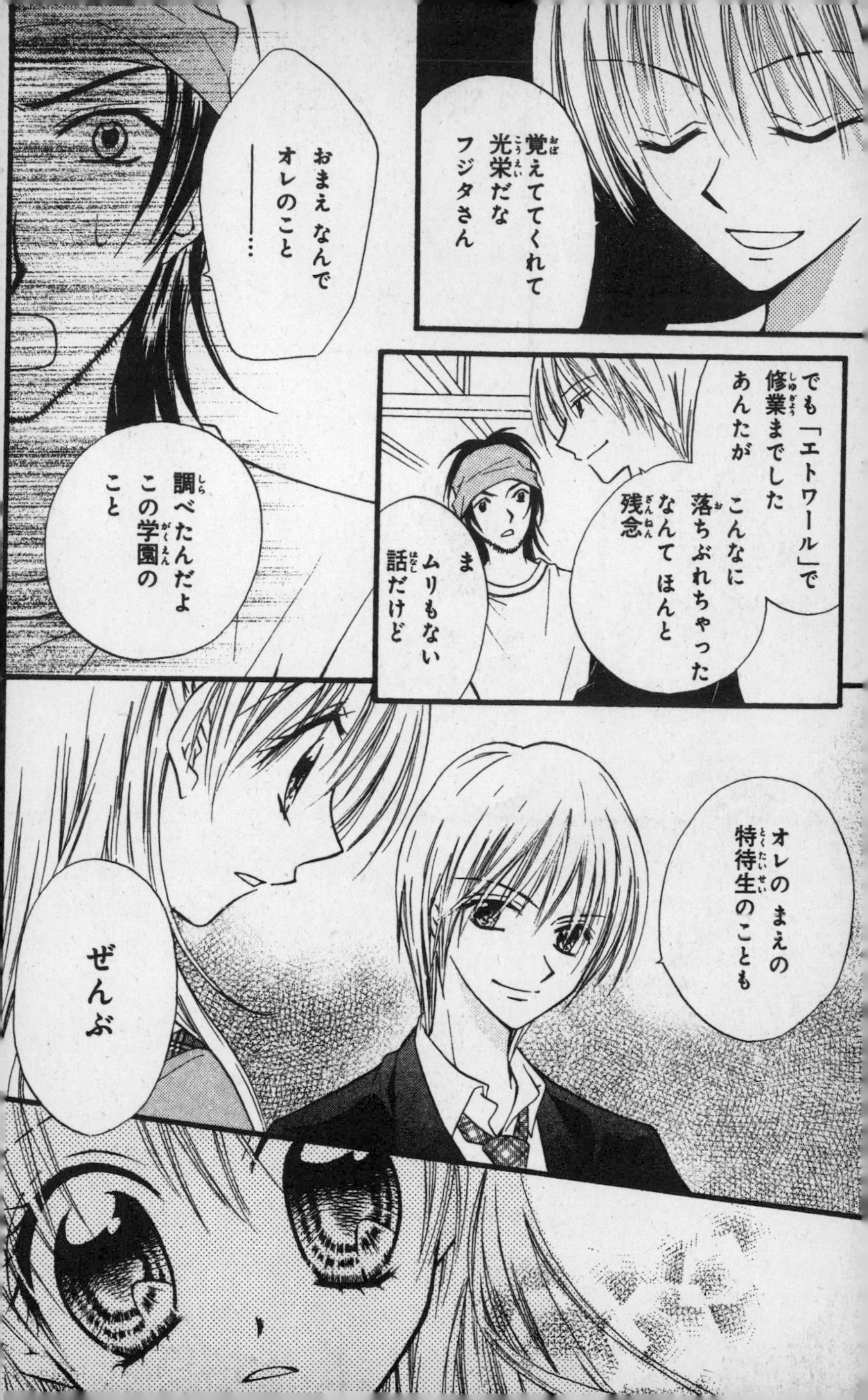
覚えててくれて光栄だな フジタさん
でも「エトワール」で修業までしたあんたが こんなに落ちぶれちゃったなんて ほんと残念
ま ムリもない話だけど
おまえ なんで オレのこと ……
調べたんだよ この学園のこと
オレのまえの特待生のことも
ぜんぶ

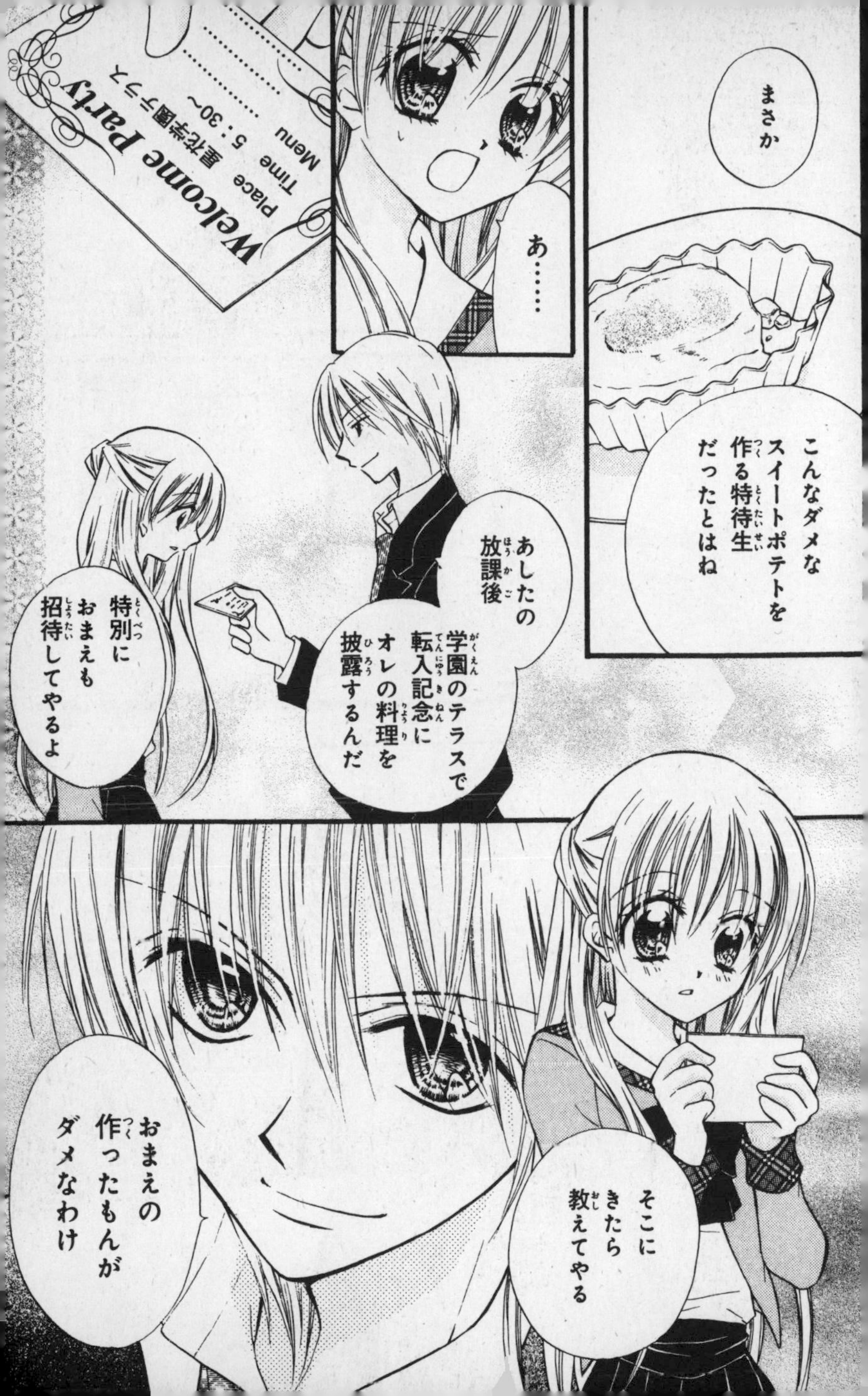
まさか
こんなダメなスイートポテトを作る特待生だったとはね
あ……
Welcome Party
Place 星花学園テラス
Time 5：30～
Menu
あしたの放課後
学園のテラスで転入記念にオレの料理を披露するんだ
特別におまえも招待してやるよ
そこにきたら教えてやる
おまえの作ったもんがダメなわけ

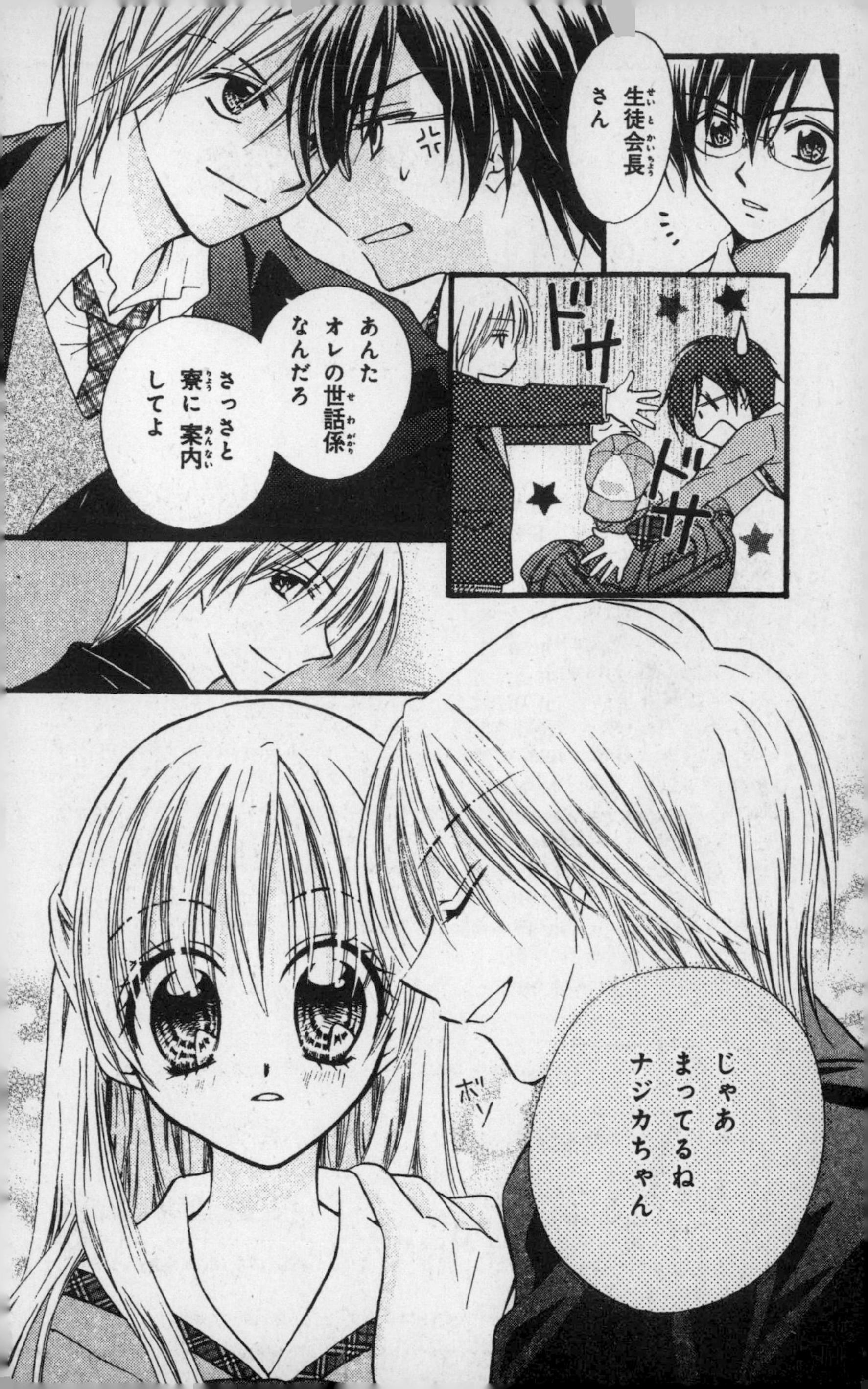

生徒会長さん
ドサ
ドサ
あんたオレの世話係なんだろ
さっさと寮に案内してよ
ボソ
じゃあまってるねナジカちゃん

MICHIYO KIKUTA

BOY CRAZY

Junior high schooler Nina is ready to fall in love. She's looking for a boy who's cute and sweet—and strong enough to support her when the chips are down. But what happens when Nina's dream comes true . . . twice? One day, two cute boys literally fall from the sky. They're both wizards who've come to the Human World to take the Magic Exam. The boys' success on this test depends on protecting Nina from evil, so now Nina has a pair of cute magical boys chasing her everywhere! One of these wizards just might be the boy of her dreams . . . but which one?

Special extras in each volume! Read them all!

VISIT WWW.DELREYMANGA.COM TO:
- Read sample pages
- View release date calendars for upcoming volumes
- Sign up for Del Rey's free manga e-newsletter
- Find out the latest about new Del Rey Manga series

RATING   T AGES 13+

DEL REY MANGA

The Otaku's Choice

TOMARE!

[STOP!]

You're going the wrong way!

Manga is a completely different
type of reading experience.

To start at the *beginning*,
go to the *end*!

That's right! Authentic manga is read the traditional Japanese way—
from right to left. Exactly the *opposite* of how American books are
read. It's easy to follow: Just go to the other end of the book, and read
each page—and each panel—from right side to left side, starting at
the top right. Now you're experiencing manga as it was meant to be!